T0390792

Regulatory Affairs in the Pharmaceutical Industry

Regulatory Affairs in the Pharmaceutical Industry

Edited by

Javed Ali
Department of Pharmaceutics, School of Pharmaceutical Education and
Research, Jamia Hamdard, New Delhi, India

Sanjula Baboota
Department of Pharmaceutics, School of Pharmaceutical Education and
Research, Jamia Hamdard, New Delhi, India

ACADEMIC PRESS
An imprint of Elsevier

ELSEVIER

Academic Press is an imprint of Elsevier
125 London Wall, London EC2Y 5AS, United Kingdom
525 B Street, Suite 1650, San Diego, CA 92101, United States
50 Hampshire Street, 5th Floor, Cambridge, MA 02139, United States
The Boulevard, Langford Lane, Kidlington, Oxford OX5 1GB, United Kingdom

Copyright © 2022 Elsevier Inc. All rights reserved.

No part of this publication may be reproduced or transmitted in any form or by any means, electronic or mechanical, including photocopying, recording, or any information storage and retrieval system, without permission in writing from the publisher. Details on how to seek permission, further information about the Publisher's permissions policies and our arrangements with organizations such as the Copyright Clearance Center and the Copyright Licensing Agency, can be found at our website: www. elsevier.com/permissions.

This book and the individual contributions contained in it are protected under copyright by the Publisher (other than as may be noted herein).

Notices
Knowledge and best practice in this field are constantly changing. As new research and experience broaden our understanding, changes in research methods, professional practices, or medical treatment may become necessary.

Practitioners and researchers must always rely on their own experience and knowledge in evaluating and using any information, methods, compounds, or experiments described herein. In using such information or methods they should be mindful of their own safety and the safety of others, including parties for whom they have a professional responsibility.

To the fullest extent of the law, neither the Publisher nor the authors, contributors, or editors, assume any liability for any injury and/or damage to persons or property as a matter of products liability, negligence or otherwise, or from any use or operation of any methods, products, instructions, or ideas contained in the material herein.

British Library Cataloguing-in-Publication Data
A catalogue record for this book is available from the British Library

Library of Congress Cataloging-in-Publication Data
A catalog record for this book is available from the Library of Congress

ISBN: 978-0-12-822211-9

For Information on all Academic Press publications
visit our website at https://www.elsevier.com/books-and-journals

Publisher: Andre Gerhard Wolff
Editorial Project Manager: Timothy Bennett
Production Project Manager: Sreejith Viswanathan
Cover Designer: Victoria Pearson Esser

Typeset by MPS Limited, Chennai, India

Working together
to grow libraries in
developing countries

www.elsevier.com • www.bookaid.org

Dedication

The book is dedicated to Late (Mrs.) Zubeda Begum and Shri Gopal Krishna Mangla.

Contents

7. Pharmaceutical regulatory requirements of nonregulated markets 163

G.N.K. Ganesh and Suresh K. Mohankumar

8. Drug product performance and scale-up process approval changes 215

Gulam Mustafa, Md Ali Mujtaba, Sabna Kotta, Abdullah Habeeballah, Nabil A. Alhakamy, Hibah M. Aldawsari, Shahid Karim and Shadab Md

List of contributors

Syed Sufian Ahmad Department of Pharmacology, School of Pharmaceutical Education and Research, Jamia Hamdard, New Delhi, India

Faraha Ahmed Department of Pharmacology, School of Pharmaceutical Education and Research, Jamia Hamdard, New Delhi, India

Hibah M. Aldawsari Department of Pharmaceutics, Faculty of Pharmacy, King Abdulaziz University, Jeddah, Saudi Arabia; Mohamed Saeed Tamer Chair for Pharmaceutical Industries, King Abdulaziz University, Jeddah, Saudi Arabia

Nabil A. Alhakamy Department of Pharmaceutics, Faculty of Pharmacy, King Abdulaziz University, Jeddah, Saudi Arabia; Mohamed Saeed Tamer Chair for Pharmaceutical Industries, King Abdulaziz University, Jeddah, Saudi Arabia

Javed Ali Department of Pharmaceutics, School of Pharmaceutical Education and Research, Jamia Hamdard, New Delhi, India

Sanjula Baboota Department of Pharmaceutics, School of Pharmaceutical Education and Research, Jamia Hamdard, New Delhi, India

Samir Bhargava Faculty of Pharmacy, DIT University, Dehradun, India

Bhavna Faculty of Pharmacy, DIT University, Dehradun, India

Shweta Dang Department of Biotechnology, Jaypee Institute of Information Technology, Noida, India

Anmol Dogra Department of Pharmaceutics, Khalsa College of Pharmacy, Amritsar, India

G.N.K. Ganesh Department of Pharmaceutical Regulatory Affairs, JSS College of Pharmacy, JSS Academy of Higher Education & Research, Ooty, India

Sonal Gupta Department of Biotechnology, Jaypee Institute of Information Technology, Noida, India

Abdullah Habeeballah Department of Clinical Pharmacology, University of Glasgow, Glasgow, United Kingdom

Shrikant Joshi Maliba Pharmacy College, Uka Tarsadia University, Bardoli, Surat, India

Gajanan Kalyankar Maliba Pharmacy College, Uka Tarsadia University, Bardoli, Surat, India

Shahid Karim Department of Pharmacology, Faculty of Medicine, King Abdulaziz University, Jeddah, Saudi Arabia

Mohammad Ahmed Khan Department of Pharmacology, School of Pharmaceutical Education and Research, Jamia Hamdard, New Delhi, India

Sabna Kotta Department of Pharmaceutics, Faculty of Pharmacy, King Abdulaziz University, Jeddah, Saudi Arabia

Shobhit Kumar Department of Pharmaceutical Technology, Meerut Institute of Engineering and Technology (MIET), Meerut, India

Sandesh Lodha Maliba Pharmacy College, Uka Tarsadia University, Bardoli, Surat, India

Shadab Md Department of Pharmaceutics, Faculty of Pharmacy, King Abdulaziz University, Jeddah, Saudi Arabia; Mohamed Saeed Tamer Chair for Pharmaceutical Industries, King Abdulaziz University, Jeddah, Saudi Arabia

Ashish Mishra Maliba Pharmacy College, Uka Tarsadia University, Bardoli, Surat, India

Suresh K. Mohankumar Pharmacy Program, Medical School, Faculty of Medicine, Health & Life Science, Swansea University, Swansea, Wales, United Kingdom

Md Ali Mujtaba Department of Pharmaceutics, Faculty of Pharmacy, Northern Border University, Rafha, Saudi Arabia

Gulam Mustafa College of Pharmacy, AD-Dawadmi, Shaqra University, Riyadh, Saudi Arabia

Jasjeet Kaur Narang Department of Pharmaceutics, Khalsa College of Pharmacy, Amritsar, India

Abhijeet Ojha College of Pharmacy, Six Sigma Institute of Technology, Rudrapur, India

Hetal Patel Maliba Pharmacy College, Uka Tarsadia University, Bardoli, Surat, India

Syed Arman Rabbani Department of Clinical Pharmacy and Pharmacology, RAK College of Pharmaceutical Sciences, RAK Medical and Health Sciences University, Ras Al-Khaimah, United Arab Emirates

Sadat Shafi Department of Pharmacology, School of Pharmaceutical Education and Research, Jamia Hamdard, New Delhi, India

Rajesh Sharma Department of Pharmaceutics, School of Medical and Allied Sciences, K.R. Mangalam University, Gurgaon, India

Shrestha Sharma Department of Pharmaceutics, School of Medical and Allied Sciences, K.R. Mangalam University, Gurgaon, India

Harmanpreet Singh Department of Pharmacy, Government Polytechnic College for Girls, Jalandhar, India

Editor biographies

Prof. Javed Ali

Prof. Javed Ali passed his BPharm and MPharm with distinction from Jamia Hamdard. He bagged gold medals in 1994 and 1996, respectively. He earned a PhD in the year 2000. He was a postdoctoral fellow at the Institute of Pharmaceutical Technology, University of Frankfurt, Germany in 2005. He has a total experience of 25 years in teaching and research. Presently, he is working as a professor at the Department of Pharmaceutics, School of Pharmaceutical Education and Research, and is also the in-charge of IP Management Cell, Jamia Hamdard, New Delhi.

Prof. Ali has been bestowed with several honors; a few of them worth mentioning include the Career Award for Young Teachers by the All India Council of Technical Education (2003); APTI-Young Pharmacy Teacher of the year (2004) by the Association of Pharmacy Teachers of India; the BOYSCAST Fellowship of Department of Science and Technology, Government of India (2005); American Association of Indian Pharmaceutical Scientists (AAiPS)-IPA Distinguished Educator and Researcher Award 2007 at the Association meeting at San Diego, United States; Research Award 2014 by the University Grants Commission, New Delhi; and Indian National Science Academy (INSA) Teachers Award 2018 by INSA, New Delhi for his outstanding teaching methodology and research outputs. In addition, he has won several awards for best paper presentations at conferences of Indian Pharmaceutical Congress, Indian Pharmacy Graduate Association, and Controlled Release Society, Indian Chapter. He has also received certificates of recognition for publications in high-impact factor journals from Jamia Hamdard.

Prof. Ali has received research grants from a large number of agencies including FIP (the Netherlands) and industries. He is actively involved in the field of drug delivery, which includes improvement in oral bioavailability of BCS classes II and IV drugs by polymeric conjugates and nanolipid-based systems, and nanoparticulate drug delivery systems for brain delivery. He is supervising scientific research at the postgraduation and the doctoral level. He has guided 76 theses of MPharm and 37 theses of PhD. Presently, 12 PhD theses are under his supervision. He is an external expert for PhD theses of a large number of Indian and foreign universities. He has written several books and has contributed several chapters in books on controlled and novel drug delivery systems of reputed Indian and international publishers. A widely traveled person, he has presented his research work in more than 100 conferences held in India and abroad. He has a list of about 350 manuscripts in reputed journals and five Indian patents granted/applied. He has an h-index of 68, i10 index of 224, and more than 17,220 citations to his credit as per Google Scholar bibliometric data in September, 2021. He has been named in the list of top 2% worldwide scientists in the field of pharmacy and pharmacology, and has also been named in the top scientists in 2019 global list across all fields by a publication of Stanford University in 2019. He has also worked as a paper coordinator of UGC ePathshala project of the Ministry of Education, Government of India for two papers of pharmaceutical sciences. He is a reviewer to a large number of reputed international and national journals and book proposals from various international publishers. He is an expert for projects review for agencies of various countries. He is on the editorial board of many renowned journals.

Prof. Ali is also actively engaged in committees of various universities/councils/accreditation bodies/public service commissions, etc. He has been an executive member of the Indian Pharmaceutical Association (Delhi Branch) from 2012 to date. He has been a member of the local organizing scientific committees of conferences. He has been delivering talks on various topics on regulatory affairs in national and international conferences/workshops and for various undergraduate and postgraduate courses. He is a resource person and has organized staff development/ refresher/short-term training programs from time to time. He is a member/life member of 20 Indian and international scientific organizations.

Prof. Sanjula Baboota

Prof. Sanjula Baboota passed her Bachelors and Masters in Pharmacy with distinction from the School of Pharmaceutical Education and Research, Jamia Hamdard in 1993 and 1995, respectively. She was a gold medalist in her postgraduate programme. She earned her PhD in the year 2002 from Jamia Hamdard. She is presently working as Professor at Department of Pharmaceutics, School of Pharmaceutical Education and Research, Jamia Hamdard. She has a total experience of about 25 years in teaching, research, and mentoring.

Prof. Sanjula teaches at undergraduate, postgraduate, and doctoral levels, and has also prepared e-content for postgraduate students on subjects like biopharmaceutics and cosmetics. Her research interests include improving oral bioavailability of BCS class II and Class IV drugs using approaches like complexation, polymeric conjugates, lipid based systems like microemulsions, nanoemulsions, solid lipid nanoparticles, and nanostructured lipid carriers. She is actively involved in formulating nanoparticulate drug delivery systems for treatment of neurological disorders and cancer. Recently the research group of Prof. Baboota has expanded their research on formulating nanocarriers of combination drugs as combination drug therapy provides additive or synergistic effect, increases the spectrum of treatment, reduces the side effects, helps in overcoming the resistance, improves patient compliance, and targets multiple pathways taking part in disease progression. Encapsulation of combination drugs in nanocarriers helps in overcoming the various biopharmaceutical challenges associated with, them thereby creating opportunities for better treatment.

Prof Baboota is actively engaged in supervising postgraduate and doctoral research work. More than 65 theses at postgraduate level and 30 doctoral research work is being guided by her. Her research work has received financial supports from all the leading sponsoring bodies in India. She has published more than 300 papers which includes original research articles, review articles, proceedings, and invited book chapters in edited books in the field of drug delivery. The work has also been presented at various national and international conferences. She has written several textbooks and has contributed chapters in books on controlled and novel drug delivery systems. Prof. Baboota's research work has received more than 11,325 citations. She has an h-index of 53 and i10 index of 156 as per the September, 2021 Google Scholar data.

Prof. Baboota has guest edited thematic issues for internationally reputed journals and also serves as regional editor and editorial board member for several international journals. She is a referee for a number of referred journal of repute and also a reviewer for book proposals of reputed international publishers. She serves as an expert for evaluation of national and international projects of different universities and funding bodies. She is also on examination panel of a number of University both in India and abroad for PhD theses evaluation.

Prof. Baboota has been bestowed with several honors, a few of them worth mentioning include AICTE Visvesvaraya Best teacher award 2021, the research award by UGC, Young Pharmacy teacher of the year award by APTI, Dr. P.D. Sethi research paper annual award for her research paper and several other best paper presentation awards. She has also received certificate of recognition for publication in high-impact factor journals and citations from Jamia Hamdard. Prof. Baboota featured in the top scientists in 2019 global list across all fields as per the data released by Stanford University and was awarded level 5 certificate in management and leadership by Chartered management Institute (CMI), United Kingdom.

Prof. Baboota has shared her research and teaching experience in several conferences, seminars, symposiums, and workshops as a chairperson and invited speaker. She is also actively engaged in various committees of the department, school, and University. She is a member/life member of several Indian and International scientific organizations.

Preface

In the current dynamic era where the healthcare domain is gaining impetus, there is a robust and holistic process applicable for any novel therapeutic moiety to reach from laboratory to bedside. Furthermore, it is owing to the guidelines governing the process that out of the plethora of entities only a handful of them reach the marketing stage and are available to the common masses. These guidelines are drafted appraising the risk−benefit analysis of the drug and laying down substantial do's and don'ts for the pharmaceutical organizations. These regulations primarily act as an interface between the pharmaceutical companies and the regulatory agencies and are instrumental in maintaining the quality of the final finished product.

For the past few years, we have always thought of coming up with a comprehensive book focusing on regulatory affairs in the Pharmaceutical Industry. The primary focus of which was to assimilate all the information available pertaining to regulatory procedures being followed in the pharmaceutical industry and the guidelines of various regulators. The present compilation of the content of the book is designed to impart advanced knowledge and skills required to learn the various concepts of regulatory affairs namely new drug, generic drug and their development, various regulatory filings in different countries, different phases of clinical trials, and submitting regulatory documents: filing process of investigational new drug (IND), new drug application (NDA), and abbreviated new drug application (ANDA). The book will also impart the knowledge about the manufacturing controls and their regulatory importance.

The book consists of nine chapters covering all the pertinent information dealing with the drug regulations and product approval process. Chapter 1, Drug Regulatory Affairs: An Introduction, is an introductory chapter on drug regulatory affairs which will make the readers aware of the importance of regulatory affairs, from the stage of production of a product to its marketing encompassing the documentation in the pharmaceutical industry. As the main goal of regulatory requirement for product approval is to establish a foundation for ensuring high-quality drug products, therefore, in Chapter 2, Regulatory Requirement for the Approval of Novel, Nanotechnology-Based Biological Products, approval process and regulatory requirements according to various regulatory authorities for API, nanotechnology-based and biologic products have been discussed. Chapter 3, International Council for Harmonisation Guidelines, enlists International Council for Harmonization (ICH) guidelines to make the readers familiar with the implications and enactment of quality, safety, efficacy, and multi-disciplinary topics applicable during drug development. In Chapter 4, Regulatory Affairs for Chemistry, Manufacturing, and Controls, regulatory details have been provided with regards to Chemistry, Manufacturing and Controls (CMC) section of a new investigational or new drug application as it is an important document to understand the physicochemical properties and getting speedy approvals in postapproval manufacturing changes of drugs. Chapter 5, Global Submissions for Drug Approvals, deals with global submissions required for drug approvals. It summarizes drug approval procedures adopted by regulatory agencies of different countries for providing marketing authorization of new drug products. In Chapter 6, Regulatory Requirements of Regulated Market, details and comparison of the marketing and distribution approval process in various countries have been discussed. Chapter 7, Pharmaceutical Regulatory Requirements of Nonregulated Markets, provides an overview of the selective underdeveloped country-specific regulatory and marketing authorization application requirements and associated processes. Chapter 8, Drug Product Performance and Scale-up Process Approval Changes, discusses general information about the in vitro drug product performance, in vivo performance including bioavailability and bioequivalence studies has been provided. The chapter also discusses in vitro-in vivo correlation, biowaivers, scale-up, and postapproval changes in accordance with regulatory guidelines. Chapter 9, Regulatory Affairs in Clinical Trials, which focuses on regulatory affairs in clinical trials, gives description of various aspects of regulations related to clinical trials in different regulated markets. The Good clinical practice guidelines, harmonization of clinical trial regulations, quality assurance in clinical trials, and ethical aspects, Pharmacovigilance, data privacy, the safety of human subjects have also been comprehended.

The unique features of the book include the following:

1. A comprehensive book covering necessary information regarding regulatory aspects of drugs, medical devices, and combination products;
2. A concise compilation of regulatory requirements of different countries;
3. Updated information as guidelines keeps on changing.

We are very thankful to Jamia Hamdard to provide facilities and the motivating environment which has helped us in bringing the present book. We are thankful to all the contributors especially during the COVID-19 pandemic time and providing in depth knowledge in their chapters with regards to various aspects of regulatory affairs. We would also like to place on record the efforts of the research team behind the timely help in order to improve the quality of the chapters namely, Dr. Bushra Nabi, Dr. Saleha Rehman, Mr. Musheer Khan, Ms. Anu, Mr. Ali Sartaj, Ms. Shaheen Parveen, Mr. Ashif Iqbaul, Mr. Mohd. Kashif Iqbaul, Ms. Zufika Qamar, Ms. Nupur Srivastava, Mr. Saurabh Mittal, and Mr. Ajay Singh in helping us in bringing up this book. We are grateful to the editorial and publishing staff members associated with Elsevier Inc. for their valuable support and guidance to ensure timely publication of the book.

Criticism and suggestions are welcome as they will help us in improving the quality of the book for the upcoming revised edition.

Editors

Javed Ali and Sanjula Baboota

Chapter 1

Drug regulatory affairs: an introduction

Jasjeet Kaur Narang[1], Anmol Dogra[1], Javed Ali[2], Sanjula Baboota[2] and Harmanpreet Singh[3]

[1]*Department of Pharmaceutics, Khalsa College of Pharmacy, Amritsar, India*, [2]*Department of Pharmaceutics, School of Pharmaceutical Education and Research, Jamia Hamdard, New Delhi, India*, [3]*Department of Pharmacy, Government Polytechnic College for Girls, Jalandhar, India*

1.1 Introduction

A substantial increase in regulations and legislations related to the assessment of efficacy, quality, and safety of drug products came into existence following the multiple tragedies—sulfanilamide elixir disaster, 1937; sulfathiazole disaster, 1941; thalidomide disaster, 1962—being a few of them (Harsha et al., 2017). However, the enactment of various Acts and laws also led to the evolution of drug regulations and their evolution over time.

1. **The 1906 Food and Drugs Act:** The Act's main motive was to prohibit the foreign and interstate movement of questionable, mislabeled, and adulterated food and drug products.
2. **Durham−Humphrey Amendment 1951:** The amendment granted the authority to Food and Drug Administration (FDA) to establish a distinction between two categories of medicines, that is prescription drugs and over-the-counter (OTC) drugs. Before this amendment, the manufacturers were free to determine the category of the drug.
3. **Kefauver−Harris Drug Amendment 1962:** According to this amendment the drug manufacturer has to prove that the product is effective based on adequate and well-controlled clinical trial before getting marketing approval.
4. **Orphan Drug Act 1983:** This Act encouraged the manufacturers of drugs to formulate medicines for diseases which occur rarely (affect less than 200,000 persons in the United States) and in return the regulatory authorities would provide the manufacturers with benefits, such as tax incentives, subsidies on clinical research, patent protection, and exclusive marketing rights.
5. **Drug Price Competition and Patent Restoration Act 1984:** The Act is commonly termed as the Hatch−Waxman Amendment. This established a pathway for the approval of generic drugs filed under the abbreviated new drug application (ANDA). This act also includes provisions for patent time increment and patent exclusivity related to the new drug applications (NDAs).
6. **Generic Drug Enforcement Act 1992:** This Act states that the drug applicant will not use the services of a person who has been convicted of a felony under federal law for conduct related to or in connection with a drug product application.
7. **Prescription Drug User Fee Act 1992:** The Act gave the authority to FDA for collecting fees from the drug firms manufacturing any drug for human administration or biological products to fund the new drug approval process.
8. **FDA Modernization Act 1997:** This act is aimed for better and improved regulation of drugs, food, devices, and biological products by enhancing advancements in technology as well as in trade and public health complexities.

The concept of regulatory affairs was also strengthened, besides setting up of stricter regulations for Good Manufacturing Practices (GMPs) and marketing authorizations.

The terms commonly used in Drug Regulatory Affairs (DRA) are mentioned below:

1. **U.S. FDA**: It is a federal agency of the U.S. Department of Health and Human Services, which has the responsibility to protect the health of the public.
2. **NDA:** It is an application which a drug sponsor files with the FDA to get marketing approval of their new drug product in the United States.
3. **Investigational New Drug Application**: In order to get permission for evaluating an experimental drug legally on human beings in the United States, an investigational new drug (IND) is filed with the FDA.

Regulatory Affairs in the Pharmaceutical Industry. DOI: https://doi.org/10.1016/B978-0-12-822211-9.00001-0
© 2022 Elsevier Inc. All rights reserved.

4. **ANDA**: In order to get approval for a generic drug product in the United States, an ANDA is filled.
5. **Generic Drug Product**: A pharmaceutical product which is comparable in terms of formulation, route of administration, strength, use, performance characteristics, and quality to the drug product of innovator is referred to as a generic drug product.
6. **Drug Master File (DMF):** It is a detailed information related to facilities, articles, as well as processes which are used in the formulation, processing, packing, and storage of one or more drugs meant for human administration, which is submitted confidentially to the FDA.
7. **Dossier**: All the technical data, which may be pertaining to the quality, administration, and clinical and nonclinical aspects of a drug product which has to be either approved, registered, or marketed in a country, is contained in a dossier.
8. **Active Pharmaceutical Ingredients (API):** The therapeutically active constituent of a pharmaceutical dosage form is referred to as API.
9. **International Council for Harmonization (ICH):** Formerly referred to as International Conference for Harmonization and then after October 2015 known as International Council for Harmonization, it is a regulatory agency which is meant to achieve harmonization globally with the view to formulate and register medicines with increased safety, efficacy, and quality.
10. **Master File Record (MFR):** It is a set of documents which comprises starting ingredients along with their quantities, methods of preparation, including the precautions to be followed while manufacturing, a detailed description of the product, and in-process quality tests, packaging, and storage conditions.
11. **Common Technical Document (CTD)**: It is a set of specification for application dossier, which is required for the registration of therapeutics. It is used across Japan, Europe, and the United States. It contains a compilation of quality, safety and efficacy information.
12. **Medical Devices**: It is defined as an article, apparatus, instrument or machine which is used either to prevent, diagnose or treat an illness or is used to detect, measure, restore, correct, or modify the body structure or function for health purpose.

1.1.1 Reason for the requirement of a drug regulatory department in the pharmaceutical industry

Among different industries, the pharmaceutical industry is reported to be the most regulated industry. For the development of efficient and safe pharmaceutical therapeutics, regulations are a very important requirement. Since the development of new pharmaceutical products takes approximately 8–15 years with an expenditure estimated to be more than 800 million dollars, development failures occurring at later stages can result in huge losses both financially and in terms of time spent. Therefore to minimize such development failures and losses to investors, existence of regulatory affairs and agencies is very important. Regulatory bodies based on their wisdom gained through guidance, market research, and previous experience play a significant role in the smooth development and marketing of pharmaceutical products with minimal product failures.

1.1.2 Responsibilities and duties of Drug Regulatory Affair professionals

The complexity in legislations worldwide associated with the growth of the pharmaceutical industry has promulgated the need for a regulatory department in each industry with a sufficient number of regulatory affair professionals. The regulatory affair professionals deal with regulatory issues and approvals (Pisano and Mantus, 2008; Kumar, 2013). The department of Regulatory Affairs is very often the first point of contact between an industry and government authorities (Harsha et al., 2017). The regulatory affair professionals in general have the responsibility to guide their industries on technical and regulatory legislations which helps in saving time and money in product development and its approval besides making sure that their industries comply with and satisfy the laws and regulations relating to them. Besides this:

1. They prepare and review standard operating procedures related to labeling, recalls, and other issues.
2. They contact the project managers of regulatory bodies.
3. They provide solutions to inquiries related to marketing.
4. They develop strategies to prevent delays in presenting the data generated from clinical studies to the regulatory bodies so as to get timely approval of new products.

The jobs performed by the regulatory affairs professionals in an active pharmaceutical ingredient (API) manufacturing company are different from those performed by a regulatory affairs professional in a formulation manufacturing company.

1. Jobs performed by a regulatory affairs professional in a company manufacturing API.

   The different jobs performed by a regulatory affairs professional in a company manufacturing API include, but are not restricted to:

   a. Filing a DMF with regulatory agencies supporting the new drug application, abbreviated new drug application, and abbreviated new drug application already filed by a formulator.

   b. Filing dossier of API for obtaining certificate of suitability (CEP).

   c. Filing any amendments or deviations from the data related to manufacturing, stability studies, etc., in DMF/dossier of specific drug with the regulatory bodies after suitable assessment.

   d. Getting customer approvals before the implementation of major changes related to the information mentioned in DMF or dossier.

   e. Submitting the prepared letter of access or letter of authorization (LoA) to the customers of API or formulators and the regulatory agencies.

   f. Preparing technical packages for a customer who can be a prospective or for an existing customer for initial testing of the API.

   g. Filing reports listing changes to the DMF, Active Substance Master File or dossier on an annual, biannual, or quinquennial basis with the regulatory bodies.

   h. Maintaining full record of every API, including amendments and annual reports.

   i. Participating in the process of drug development by guiding the research and development scientists on various guidelines, regulations, and laws.

2. Jobs performed by a regulatory affairs professional in a formulation manufacturing company.

   The different jobs performed by a regulatory affairs professional in a formulation manufacturing company includes, but are not restricted to:

   a. Filing an NDA or an ANDA related to formulations with regulatory agencies with the purpose of getting marketing approval.

   b. Filing any amendments or deviations to the data pertaining to manufacturing, stability studies, etc. in NDA or ANDA with the regulatory bodies after suitable assessment before their approval or after getting approval.

   c. Filing reports listing changes if any in the NDA or ANDA annually or biannually with the regulatory agencies.

   d. Reporting any adverse effects associated with the use of the formulation, which have either occurred or have chances to occur.

   e. Maintenance of the drug products' history, including amendments and annual reports.

   f. Involved in design and revision of labels of drug products and leaflets used for packaging.

   g. Participating in the process of drug development by guiding the research and development scientists on various guidelines, regulations, and laws.

Regulatory inspectors while inspecting the premises where pharmaceutical products are being manufactured, spend a substantial amount of time checking all the related documentation and records. Therefore documentation is a very important and inseparable part of regulatory affairs. It is a very important tool which helps the regulators to get information on the manufacturing processes done in the past and those being done currently. Besides this, maintenance of proper records is also a mandatory requirement as per GMP regulations (Patel and Chotai, 2011)

DRA is an important department existing in regulated pharmaceutical industries which acts as an important link between pharma industry and regulatory authorities to ensure that pharmaceuticals are manufactured and distributed as per the required legislation (Harsha et al., 2017). A regulatory affair is a unique synergy of internal departments of an industry with the regulatory bodies which starts with the conceptualization of a product to be developed by that industry and ends with the development of marketing and postmarketing strategies of that product. The desire of governments to safeguard the health of its citizens by ensuring safety and efficacy of drugs has resulted in the advent of regulatory affairs and regulatory affairs department in pharmaceutical companies (Itkar and Vyawahare, 2015; Sreedhar et al., 2005). Fig. 1.1 illustrates the concept and purpose of regulatory affairs.

The following are a few responsibilities and activities performed by a DRA department:

- Formulation of a regulatory strategy.
- Preparation, submission, and maintenance of regulatory documents.

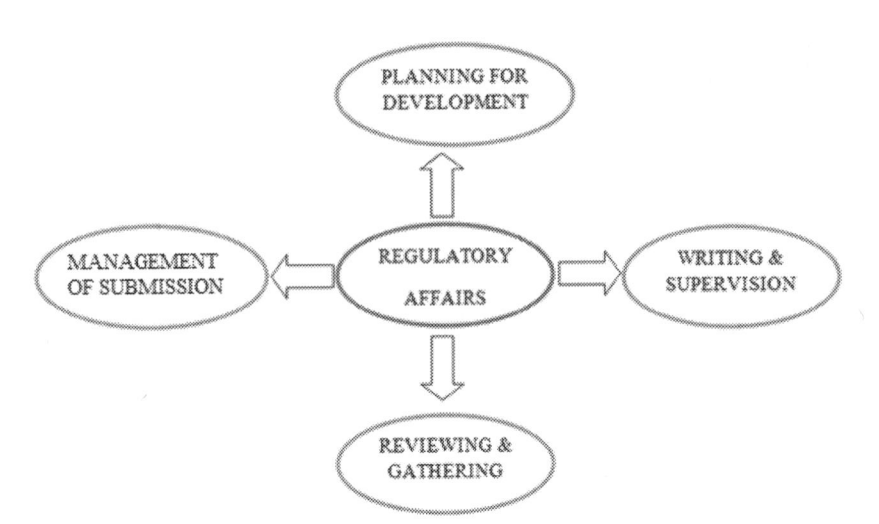

FIGURE 1.1 Concept of regulatory affairs. *(Adapted with modification from "Regulatory affairs- an overview", Shah and Mistry, 2012, https://www.pharmatutor.org/articles/an-overview-of-regulatory-affairs-and-its-importance-in-pharmaceuticals-other-industries, Pharmatutor with permisssion.*

- Meeting various regulatory authorities and corresponding with them regarding study updates, safety reports, and any amendments or supplements.
- During the conduct of clinical trials being engaged in filling dossiers, updating data regarding safety of product, adverse drug events, protocol modification if any, meeting the regulatory agencies and giving updates, taking advice, and reporting any change in strategies.
- After the conduct of clinical trials preparing for submission of an NDA, interacting with the regulatory bodies during its review, negotiation of label, and launch of the product.
- After launching a product, reporting any changes in case done and gathering report related to the safety of the product.

1.1.3 Different regulatory agencies regulating pharmaceutical industries worldwide

To regulate the pharmaceutical products, various regulatory bodies exist worldwide. In the United States, FDA is the regulatory body, the purpose of which is to not only protect but also promote the health of the public by checking, supervising, controlling, and certifying the efficacy and safety of food products; drugs meant for human and veterinary application; medical devices; and biological products besides ensuring the safe use of cosmetic products and products that emit radiation. It has its headquarters in White Oak, MD (https://www.federalregister.gov/agencies/food-and-drug-administration).

A similar regulatory role is played by The Medicines and Health Care Products Regulatory Agency (MHRA) in the United Kingdom. It is an executive agency of the Department of Health and Social Care and its function is to ensure the safety of the medicines, blood components for transfusion, and medical devices. Besides having the responsibility to ensure that the medicines, medical devices, and blood components used for the purpose of transfusion conform to the desired safety, efficacy, and quality standards, the agency also has a pivotal role to play in ensuring the safety and security of supply chain for drugs, medical devices, as well as blood components, aiding in educating both public and healthcare professionals regarding the benefits as well as risks associated with their use. This would ultimately ensure their safety and effectiveness, promote worldwide harmonization for safe and effective use of biological medicines, and also support research and innovation, which could have beneficial effect on the health of people (https://www.gov.uk/government/organisations/medicines-and-healthcare-products-regulatory-agency/about).

Therapeutics Goods Administration is the regulatory body responsible for regulating the therapeutic goods and other therapeutic goods (OTGs) in Australia with the view to ensure their safety and effectiveness for public use. It is a part of the Australian Government Department of Health. Therapeutic goods include medicines (prescription and OTC and complementary medicines), biological products, and medical devices (instruments, sterile bandages, pacemakers, implants, and appliances). The OTGs include disinfectants and tampons. It is mandatory that all the products for therapeutic use which have to be sold in Australia have to be recorded in the Australian Register of Therapeutic goods (https://www.tga.gov.au/tga-basics).

The Central Drug Standard Organisation (CDSCO) is the regulatory body for ensuring the safe use of therapeutics including medical devices in India. It is a body under the Directorate General of Health Services, Ministry of Health &

Family Welfare, Government of India, and is the National Regulatory Authority of India. Its headquarters are located in New Delhi 110002, and it has six zonal offices, four subzonal offices, 13 port offices, and seven laboratories in different parts of the country. Under the Drugs and Cosmetics Act, the responsibilities of CDSCO include drug approvals, setting standards for drugs, conducting clinical trials, controlling quality of drugs imported besides coordinating the activities of State Drug Control Organizations. It also gives advice to State Drug Control Organizations in order to achieve uniform implementation of the Drugs and Cosmetics Act. The CDSCO also has another important role which includes granting licenses of special categories of critical drugs, such as vaccines, sera, and blood products, along with regulatory bodies of the state (https://cdsco.gov.in/opencms/opencms/en/Home/).

Health Canada is a federal department responsible for ensuring good health of people in Canada. The Health Products and Food Branch is a national authority which regulates, evaluates, and monitors the quality, efficacy, and safety of drug products, biologics, gene therapies, as well as other products pertaining to health for sale in Canadian markets, including diagnostic products (https://www.canada.ca/en/health-canada/services/drugs-health-products/drug-products/fact-sheets/drugs-reviewed-canada.html). Prescription and nonprescription drugs, disinfectants, as well as sanitizers which claim as disinfectants are included in the category of drug products. It is responsible for managing the benefits and risks associated with the use of foods as well as health products in Canadian public.

In Europe, the agency responsible for the evaluation of medicinal products is European Medicines Evaluation Agency or European Medicines Agency (EMA). From 1995 to 2004, the name of European Medicines Agency was European Agency for the Evaluation of Medicinal Products. In the year 1995, EMA was established with funds from pharmaceutical industry, European Union and with indirect subsidy from member states. The purpose of establishing it was to harmonize the work of national medicine regulatory bodies which were already in existence. As part of the European centralized procedure, the pharmaceutical companies are required to submit a single application for authorization to market their products with the EMA. After being granted by the European Commission (EC), it has validity in all the member states of EU/EEA.

In Japan, the regulations and legislations related to the pharmaceutical affairs are laid down by the Ministry of Health, Labour and Welfare (MHLW), commonly known as *Kōrō-shō*. It is a ministry at the cabinet level in the Government of Japan and is entrusted with the responsibility to provide services related to health, welfare, and labor. The ministry comprises many sections, the Pharmaceutical and Food Safety Bureau being one of them (https://www.mhlw.go.jp/english/org/detail/dl/organigram.pdf). Although the Pharmaceutical Affairs Law and related ordinances play an important role in regulating clinical trials as well as granting approvals for new drugs in Japan, the final decision regarding approval of drugs against the filed NDAs or halting of clinical trials for drugs for which INDs application have been filled rests with the MHLW (Ono, 2007).

1.1.3.1 International Council for Harmonisation

The year 1990 marked the establishment of the International Conference on Harmonisation (ICH) of Technical Requirements for Registration of Pharmaceuticals for Human Use which came into existence in April at a meeting in Brussels. After October 2015, its name changed to International Council for Harmonisation. It is a unique council which brings together both the pharmaceutical industry and the regulatory authorities on a common platform to discuss technical as well as scientific aspects of pharmaceutical products. ICH was established with the mission to achieve harmonization globally with the view to formulate and register medicines with increased safety, effectiveness, and high quality. At present ICH includes 17 members and 32 observers (https://www.ich.org/).

ICH was constituted with the mission to develop technical guidelines and requirements and condition necessary for getting a pharmaceutical product registered, the ultimate aim of which was to build increased harmonization for promoting public health (Theresa, 2017). The importance of attaining harmonization lies in the fact that it eliminates unwanted delays in the worldwide development as well as availability of new pharmaceuticals and therapeutics while maintaining optimized standards of safety, efficacy, quality, and regulatory procedures with the view to protect health of people. It also facilitates a more rational and logical utilization of resources.

1.1.3.2 Organization of ICH

The MedDRA Management Committee and The Maintenance and Support Services Organization, contracted by the ICH, are responsible for the maintenance, development, and distribution of the Medical Dictionary for Regulatory Affairs (MedDRA). MedDRA comprises specialized medical terms to facilitate in global sharing of regulatory information related to medical products, such as pharmaceuticals, vaccines, and drug-device combination products, meant for human administration (https://www.ich.org/page/meddra).

1.1.3.3 Process of harmonization

The process of harmonization starts with a concept paper which is a brief summary of the proposal. Depending on the activity for which harmonization is required, the harmonization activities of ICH are classified into four categories:

1. Formal ICH procedure
2. Q&A procedure
3. Revision procedure
4. Maintenance procedure

A business plan, the purpose of which is to outline the expenses and advantages of harmonizing the topic for which the Concept Paper is proposed, may also be required depending on the harmonization activity category.

A formal ICH procedure requires concept paper and business plan; in a Q&A procedure, concept paper is required; however, in certain cases, business plan may also be required; in the revision procedure also the concept paper is required and in the maintenance procedure concept paper is required except for M2 recommendations maintenance (https://www.ich.org/page/process-harmonisation).

1.1.3.4 ICH guidelines for pharmaceuticals

The ICH provides guidance documents in the form of Quality guidelines, Safety guidelines, Efficacy guidelines, and Multidisciplinary Guidelines also commonly referred to as QSEM guidelines, which are aimed at improving the efficacy of pharmaceuticals without compromising on their safety. The QSEM guidelines are given in flowcharts in Fig. 1.2A−D.

1.2 Pharmaceutical regulatory affairs: documentation

The concept of GMP came into existence in the 1970s, with the aim to ensure the production of safe and good quality drugs consistently (Jain and Jain, 2017). Documentation is a very important part of GMP compliance. It ensures traceability and accountability of all activities related to manufacturing and testing of products (Patel and Chotai, 2011). A number of records have to be prepared and retained by companies in order to meet the GMP regulations. Among the different records, Dossiers, DMFs, MFR, and batch production records are important.

1.2.1 Dossiers

A comprehensive scientific document which is used for obtaining approval of drug for global licensing by different health authorities is known as a dossier. A number of interrelated activities are involved in the making of a dossier. These include planning, scheduling, creating, organizing, copying, typing, formatting, collaborating with other services and suppliers, and at the end shipping the document to the desired site.

In dossiers the supportive documentation which is asked generally comprises:

1. Administrative data:

    All the documents relating to the payment of fees, the samples, as well as the licenses related to manufacturing and copies of approval of marketing authorizations, including valid GMP certification and details of the last inspection date are included in the administrative data provided.

2. Information pertaining to the product:

    Trade name of the therapeutic product and its composition (both qualitative and quantitative), and also the data pertaining to the pharmaceutical form and clinical particulars are included. The clinical particulars consist of information related to the therapeutic indications, administration methods, posology, any special precautions and warnings regarding its use, any contraindications and drug interactions or any other interaction, effects during lactation and pregnancy, side effects, and information related to overdose.

3. Information related to the product pharmacology

    This is further categorized into information related to the:

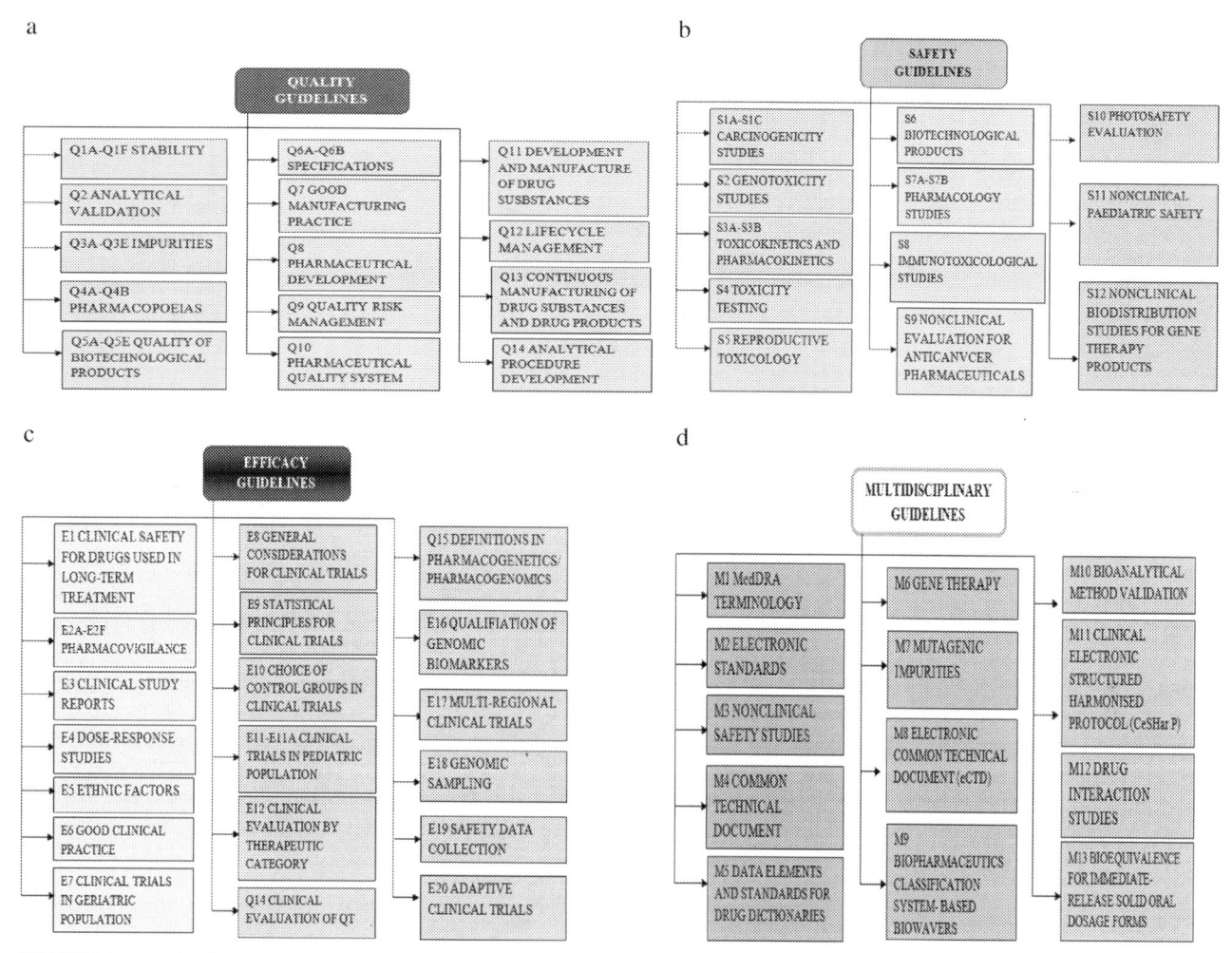

FIGURE 1.2 (A) Quality guidelines, (B) safety guidelines, (C) efficacy guidelines, and (D) multidisciplinary guidelines.

a. Pharmacodynamics: Information and data related to mechanism of action, effect on the respiration, hepatic function, blood circulation, etc. are included. For all the pharmacodynamic studies undertaken, a summary of protocol, results, and result analysis should be provided.

b. Pharmacokinetics: Information related to the bioavailability of the formulation as well as related relevant clinical data, such as plasma drug concentrations, clearance, metabolism, absorption, and excretion are provided. Data related to both single-dose administrations and multiple-dose administrations should be documented. It is also desirable to include information about the plasma concentrations at which the drug product exhibited therapeutic effect and side effects. For all the pharmacokinetic studies undertaken, a summary of protocol, results, and result analysis should be provided.

c. Toxicity studies: Information related to acute toxicity, subacute toxicity, and chronic toxicity is provided.

d. Reproductive function studies: Information related to the fertility, teratogenicity, embryotoxicity, and pre- and postnatal action of the drug product is included.

e. Pharmacodynamic properties: Information related to the mode of action, ED50 in different animal species, and any additional pharmacodynamic studies undertaken to ascertain the adverse effects, and also information derived from studies pertaining to tolerance and drug interactions are included.

Besides the above-mentioned data, information on mutagenic studies, clinical trials, and carcinogenic studies is also included.

4. Pharmaceutical information of the product:

The information in this relates to excipients present, incompatibilities, shelf life, nature and contents of containers, special precautions for use in case applicable, and instructions for handling and use. Submission of detailed information about the manufacturing process is also a requirement in some countries. In this case, information related to batch size, manufacturing formula, process of manufacturing, and information related to the validation in case the process of manufacturing is critical or is a nonstandard process is required to be submitted.

The information related to the active substances include:

1. Specifications and tests conducted routinely for:
   a. active substance(s) mentioned in a pharmacopoeia;
   b. active substance(s) not mentioned in a pharmacopoeia;
   c. characteristics;
   d. tests for identification;
   e. tests for purity (physical, chemical, other tests), which would also include the limits for named, total, single and unidentified single, as well as unidentified total impurities.
2. Scientific data which includes:
   a. Nomenclature: In this chemical name, international nonproprietary name (INN), synonyms, and laboratory code are mentioned.
   b. Description: This includes information about physical form, molecular formula, structural formula with data related to conformational status for macromolecules, relative molecular mass, and chirality.
   c. Manufacture: This includes information about name(s) and address(es) of the manufacturing source(s); synthetic or manufacturing route with a mention of the process flowchart, process description, with information related to the in-process controls, catalysts, and data related to solvents, reagents, and other auxillary substances. Besides this information related to the stages of purification and criteria for reprocessing used for purification steps along with the date should also be mentioned.
   d. Quality control during manufacture: This includes information regarding the starting materials and wherever applicable control tests on intermediate products.
   e. Development chemistry: This includes information related to potential isomerism, proof of chemical structure (synthetic route, key intermediates, elemental analysis, mass spectrum, NMR (nuclear magntic resonance), IR (infrared spectroscopy), UV (ultraviolet spectroscopy), and others), physicochemical evaluation, and complete evaluation of the primary reference material. Besides these data related to the analytical validation, comments on the selection of tests conducted routinely and standards are also included.
   f. Impurities: This includes impurities that may originate from the process of synthesis, during production or purification of a product. It also mentions the analytical tests for their detection and their limit of detection.
   g. Batch analysis: This includes information related to date and place of manufacture, size of batch, as well as details of batches evaluated, including those utilized for preclinical and clinical testing, test results, and results of analysis of reference materials.

The information related to the excipients include:

1. Specifications and routine tests: This includes information related to excipients mentioned in pharmacopoeia and also the excipient(s) not mentioned in a pharmacopoeia. The information included pertains to details of characteristics, tests for identity, purity, and assay wherever admissible and other tests.
2. Scientific data: This includes data related to excipient(s) which are used for the first time in medicinal products.
3. Packaging material (immediate packaging): This includes data related to specifications, tests done on a routine basis, and scientific data. The information included in specifications and tests conducted on a routine basis include the material type used, construction, as well as quality specifications (routine tests) and methods for conducting tests. On the other hand development studies on packaging components and results of batch analysis are included in the scientific data.

Besides the above data, information on the control tests on the finished product are also mentioned. This includes the details of the product specifications, tests for relevance at the time of manufacturing, general characteristics, specific standards, control methods which include detailed procedures (including microbiological and biological methods wherever applicable) of tests used for identification, and quantitative determination for the active substance(s). Besides this control tests used for the identification and determination of excipients should also be described.

Scientific data related to an analytical validation of procedures, including reason for the selection of tests conducted on routine basis and standards (e.g., working standards) and batch analysis which in turn includes information, such as date and place of formulation development, size of batch, application of batches tested, results obtained, and analytical results of reference material, primary and others are given.

A dossier also contains information on tests for stability conducted on active substance(s) (i.e., batches tested, test methods and analytical procedures, validation, test results, and conclusion) and information related to the tests for stability on the finished product, such as Quality specifications for the shelf life proposed, batches tested, characteristics evaluated, test procedures, results, and conclusions.

The name and the address of the marketing authorization holder, marketing authorization number, date of first authorization/renewal of authorization, and date of (partial) revision of the text are included.

1.2.1.1 Pharmaceutical dossier

It includes detailed scientific documentation and extensive data related to a particular drug which has to be submitted to the regulatory agency for getting approval for manufacturing, marketing, use, distribution, or sale of a product. The information present includes complete formula of the formulation including its inert excipients, method of preparation, including in-process quality controls as well as information related to analytical control of active ingredients and excipients, such as specifications and methods, stability tests, and their procedures and results. The dossier has to be prepared as per the format which is accepted globally and includes the Common Technical Dossier (CTD) and the ASEAN Common Technical Dossier (ACTD) format, which helps in reducing time and extra efforts involved in registration of a single drug in many countries. The CTD contains five modules which relate to the Quality, Safety, Efficacy, and Toxicity of the drug and are acceptable by all the main regulatory bodies, that is the United States, the European Union, and Japan. In the ACTD and CTD, the information given is written unequivocally and is easy to perceive by the reviewer.

1.2.1.2 Preclinical dossier

A preclinical dossier includes elaborated studies related to pharmacodynamic, toxicology, and pharmacokinetics.

1.2.2 Drug master file

It is a set of documents or a file which needs to be presented to the FDA and contains detailed and confidential information which relates to articles, facilities, or processes which have been utilized for the purpose of formulation, processing, packaging, and storage of drugs meant for human use. It is not a requirement as per law or the FDA regulation. It is a document which is filled based on the holder's discretion (https://www.fda.gov/drugs/drug-master-files-dmfs/guideline-drug-master-files-dmf). It contains compiled data of drug product chemistry, manufacturing, packaging, storing, impurity profile, stability, etc. It contains complete information about the active pharmaceutical ingredient (API) and the finished dosage forms (Drug Master Files: Guidelines, Center for Drug Evaluation and Research, Food and Drug Administration, Department of Health and Human Services, 1989).

1. Parts of DMF:
     The content of DMF consists of two parts:
   a. Applicant's part: It is also called an open part which comprises nonconfidential information. This information provides access to the license holder for marketing.
   b. Restricted part: It is also called a closed part, which comprises confidential information. This information is supplied to the authorities only and contains details about the manufacturing procedures
2. *Types and content of DMF:*

In pharmaceuticals, DMFs are of five types (Drug master files: Guidelines, Center for Drug Evaluation and Research, Food and Drug Administration, Department of Health and Human Services, 1989). Table 1.1 lists various types of DMFs.

1.2.2.1 Type I: Manufacturing site, facilities, operating procedures, and personnel

A Type I DMF is advisable for persons residing outside the United States to help the FDA in the conduct of site inspections of their manufacturing establishments. It should give details of the manufacturing site, such as actual address of the site, its aerial photograph, a map which shows its location with respect to the nearest city and a diagram of the manufacturing site, equipment capabilities, and layout of operations. The details of major equipment, such as their location and applications should be mentioned. A mention of the model and make is not needed normally except in cases where the equipment is unique or new. Besides this, diagrammatic representation of the main production and processing areas is provided as it is useful for understanding the operational layout. Normally domestic facilities are not required

TABLE 1.1 Various types of drug master files (DMFs).

S. no.	Type of DMF	Information included
1	Type I	It comprises information of plant and includes details regarding manufacturing site, functional procedures, and personnel. Now a days the FDA does not accept type I DMFs.
2	Type II	This part comprises drug substances, intermediates of drug substance, and substances used in their formulation.
3	Type III	This part comprises information to be submitted for packaging materials. Any information that the manufacturer does not want to disclose to the applicant or sponsor can be put in type III DMFs.
4	Type IV	This part contains details of excipients, colorant, flavor, essence, and materials required for manufacturing.
5	Type V	This part contains reference information accepted by the FDA.

to be described in a Type I DMF. They are only required to be mentioned in special cases when the applicant is not registered and not inspected routinely.

1.2.2.2 Type II: Drug substance, drug substance intermediate, and material used in their preparation, or drug product

A Type II DMF should, in general, contain information related to a single drug intermediate, drug substance, drug product, or type of material used in their production. It summarizes all the major steps followed in the formulation, besides providing information about controls of drug substances and drug intermediates.

"Guideline for Submitting Supporting Documentation in Drug Applications for the Manufacture of Drug Substances" and "Guideline for the Format and Content of the Chemistry, Manufacturing, and Controls Section of an Application" gives an elaborated guidance on the contents and information in Type II DMF for drug substances and intermediates.

1.2.2.2.1 Drug product

In case the information related to procedures for formulation and controls for finished drug products cannot be submitted in other regulatory applications, such as IND, NDA, ANDA, or an export application, it can be submitted in DMF format. The applicant or sponsor filling a DMF for a dosage form should refer "Guideline for the format and content of the Chemistry, Manufacturing and Controls section of an Application," "Guideline for submitting Documentation for the manufacture of and Controls for Drug Products," and "Guideline for submitting samples and analytical data for methods validation" for guidance.

1.2.2.3 Type III: Packaging material

Identification of all the packaging materials should be done based on their intended use, components, composition, as well as its controls and specifications for release. Besides this, names of suppliers of individuals involved in the fabrication of components used in the preparation of materials used for packaging, including their specifications for acceptance should also be mentioned. The applicants are required to refer to "Guideline for submitting documentation for packaging for human drugs and biologics" before submitting data supporting the acceptability of the packaging material for the use for which it is intended. In Type II DMF, toxicological data on the packaging materials can also be submitted in case it is not available as a cross reference to any other document.

1.2.2.4 Type IV: Excipient, colorant, flavor, essence, or material used in their preparation

The information in Type IV DMF includes identification and characterization of all the additives by their manufacturing method, methods of testing, and release specifications. It also includes toxicological data of additives in case it is not available as a cross reference to another document. Guidelines which are suggested for preparing Type II DMF can also be used for making Type IV DMF. Usually 21 Code of Federal Regulation (CFR) Parts 70–82, which relate to the FDA regulations for color additives; 21 CFR Parts 170–173, which relate to direct food additives, 21 CFR Parts 174–178, which relate to indirect food additives; and 21 CFR Parts 181–186, which relate to food substances along with the official compendia may be utilized as sources for safety, specifications, and release tests.

1.2.2.5 Type V: *Food and Drug Administration–accepted reference information*

The use of Type V DMFs are discouraged by the FDA for submitting information which is either miscellaneous or duplicate or which is included in Type I–IV DMFs. In case any applicant or holder wants to submit any data to support a previously submitted data in DMF, he should submit a letter of intent to the DMF staff after which the FDA would contact the concerned holder to discuss the proposed submission.

Besides the above contents, the other information present in DMF includes:

1. Information pertaining to the assessment of environment: In case of types II, III, and IV DMFs, a commitment and assurance by the firm should be given regarding the fact that operation of all its facilities would be done while complying with the environmental laws which are applicable.
2. Information related to design of the stability study, data, its interpretation, as well as other information has to be submitted, as and when admissible, as mentioned in the "Guideline for Submitting Documentation for the Stability of Human Drugs and Biologics."
3. A list of names of individuals who have the authority to add any data or information in the submitted DMF along with the details of the reference number, volume number, as well as page number on which the authorized person can add information. In cases, where the holder allows the authorization for only selected drug products, the drug products name and its application number has also to be mentioned.

The contents presented in DMF can be used as supportive material for the IND, NDA, and ANDA but cannot act as an alternative for IND, ANDA, NDA, or export application.

3. *Purpose of using DMF*

    DMF is used either to maintain secrecy of proprietary data for the holder or to review the data by the FDA to support applications submitted by one or more applicants.
4. *Requirement of DMF submission*

    The individual DMF should include a transmittal letter, administrative information, and special information if needed. DMF should be submitted in English language.
5. *Design of DMF*

The design and contents of the DMF with their amendments are given in Tables 1.2 and 1.3.

TABLE 1.2 Transmittal letter (cover letter).

Original submission	Amendments
1. Identification of submission—authenticity, kind of DMF—its content and objective	1. Identification of submission modification regarding DMF number
2. Recognition of application —sponsor name and address and other relevant documents	2. Recognition of application—details of aim/objective of submission, such as updates and revised formula
3. Signature of the authorized holder	3. Signature of the authorized holder

TABLE 1.3 Administrative information.

Original submission	Amendments
1. Name and address of the following: Corporate headquarters, DMF holder, manufacturing/processing facility, contact details for correspondence from the FDA or Agent(s) if any	1. DMF holder name, DMF number, and correspondence name and address
2. The responsibilities assigned to each person	2. Section affected and/or DMF page number
3. Statement of commitment	3. Individual's name and address, whose IND, ANDA, NDA, and export application depends on amendment subject
—	4. Number and particular items of each IND, ANDA, NDA, and export application

6. *Formatting, assembling, and delivery of DMF*

A copy of the DMF should be retained with DMF holder/agencies and it should be arranged in the same order as submitted. Each volume of DMF is not greater than 2 inch thick and in case of multivolume, each volume should be numbered. For example, if there are four volumes, then volumes are numbered as 1 of 4, 2 of 4, 3 of 4, and 4 of 4.

DMF is prepared in the United States with standard paper size and length not less than 10" or not more than 12". If floor plan, synthesis diagram, batch formula, and manufacturing instruction are to be printed, then larger pages than the standard can be used.

7. *Authorization to DMF and letter of Authorization:*

It refers to a drafted report given by the holder or nominated representative to the FDA. LoA permits the FDA to review the DMF which is only reviewed when LoA is submitted.

8. *Review of the DMF*

The FDA takes 2–3 weeks' time to review the administrative content of the DMF submitted. An acknowledgment letter with a DMF number is dispatched to the candidate after the FDA is satisfied with DMF contents. On the contrary, in case the FDA is not satisfied with the administrative content, it notifies the deficiencies to the holder, which have to be corrected.

The DMF is reviewed by a reviewer as per the flowchart given in Fig. 1.3

The FDA reviews the technical part of the submitted DMF only after:

1. Submission of LoA in duplicate with DMF number to the FDA.
2. Submission of one copy of LoA by the DMF holder to the customer, who is the authorized party.
3. Submission of an application along with a copy of LoA by the customer to the FDA.

1.2.3 Master formula record

It is a master set of documents for a given pharmaceutical product, which is usually prepared by research and development team of a company. It contains a list of starting material with their quantities, preparation method, packaging material, precautions required during manufacture, full description of the product, in-process quality controls, and storing conditions (Patel and Chotai, 2011).

MFR is made to obtain entire information of the finished pharmaceutical product, that is, starting from raw material used to final packaging of the finished pharmaceutical product. It is a very important form of a record that can be checked after regular interval of time to minimize errors and get a safe product. It acts as a standard for preparing batch manufacturing record, which is to be prepared during preparation of each batch of given finished pharmaceutical product (Pharmaceutical Inspection Co-operation Scheme PE 009-3, 2006).

1. *Preparation of MFR*

Production department in association with formulation and development (F&D) department generally prepares MFR. It is either prepared by the qualified staff, such as manufacturing chemist or analytical chemist, depending upon their experience or it is prepared from the documents obtained through batch manufacturing record of batch

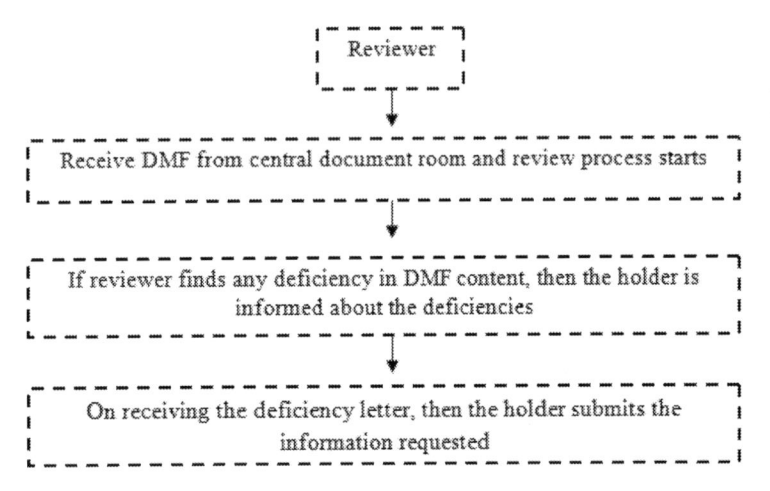

FIGURE 1.3 Review of drug master file (DMF). (*Adapted with modification from "Drug Master Files", Cyclone pharmaceuticals", 2015, https://www.https://www.slideshare.net/ cyclonepharma/dmf-drug-master-file.*)

size. Production Manager is responsible for checking of the MFR. The final approval and final authorization of the MFR is the responsibility of the QA manager and General Manager of QA/QC department, respectively. Their names and designations shall be mentioned below their signatures along with the date of signing the document.

2. *Parts of MFR*

MFR is divided into two parts (Patel and Chotai, 2011):

a. Manufacturing part;
b. Packaging part.

The first page of both parts contains the following details:

a. Name, address, and logo of the company;
b. Formulation and its strength;
c. Brand name and product's generic name;
d. Code of product and description of product;
e. Label claim;
f. Size of batch;
g. Shelf life;
h. Storage condition;
i. Drug schedule—whether "H" or "G" drug;
j. Authorization of MFR by responsible staff.

The second page of manufacturing part contains the flowchart describing the entire process, which includes the stage-wise movement of material from dispensing of material to transfer of a batch to finished stores. Besides this, it also contains the list of equipment, machines, and apparatus used.

The third page contains any special precautions to be taken during manufacturing and packing of the product besides containing the batch manufacturing formula.

The fourth page contains a stage-wise and step-wise manufacturing process and at the end of each process. The yield obtained is mentioned with acceptable limits and the result of in-process quality checks.

The packaging part of MFR enlists the packaging material for given batch size, including quantities, sizes, and types.

3. *Contents of MFR*

The MFR comprises the following contents:

- Name of the product, its logo, and manufacturing company address;
- The generic name, brand name, patent or proprietary name, name of dosage form, strength, composition, shelf life, and batch size;
- Equipment and machines with their capacities used for manufacturing and the manufacturing location;
- Quantities of material used for manufacturing, steps of manufacturing, and precautions during manufacturing;
- Step-wise details about the instructions to be followed during processing along with the time taken by each and every processing step;
- Expected final yield and also intermediate yield statement with acceptable limits;
- In-process control measures with their acceptable limits;
- Special mention of ingredients that have a possibility of disappearing during the manufacturing process;
- Methods of cleaning, sanitization, sterilization, etc.;
- Details of packaging materials, such as bottle and boxes;
- Labeling details, storage conditions, and packaging material and packaging techniques used;
- Any special precaution and instructions if applicable.

1.2.4 Batch manufacturing formula record

The batch manufacturing record is the required quality and GMP documentation record of manufacturing and control for each batch. It contains the following (Patel and Chotai, 2011; Pharmaceutical Inspection Co-operation Scheme PE 009-3, 2006):

1. Serial number and dates;
2. Brand name of the dosage form;
3. Batch number or lot number;
4. Batch size or lot size;
5. Reference of the specification of ingredients;
6. Name of the ingredients;
7. Quantity of the ingredients to be added (in mg/mL or /tablet or /capsule or /g as the case may be), overages to be added (in %);
8. Date on which the manufacturing started and date on which the manufacturing completed;
9. Manufacturing date and expiry date;
10. Maximum retail price;
11. Reference detail of MFR;
12. Date and time for each manufacturing step along with the name and signatures of personnel present during the production and conduct of analytical procedures;
13. Name of all the operators and concerned staff who are involved in performing the different processes;
14. Details of quality and grade of all the ingredients verified by the quality control department;
15. Time consumed in carrying out each and every step of the production, such as blending time and stirring time;
16. Information and data pertaining to environmental factors, such as temperature and relative humidity and standards of quality assurance, wherever applicable;
17. Date and time of taking test samples for analysis along with results of evaluations done both during production and after production, such as hardness test and disintegration test, wherever applicable;
18. Inspection records;
19. Washing records of all the equipment, machinery, and other applicable things;
20. Information about theoretical yield, yield which is allowable and admissible, and yield actually obtained along with a variation record containing clarifications in case any;
21. Reprocessing details in case applicable;
22. Details of packaging materials along with a sample of the printed packaging material.

1.2.5 Distribution record

These are defined as record consisting of data associated with distribution of drugs from the manufacturer to the distributors. Such records are required for meeting the GMP regulations (available from https://www.fda.gov/media/71518/download).

1.2.5.1 Objective

The objective of such record is that if there occurs any adverse drug reaction or some quality defect, then such batches are promptly withdrawn from the market by the manufacturer.

1.2.5.2 Contents of distribution record

The distribution record has the following contents:

1. Product information: It gives information regarding product name, manufacturer identity, batch number, strength, and type of dosage form.
2. Transaction information: It gives information regarding sales transfer, return of any product, or any other documents related to the product, such as quantity, invoice number, and invoice date.
3. Distribution information: It gives information regarding distribution of product (selling/transferring) to other group or party. It involves the name of the person who will distribute the product and also the signature of the person.
4. Recipient information: It tells about the party/person receiving the product. It involves name, address of the recipient, and signature and also the data collected.

1.3 Applications filed by the Drug Regulatory Affairs department

The various applications filed by the DRA department include IND, NDA, ANDA, biologics license application (BLA), Trademark registrations, and GMP certifications, etc.

1.3.1 Investigational new drug application

The current regulatory conditions requires that before a drug can be transported or distributed, a marketing approval for the same has to be taken by the pharmaceutical company or sponsor. Since a sponsor has to ship its new investigational drug to many clinical investigators in different states, he requires an exemption from such regulation. The exemption can be obtained by filing an IND with the FDA (https://www.fda.gov/drugs/types-applications/investigational-new-drug-ind-application).

In other words, an IND application filed with FDA is legal means by which any sponsor or pharmaceutical facility can obtain permission to either transport an experimental or investigational drug across different states to clinical investigators or start clinical trials in humans, before obtaining approval for marketing of the same. The regulations are mainly given in 21 C.F.R.312.

IND falls into two categories:

- Commercial IND: This is filed by a pharmaceutical company to get marketing approval for new drug. A commercial IND application is submitted by a sponsor, which is in most of the cases a corporate body, who wishes to commercialize his product. For a commercial IND submission, the sponsor has to select "Commercial IND" option in the Form 1571 Field 6B of IND.
- Research (noncommercial) IND: To study either an unapproved drug or an approved drug for a new application or in a new population set, a physician can submit a research IND. A research IND, the sponsor is an academic institution, individual investigator, or a nonprofit organization.

IND is of the following types:

1. An Investigator IND: This type of IND filling is initiated by a clinician who not only initiates a clinical investigation using the experimental drug but also conducts the investigation in which the investigational drug is dispensed or administered under his immediate direction.
2. Emergency Use IND: This IND authorizes the application and administration of an experimental drug in an emergency situation when there is no time for submitting an IND which complies with the Sec. 312.23 or Sec. 312.20 of the 21 CFR. It can also be used in cases where there is no existence of a study protocol which is approved or also in those cases where the patients do not fulfill the existing study protocol criteria.
3. Treatment IND: For experimental drugs showing promising results in clinical testing for immediately life-threatening conditions or serious diseases, a treatment IND is filed during the time final clinical study is being conducted and when the FDA is reviewing the application for approval for marketing.
4. Screening INDs: They are filed for screening multiple, closely related compounds, such as different salts, esters, and other derivatives of drug that are different chemically but show similarity pharmacodynamically. Each preferred compound is then developed under a separate IND.

The information furnished in an IND application must be in three broad areas:

- Animal Pharmacology and Toxicology Studies—This includes data and results of preclinical studies conducted to permit an assessment of whether or not the drug is safe for initial testing in human subject. Besides this, any previous studies with the drug used in humans, often in foreign countries, are also mentioned.
- Manufacturing Information—This includes data and other relevant information regarding the manufacturer, composition, stability, and manufacturing controls pertaining to the drug and drug product. This information is assessed for ensuring whether or not the manufacturing company can produce and supply consistent drug batches adequately.
- Clinical Protocols and Investigator Information—This includes all the protocols for the clinical studies proposed in detail so that assessment can be made about whether or not the initial clinical trials would expose the humans to unnecessary risks. In order to ascertain whether the clinical investigators are qualified enough to oversee the administration of experimental drug and to perform other clinical trial duties, information regarding their qualification is also included. Besides this, commitments to get informed consent from human subjects under study, to obtain review of the investigation during its conduction by the institutional review board, and to comply with the investigational new drug regulations are also given.

After submitting an IND, the sponsor of the study has to wait for 30 calendar days before starting any clinical trial. In this tenure, the FDA has time to assess the IND for safety to ascertain that the human subjects under study are not exposed to any kind of unreasonable risk.

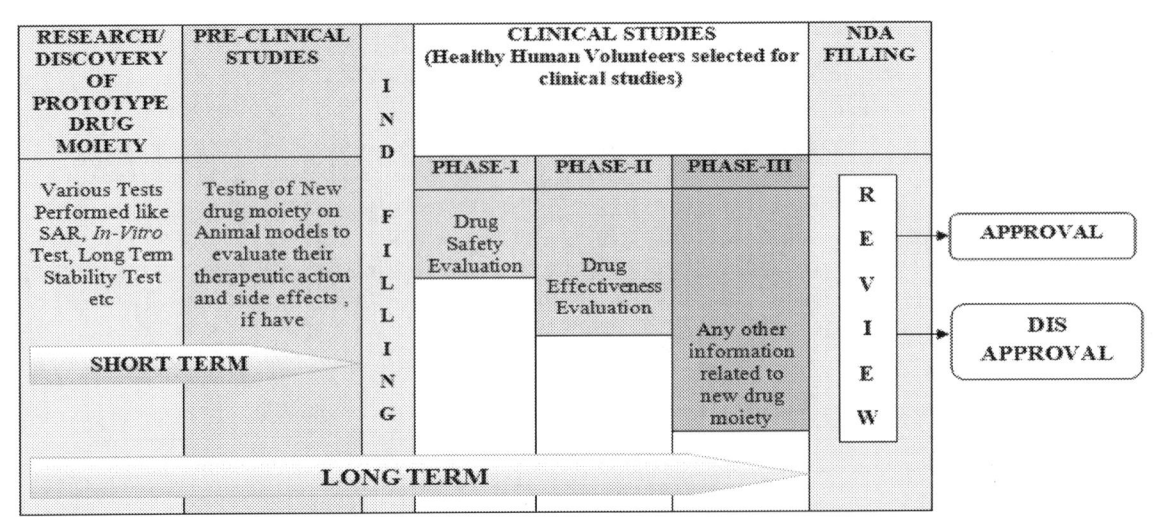

FIGURE 1.4 Schematic representation of new drug application (NDA) filing timeline. *(Adapted with modification from "Non clinical drug development-New Drug Application", S Gokulakrishnan, 2019, https://www.slideshare.net/GokulKrishnan170/new-drug-application-nda-175661807 and "New Drug Application-NDA", S. K. Savale, https://www.slideshare.net/sagarsavale1/new-drug-application-nda, 2016).*

1.3.2 New drug application

The filing of an NDA is the final step related to a new drug approval adopted by a sponsor. It is an application filed to the FDA by the sponsors of the new drug to seek approval for marketing their product in the United States. It is an exhaustive document consisting of 20 sections covering information ranging from process of manufacturing of the new drug to information related to the animal and human studies conducted using the new drug (NDA) (available from https://www.fda.gov/drugs/types-applications/new-drug-application-nda).

1.3.2.1 Goals of new drug application

The NDA has the following goals:

1. To check whether or not the new drug is safe and effective for use for which it is recommended.
2. To check whether or not the advantages of using the new drug outweigh the risks involving its use.
3. To check the appropriateness and completeness of the labeling recommended for the new drug with a check on its contents.
4. To check the adequacy of the processes followed in the formulation GMPs of the therapeutic agent as well as their controls in preserving the strength and identity of the drug.

1.3.2.2 When will we go for new drug application?

The NDA filing process is started after getting satisfactory results from the preclinical and clinical studies (Fig. 1.4).

1.3.2.3 Content and format of an new drug application application

The application for NDA besides having **Form FDA-356h** has 20 sections in which the applicant has to submit data for getting approval of drug product. The Form **FDA-356h**, besides acting as a checklist, certifies the fact that the sponsor has agreed that he will meet all legal and regulatory requirements (Guidance for Industry Submitting Marketing Applications According to the ICH-CTD Format—General Considerations. Available from: https://www.fda.gov/media/71666/download). The contents of an NDA application are given in Table 1.4.

For filling an NDA, the applicant has to submit three copies, namely archival copy, review copy, and a field copy (https://www.accessdata.fda.gov/scripts/cdrh/cfdocs/cfcfr/CFRSearch.cfm?fr = 314.50).

A. Archival copy

The copy which serves as a source of reference for the reviewers of the FDA includes a full copy of the submitted application. The reviewers can use the copy to get information and data not mentioned in their review copy, which contains only a particular section of the NDA. The archival copy has the following contents:

TABLE 1.4 Contents of new drug application (NDA).

S. no.	Name	Section of NDA
1	Index	I
2	Labeling	II
3	Application summary	III
4	Chemistry, manufacturing, and controls (CMC)	IV
5	Nonclinical pharmacology and toxicology	V
6	Human pharmacokinetics and bioavailability	VI
7	Clinical microbiology	VII
8	Clinical data	VIII
9	Safety update reports	IX
10	Statistics	X
11	Case report tabulations	XI
12	Case report forms	XII
13	Patent information	XIII
14	Patent certification	XIV
15	Establishment description	XV
16	Debarment certificate	XVI
17	Field copy certification	XVII
18	User fee coversheet	XVIII
19	Financial disclosure	XIX
20	Other	XX

1. *Cover letter*
2. *Form FDA-356h*
3. *Index*

   A comprehensive index by page number and volume number for summary, technical sections, and any supporting information has to be given in archival copy.

4. *Summary*

   It requires detailed information so as to provide a general insight of the application regarding the data and information included in it.

5. *Technical sections*

   It includes the required details of technical data and information for the FDA to analyze and judge whether to approve or disapprove the NDA application.

   a. Chemistry, manufacturing, and controls section:

      This section includes the information relating not only to the composition but also furnishes details of manufacture as well as specifications of the active drug and its formulation.

   b. Nonclinical pharmacological and toxicological section:

      The section includes information related to the following studies:

      i. *Pharmacology studies*:

         This section includes studies relating to the drug pharmacological actions in relation to its expected therapeutic indication followed by studies which are related to the possible adverse drug reactions and interactions with other drugs.

      ii. *Acute toxicity studies*:

         Details, such as age of the animals in the study, dosing procedure, and volume of doses should be clearly specified.

    iii. *Subchronic/chronic/carcinogenicity studies*:

        All the studies assessing the drugs subchronic toxicity, chronic toxicity, and carcinogenicity are included in this section. The results of the study should include observed effects, mortality, food /water consumption, body weight, physical examination, blood chemistry/urine analysis/Absorption, Distribution, Metabolism, and Excretion data.

    iv. *Reproduction studies*:

        This section contains information related to the drug effects on reproduction and on the fetus which is under development.

    v. *Mutagenicity studies*:

    This section includes results of mutagenicity studies carried on either in vitro or in vivo nonmammalian cell system or in in vitro or in vivo mammalian cell system.

  c. *Human pharmacokinetics and bioavailability section*:

    This includes all studies related to biopharmaceutics of the drug conducted in humans.

  d. *Microbiology section*:

    For all antiinfective and antiviral drugs, the NDA includes a section on microbiological data. This technical section includes a narration of the biochemical basis of the drugs action on microbial physiology.

  e. *Clinical data section*:

    This is the most complicated NDA section, which consists of the clinical investigations of the drug. It includes narration and analysis of each study relating to the clinical pharmacology of the drug and toxicology data.

  f. *Statistical section*:

    This describes the statistical evaluation of clinical data.

  g. *Pediatric use section*:

    This section describes the findings of the investigation of drug for administration in pediatric population.

6. Samples and labeling:

    The applicant has to submit four representative samples of drug product which is proposed to be marketed, the sample of drug utilized in the drug product and sample of blanks and reference standards except those that are mentioned in the official compendias. Besides this, in case the FDA asks, the applicant has to submit finished market package samples. Also included in the archival copy are either four copies of drafts of labels or 12 copies of final labeling which is printed.

7. *Three copies of chemistry, manufacturing, and control section (CMC), methods validation package*

8. *Case report tabulations and case report forms.*

B. Review copy:

    Besides an archival copy, the applicant also has to submit a review copy. In a review copy each of the technical sections are bound separately along with a summary copy and application form.

C. Field copy:

The field copy submitted by the applicant contains the CMC, application form copy, and a summary copy besides containing a certification that the CMC section included in the field copy is a true and original copy of the section as given in the review and archival copies of the NDA.

1.3.2.4 Review of new drug application

Under the Food and Drug Administration Modernization Act (FDAMA), the review of the NDA based on its anticipated potential in diagnosis and treatment is classified (Chen, 2019) as follows:

1. *Standard review*: All drug products which are similar to those drug products already available in the market (also referred to and considered as standard) are considered non-priority applications and are subjected to standard review. In case of a standard review, the FDA has to complete application review within 6 months after the filing date.

2. *Priority review*- If the drug product for which the NDA is filed shows a marked improvement in either prevention, treatment, or diagnosis of a disease, it is taken for priority review. The goal of the FDA under priority review is to take action within 6 months of NDA filing.

Besides the option for priority review, the other methods used by the CDER for expediting the review process include:

- Fast track approval:

    To promote the development process and to allow expedited review of medicines which are used for treating either serious conditions or which provide a medical treatment to a disease with no treatment available earlier. This approval process is used for making the new and important medications available to the patient at the earliest.
- Breakthrough therapy:

    This process of review is aimed at expediting the formulation and review of medications meant for treatment of conditions which are serious, and the results of clinical studies done preliminarily indicate that the drug has the potential to provide substantial improvement on the clinically significant endpoints as compared to the available therapies.
- Accelerated approval:

This review was instituted by the FDA in 1992. This allows expedited approval of drugs meant for treatment of serious medical ailments with unmet medical needs on the basis of surrogate endpoint.

After the completion of the review of NDA application by the FDA, the FDA gives its response to the applicant in the form of action letters, which are of the following three types:

1. An approval letter
2. An approvable letter
3. A nonapprovable letter

1.3.3   Abbreviated new drug application

The approval of a generic drug product requires the filing of an ANDA by the applicant. Any drug product for which an equivalence can be established with the innovators' product in terms of safety and effectiveness is referred to as a generic drug product. In comparison to the innovators' formulation, the cost of the generic product is less, thereby making it affordable and a substitute with a reduced cost (ANDA; https://www.fda.gov/drugs/developmentapprovalprocess/howdrugsaredevelopedandapproved/approvalapplications/abbreviatednewdrugapplicationandagenerics/default.html).

1.3.3.1   *Goals of abbreviated new drug application*

ANDA is filed with the following goals:

1. To reduce the delay in getting drug approval.
2. To facilitate an environment of healthy competition with avoidance of increase in prices of drugs.
3. To facilitate getting approval of generic drugs by manufacturers based on the establishment of their bioequivalence with the innovators' drug product without carrying out any preclinical and clinical studies.

1.3.3.2   *Content and format of abbreviated new drug application*

The items that should be included in an ANDA are as follows:

1. Application form: The applicant has to fill up and submit a signed application form, which gives details related to the applicant's name and address.
2. Table of content: Index is also included and should show both the page and the volume number for each item.
3. Basis for ANDA submission: An ANDA must contain a reference listed drug, which is usually a drug that the FDA selects as a reference standard for the conduct of bioequivalence testing. Besides the reference listed drug name, dose, and strength, a statement on exclusivity is also included in this section.
4. Conditions of use: The conditions for which the drug will be used should be mentioned.
5. Active ingredient:-

    The information which shows that the API of the formulation is same as that of the reference listed drug should be included. For a combinatorial formulation, the information should be provided for each of the drug candidates present in the combination.
6. Route of administration, dosage form, and strength: All the data which proves that the drug product for which an ANDA is being filed has the same administration route, strength, and formulation as the reference listed drug should be included in this section.

7. Bioequivalence: It includes all the information which proves the bioequivalence of the proposed drug product to the reference listed drug besides containing a thorough description of the statistical and the analytical procedures used in the conduct of the in vivo bioequivalence study mentioned in the ANDA.
8. Labeling: This part comprises both a copy of the labeling proposed for the formulation for which an ANDA is filed and a copy of the labeling approved for the listed drug.
9. CMC: This part of ANDA provides information related to the contents, method of formulation, specifications, and the methods used for the analysis of the drug and its formulation.
10. Human pharmacokinetics and bioavailability: This section must contain full reports of all the bioavailability and bioequivalence studies that show that the product complies with the regulations published by the FDA.
11. Samples: All samples of the finished product should be made available to the FDA as four individuals in sufficient quantity so that the test given in application can be performed at least three times.
12. Analytical methods: This contains all the analytical methods, validation methods, stability indications as given in the CMC section of the application.
13. Labeling: This consists of 4 copies of draft or 12 copies of the final printed label intended to be put on the product.
14. Case report and tabulations: This contains case report forms of bioequivalence studies and safety data, including side effects or any other noted side effects. These reports are to be included only if they are found to be necessary by the personnel of the division of the bioequivalence.

1.3.3.3 Approval time for abbreviated new drug application

Within a period of 60 days of receipt of ANDA application by the FDA, the FDA determines whether or not the application is fit to be considered for filing. In case of the FDA being satisfied with the quantum of information given by the ANDA application by the applicant, it will file the application. However, if the FDA is not satisfied, it would notify the applicant in writing regarding refusal to file along with the reason for the same. Upon receipt of the refusal letter, the applicant can within 30 days of the receipt of the refusal letter from the FDA can request the FDA to review ANDA again. A pictorial representation of the ANDA approval process is given in Fig. 1.5.

1.3.3.4 Generic drug product development

Generic drug products are defined as the substitutes of brand name drugs having the same dosage form, strength, safety, efficacy, and the route of administration as the original formulation. A drug product which is of generic origin needs to be affordable and accessible with low prices (IMS Health Data, 2003; Shargel and Kanfer, 2013).

Formulation of a generic dosage form involves a group of tasks which start with the understanding of opportunities of the market and ends in the manufacture, sale, and distribution of a generic product (IMS Health Data, 2003).

1.3.3.5 Selection criteria for formulation of a generic drug product

The different factors that determine the choice of generic drug product for formulation include (Parker et al., 1991; History of the Food and Drug Administration, 2003) the following:

1. Availability of API.
2. Timing: The manufacturer of the generic drug product requires some lead time for making the product and submitting it to the USFDA for approval.
3. Technology: The choice of generic drug depends on the availability and cost of technology.
4. Formulation: The manufacturing of generic drug also depends on the accessibility of raw material, its purity, polymeric state, size of particles, and any patent filed by the innovator.
5. Experience: The choice of generic drug product also depends on the experience and expertise of manufacturing a particular drug product. For example, some manufacturers have experience in producing immediate and modified release solid and oral dosage form only, whereas other manufacturers produce transdermal or inhalational drug products.

1.3.3.5.1 Generic drug approval process

The office of the FDA is responsible for the generic dosage form approval. A formulation which is generic is only approved if (Approved Drug Products with Therapeutic Equivalence Evaluations "Orange Book," 2003):

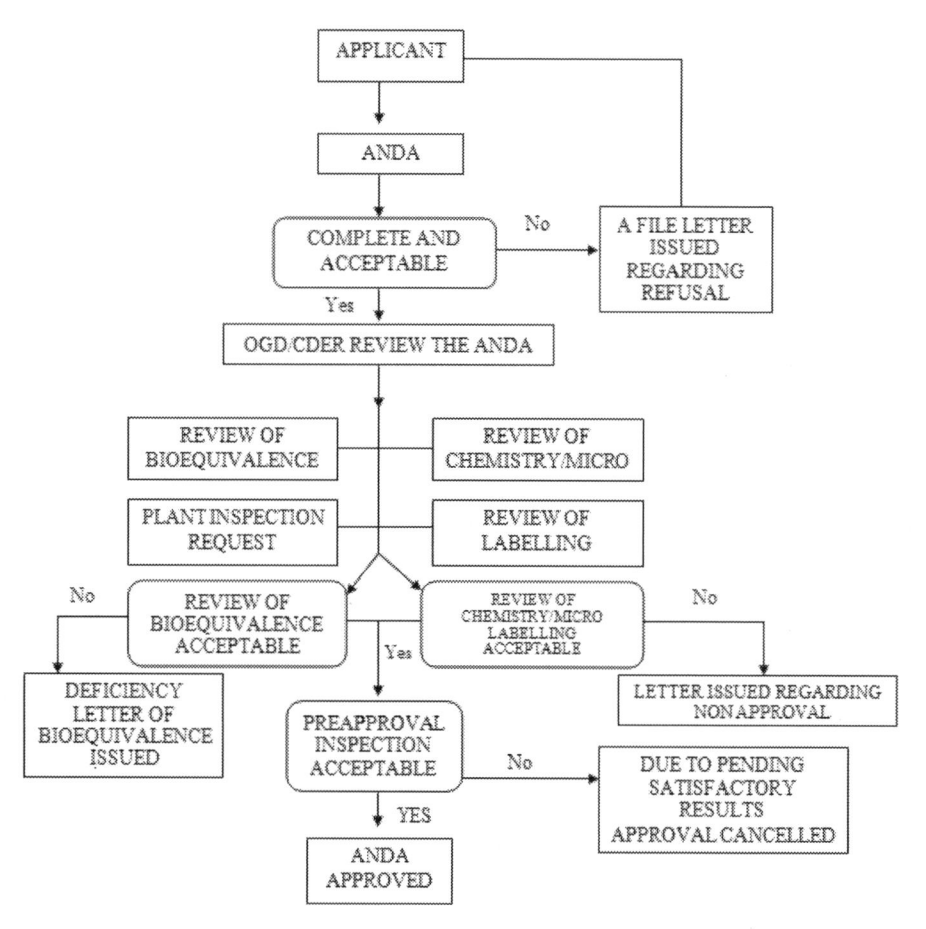

FIGURE 1.5 Schematic representation of the abbreviated new drug application (ANDA) approval process. *(Adapted with modification from "Regulatory Requirements and Registration Procedure for Generic Drugs in USA" by Rafi N, Sandeep DS, Narayanan AV, 2018, Indian J of Pharmaceutical Education and Research,52 (4):544-9 with permission).*

1. It has the same API as in the reference listed drug product.
2. It contains the same strength, concentration, dosage form, and route of administration.
3. It is bioequivalent.
4. It is pure.

1.4   Hatch−Waxman Act and amendments

The Hatch−Waxman also referred to as "The Drug Price Competition and Patent Term Restoration Act" was enacted in 1984. The act amended Section 505(j) codified as 21 U.S.C. Section 355(j), of the Federal Food, Drug, and Cosmetic Act. The Act gives guidelines and the procedure the drug manufacturing companies have to adopt to file an ANDA for getting their generic formulation approved from the FDA (Mossinghoff, 1999).

The Hatch−Waxman Act was introduced with the following objectives:

1. To decrease the cost of approval of generic drug product;
2. To facilitate and allow early experimental use of generic drug product;
3. To motivate the manufacturers of generic drugs;
4. To compensate the branded drug manufacturer for the time lapsed from the term of a patent while completing the regulatory formalities for drug approval.

Hatch−Waxman Act's Title I brought amendment in the United States Federal Food, Drug, and Cosmetic Act (FD&C Act). Section 505 introduced the concept of ANDA, which permitted the approval of generics on the basis of bioequivalence. Changes regarding patent law were made to the U.S. Code Title 35 by Title II of the Act. The drug innovators were awarded a new time span pertaining to data exclusivity, which was five years after the approval of their drug for marketing by the FDA. During this five-year tenure, no generic versions of the innovators' products were given approval by the FDA.

Hatch—Waxman Act created abbreviated processes that allow the manufacturer of a generic drug to obtain the FDA approval. According to this Act, approval is granted to ANDA on the basis of evidence that the generic formulation is a "bioequivalent" of a formulation for which the FDA has approved a full NDA, without any further need for carrying out animal experiments to establish that the generic formulation is both safe and effective.

The Act was useful both for the innovators and for the generic drug manufacturers. The drug innovators were awarded a new time frame of data exclusivity, which was five years after approval of their drug for marketing by the FDA. During this five-year tenure, no generic versions of the innovators' products were given approval by the FDA (Garth et al., 2013). Besides this, the life of the patent was also extended by the time period during which the product was under review by the FDA (Schacht and Thomas, 2004). Besides this, a three-year exclusivity period was granted for better versions of brand pharmaceuticals, which required additional clinical studies for the FDA approval. It was notified that during this exclusivity period, no manufacturer of generic products can get approval from the FDA marketing of generic versions of the improved drugs.

Besides providing protection to the innovators, the act also gave incentives to generic companies to file ANDAs (Garth et al., 2013). It also gives the "research exemption" protection to generic manufacturers. It is the time during which the generic company has to learn all processes for which can be sued by the innovator for infringement. These activities include method of manufacture not only of the drug and the test batch but also how to conduct its bioequivalence study (Garth et al., 2013; Schacht and Thomas, 2004).

According to the provisions of the act, the innovator company has to give the FDA the data regarding the patents which could possibly cover its drug. These data are not evaluated by the FDA. The FDA, however, provides a list of all such patents provided by the innovator publicly in the Orange Book (Schacht and Thomas, 2004).

According to the provisions of the act, whenever a generic drug manufacturer is equipped with desired data to submit an ANDA application for approval, the company has to announce the relation of its drug product to the list of patents given in the Orange Book. In this regard, four patent certifications exist.

1.4.1 Orange Book

The formal name of "Orange Book" is Approved Drug Products with Therapeutic Equivalence Evaluations (Chen, 2020). It is an electronic database which is freely available and consists of a list of drugs approved by the FDA along with patent and exclusivity information. In case of withdrawal of safety or efficacy approval of drugs, the drugs are excluded from the Orange Book. An Orange Book is a reliable tool for medical professionals and researchers not only for finding information related to the FDA-approved drugs, but also to search for generic formulations which are equivalents to proprietary drugs as well as to information on patents and drug exclusivity (Orange Book and its Applications, 2019).

To get a drug approved by the FDA, the applicant of an NDA needs to deposit the information as listed below:

1. Patent number and its expiry date
2. Product type
3. Patent holder name

The Orange Book has different codes which are given in Table 1.5.

1.4.1.1 Main uses of Orange Book

Orange book has the following uses which are documented as follows (Orange Book and its Applications, 2019):

- To retrieve information, such as date of drug application, date of approval, and list of related patents, and to confirm whether the patents relate to drug substance (DS) or drug product (DP).
- To find out the dates of expiry of the corresponding patents.
- To get information on drugs of the innovators and to find out information about the corresponding generic drugs which have been approved.
- It helps the pharmaceutical industries to take important decisions and make appropriate strategies regarding whether they should enter the market for sale or have to modify their existing product before entering the market.
- It helps to identify the period of patent exclusivity as well as respective deadlines for any drugs which have been approved. Example: From Orange Book information, such as the 7 years drug exclusivity period for the Orphan Drug, the 5 years' time period for New Chemical Entity (NCE) Exclusivity, the 3 years' time period for the NCE Exclusivity drugs, and 6 months' time period for pediatrics can be known.

TABLE 1.5 Codes given in the Orange Book.

S. no.	Code assigned	Drug product designated
1	A	This code is applicable to those drug products which are therapeutic equivalents to other drug products. For these products, sufficient evidence in the form of in vitro and in vivo data is available in support of their bioequivalence.
2	AA	This code is applicable to those drug products which are present in conventional dosage forms but do not show any bioequivalence problems.
3	AB	This code is applicable to drug products which meet necessary requirements of bioequivalence.
4	AN	This code is applicable to solutions and powders used for aerosolization.
5	AO	This code is applicable to injectable oil solution.
6	AP	This code applies to aqueous solutions and, in certain cases, nonaqueous solutions meant to be administered as injectables.
7	AT	This code applies to products to be applied topically.
8	B	This code applies to those drug products that the FDA, at this time, does not consider therapeutically equivalent to other available pharmaceutically equivalent products.
9	B*	This code applies to those drug products which require further investigation and review by the FDA to establish therapeutic equivalence.
10	BC	This code applies to formulations (capsules, tablets, and injectables) which are administered for releasing the drug for an extended duration.
11	BD	This code applies to active pharmaceutical ingredients and formulations whose problems related to bioequivalence have been documented.
12	BE	This code applies to those dosage forms which are meant for oral administration and for providing a delayed release of the drug.
13	BN	This code applies to drug products administered in aerosol–nebulizer dosage form.
14	BP	This code applies to active pharmaceutical ingredients and dosage forms which exhibit potential problems related to bioequivalence.
15	BR	This code applies to suppositories or enemas that are used to deliver drugs meant for systemic absorption.
16	BS	This code applies to drug formulations which have deficiencies in drug standard.
17	BT	This code applies to topical drug products which are associated with bioequivalence issues.
18	BX	This code applies to formulations for which insufficient information is available for determination of therapeutic equivalence.

- It helps to identify the polymorphs which exist for patented drugs of the innovators, based on which the drug patented by the innovator can be challenged in order to avail the benefit of market exclusivity for 180 days by filing an ANDA in the United States.

1.4.2 Biologics license application

The BLA is required by the sponsor to permit introduction of a biological product into interstate commerce according to the provisions of Section 351 of the Public Health Service (PHS) Act of the United States. A biological product consists of large and complex molecules generally produced through biotechnology using living system, such as microorganism, plant cell, or animal cell. A large number of products, such as blood and blood components, allergenics, gene therapy, tissues, somatic cells, recombinant therapeutic proteins, and vaccines come under biological products. The BLA is regulated under 21 CFR 600–680. A BLA can be given by any legal person or entity which is involved in manufacturing of biological product or an applicant who takes full responsibility for compliance of biological product with the required standards.

The FDA form 356h which is used for NDA submission is also used for BLA submission. Following are the requirements for BLA as specified in the FDA form 356h

- Summary of the necessary information;
- Applicant information;
- Product/manufacturing information, including information related to the chemistry and controls of the product;
- Summary of data related to the validation of different procedures used in the product manufacturing;
- Preclinical studies data;
- Clinical studies data, including data pertaining to safety and efficacy of the product;
- A draft of labeling of the product;
- An elaborate description of the facility used for manufacturing the product;
- Mention of the case reports related to the clinical experience of the manufacturer;
- Information about the serious events as well as case report forms;
- Index.

After getting the BLA, the FDA authorities first evaluate it for its completeness. The FDA then reviews the BLA application to get complete understanding of the quality, efficacy, and safety of the proposed biological product. Generally it takes around 8 months for the FDA to decide on BLA application after its submission (Parkman and Hardegree, 1999).

1.4.3 Marketing Authorization Application

A manufacturer who wants to seek authorization for marketing his medicinal product, either new or generic has to submit a Marketing Authorization Application (MAA). The process of MAA is equivalent to the process of NDA. MAA has to be submitted to the Medicines and Healthcare products Regulatory Agency in the United Kingdom and the Committee for Medicinal Products for Human Use of the European Medicines Agency, which is a special agency of the European Commission.

1.4.4 Scale-up, process approval changes, and postmarketing surveillance

An NDA approval and an ANDA approval are the first steps required for a new drug product and a generic drug product for commercialization, respectively. However, changes in the CMC section are also done many a time even after getting the NDA and ANDA approval. Such changes can even continue throughout the life span of the drug product. Besides this, alteration in size of batch of an NDA- or an ANDA-approved formulation following changes in the market forecast, qualification of a new source for the active therapeutic agent, optimization of the process of manufacturing of the drug product, replacement of the initial container-closure system with an advanced version or advent of advanced methods of analysis, and specifications are few reasons for undertaking changes in an approved NDA or an approved ANDA. However, since these changes can have a tremendous influence on the strength, identity, purity, quality, potency, and ultimately safety and efficacy of the final drug product, all such changes need to be thoroughly evaluated [FDA. Center for Drug Evaluation and Research, Guidance for Industry: Immediate Release Solid Oral Dosage Forms. Scale-up and Post-Approval Changes: Chemistry, Manufacturing and Controls, In Vitro Dissolution Testing, and In Vivo Bioequivalence Documentation (SUPAC-IR), 1995].

The FDA has provided guidance documents which contain recommendations to holders of approved NDA and approved ANDA who are interested in doing postapproval changes in accordance with section 506A of the Federal Food, Drug, and Cosmetic Act (the Act) and Section 314.70 (21 CFR 314.70).

Before the advent of the FDAMA, Scale-up and postapproval changes (SUPAC) which served as an important milestone for the drug industry was the ground for FD&C Act revision. The SUPAC elaborated the 21 CFR part 314.70 and described more elaborately the types of changes as well as the category under which they have to be reported [Guidance for Industry. Immediate Release Solid Oral Dosage Forms Scale-Up and Post-approval Changes: Chemistry, Manufacturing, and Controls, In Vitro Dissolution Testing, and In Vivo Bioequivalence Documentation. Center for Drug and Research (CDER), November 1995, CMC (Chemistry, Manufacturing, and Controls) 5].

According to the SUPAC guidance, the most likely areas where the passivity of change is observed include the drug product composition, change in the formulation site of the dosage form, drug products scale-up, equipment used in the manufacture of the drug product, and packaging.

TABLE 1.6 Three levels of changes as given by the Food and Drug Administration.

Level	Definition
1	It includes all those changes which are unlikely to influence the quality and performance of the formulation in a detectable way.
2	It includes all those changes whose influence on the quality and performance of the formulation could be significant.
3	It includes all those changes that are expected to significantly influence the quality as well as performance of the formulation.

According to SUPAC, all the changes were categorized according to "levels." The guidance also enlisted the requirements for each designated level. According to the SUPAC guidance, three levels of changes are described, which are given in Table 1.6.

Changes categorized in Level I include a small change in the amount of the excipient added (e.g., lactose), which is not likely to have any influence on altering the quality or performance of the formulation. On the other hand, changes described in level 3 include a condition in which an alteration in the excipients (qualitative or quantitative) is beyond a permissible limit, especially for formulations exhibiting a therapeutic range, which is narrow. For such changes, a bioequivalence evaluation has to be conducted in vivo to establish that no alteration is occurring in the quality as well as the performance of the formulation after implementation of the proposed modification.

Besides this, the guidance also describes the suggested chemistry, production, and control tests; in vitro dissolution tests; and bioequivalence tests for each designated level. Information and guidance describing the documents which are required to be provided in support of the change is also provided in SUPAC.

1.4.5 Food and Drug Administration Modernization Act

On November 21, 1997, the FDAMA was signed, which later became law. The FDAMA was aimed to clarify the current FD&C Act, besides defining the regulatory requirements required for commercialization of drugs approved in the United States (Guidance for Industry. Changes to an Approved NDA or ANDA. U.S. Department of Health and Human Services, Food and Drug Administration, Center for Drug Evaluation and Research (CDER), November 1999, CMC).

The FDAMA is defined for four reporting categories, which are summarized below:

1. *Prior approval supplement*: This includes all the major changes for which approval of the FDA is required before implementation.
2. *Supplement*: *changes being effected (30 days):* This includes all the moderate changes for which a notice period of 30 days is required prior to their implementation.
3. *Supplement: changes being effected (0 day)*: This includes all the changes which are moderate and be immediately implemented.
4. *Annual report*: This includes all the changes which are minor and can be immediately implemented as well as filed in the subsequent Periodic Report.

1.4.6 Postmarketing surveillance

Postmarketing surveillance is conducted by manufacturers after the formulation is approved by the regulatory agency for marketing. It is an important part of pharmacovigilance and is a practice undertaken to monitor the safety of a drug or a medical device after it has been marketed. The U.S. Federal Code of Regulations, 21 CFR 314.80, has set forth the requirements for reporting postmarketing events, the principal part being the condition-related *adverse drug experiences (ADEs)* reporting (Guidance for Industry. Postmarketing Adverse Experience Reporting for Human Drug and Licensed Biological Products: Clarification of What to Report. Food and Drug Administration, August 1997).

21 CFR defines an ADE as any adverse experience which is linked with the application of a drug in humans, irrespective of whether it is linked to drug or not. Adverse experiences that occur during the use of the formulation professionally or those that are related to abuse, intentional or accidental overdose of the drug, or drug withdrawal, or which result from failure of achieving a pharmacological effect which was otherwise expected are all included in ADEs (Food and Drug Administration, June 1993. http://www.fda.gov/cder/guidance/5427dft.pdf).

The reporting of ADE is done by three people:

1. A reporter,
2. A manufacturer, and
3. The FDA.

A reporter is any person, be it a doctor, patient, nurse, pharmacist, or any person who is aware of the occurrence of the ADE and reports the ADE. The ADE can be reported by him/her either to the manufacturer of the formulation or to the FDA directly. In case the reporter reports the ADE to the manufacturer, then it is the duty of the manufacturer to investigate it and further report it to the FDA. In cases where the FDA is reported of the ADE directly by the reporter, the FDA notifies the same to the manufacturer, who shall investigate the ADE. Investigations involving occurrence of ADE may lead to contacting the physician of the patient or the person who prescribed in case different from the physician and also contacting the pharmacy involved. Besides this, testing of all the retained samples from the lot of drug product that the patient used is also a part of the investigation. After completing the investigations, it is the responsibility of the manufacturer to submit all the information in a report to the FDA.

1.4.7 Good manufacturing practice certification

GMP certification certifies that the pharmaceutical products are made as per quality standard norms as required in GMP. GMP refers to good manufacturing practice, the term used globally for the control and management of manufacturing, testing, and overall quality of pharmaceutical products. It is also sometimes referred to as "CGMP," where C stands for "current" because all the manufacturing methods, testing methods, designs, and control are dynamic and change or evolve with time. GMP certification deals with matter concerning documentation, record keeping, personnel qualifications, sanitation, cleanliness, equipment verification, sanitation, complaint handling, and process validation. By following GMP certification, a manufacturer eliminates the risk of rejection of pharmaceutical product following final testing. In GMP a quality assurance approach is followed, which provides a guarantee that the drug products are of good quality which meet all the required standards of quality are produced consistently and comply with the requirements of market authorizations.

WHO has made guidelines for GMP. Various countries have defined their own requirements for GMP based on WHO GMP. GMP guidelines require a quality way to deal with manufacturing thus ensuring organizations to limit or eliminate any instances of accidental contamination and mistakes. Finally, it ensures the ultimate consumer for buying a safe and quality product. GMP certification is also a legal requirement for manufacturer for certification of their products which if not complied may lead to seizure, fines, and prison (Signore and Jacobs, 2016).

1.4.8 Application for getting a certificate of pharmaceutical product

The certificate of pharmaceutical product (CPP) is issued by the exporting country as per the format approved by the WHO to the requesting country thus establishing the status of the pharmaceutical product for sale and distribution in the exporting country. This certificate is always issued for a single product as the manufacturing and other information may vary for different types of dosage forms and strengths. CPP usually expires in 24 months from the date of issue and a new application needs to be submitted after that. These certificates cannot be reissued.

1.4.8.1 Contents of certificate of pharmaceutical product

The main contents of CPP include:

- Certifying (exporting) country;
- Requesting (importing) country;
- Name, dosage form, and composition of the pharmaceutical product (amount of drug in each dose);
- Information pertaining to registration (licensing) and marketing status of the product in the country in which it is to be exported;
- Product license number (including details of license holder, manufacturing details of the license holder (if any), and issue date;
- Summary of technical data on the basis of which the product has been given license (in case asked by the issuing authority);
- Current information of the product;
- Applicant details for the CPP;
- GMP compliance report of manufacturing site.

In some countries, examples of which include Italy, CPP is not issued if in the exporting country, the pharmaceutical product is not licensed. In these cases, a Certificate of Exportation, instead of a CPP, a Certificate of Exportation is issued, which has contents and format which are similar to CPP (https://www.who.int/medicines/areas/quality_safety/regulation_legislation/certification/modelcertificate/en/).

1.4.9 Patent certifications

There are four options or patent "certifications," which are named after Section 505(j)(2)(A)(vii)(IV)) as Para I, Para II, Para III, and Para IV certifications (Mossinghoff, 1999), which are:

1. Para I certification—When no patent data analogous to such patents has been filed or listed. In this case an ANDA can be approved immediately by the FDA and one or more applicant can enter. However, it is the responsibility of the ANDA applicant to certify that the patent information which has been submitted by him has not been submitted by any innovator for Orange Book listing.
2. Para II certification—When patent data analogous to such patents has expired. The FDA can approve the ANDA application immediately in this case also and one or more than one can enter the market.
3. Para III certification—When patent data analogous to such patents has not expired but will expire on a particular date later. The FDA in this case can give approval to the ANDA application which will be effective on the date of patent expiry. In this case also one or more than one can enter the market. In the patent certification the applicant is clearly required to mention the date of expiry of the patent.
4. Para IV certification—When patent data analogous to such patents is either invalid or cannot be infringed by the generic drug produced. The applicant submitting an ANDA has to give a notice to the innovator in this case. The first generic manufacturer and applicant who succeeds in a Paragraph IV challenge to a patent is rewarded with a period of 180 days of marketing exclusivity in accordance with the Hatch−Waxman scheme. During this time, the FDA does not have the authority to issue a final ANDA approval to any other generic manufacturer (21 U.S. Code Section 355. New drugs). During this tenure of market exclusivity, duopoly exists, in which the innovator with NDA and generic drug manufacturer who is the first filer of the ANDA are the only two companies who have the right to formulate as well as market formulation listed in the Orange Book, even in a condition when all the patents related to that product have been invalidated (Ohly, 2010). The Hatch−Waxman Act postulated the 180-day marketing exclusivity period with the purpose to motivate challenges of Paragraph IV by providing benefits to the generic applicants who were first filers for bearing not only the risks but also the cost involved in filing litigations, challenging the patents which were either weak or not obtained properly, or those which involved the defending of noninfringing products (Schacht and Thomas, 2004). The manufacturers of the generic formulations at one time were benefitted with the 180-day exclusivity period since as they could commercialize their drug products at a notably increased price, which could be attributed to the presence of multiple generics in the market (Avery, 1998). Besides this, another incentive was the grant of a stay for a period of 30 months on approval given by the FDA in cases where the NDA holder filed a case against ANDA for violation of patent within a period of 45 days after receiving intimation in the form of a notice of the Paragraph IV certification. The period of stay starts from the time and date of notification and can be shortened or lengthened by the court.

1.4.10 Trademark registration

A trademark, which is a type of intellectual property, is a design, phrase, word, and/or symbol that recognizes and differentiates the source of the goods of one firm from those of the others. A few examples are slogans, brand names, and logos. Trademarks do not lapse like copyrights and patents, after some years. Trademark rights last forever as long as specific documents and fee is paid at regular intervals of time.

There are two main advantages of trademarks—the first being to prevent consumer confusion which is especially important in the context of OTC purchases; and second is to encourage competitors to make their own trademarks, this is especially important. The brand name is associated with the goodwill of the company.

According to section 13 of the Indian Trade Marks Act, 1999, words that are used frequently for a single chemical compound or entity or INNs cannot be registrable as trademarks. However, brand names or common names can be registered. Pharmaceutical companies, in order to avoid the provisions of section 13, use either the main component of their formulation or the name of disease for which the formulation is made or the organ for which the formulation is made to create brand names for their products.

Besides relying on the product name, pharmaceutical firms also rely on the nonconventional trademark protection for their products. An example which is very common includes the protection of the heartburn medicine Nexium, as the "purple pill" by AstraZeneca. The company registered the distinctive purple and gold color of the medicine besides preventing other manufacturers from launching purple-colored medicines for treating heartburns in the United States.

Since confusion in pharmaceutical trademarks can have a serious impact on human lives, courts are adopting a stricter approach. Therefore, a few things which should be considered while choosing a brand name for pharmaceutical products are:

1. Avoidance of terms or words which have either become common or are descriptive;
2. Avoidance of suggestive words or terms;
3. Conducting a search on the Trade Marks Registry website to check for previous registrations or applications which would in turn avoid the risk of infringement;
4. Conducting a Google search to know about drugs already present in the market to avoid similarity in names, packing, or looks similar to existing products.
5. Avoidance of terms or marks which refer to inactive ingredients as it may be misleading.
6. No phonetic similarity should be there with a previously available drug product. Example: In the Case of Pfizer Ireland Pharmaceuticals vs Intas Pharmaceuticals and another 2004 (28) PTC 456, the Intellectual Property Appellate Court considered the words LIPITOR (name of the drug product of Pfizer) and LIPICOR (name of the drug product of Intas) to be phonetically similar. It held that the popular drug of Pfizer Lipitor was being made and sold at a cheaper price by Intas as no cost of research was involved and restrained Intas from manufacturing and selling the drug.

Although registration is not mandatory for all trademarks, its registration with the U.S. Patent and Trademark Office's (USPTO's) has many advantages, including a notice to the general public regarding the claim of the registrant for ownership of the mark, a presumption that the registrant has an ownership across the nation, as well as the exclusive right to utilize the mark on the goods or services mentioned in the registration. Service marks are a type of trademarks which are used for the identification of services.

For getting trademark registration, the interested individual has to apply online in USPTO. Once registration certificate is obtained, one has to file specific maintenance documents for registration and at regular intervals pay fees to keep their registration valid. The filing deadlines for these documents are calculated based on the date of registration mentioned on the registration certificate. If documents are not filed by the deadline, the registration will expire or be canceled and cannot be reinstated. The only option left is to file a new application (https://www.uspto.gov/).

The different symbols used for designating the trademarks include:

- For an unregistered trademark the symbol is in superscript,
- For an unregistered service mark the symbol is the letters "SM" in superscript like^{SM}, and
- For a registered trademark the symbol is the letter "R" surrounded by a circle like®.

1.4.11 Copyright registration

A copyright provides protection to works of authorship, including musical, dramatic, literary, computer software, and architecture artistic works, such as songs, poetry, novels, movies which are original. In Copyright law, an author's creative expression(s) are protected, although there is no protection of ideas.

In the pharmaceutical context, the word-by-word copying of a brand label by a generic company for its label does not come under copyright infringement since it is an FDA mandatory requirement. In the pharmaceutical industry, copyright issues usually arise in product monograph, which are documents appearing publicly and are prepared for making the information related to the safe and effective use of drugs to doctors, pharmacists, and patients. Besides this the marketing and training materials produced by the pharmaceutical companies also need to be protected from copying by their competitors.

Copyright registration can help pharmaceutical companies protect their packing material, design of outer carton as well as appearance pharma products from being copied or duplicated.

The copyright protection for the work created by a person generally lasts for 70 years after life of the creator. If the work was "works for hire," then protection exists for 95 years from the date of publication or 120 years from the date of creation, whichever is shorter. A copyright can be registered online at the United States Copyright Office's website, which requires depositing a copy of the work for which copyright registration is sought through electronic Copyright

Office registration system. The Copyright Office then reviews applications for any discrepancies or absence of copyrightable subject matter after which it issues a registration certificate (http://www.copyright.gov/).

1.4.12 Design registration in pharmaceutical context

"Design" includes shape, pattern, configuration, ornament or arrangement of colors, as well as lines applied either in two-dimensional form or three-dimensional form or in both forms to any article using any industrial process or method which can be mechanical, manual, or chemical, separate or a combination which are only judged by the eyes of individuals and are meant for improving the product appeal. The pharmaceutical products can protect their product design in case it is original and new by filling for a design registration.

1.5 Conclusion

Based on the information provided in this chapter, it can be concluded that regulatory affairs is a very salient part for the development and quick launching of pharmaceutical products by the pharmaceutical companies in the market. Most of the pharmaceutical industries whether multinational companies or small-sized companies have a drug regulatory department. The pharmaceutical industries should keep themselves abreast of the revisions in the regulations to help them to produce good quality products, which are safe and effective and which could be easily commercialized.

References

Approved Drug Products with Therapeutic Equivalence Evaluations, "Orange Book," 2003. <http://www.fda.gov/cder/ob/default.htm> (accessed 20.04.20.).

Avery, M., 1998. Mova Pharm. Corp. v. Shalala, 140 F.3d 1060. Supra, Note 7, 178.

Chen, J., 2019. New Drug Application. Available from: <https://www.investopedia.com/terms/n/new-drug-application-nda.asp> (accessed 19.04.20.).

Chen, J., 2020. Orange Book. Available from: <https://www.investopedia.com/terms/o/orange-book.asp> (accessed 20.04.20.).

Drug master files: Guidelines, Center for Drug Evaluation and Research Food and Drug Administration, Department of Health and Human Services, September 1989. Available from: <https://www.fda.gov/drugs/guidances-drugs/drug-master-files-guidelines> (accessed 20.04.20.).

FDA, November 1995. Center for Drug Evaluation and Research, Guidance for Industry: Immediate Release Solid Oral Dosage Forms. Scale-up and Post-Approval Changes: Chemistry, Manufacturing and Controls, In Vitro Dissolution Testing, and In Vivo Bioequivalence Documentation [SUPAC-IR].

Food and Drug Administration, June 1993. MedWatch FDA Form 3500 = 3500A. p. 298 <http://www.fda.gov/cder/guidance/5427dft.pdf>.

Garth, B., Lixin, Y., Liang, H., 2013. Development of the generic drug industry in the United States after the Hatch-Waxman Act of 1984. Acta Pharm. Sin. B 3 (5), 297−311.

Guidance for Industry. Submitting Marketing Applications According to the ICH-CTD Format—General Considerations. Available from: <https://www.fda.gov/media/71666/download> (accessed 19.04.20.).

Guidance for Industry. Immediate Release Solid Oral Dosage Forms Scale-Up and Postapproval Changes: Chemistry, Manufacturing, and Controls, In Vitro Dissolution Testing, and In Vivo Bioequivalence Documentation. Center for Drug and Research (CDER), November 1995, CMC 5.

Guidance for Industry. Postmarketing Adverse Experience Reporting for Human Drug and Licensed Biological Products: Clarification of What to Report. Food and Drug Administration, August 1997.

Guidance for Industry. Changes to an Approved NDA or ANDA. United States Department of Health and Human Services, Food and Drug Administration, Center for Drug Evaluation and Research (CDER), November 1999, CMC.

Harsha, Y.S., Reddy, V.S., Mary, D., 2017. Role of regulatory affairs in a pharmaceutical industry. Int. J. Pharm. Res. Bio-Sci. 6 (2), 170−177.

History of the Food and Drug Administration, 2003. Center for Drug Evaluation and Research. Available from <http://www.fda.gov/cder/about/history/> (accessed 20.10.20.).

IMS Health Data, February 21, 2003. Wall Street Journal.

Itkar, S.C., Vyawahare, N., 2015. Drug Regulatory Affairs, third ed.

Jain, S.K., Jain, R.K., 2017. Evolution of GMP in pharmaceutical industry. Res. J. Pharm. Technol. 10 (2), 601−606.

Kumar, B.J., 2013. Overview of drug regulatory affairs and regulatory profession. Int. J. Drug. Regul. Aff. 1 (1), 1−4.

Mossinghoff, G.J., 1999. Overview of the Hatch-Waxman Act and its impact on the drug development process. Food Drug Law J 54 (2), 187−194.

Ohly, D.C., 2010. The Hatch-Waxman Act: Prescriptions for Innovative and Inexpensive Medicines: 50 Comment, The Dubious Value of Hatch-Waxman Exclusivity, supra, Note 7 (duopoly), 558.

Ono, S., 2007. Ministry of Health, Labour and Welfare (MHLW) of Japan, Wiley Encyclopedia of Clinical Trials. John Wiley & Sons, Inc.

Orange Book and Its Applications, 2019. Available from: <https://www.legaladvantage.net/blog/orange-book-and-its-applications/> (accessed 20.04.20.).

Parker, R.E., Martinez, D.R., Covington, T.R., 1991. Drug product selection: part 1: history and legal overview. Am. Pharm. 31, 72−77.

Parkman, P.D., Hardegree, M.C., 1999. Regulation and testing of vaccines. In: Plotkin, S.A., Orenstein, W.A. (Eds.), Vaccines, 3rd ed. Saunders, Philadelphia, pp. 1131–1143.

Patel, K.T., Chotai, N.P., 2011. Documentation and records: harmonized GMP requirements. J. Young Pharm. 3 (2), 138–150.

Pharmaceutical Inspection Co-operation Scheme PE 009-3, 1 January 2006: Guide to Good Manufacturing Practice for Medicinal Products. (© PIC/S January 2006) Pharmaceutical Management and Regulatory Affairs.

Pisano, D.S., Mantus, D.S., 2008. Textbook of FDA Regulatory Affairs a Guide for Prescription Drugs, Medical Devices, and Biologics, 2nd ed.

Schacht, W.H., Thomas, J.R., 2004. The Hatch-Waxman Act: Legislative Changes Affecting Pharmaceutical Patents. CRS Report for Congress. Available from: <https://www.everycrsreport.com/files/20040430_RL32377_50eabc4c91070b82434d6911a1f409b8292345b1.pdf> (accessed 20.04.20.).

Shargel, L., Kanfer, I., 2013. Generic Drug Product Development Solid Oral Dosage Forms, 2nd ed. CRC Press.

Signore, A.A., Jacobs, T., 2016. Good Design Practices for GMP Pharmaceutical Facilities, 2nd ed. CRC Press, pp. 180–200.

Sreedhar, D., Subramanian, G., Reddy, M.S., 2005. Need for the Introduction of Regulatory affairs in the Pharmacy Curriculum. Health Administrator XIX (1), 51–52.

Theresa, M., 2017. International regulation of drugs and biological products. In: Gallin, J.I., Ognibene, F.P., Lee Johnson, L. (Eds.), Principles and Practice of Clinical Research. Academic Press, p. 88.

Chapter 2

Regulatory requirement for the approval of novel, nanotechnology-based biological products

Shobhit Kumar[1], Javed Ali[2] and Sanjula Baboota[2]

[1]Department of Pharmaceutical Technology, Meerut Institute of Engineering and Technology (MIET), Meerut, India, [2]Department of Pharmaceutics, School of Pharmaceutical Education and Research, Jamia Hamdard, New Delhi, India

2.1 Introduction

Drugs are often as old as a community, and therefore, over time, the ideas about how to guarantee their consistency have developed slowly. "Like for example, a compound preparation called "Mithridatium," including 41 individual components, was cooked by Mithridates (120 BCE), King of Pontus, and was kept as a panacea until as late as 1780s for nearly all diseases. Regulation of recent drugs began only after the breakthrough developments within the life sciences in the 19th century.

Medicinal goods, medical equipment, and dietary supplements are all subject to government legislation aimed at safeguarding public health. Every industry must obey regulations in order to manufacture high-quality, safe, and efficient drug products. The regulatory affairs department is an important part of a pharmaceutical company's organizational structure. Regulatory practitioners are in charge of sending dossiers for registration at the end of the product development process. The contents of product dossier are listed in Table 2.1.

A pharmaceutical company's regulatory affairs department is in charge of obtaining approval for new products (Green, 2009). The various regulatory agencies are listed in Table 2.2. Working with project teams and interacting with regulatory healthcare bodies, such as the Food and Drug Administration (FDA) or the International Council for Harmonisation (ICH), is managed by regulatory affairs liaisons. Regulatory affairs establish common principles and responsibilities that support decision making for pharmaceutical products by providing a strong scientific database, efficient organizational arrangements, and procedures. The main goal of the regulatory affairs is to establish a foundation for ensuring high-quality drug products (Munteanu et al., 2013).

A number of functions are necessary for effective regulation of drugs. Significant functions include (1) the evaluation of animal and clinical trial safety and efficacy results, (2) the inspection and licensing of manufacturing facilities, (3) the observation of adverse drug reactions for medicinal products, and (4) the quality control of products promotion and advertisements to ensure that drugs are safe and effective. Drug regulators of different countries have the sole responsibility of evaluating the information collected during the clinical trials of new medicine which assure the safety, efficacy, and quality.

The present chapter expresses regulatory requirements for active pharmaceutical ingredients (APIs), novel drug delivery systems, nanotechnology products, and biologics.

2.2 Regulatory requirements and active pharmaceutical ingredients approval process

APIs are substances that are intended to provide pharmacological action and diagnostic action, reducing, treating, and preventing diseases. These substances also affect the body's structure and function. Consistency of the APIs used in formulations decides the quality of a major part of the finished pharmaceutical product. A proper supplier system is needed

© 2022 Elsevier Inc. All rights reserved.

TABLE 2.1 Product dossier.

Section	Content
S1	General information
	• Structure
	• Properties
	• Nomenclature
S2	Manufacture
	• Manufacturing site
	• Details of procedure
	• Control of substances
	• Validation of process
	• Manufacturing process development
S3	Characterization
	• Structure elucidation
	• Impurities
S4	Control of active pharmaceutical ingredients/drug substance
	• Validation of analytical methods
	• Batch analysis
	• Specification for validation
S5	Standards
S6	Packaging information
S7	Stability information

TABLE 2.2 Various regulatory agencies in different countries.

Country	Regulatory authority
United Kingdom	Medicines and Healthcare Products Regulatory Agency (MHRA)
United States	U.S. Food and Drug Administration (USFDA)
India	Central Drugs Standard Control Organisation (CDSCO)
Australia	Therapeutic Goods Administration (TGA)
Canada	Health Canada
South Africa	Medicines Control Council (MCC)
Sri Lanka	Ministry of Health, Nutrition and Indigenous Medicine
Korea	Ministry of Food and Drug Safety
New Zealand	New Zealand Medicines and Medical Devices Safety Authority
Switzerland	The Swiss Agency for Therapeutic Products (SWISSMEDIC)
Japan	Ministry of Health, Labour and Welfare (MHLW) and Pharmaceuticals and Medical Devices Agency (PMDA)
China	National Medical Products Administration (NMPA)

to ensure reliable procurement of APIs of acceptable quality while also protecting the public health. This will be achieved by a structured inspection process and quality evaluation.

2.2.1   Registration of active pharmaceutical ingredients

New drug approval laws necessitate the use of a new drug application (NDA). The manufacturing processes and in-process controls for the new drug product are listed in NDA. It also contains all of the drug's components as well as full information on the drug's structure. The drug manufacturer must provide sufficient data in an NDA to prove that the drug substance used for the specific formulation of interest would not affect the formulation's safety or effectiveness in any way. Furthermore, it is important to include details about the drug product when submitting an abbreviated new drug application (ANDA). All of the data are mentioned in the drug master file (DMF).

2.2.2   Drug master file

A DMF is a document that provides comprehensive details about the facilities or procedures used in the manufacturing of drugs (Thambavita et al., 2018). The FDA receives a DMF after which they check it for administrative material. The FDA takes about 2−3 weeks to review a DMF. In case where FDA finds DMF appropriate, the FDA issues a letter of acknowledgment. On other hand if FDA considers the DMF inappropriate, it notifies the holder regarding deficiencies. The types of DMFs are listed in Table 2.3. There are five types of DMF. Type I DMF comprises information of the manufacturing site, working process, and SOP, whereas type II consists of information regarding drug substance intermediate and drug substance. Type II is submitted structure among all and can integrate measurements for another entity that would report an ANDA from medications produced under contract. Type III comprises packaging materials data. Type IV comprises data of excipients and other substances employed in formulation. Type V consists of all referred drug-specific information not found in previous types of DMFs. It comprises FDA-accepted reference data. DMF submitted to National Pharmaceutical Control Bureau (NPCB) should contain the information as required. Only when a new application for product registration is being checked, the technical contents of a DMF are investigated. The DMF must be maintained and revised by the API manufacturer (Matsuhama et al., 2016).

2.2.3   Recent changes in the drug master file rules

If a DMF does not exist in common technical data (eCTD) format and is present in paper format with the FDA, resubmission is not required. From May 5, 2018, onward if changes are needed to be done in existing DMFs, then it has to be done in eCTD format only. DMF holder will have the similar DMF number. If the existing number is four-digits, for example, 6789, then DMF holder will need to add zeroes to the left to convert the DMF number to a six-digit format, which makes it 006789 when the DMF is converted to eCTD format. If there are some changes made by the DMF holder in the file that already exists in eCTD form, then the updated or modified areas should be specified in the cover letter (https://www.fda.gov/drugs/cder-small-business-industry-assistance-sbia/cder-sbia-chronicles-submitting-master-files-ectd-format-when-and-how-comply-5252017-issue; https://www.fda.gov/media/105733/download). The CTD is divided into five parts. Module 1 is unique to an area, while modules 2, 3, 4, and 5 are meant to be universal.

TABLE 2.3 Types of drug master files.

Type	Information provided
I	Manufacturing location and SOPs
II	Drug substance intermediate
III	Packaging material
IV	Excipient and other substances employed in formulation
V	FDA-accepted reference data

2.2.4 Responsibilities of active pharmaceutical ingredients manufacturer

Any changes related to specific Marketing Authorization Holder (MAH) must be submitted in duplicate to the NPCB. The date(s) affected should all be included in reference. This notification should be given well in advance of the modification to allow MAH to supplement or modify any affected applications as appropriate. While a DMF is not needed for these active ingredients, the finished MAH must provide proof that the drug was obtained from a reputable source and meets the relevant pharmacological requirements on a consistent basis. Any nonpharmacological specifications must be reviewed by the NPCB to assess their correctness and acceptability in assessing the substance's consistency. The impurities that generated during API manufacturing should also be reported.

2.2.5 Letter of access

The following is mentioned in the letter of access:

- Name of product
- Product composition
- Dosage form
- A declaration that any alteration in API requirements that would possibly disturb the quality of product will be reported to both the local MAH and the NPCB.

After receiving the DMF, a reference number will be given to the product registration applications for potential correspondence. The assigned reference number should be listed by the MAH and API manufacturer. If there is a deficiency in the restricted part of the DMF, then NPCB will contact the API manufacturer directly (https://www.npra.gov.my/images/Drug-Registration-Guidance-Document/July-2013/Complete_DRGD_with_appendices_update_July13_SAVE_AS_PDF.pdf).

2.2.6 Regulatory requirement for drug approval in the United States

The FDA participates in strategic discussions with the other US government organizations through Interagency Policy Coordination Committee on Emerging Technology and other platforms. The FDA also contributes to the broader policies of the US government related to nanotechnology and to manage its policy activities where necessary. FDA is also collaborating with international regulatory counterparts to exchange viewpoints and information on drug products regulations and their planned uses. The FDA develops guidelines to interpret the policy of agency on a regulatory problem for its employees, applicants, sponsors, and the public. These guidelines interpret the applicable legislative and regulatory references. These guiding documents give the guidance on the technical information that is necessary to fulfill such standards. The FDA may adapt recommendations to particular confluence of product-class legislation, degree of scientific expertise applicable to such applications and the possible nature of human and animal health consequences (https://www.fda.gov/science-research/nanotechnology-programs-fda/fdas-approach-regulation-nanotechnology-products).

The process of drug approval in the United States is one of the tedious processes (Fig. 2.1) and has the most stringent rules and regulations, which must be followed by the sponsors to get the approval of foreign drugs in the US market (Holbein, 2009). The U.S. Food and Drug Administration (USFDA) works to ensure the safety and effectiveness of medications, vaccines, biological products, medical devices, cosmetics, dietary supplements, and tobacco products, among other things. The USFDA is an agency which works to protect public health by assuring safety and efficacy of drug products, to regulate tobacco products, and so on.

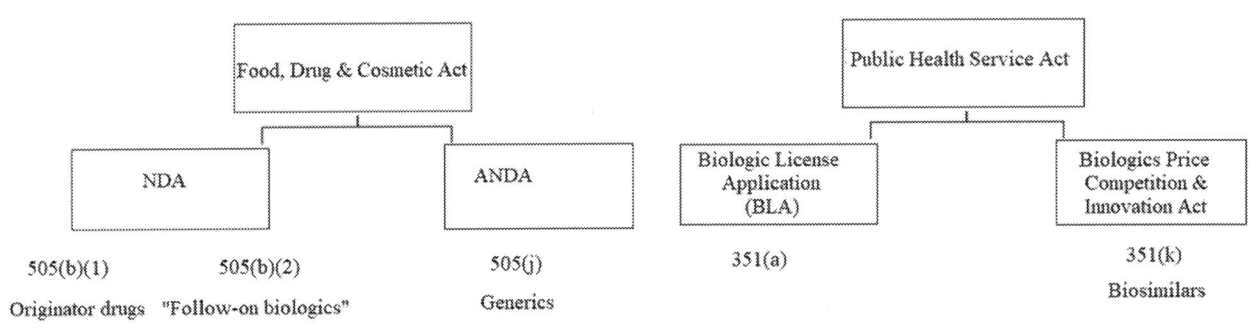

FIGURE 2.1 The FDA approval pathways.

The FDA organization comprises several offices and centers:

1. Office of Commissioner of Food and Drugs
2. National Center for Toxicological Research
3. Office of Regulatory Affairs (ORA)
4. Center for Veterinary Medicine
5. Center for Tobacco Products
6. Center for Food Safety and Applied Nutrition
7. Center for Drug Evaluation and Research (CDER)
8. Center for Devices and Radiological Health (CDRH)
9. Center for Biologics Evaluation and Research (CBER).

As per the section 510 of the Federal Food, Drug and Cosmetic (FD&C) Act or subpart B of 21 code of Code of Federal Regulation (CFR) 207 "it is required that the companies/firms that manufacture, compound, or the methods used to produce the drugs in US or import foreign drugs must register themselves with the FDA and list all the drug products that has been manufactured, compounded, prepared or processed for marketing in US" The importers must designate a US agent during the registration of foreign drugs and the agent should be in the United States. The registrant should submit a required listed information at the time of registration of a drug product, additionally one has to update the listing information in the month of "June and December of each year" in which they should include the information for those drugs which have not been updated earlier (https://www.accessdata.fda.gov/scripts/cdrh/cfdocs/cfCFR/CFRSearch.cfm?CFRPart = 207&showFR = 1).

Various forms of drug applications must be submitted to the FDA in order for the drug to be approved:

2.2.6.1 Investigational new drug

This application is submitted to FDA to get approval for conducting clinical trials in humans based on the preclinical results obtained. The types of investigational new drug (IND) are listed in Table 2.4.

Section 312 of the 21 code of CFR sets out the specifications for the content and structure of an IND application. A sponsor (commercial organization) or an investigator who plans to conduct a clinical trial should request an "Investigational New Drug Application." Following are the IND content and format:

- Form FDA 1571
- Table of contents
- Investigational plan
- Introductory report
- Investigator's catalog
- Procedures
- Information regarding manufacturing
- Data of pharmacology
- Earlier human experience
- Toxicology data
- Supplementary information

TABLE 2.4 Types of investigational new drugs (IND).

Type of IND	Description
Investigator IND	This form of IND is sent by a doctor who is in charge of the investigational drug.
Treatment IND	It is used to apply experimental medicines that have shown promise in clinical trials.
Emergency use IND	This helps the drug regulatory agencies to approve the use in an emergency situation of an experimental drug which may take a long time for IND submission.

2.2.6.2 *New drug application*

After successfully performing the clinical trials if the drug product is found to be relatively safe and effective and does not contain any potential risk and is also safe to use, the sponsor can file for NDA. Only if the drug successfully completes all three phases of clinical trials will an NDA be submitted and covers all information regarding animal and human study, data interpretation, drug pharmacokinetics and its development, and proposed labeling. Approval of an NDA is usually issued within two years on average, although this process can take more than two months to several years. After the approval of an NDA, the revolutionary company is authorized to market the drug and is considered to be in Phase IV trials. NDA is an integral aspect of the drug approval process that must be submitted to the USFDA prior to commercialization. Prior to commercialization, an NDA must be sent to the USFDA as part of the drug approval process. The flowchart of NDA is presented in Fig. 2.2.

2.2.6.2.1 Goal of new drug application

NDAs provide the following details for FDA reviewers to make an informed decision:

- Appropriate labeling
- Safety
- Efficiency
- Quality maintenance
- Methods used in manufacturing

2.2.6.2.2 New drug application contents

1. Description of drug
2. Chemical and pharmaceutical information
3. Pharmacology studies
4. Information on prescription
5. Pharmacokinetics
6. Clinical trials
7. Regulatory status in other countries
8. Toxicology studies
9. Samples and testing protocols.

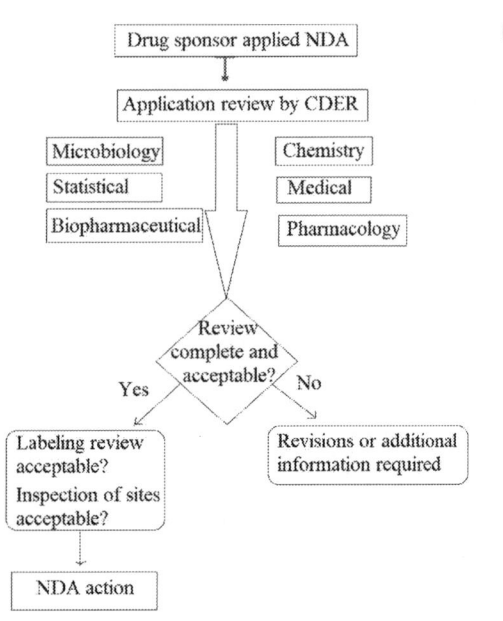

FIGURE 2.2 Flowchart of new drug application (NDA).

2.2.6.3 Abbreviated new drug application

This application is submitted to get the approval for generic drugs. The major goals of ANDA are to reduce drug price and reduce time of drug development. The sponsors who have applied for ANDA are not required to conduct clinical trials. However, they must show that their medication is bioequivalent to the previously accepted reference drug. Generic drugs are safe, economic, cost-effective alternative for a reference/brand name drug product (Hu et al., 2019). They may have different inactive ingredients and color of medicine. Preclinical testing is not needed for generic drug applications to assess the safety and efficacy of the generic drug. Once the application gets approved, the generic drug manufacturer can manufacture the product.

In the Orange Book the FDA has listed all the drug products which are eligible to be the reference listed drugs (RLDs) for which ANDA can be submitted for the generic version of that drug product (Fig. 2.3). RLDs are the listed drug product specified under the section 505 (c) of the FD&C Act based on the result submitted of the bioequivalence studies conducted to show the sameness with the brand name drug product (https://www.fda.gov/drugs/drug-approvals-and-databases/orange-book-data-files).

Generic drug manufacturer should file one of the four possible patent certifications while filing an ANDA mentioned in the Orange Book:

Para 1 certification: There is no patent for the drug mentioned in the Orange Book in this case.

Para 2 certification: The patent for the brand drug product is listed in the Orange Book, but it has expired.

Para 3 certification: The patent is listed and is legitimate, but the applicant must seek permission to sell the generic drug after the patent expires.

Para 4 certification: The most critical of all, the generic applicant can either challenge the validity of the innovator drug patent or claim it to be fake.

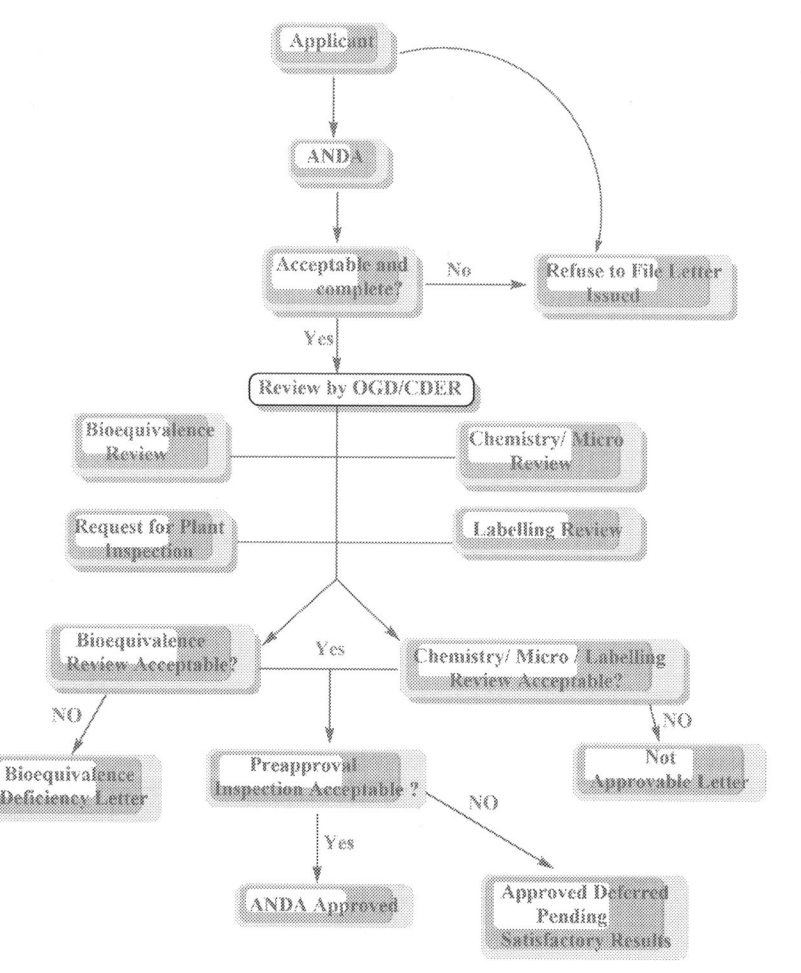

FIGURE 2.3 Flowchart showing ANDA approval process (Vishal et al., 2014).

2.2.6.3.1 Content and format of abbreviated new drug application

- *Reason for sending an ANDA*
- *Application form*: An application to market an abbreviated new drug for use has been submitted, which ANDA applicants must fully complete and sign for their submissions.
- *Usage conditions*
- *Administration route*
- *Active ingredients*: A detailed information regarding drug product should be provided. Details on the composition and function of each ingredient of their generic drug product should be given by applicants, including any solvents and processing aids used during the manufacture of the drug product.
- *Bioequivalence*: Applicants should submit summary data related to the determination of bioequivalence. The applicant summarizes different aspects of the bioequivalence application, including the design and results of in vivo and in vitro bioequivalent studies, as well as the results of in vitro dissolution experiments. In addition, applicants can apply review tables for all research carried out whether the studies have passed or failed.
- *Labeling*: Labeling information contains labeling for drug product.
- *Chemistry, manufacturing, and control*
- *Patent certification*: It contains information regarding patent certification.

The "Hatch—Waxman Act of 1984" regulates the USFDA's generic drug approval process and has resulted in a wave of generic drugs entering the market (Gupta et al., 2016). The pharmaceutical industry was dominated by brand-name drug manufacturers, also known as innovators, prior to the passage of this Act. Generic drug firms have rarely competed with them in the past, opting instead to invest in the already proven products on the market. Hatch—Waxman Act has the following objectives:

- *Redeem the drug approval delay:*
  Earlier the innovators used to face a lot of delay in the drug approval process for NDA which caused a lot of financial losses for the brand drug manufacturers.
- *To encourage healthy competition and prevent drug price increases*:
  Prior to the enactment of this Act, generic drug manufacturers had no way to enter the market until the innovator's patent term had expired and there were no provisions for questioning the validity of the innovator's patent. There were also little benefits anticipated from generic drug manufacturers investing large sums of money to launch a new version of the same drug after its patent had expired. This product monopoly kept competition at bay, resulting in high drug prices as requested by the innovator. Market exclusivity and successful patent life have been extended from 8.5 years (in the 1980s) to 13 years and nowadays to approximately 16—17 years.
- *Make life easier for generic manufacturers*:
  Before this Act, generic drug manufacturers had a difficult time completing all of the clinical trials required by brand name manufacturers in order to get their generic license. Now they only have to perform the bioequivalence/ bioavailability studies to show that the generic version of the brand name drug is bioequivalent, safe and effective just like the reference drug (Lee et al., 2016).

Biologics license application:
The Federal FDA has the power to control biologics under the Public Health Services Act. Vaccines, blood and blood byproducts, some monoclonal antibodies, and tissue and cellular products are all regulated by the FDA. Biologics are controlled by CDER and FDA's Center for Biologics. The FDA evaluates biologics for marketability by filing a biologics license application. It has its own set of specific criteria, despite being similar to NDA. Under the relevant legislation, the applicant must include the details in an appropriate format.

2.3 Novel drugs and their regulatory requirements

Novel drugs have the potential to be important new treatments for improving patient care. The introduction of new medications and bioproducts also means that new clinical therapy for patients and developments for the public in healthcare. Therefore, CDER encourages technological advancement and assists in accelerating development of new medicines. Annually CDER develops a huge variety of novel medicines and biologics. Some products are novel and improved products which were never utilized in medical treatment. All credit goes to CDER new drug therapy approval which occurred in the year 2017. In 2020, CDER approved many novel molecules [Tazverik (to treat epithelioid sarcoma), Tepezza (to treat thyroid eye disease), and Ayvakit (for management of gastrointestinal stromal tumor)], new bioproducts and vaccines (https://www.fda.gov/drugs/new-drugs-fda-cders-new-molecular-entities-and-new-therapeutic-biological-products/novel-drug-approvals-2020).

2.3.1 Rules for approval of novel drugs

To speed up the development and approval of new drugs, the CDER employs a number of regulatory pathways. These routes take a variety of approaches to improve the development efficiency and speed up the process. The medicine approval process is performed within a formal system comprising:

- *Review of the desired condition and therapies available*—Disease for which medication prepared is evaluated by reviewers of the FDA. They also analyze the treatment therapy that gives the framework for assessing the problems and therapeutic effect of a drug.
- *Evaluation of advantages and risks from clinical data*—It is the responsibility of FDA to evaluate the clinical data of drugs.

2.3.2 Approaches for approval

In almost all cases, medicines that qualify for these pathways must address serious, rare, or difficult-to-treat diseases, and should offer substantial improvements over available remedies. The following are examples of accelerated pathways in the United States:

2.3.2.1 Fast track

Drugs that have been designated as fast track have the potential to address unmet medical needs. CDER designated nearly 39% of novel drugs as fast track in 2017. The goal of fast track approval is to obtain essential new drugs to patients as soon as possible. Fast track treats a wide variety of severe illnesses. Any medication being developed to cure or avoid a disease for which there is currently no treatment is clearly aimed at an unmet need. If therapies are available, a quick-track treatment should demonstrate more benefit over the treatment already available, including:

- demonstrating superior efficiency,
- avoiding severe adverse effects of existing therapy,
- enhancing the diagnostic system of severe disorder resulting in better outcomes,
- reducing the toxicity of existing medication, and
- Resolving the predicted community health needs.

Fast track expedites the production and evaluation of new drugs. When a medicine achieves Fast Track approval then fast and regular contact is promoted between the FDA and a drug manufacturer during the entire product production and evaluation process. If there is any problem and doubt then it is quickly resolved by regular contact often resulting in fast approval of medicine.

2.3.2.2 Breakthrough therapy

A medicine is referred as a breakthrough therapy when this medicine is used alone or in combination with one or more other medicine for the treatment of chronic disease. The classification of breakthrough therapy is meant to help speed up the production of a possible new therapy.

2.3.2.3 Priority review

A priority review is a program run by the USFDA that speeds up the approval process for medications that are likely to have a major effect on disease care. Under the Prescription Drug User Fee Act (PDUFA), the FDA committed to clear targets for reducing drug approval time. A medication is granted priority review if the CDER concludes that it has the potential to make a major advance in medical care. The FDA has developed a two-tiered review system: norm and priority.

2.3.2.4 Accelerated approval

The FDA's accelerated approval program gives it more leeway in choosing which endpoints to use when approving a medication that improves on existing therapies for a severe disease. Drugs that can bring major advances to patients are accepted earlier than those that are typically approved. For accelerated clearance, a surrogate endpoint is used. A surrogate endpoint is also referred to as marker which is a laboratory test and indicator believed to indicate therapeutic benefit, but not a therapeutic benefit indicator in itself. Similarly, an intermediary medical endpoint is a therapeutic impact indicator that is deemed fairly likely to estimate a medicine's therapeutic benefit (Ritter, 2008).

2.3.3 CDSCO and rules for novel drug marketing

CDSCO is India's national regulatory organization. The Drug Controller General of India (DCGI), which is part of the CDSCO, regulates pharmaceuticals and medical devices. Drug Technical Advisory Board (DTAB) and Drug Consultative Committee (DCC) advise DCGI. Drug and Cosmetic Act of 1940 established the CDTL in Kolkata as a national statutory laboratory for quality control of drugs and cosmetics, which is in India, the drug enforcement authorities' oldest quality control laboratory. In the Ministry of Health and Family Welfare, it reports to the Director General of Health Services. The Common Technical Document (CTD) is only a format for CDSCO to send information. Although adhering to the CTD's overarching framework is critical, it should be remembered that no set of guidelines will cover all possible scenarios.

2.3.3.1 Rules for novel drug marketing

For ease of understanding, the new drug approval process is divided into three stages:

- The first step is premarketing, which includes research, production, and clinical trials. To ensure effectiveness and safety, preclinical trials of a medication are performed. Applications are sent to the relevant government agency for the execution of clinical trials. After that it is possible to perform clinical trials (Phase I to Phase IV). These experiments are also carried out in order to optimize dose of drug.
- Second phase for marketing authorization of drug: Following the completion of the medication's clinical trials, an application for approval of the drug for sale is sent to the country's competent authority. The competent authority can only review the application and approve the drug for sale if it is found to be safe and effective in humans.
- Third is for postmarketing: After approval of drug, regulatory authorities require drug companies to monitor drug safety. Through this phase, consumers and health professionals report problems.

2.4 Guidelines on approval of novel drug delivery systems

Prior to marketing of modified release drug products there is a requirement for conducting comparative clinical trials and bioequivalence studies with immediate release formulations. Bioavailability studies for changed release dosage forms are recommended, and they should be planned to ensure the following:

1. Product complies with the statements on the amended release mark.
2. Active drug material is not released at a sufficient rate and duration, resulting in dose dumping.
3. The output of the adjusted release product and the reference immediate release product delivered by similar route in multiple doses is not significantly different.
4. There must be a discernible difference in performance between the modified release product and the regular release product when used as a reference product.

Single dose or single and multiple dose based on modified release products that are likely to accumulate or unlikely to accumulate both in the fasted and nonfasted states will be the study design for in vivo bioequivalence/bioavailability studies of modified release doses styles. If the effect of food on the reference product is unclear, two separate two-way crossover tests, one fasted and the other fed, may be performed (or if it is understood that food affects its absorption). A three-way crossover study may be appropriate if the reference product is proved to be unaffected by food with certainty (e.g., from published data).

2.5 Regulation for nanotechnology products

API when loaded in a nanocarrier is likely to show different pharmacokinetics/pharmacodynamics as compared to pure compound. That is the root cause of complexity of evaluation of quality, safety, and efficacy attributes of nanocarriers. Materials at nanoscale dimensions may show novel or changed physicochemical properties that can allow the creation of novel products. Nanotechnology applications become interesting after alteration in physicochemical properties of products.

FDA may allow the safe production of products with novel and beneficial properties through improving its scientific knowledge and resources available to determine the effectiveness and safety of goods. The main intention of FDA is to establish consistent and reliable regulatory processes. Regulatory strategy adopted by the FDA should have the following attributes:

2.5.1 FDA's methodology for various product classes

In case when therapeutic agents do not harm then these are considered as safe. But therapeutic agents are tested not only on the basis of their level of risk but also on the basis of their expected utility. Many FDA-regulated products have different standards for protection or efficacy. The effect for different product classes and applications of nanomaterials can be different regulatory outcomes even if objective measures of risk are same.

- *In case where premarket review authority exists*

    There are many products, such as novel medicine, new veterinary medicine, biological products, food excipients, dietary ingredients, some human devices, and coloring agents, which have to undergo premarket review examination. Applicants will have to submit information associated with product's safety, efficiency, and regulatory status during processes of premarket review. Processes of individual premarket review require consideration of the necessity of additional information on safety and efficacy (as needed) of nanoproducts.

- *In case where regulatory authority does not authorize premarket analysis*

    There are certain FDA-regulated products, such as cosmetics (except coloring agent), whose premarket review is not compulsory. In this type of cases, the FDA depends on data which is obtained by public, adverse effect reports (where required), and on postmarket surveillance programs. FDA provides oversight through this information. Where applications related to nanotechnology are concerned, FDA recommends manufacturers to communicate with the agency before marketing their products. FDA may guide industries to review safety data and create postmarketing safety inspection through such communication.

- *Postmarket monitoring*

    Markets of nanomaterial containing products will be monitored by the FDA. FDA will also take steps to protect customers when appropriate.

    Manufacturers must focus on ensuring that their item meets relevant safety standards and other specific specifications, even if items are under the premarket inspection or authorization. Hence, companies should work with latest information during manufacturing the product. Industry must also keep monitoring goods after their marketing. Industry should contact the FDA sooner rather than later to address issues, such as regulatory status, protection, effectiveness, or unique characteristics of products containing nanomaterials, or even issues involving nanotechnology application. Methodologies and information can be clarified through this initial communication. These methodologies and information are essential to fulfill the obligations of sponsors. Extra meetings with people and seminars can be arranged for the development of regulatory science, to recognize requirements for material information, and to obtain feedback on particular issues.

2.5.2 Data required for nanopharmaceuticals evaluation

For marketing a nanopharmaceutical product the following information should be submitted to the regulatory authority (Guidelines for Evaluation of Nanopharmaceuticals in India, Government of India New Delhi, October 2019):

A. Introduction
   1. Description of nanopharmaceutical
   2. Indication
   3. Category to which it belongs
   4. Rationalization for formulation
B. Information on pharmaceutical and chemical properties
   1. Ingredients information
      a. Chemical name, generic name, international nonproprietary name
      b. Data on nanomaterial utilized, excipient
      c. Nanopharmaceutical rationality

2. Physiochemical characterization data of nanopharmaceuticals
   a. Individual component(s) description
   b. Chemical name, structure, crystal structure of drug, and nanomaterial(s)
   c. Empirical formula (drug and nanomaterials)
   d. Molecular weight (drug and nanomaterials)
   e. Description of the product with
      i. Nano-size range by number and/or intensity distribution, average size and polydispersion index, and percentage of particle under each distribution with standard deviation
      ii. Shape, surface texture information
      iii. Surface charge with standard deviation (zeta potential)
      iv. Percentage of drug loading with standard deviation
      v. Encapsulation efficiency, loaded versus free drug content, with standard deviation
      vi. Osmolality (wherever applicable)
      vii. Solubility/dispersion information (for injectable product)
      viii. Colloidal stability information for injections (06 batches)
      ix. State of drug (API) in nanomaterial (chemically conjugated/loaded/complexed with the nanocarrier)
      x. Scalable Good Manufacturing Practice (GMP) process description of the nanopharmaceutical preparation
      xi. Average pH (wherever applicable)
      xii. Viscosity (wherever applicable)
      xiii. Mechanical integrity (as applicable)
      xiv. Endotoxin/microbial load level for parental nanoformulations
      xv. Residual solvent content as per ICH guidelines
      xvi. Sterilization protocol
      xvii. Waste disposal method.
3. Analytical data (nanocarrier/API/nanopharmaceutical)
   a. Size (Scanning electron microscopy, transmission electron microscopy, atomic force microscopy, etc.)
   b. Quantitative elemental analysis
   c. Mass spectrum analysis
   d. Nuclear magnetic resonance spectra (state of the API as encapsulated or chemically bonded, or intercalated may be identified and specified)
   e. Fourier-transform infrared spectroscopy spectra
   f. Fluorescence spectra
   g. Raman spectra
   h. Ultraviolet–visible spectroscopy spectra
   i. X-ray diffraction analysis
   j. Identification of polymorphic changes (during the shelf-life of the product)
4. Monograph specification
   a. Defined criteria for unique identification of nanopharmaceutical
   b. Impurities identification and quantification
   c. In vitro/in vivo release kinetics of API
   d. In vitro/in vivo degradation kinetics of nanopharmaceutical in various simulated media
   e. Stability data
5. Validation of analytical method
   a. Method of assay
   b. Procedure for estimation of impurity
   c. Procedure for estimation of residual solvent impurities
   d. Dissolution test method
6. Stability data
7. Data on nanopharmaceutical formulation
   a. Dosage form
   b. Administration route
   c. Composition
   d. Analytical method validation

      e. In-process quality control check
      f. Ingredients compatibility study
      g. Procedure regarding surface functionalization/modification
      h. Specification related to finished product
    8. Relative assessment of innovator product (if applicable)
      a. Container and closure system
      b. Content uniformity
      c. Impurities
      d. pH
    9. Stability estimation in market-intended pack
    10. Specifications for packaging
    11. Validation of procedure
 C. Animal pharmacology
    1. Pharmacokinetics
    2. Summary
 D. Toxicity studies in animal
    1. Carcinogenicity
    2. Genotoxicity
    3. Hypersensitivity
    4. Systemic toxicity studies
 E. Human pharmacology
    1. Pharmacological effects
    2. Pharmacokinetics
    3. Pharmacodynamics
 F. Therapeutic exploratory trials
 G. Therapeutic confirmatory trials
 H. Bioavailability/bioequivalence studies
 I. Nanopharmaceutical's regulatory status in other countries
    1. Approval status
    2. Name of countries where marketed
    3. Information on prescribing
    4. Restrictions on use
 J. Labeling information

2.6 Biologics and its regulatory guidelines

A relatively new and emerging group of drugs is biologics. Biologics may comprise nucleic acids, proteins, sugars, or mixture of these compounds. Sometimes, they can be living organisms, such as cells and tissues. Biological products are prepared using natural resources, such as human, animal, and microorganism. Biotechnological method may be used for the manufacturing of bioproducts. All are important for the prevention, diagnosis, or recovery of a disorder or human condition. Biologics are utilized to treat various diseases and disorders, including anemia. Retacrit (epoetin alfa-epbx) has been approved by the USFDA as a biosimilar to Epogen/Procrit (epoetin alfa) for the treatment of anemia. There are various innovative biologics products. Few of them are listed in Table 2.5. Biologics are regulated by the FD&C Act and the Act on Public Health Service. These require specific guidance to monitor the development of biological medicine, and their application in clinical therapy is permitted by regulatory authorities.

2.6.1 International standards for regulation of biologics

Various regulatory bodies are attaining experience in the process of approval. WHO has defined global regulatory standards required for the approval of all biological medicines. Regulators will ensure that the biologics available to patients are as safe and efficient as possible by adhering to these requirements (https://www.iapo.org.uk/sites/default/files/files/factsheet2.pdf). In addition, not only new biologics, but also those approved prior to the development of the WHO and other national guidelines, should be covered by the WHO guidelines. All these goods have been licensed via a regulatory path. In cases where small-molecule drugs may not meet up-to-date quality expectations, clinical trial facts, and

TABLE 2.5 Various Food and Drug Administration–approved biosimilar products.

Biosimilar products	Reference product	Month and year of approval
Hulio	Humira (adalimumab)	July 2020
Nyvepria	Neulasta (pegfilgrastim)	June 2020
Avsola	Remicade (infliximab)	December 2019
Ziextenzo	Neulasta (pegfilgrastim)	November 2019
Abrilada	Humira (adalimumab)	November 2019
Ruxience	Rituxan (rituximab)	July 2019
Hadlima	Humira (adalimumab)	July 2019
Zirabev	Avastin (bevacizumab)	June 2019
Kanjinti	Herceptin (trastuzumab)	June 2019

postmarket scrutiny plans, the WHO argues that these goods need to be reassessed to ensure that they meet the new requirements. For example, in the United States, the FDA has developed an approval pathway explicitly for biosimilars, although certain products deemed "follow-on biologics" have been licensed in the past via a mechanism reserved for products closely related to originators that do not fit into the generic category.

2.6.2 U.S. Food and Drug Administration biologics team

In year 1997, USFDA biologics team was formed with the aim to maintain biological products quality. This team includes the following:

1. CBER certified inspectors,
2. Certified ORA investigators, and
3. Officers representing both CBER and ORA.

2.6.3 Postlicensing monitoring

2.6.3.1 Product release

By controlling the production process of biologics, it is necessary to ensure consistent quality. This requires that genetic consistency be systematically controlled and the level of genetic impurities of cells reprogrammed for biological production be minimized; and that the occurrence of biotoxins or viral contamination be prevented. Therefore, proper monitoring process is needed throughout the manufacturing. Biological samples are tested as per the specifications given by the National Control Authority. The National Control Authority also evaluates the protocols and standards followed by company manufacturers. Batch protocols are critically reviewed by the authority. In-process control and control tests should be compliant with given specifications. In patients with the intended disease or disorder, all biologics must undergo clinical trials.

2.6.3.2 Inspections

Manufacturing plant should be inspected periodically by the control authority to confirm that the premise is in accordance with the requirements of GMPs.

2.6.3.3 Postlicensing surveillance

Everybody, including doctors, patients, nurses etc., is free to report the events of adverse drug reaction associated with the new biological product. Authority is expected to take action for it by analyzing the adverse reaction, assessing and take opinions from experts, if required. If there is reporting of an adverse reaction for an imported product, then WHO should be notified. The operation of a monitoring system for adverse reaction is done on the basis of Council for International Organizations of Medical Sciences (CIOMS) report.

2.6.3.4   Recall and revocation

Authorities have the power to recall batches, revoke approvals and also ensuring that the concerned manufacturer is informed accordingly.

2.6.3.5   Approval of changes in manufacturing

If there are any modifications made by the manufacturer regarding process, packing, quality assurance, labeling, and so on, then proper data should be presented by the manufacturer to the authorities about the updates and consistency of the product.

2.6.3.6   Approval of new patterns

If there are any changes in the route of administration, dosage regimen, frequency of dosing, and so on, then it is to be reported by the manufacturer to the National Control Authority (https://www.fda.gov).

2.7   Conclusion

Safeguarding public health is the main goal of drug policy. It is the responsibility of regulatory authorities to confirm that regulations are followed by pharmaceutical companies. There are regulations which include manufacturing of drugs in compliance with the rules in order to protect them and the well-being of the patient. General requirements and guidelines should be followed as specified for approval of API, novel drug delivery systems, nanotechnology products, and biologics.

References

Green, J.D., 2009. Regulatory Affairs introduction. Toxicol. Pathol. 37 (3), 361–362.

Guidelines for Evaluation of Nanopharmaceuticals in India, Government of India New Delhi, October 2019.

Gupta, R., Kesselheim, A.S., Downing, N., Greene, J., Ross, J.S., 2016. Generic drug approvals since the 1984 Hatch–Waxman Act. JAMA Intern. Med. 176 (9), 1391–1393.

Holbein, M.E., 2009. Understanding FDA regulatory requirements for investigational new drug applications for sponsor-investigators. J. Investig. Med. 57 (6), 688–694.

Hu, M., Babiskin, A., Wittayanukorn, S., et al., 2019. Predictive analysis of first abbreviated new drug application submission for new chemical entities based on machine learning methodology. Clin. Pharmacol. Ther. 106 (1), 174–181.

Lee, C.Y., Chen, X., Romanelli, R.J., Segal, J.B., 2016. Forces influencing generic drug development in the United States: A narrative review. J. Pharm. Policy Pract. 9, 26.

Matsuhama, M., Takishita, T., Kuribayashi, R., Takagi, K., Wakao, R., Mikami, K., 2016. Similarities and differences of international practices and procedures for the regulation for active substance master files/drug master files of human use: Moving toward regulatory convergence. J. Pharm. Pharm. Sci. 19 (2), 290–301.

Munteanu, C.R., Dorado, J., Matei-Ilfoveanu, I., Nita, S.A., 2013. Regulatory affairs issues and legal ontologies in drug development. Front. Biosci. (Elite Ed.) 5, 446–460.

Ritter, J.M., 2008. Drug regulation & therapeutic efficacy. Br. J. Clin. Pharmacol. 65 (6), 801–802.

Thambavita, D., Galappatthy, P., Jayakody, R.L., 2018. Regulatory requirements for the registration of generic medicines and format of drug dossiers: procedures in Sri Lanka in comparison with selected regulatory authorities. J. Pharm. Policy Pract. 11, 14.

Vishal, P., Rahulgiri, G., Pratik, M., Kumar, B.J., 2014. A review on drug approval process for United States, Europe and India. Int. J. Drug. Reg. Aff. 2 (1), 1–11.

Chapter 3

International Council for Harmonisation (ICH) guidelines

Bhavna[1], Abhijeet Ojha[2] and Samir Bhargava[1]

[1]Faculty of Pharmacy, DIT University, Dehradun, India, [2]College of Pharmacy, Six Sigma Institute of Technology, Rudrapur, India

3.1 Introduction

The International Council for Harmonisation (ICH) is a specialized necessity of drugs for human utilization and its selective job is to bond the administrative experts and drug manufacturers to talk about the reasonable and focused parts of medication utilization. The working of the ICH reflects its operations for the progress relating to high-quality and safe dosage forms, which can be registered efficiently as per the highest standards. In the guidelines, revisions are generally given as R1, R2, R3, and so on. ICH functioning involves receiving of regular inputs from the global Pharmaceutical Industry and several stakeholders, which in turn effects requirements by regulators. The ICH, since its inception until today, has harmonized the drugs and pharmaceutical-related policies through several regulatory offices of several nations. Hence, there is avoidance of replication in clinical trials for a drug specifically in humans and reduces utilization of numerous resources during drug development.

3.1.1 Opportunities and difficulties

The ICH has progressively advanced and its initiation was done in April 1990, to react to the undeniably general face of medication improvement. The underlying target of ICH was planning the administrative exercises of the European, Japanese, and the U.S. bodies to examine and concur with the logical and specialized perspectives emerging out of item enrollment. As of late, this was enhanced by the expansion of Health Canada and Swissmedic, to the center ICH Steering Advisory Group (Huynh, 2010). The ICH's fundamental goal is to achieve more prominent harmonization globally to guarantee public health protection convincingly, and great prescriptions are created and registered most effectively.

In the current scenario of globalization of medication schemes, experts from Japan, Europe, the United States and investigation-based organizations believed to join the activities and facilities to protect the drug-testing programs without negotiating with public health (Fernand, 1996).

3.1.2 History of ICH

ICH was previously held for harmonizing regulatory requirements in 1980 by the European Union, while in the year 1989, countries such as Japan, Europe, and the United States planned for harmonization. In April 1990, the technical necessity for the harmonizing process of pharmaceuticals for human use was created at the ICH convention in Brussels. The meeting was held on October 23, 2015, in the inaugural assembly and ICH was established as an international association to act as a legal entity under the Swiss Law (Zachary, 2015).

3.1.2.1 Missions

1. ICH condensed the repetition of testing approved throughout the research and development of newly developed medicines for humans. The mission of ICH is to accomplish harmonization for the analysis and application of its official recommendations and necessities for pharmaceutical product record-keeping (Gupta et al., 2014).
2. ICH is an exclusive commission that organizes the drug-controlling jurisdictions and also monitors the industries of pharmaceuticals for countries, such as Japan, Europe, and the United States.

Regulatory Affairs in the Pharmaceutical Industry. DOI: https://doi.org/10.1016/B978-0-12-822211-9.00008-3
© 2022 Elsevier Inc. All rights reserved.

3. Regulatory harmonization proposes multiple straight profits too, individually to regulatory establishments and the pharmaceutical industries through useful effects for safeguarding public well-being. The fundamental benefit comprises the prevention of repetition in the clinical trials for humans and reducing the usage of examination without negotiating welfare.

3.1.2.2 ICH organizational structure

The structure of ICH has been framed as shown in Fig. 3.1. Each committee is composed of a specific objective.

1. *Steering Committee*

The Steering Committee is a hierarchical organization that deals with ICH rules and manages the strategies and cycles aimed at ICH, chooses subjects, and monitors the progress of harmonization activities. Each of the six parties of ICH (EFPIA, EU, FDA, JPMA, MHLW, and PhRMA) as given in Fig. 3.2 has two seats in the ICH Navigating Committee. The eyewitnesses to the Board of trustees are WHO, Health Canada, and EFTA. Every one of the spectators chooses noncasting ballot supporters to show up in the ICH Steering Committee gatherings. IFPMA likewise partakes as a noncasting a ballot part in the directing committee (ICH Introduction Organization and Guidelines — A precise insight, no date).

2. *ICH Coordinators*

The Coordinators function under the ultimate administration of the ICH and are assigned during each of the six gatherings. The ICH Facilitator serves as the primary connection with the ICH Secretariat (Coordinators, no date; ICH association, Annual Report, 2018). Because of auxiliary dissimilarities inside the European Union and MHLW, the technical facilitators (from ICH) are moreover chosen from European Medicines Agency and Pharmaceuticals and Medical Devices Agency separately.

3. *ICH Secretariat*

The ICH Secretariat workplace is in Geneva and is working from IFPMA office, and is prevalently bothered about arrangements, documentation, and organizing meetings for the Steering Committee. When it is time for ICH Conferences, the Secretariat emerges with responsibility for specialized documentation and equates with presenters

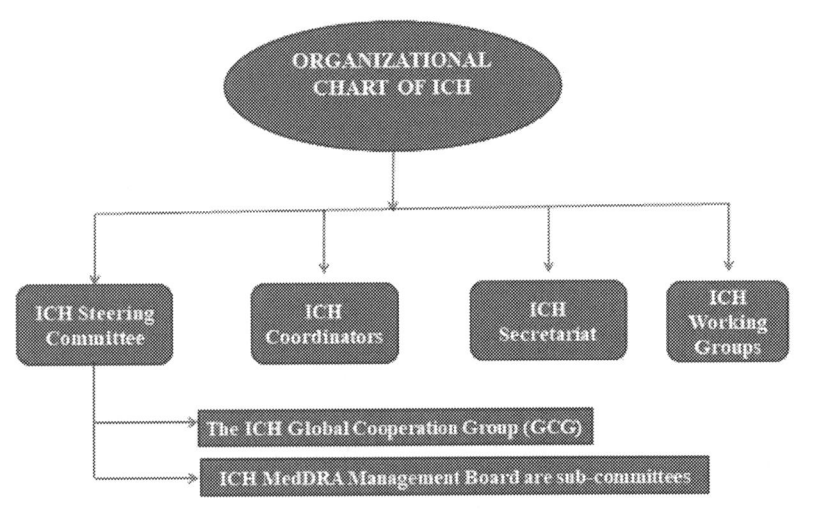

FIGURE 3.1 Organizational chart of International Council for Harmonisation (ICH).

Steering Committee	EFPIA: European Federation of Pharmaceutical Industries and Associations.
	EFTA: European Free Trade Association
	EU: European Union
	FDA: Food and Drug Administration
	IFPMA: International Federation of Pharmaceutical Manufacturers & Associations
	JPMA: Japan Pharmaceutical Manufacturers Association
	MHLW: Ministry of Health, Labour and Welfare
	PhRMA: Pharmaceutical Research and Manufacturers of America

FIGURE 3.2 Steering Committee of International Council for Harmonisation (ICH).

for conference. The ICH Secretariat additionally offers authoritative help for ICH Global Cooperation functions and ICH Medical Dictionary for Regulatory Affairs (MedDRA) Governance Board.

The Steering panel consists of:

1. *Global Cooperation Group (GCG)*: The council of GCG was established in 1999 and is one of the subcommittees for ICH Steering (Navigating) Committee. The aim of the committee is developing awareness regarding guidelines for ICH outside the three ICH provinces. In the later years, for perceiving and to connect effectively with other harmonization activities, the agents of five Regional Harmonization Initiatives were welcomed for connecting with GCG. The relationship is required for conversations with different offices—Asia Pacific Economic Cooperation (APEC), Association of Southeast Asian Nations (ASEAN), East African Community (EAC), Gulf Co-operative Council (GCC), Pan American Network for Drug Regulatory Harmonization (PANDRH), and South African Development Community (SADC). In the year 2007 the GCG agreed for the expansion, and the controllers of different nations with a background of following ICH guidelines were welcomed. Countries such as Brazil, Australia, China, Russia, India, Singapore, Republic of Korea, and Chinese Taipei were included as they implemented ICH and have contributed during the creation and clinical exploration.
2. *Management Board of MedDRA*: The ICH Steering Committee likewise chooses the MedDRA Management Board, which has responsibility for directing MedDRA; it is an ICH normalized word reference for medicinal vocabulary. The panel accomplishes trainings for the MedDRA as "Maintenance and Support Services Organization," which is free for all regulators from academics, healthcare providers, and merchant of MedDRA.

The managing board is composed of:

1. Members of ICH Parties from the European Union, FDA, EFPIA, JPMA, MHLW, PhRMA,
2. Member from Medicines and Healthcare items Regulatory Agency (MHRA) from the United Kingdom and also from Health Canada,
3. World Health Organization as Observer,
4. International Federation of Pharmaceutical Manufacturer and Association (IFPMA) (as observer), and
5. *Working group*.

   During the principal period of exercises, the specialized themes that have been assigned for harmonization require the SC to delegate a Working Group, which surveys the distinctions in prerequisites between the three districts and creates a logical assent needed to accommodate those distinctions. The Working Group does not have a static "participation" yet everyone among these six parties must be designating a Topic Leader in association with this subject (ICH Association, Annual Report, 2018).

There are various kinds of working gatherings mentioned under ICH and also have recognition:

1. *Expert Working Group (EWG)*: The group has been started with building up an orchestrated rule which provides the chance for aiming the work of Concept Paper and Business Plan.
2. *Implementation Working Group (IWG)*: It has been assigned toward the buildup of Question and Answers to empower the execution of existing rules.
3. *Informal Working Group*: This group has been framed before any authority ICH harmonization action with the expectations of advancing/concluding a Concept Paper, just as building up of Business Plan.
4. *Discussion Group*: This group was set up to give explicit logical perspectives, for example Gene Therapy Discussion Group (GTDG), ICH, and Women Discussion Group.

3.1.3 Progression of ICH harmonization

In the process of ICH, the system stays with support of the Steering Committee and initiated with Concept Paper and Business Strategy. Here, the EWG through enrollment is set as per the Concept Paper. The EWG attempts to build up a draft of rules for usage in the ICH regions (Overview of ICH, 2019). The ICH harmonization is directed in five phases:

Step 1: Consensus building
   This step follows the setting up of the EWG attempts for an agreement draft of the specialized archive and given the goals to be established by use of Concept Paper. In this process the work by is directed via email, video chats, and Web gatherings. Whenever supported by the SC, the EWG will likewise meet twice a year in the SC groups. In between these meetings the EWG investigates that the advancement of the draft is made to the SC consistently.

At the point when agreement on the draft is made available to each of the six party's EWG individuals, the EWG signs the Step first—Step first expert's sign-off sheet. In the progression, the first expert's provide text with the signatures of the EWG members and then given to the Steering (Navigating) Commission for selection which is a second step for the ICH cycle.

Step 2: Classification

Step 2A: Confirmation of Consensus on Technical Document: The step 2A is achieved once this Steering Committee approves that there is adequate logical agreement regarding specialized issues aimed at the Technical Document. This agreement remains affirmed through any of the individuals from the SC among the six ICH gatherings for marking and providing consent.

Step 2B: Adoption of draft rule by Regulatory Parties: Based on the Technical Document, the three ICH administrative groups will take important steps to build up a draft for the Guideline. Step 2B gets in hold only when the members form the regulatory party and approve the draft for the Guideline.

Step 3: Regulatory consultation and discussion

This phase arises in three different stages as: consultation by regional regulator, discussion regarding the consultation, and final decision taken by the Step 3 Experts.

Stage I: Regional Regulatory Consultation

This encapsulates entire logical agreement and leaves the ICH cycle and then turns into the theme of a typical wide-running administrative interview in three locales. In European Union, it is distributed as draft CHMP Guideline, in Japan it is used by MHLW for interior in addition to outside discussion, and in United States it is a draft direction in Federal Register. Administrative specialists and industrial relationships in nonspecific ICH areas may provide likewise remark on the draft of conference records which will be noted to ICH Secretariat.

Stage II: Discussion of Regional Consultation Remarks

This will be for acquiring all remarks from the conference cycle; the EWG attempted to address the remarks to finalize the agreement to get the Draft Guideline by Step 3 Experts.

Stage III: Finalization of Step 3 Experts Draft Guideline

After concern of the discussion outcomes by the EWG, the agreement reaches among the specialists in a modified form of Step 2B draft Guideline. While Step 3 Expert Draft Guideline is retained by the authorities of the administrative groups of ICH, Step 3 Expert Draft Guideline with the signatures of EWGs is then submitted to the Steering Committee for approval to proceed to Step 4 of the ICH cycle.

Step 4: Adoption of an ICH Harmonized Tripartite Guideline

This progression exists by the decision of the Steering Committee to provide satisfactory agreement regarding the draft Guideline. The last document provided at Step 4 is adopted through the signatures by the SC of the administrative gatherings for the harmonization as per the ICH Harmonized Tripartite Guideline at Step 4 of the ICH process.

Step 5: Implementation

The harmonized tripartite guideline moves promptly toward the last stage of the progression for the administrative execution. This progression is completed by similar national/regional strategies that are applied to added regional regulatory guidelines and necessities, for countries such as Japan, the European Union, and the United States (Overview of ICH, 2019).

3.2 Outlines of ICH guidelines

The ICH guidelines have been framed to accelerate harmonization of technical requirements (internationally) for ensuring the safety, effectiveness, and higher quality of medicine (Fig. 3.3). There are four major classes (quality, safety, efficacy, and multidisciplinary) into which the ICH guidelines are divided and named as "QSEM."

S.No	Guidelines	Frameworks
1.	Quality (Q)	Related to chemical and pharmaceutical Quality Assurance
2	Safety (S)	Related to *in vitro* and *in vivo* preclinical studies
3.	Efficacy (E):	Related to clinical studies in human subject
4.	Multidisciplinary topics (M)	Related to cross-cutting problems and includes that topic which doesn't get fitted exclusively into any of the above mentioned categories

FIGURE 3.3 List of International Council for Harmonisation (ICH) guidelines and their frameworks.

3.2.1   Quality guidelines

The quality guidelines are based on "Harmonization accomplishments in the Quality region" and include crucial attainments, provided for conducting the stability studies, for analyzing contaminants by testing and for an additional adaptable method to give pharmaceutical quality based on Good Manufacturing Practice (GMP) hazard management (Ur-Rahman, 2017). The stability guidelines are from Q1A (R2) to Q1F which are mentioned in Fig. 3.4 with the other guidelines of quality (ICH: Quality guidelines, no date; Khagga et al., 2019).

Q1A(R2) - STABILITY TESTING IN NEW DRUGS AND PRODUCTS(REVISED GUIDELINE) **Q1B -** PHOTOSTABILITY TESTING **Q1C -** STABILITY TESTING FOR NEW DOSAGE FORMS **Q1D -** BRACKETING AND MATRIXING DESIGNS FOR STABILITY TESTING OF DRUG SUBSTANCES AND DRUG PRODUCTS **Q1E -** EVALUATION OF STABILITY DATA **Q1F -** STABILITY DATA PACKAGE FOR REGISTRATION IN CLIMATIC ZONES III AND IV
Q2(R1) - VALIDATION OF ANALYTICAL PROCEDURES: TEXT AND METHODOLOGY **Q2A -** DEFINTIONS AND TERMINOLOGY:ANALYTICAL VALIDATION **Q2B -** METHODOLOGY
Q3A(R2) - IMPURITIES IN NEW DRUG SUBSTANCES **Q3B(R2) -** IMPURITIES IN NEW DRUG PRODUCTS **Q3C(R5) -** IMPURITIES: GUIDELINE FOR RESIDUAL SOLVENTS
Q4 - PHARMACOPEIA
Q5A(R1) - VIRAL SAFETY EVALUATION OF BIOTECHNOLOGY PRODUCTS DERIVED FROM CELL LINES OF HUMAN OR ANIMAL ORIGIN **Q5B -** QUALITY OF BIOTECHNOLOGICAL PRODUCTS: ANALYSIS OF THE EXPRESSION CONSTRUCT IN CELLS USED FOR PRODUCTION OF R-DNA DERIVED PROTEIN PRODUCTS **Q5C -** QUALITY OF BIOTECHNOLOGICAL PRODUCTS: STABILITY TESTING OF BIOTECHNOLOGICAL/BIOLOGICAL PRODUCTS **Q5D -** DERIVATION AND CHARACTERISATION OF CELL SUBSTRATES USED FOR PRODUCTION OF BIOTECHNOLOGICAL/BIOLOGICAL PRODUCTS **Q5E -** COMPARABILITY OF BIOTECHNOLOGICAL/BIOLOGICAL PRODUCTS SUBJECT TO CHANGES IN THEIR MANUFACTURING PROCESS
Q6A - SPECIFICATIONS: TEST PROCEDURES AND ACCEPTANCE CRITERIA FOR NEW DRUG SUBSTANCES AND NEW DRUG PRODUCTS **Q6B -** SPECIFICATIONS: TEST PROCEDURES AND ACCEPTANCE CRITERIA FOR BIOTECHNOLOGICAL/BIOLOGICAL PRODUCTS
Q7A - GOOD MANUFACTURING PRACTICE GUIDE FOR ACTIVE PHARMACEUTICAL INGREDIENTS
Q8(R2) - PHARMACEUTICAL DEVELOPMENT
Q9 - QUALITY RISK MANAGEMENT
Q10 - PHARMACEUTICAL QUALITY SYSTEM
Q11 - DEVELOPMENT AND MANUFACTURE OF DRUG SUBSTANCES CHEMICAL ENTITIES AND BIOTECHNOLOGICAL/BIOLOGICAL ENTITIES
Q12 - TECHNICAL AND REGULATORY CONSIDERATIONS FOR PHARMACEUTICAL PRODUCT LIFECYCLE MANAGEMENT
Q13 - CONTINUOUS MANUFACTURING OF DRUG SUBSTANCES AND DRUG PRODUCTS
Q14 - ANALYTICAL PROCEDURE DEVELOPMENT

FIGURE 3.4   Revised "Quality Guidelines" (ICH: Quality guidelines, no date; Khagga et al., 2019).

3.2.1.1 Q1 Guidelines

"Q1A (R2): Stability Testing in New Drugs and Products (Revised Guidelines)" (ICH Q1A (R2), 1996): The guidelines embody basic stability records for novel drug molecules; however, it excludes abundant adaptability toward incorporating the extensive choice of applied situations that could be experienced because of explicit scientific concerns and qualities of the materials that must be assessed. This parameter of the guideline is changed a second time and gives proposals on stability testing procedures with temperature, humidity, and preliminary period meant for climatic zones I and II. This modified text deliberates the necessities for stability testing of climatic zones III and IV and for limiting dissimilar storage situations aimed at the suggestion for worldwide dossier (ICH Q1A (R2), 1996).

3.2.1.1.1 "Stability Testing Designed For New Formulation and Dosage Form"

The combined ICH Tripartite Guideline on Stability testing for new drug substances and products was released on October 27, 1993 (ICH Q1A (R2), 2003). An annex is an exceptional type document having ICH basic stability guidelines and protocol. The recommendation was based on what must be presented regarding the stability of the newly developed delivery forms by the owner of the drug substance and products.

On the basis of the information and facts related to the behavioral properties of the drug substance and also from the results obtained from clinical formulation studies, the stability studies of the drug products are conducted. It should describe the appropriate changes in the storage and justification for the assortment of quality required in the formal stability studies (ICH Q1A (R2), 2003).

New dosage form It is a category of drug product, which is composed of dissimilar pharmaceutical products. However, this consists of a similar active substance as present in the existing products, permitted by the appropriate regulations. These types of the products also consist of different administration route (e.g., oral to parenteral) and comprise a special type of function or delivery system, such as an instant (immediate) release tablet to a reformed (modified) release tablet. Some dissimilar dosage forms of the similar route of administration are also manufactured (e.g., capsule, tablet suspension to solution) (ICH Q1C, 1996).

The main motive of this guideline is to explain the requirements for calculating stability data for the new dosage form and also for drug products which is adequate toward the registration submission within the European countries, Japan, and the United States. The recommendations notify the information related to the submission in the registration submission necessary for the novel dosage form and also included drug products.

Stability testing is useful for making available the information related to ways the quality of any new dosage form included with drug product changes with time. This also depends on a range of environmental factors, such as temperature, humidity, and light. It furthermore provides help in establishing re-test duration meant for the medication product or its shelf life, with recommendations for storage environments. This guideline is defined by the selection of assessment conditions, based on the examination of different impacts by the climatic regions (EC, Japan, and the United States) as mentioned in Fig. 3.5. In any part of the world, the average kinetic temperature can be obtained from climatic data. The world can be separated into four climatic zones, that is I to IV.

The main advantage of stress testing for any drug substance is to recognize a suitable degradation product, which aids in setting a degradation pathway and the inherent stability of the molecule, and recognize the stability signaling potential of analytical steps used. The characteristics of stress evaluation will highly depend on the single dosage form and the involved formulation. Stress evaluation on formulation is applicable on solitary batch. The testing should be on the temperature (in $10°$ increments, e.g., $50°$, $60°$, etc., and above for accelerated study) and humidity (e.g., RH $> 75\%$) that are suitable, oxidation, and photolysis of the drug under study. The evaluation supports estimation of sensitivity

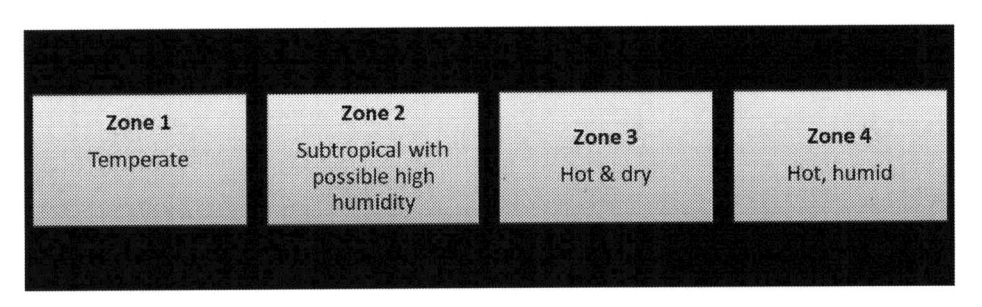

FIGURE 3.5 Climatic zones as recommended in the International Council for Harmonisation (ICH) Guidelines.

within the drug substance due to hydrolysis through an extensive range of pH values when it is in solution or suspension. The essential part of stress evaluation should be photostability testing. During a look into the degradation product under stress, situations will be useful in setting up the degradation pathway and also for developing and validating required analytical procedures (ICH Q1A (R2), 2003). The guideline primarily is studied under:

Photostability studies The information generated by photostability studies is used for the submission of registration applications for novel molecular entities and related drug products. This guideline does not have concerns with the photostability during the management of drugs and such applications are not included in the original guideline.

A regular approach that is followed for photostability testing is suggested as follows:

1. Testing on drug constituents,
2. Testing of unprotected drug product external to actual pack and if required, and
3. Testing of the drug product in the actual pack (Somvanshi and Satbha, 2015).

Selection of batches: The data collected from the stability studies should be produced on at least three initial batches of the drug product. The initial batches should have a similar formulation and packaged in a similar container closure system as introduced for marketing. The procedure for manufacturing applied for the prime batches should apply to the production batch, arrange for product of similar quality, and get similar provisions as for marketing. Hence, two out of three batches are required to be pilot scale batches, while the third batch can be a small one, if acceptable. Stability studies should be performed for each strength and container size of the drug product unless matrixing or bracketing is applied (Chinchole et al., 2014).

Container closure system: Stability testing should be accomplished on the dosage form packed in the container closure system planned for marketing (comprising suitable or any secondary packaging) and container label. If any existing study is performed on a drug product outside of the actual container or its different packaging materials, such a study could be an important portion of stress evaluation for dosage form. Hence it can be recognized as important ancillary information correspondingly (Chinchole et al., 2014).

Specifications: Specifications may include a catalog of tests, reference of the analytical process, and introduced recognition criteria. It consists of dissimilarly introduced criteria used for release and shelf half-life provisions, as proposed in the ICH guidelines Q6A and Q6B. Except these, it also includes specifications for degradation products in any drug product (medicament) as described in Q3B. Hence for evaluating different qualities of medicament, stability studies included must be prone to alter through storage and are appropriate to improve quality, safety, and efficacy (QSE). As required the testing/evaluation should comprise the physical, chemical, biological, and microbiological properties; contents of preservatives, such as antioxidants and antimicrobial preservatives; and functionality tests for a dose delivery system. The analytical process should be certified and stability of the product should be indicated. The results of the validation studies will depend on whether and to what amount of repetition should be executed (Chinchole et al., 2014).

Testing frequency—For long-term studies, the frequency of testing should be adequately set up as per the stability profile of any drug product. Those products having a shelf life of at least 12 months, it is necessary to propose occurrence of testing at storage condition for prolong tenure and should be tested at a period of 3 months during 1st year then every 6 months for the 2nd year and then annually, followed later by purposed shelf life.

(ICH Q1A (R2), 2003)

For accelerated storage circumstances, it requires at least 3 points including the initial and final time points such as 0, 3, and 6 months. There is an exception (according to development knowledge) resulting from accelerated testing appropriateness, which is necessary to use significant changes criteria while performing increased testing either by mixing samples at concluding points or by adding a 4th-time point in the study design. As a result of noteworthy changes during accelerated storage conditions, the testing is called an intermediate storage condition test. In this at least 4 points are required which includes the initial and final time points such as 0, 6, 9, 12 months, as recommended for 12 months study.

(ICH Q1A (R2), 2003)

Matrixing or bracketing, that is reduced design, in which the frequency of testing is decreased or a combination of few factors are not tested at all and can be applied if required (Chinchole et al., 2014).

Storage condition—Usually, evaluation of a drug product during storage condition having suitable durability is verified for thermal stability while the vulnerability to test moistness or possibility of solvent loss. The required duration and storage condition of the studies were selected appropriately for the storage, shipments, and subsequent use.

The test that should be performed for the long-term covers 12 months on a minimum of three primary batches during the proposed period and that should be continued for a long time which is appropriate for the duration of shelf life. The obtained information from the accelerated storage situation, if convenient from the moderate storage circumstances can be used to estimate the outcome of short-term differences outside the labeled condition (Example, during shipping).

The following conditions for storage are mentioned in Fig. 3.6, which are approved as stability studies during mentioned circumstances for the shelf life and are projected for labeling.

(ICH Q1A (R2), 2003)

Note: *It is up to the applicant to choose whether long-term stability studies are accomplished at $25 \pm 2°C/60\%$ RH $\pm 5\%$ RH or $30°C \pm 2°C/65\%$ RH $\pm 5\%$ RH.*

If $30°C \pm 2°C/65\%$ RH $\pm 5\%$ RH is the long-term condition, there is no transitional situation.

The storage of original drug products packaged in various types of containers (ICH Q1A (R2), 2003). See Fig. 3.7.

Stability commitment Stability data accessible for the long-term studies applied on main batches did not cover the projected shelf life accepted during the time of approval. A document should be released for stability studies approved previously to strongly set up the shelf life.

Study	Storage Condition	Minimum time period covered by data at submission
Long term	25°C ± 2°C/60% RH ± 5% RH or 30°C ± 2°C/65% RH ± 5% RH*	12 months
Intermediate	30°C ± 2°C/65% RH ± 5% RH	6 months
Accelerated	40°C ± 2°C/75% RH ± 5% RH	6 months
* If claimant, chooses 30°C ± 2°C/65% RH ± 5% RH for long-term condition then there is requirement of intermediate condition.		

FIGURE 3.6 General storage conditions for drug products.

Drug products packaged	Study	Storage condition	Minimum time period covered by data at submission
Impermeable containers	....	At any controlled or ambient humidity condition	....
Semipermeable containers	Long term	25°C ± 2°C/40% RH ± 5% RH Or 30°C ± 2°C/35% RH ± 5% RH	12 months
	Intermediate	30°C ± 2°C/65% RH ± 5% RH	6 months
	Accelerated	40°C ± 2°C / not more than (NMT) 25% RH	6 months
Refrigerator	Long term	5°C ± 3°C	12 months
	Accelerated	25°C ± 2°C/60% RH ± 5% RH	6 months
Freezer	Long term	- 20°C ± 5°C	12 months
Below -20°C	Treated on a case-by-case basis	....	....

FIGURE 3.7 Storage conditions of new drug products (Q1A (R2), 2003).

During the submission, it requires the data for long-term stability to have three production batches that cover the introduced shelf life, show any postapproval commitment is recognized as unnecessary. Else any of the following commitments should be applied.

1. "Information obtained from the stability studies during submission having at least 3 production batches, the obligation should be performed for the long-term studies through which the suggested shelf-life and accelerated studies for 6 months are carried out" (Q1A (R2), 2003).
2. "Information obtained from stability studies of less than 3 production batches, the obligation should be generated to keep the long-term studies via propose shelf-life and 6 months of accelerated studies and to locate extra production batches, to a total having at least 3, during long-term studies via suggested shelflife and 6 months of accelerated studies" (Q1A (R2), 2003).
3. "If stability data on production batteries do not require during submission then obligation should be generated for the first 3 production batches based on the long-term stability studies why the suggested shelf-life and 6 months of accelerated studies" (Q1A (R2), 2003).

On the commitment batches, the stability protocol applied should be as similar to the primary batches. However, it is scientifically approved.

If there is a requirement of intermediate testing for considerable change during accelerated storage conditions for primary batches, testing should be calculated for the commitment batches at either the intermediate or the accelerated storage condition. Despite having serious changes happening during accelerated storage conditions to the commitment batches, testing should be necessary during intermediate storage conditions.

Evaluation For demonstration and analysis of the stability information, there should be systematic approaches acquired. These approaches consist of suitable results from the chemical, physical, microbiological, and biological tests. This includes exceptional properties of the dose form such as the dissolution rate of solid dosage forms.

The stability studies are proposed to establish, on at least three minimum batches of any drug product. The suitable instructions are applied as shelf life and storage labels to all upcoming batches of the drug product which will be manufactured and packaged under the same situation. A little degradation is found in the obtained data at also a small variability that is clear by observation of data (for accepting requested shelf life).

Generally, it is unnecessary, to conduct the formal statistical analysis dead provider clarification for the fault should be adequate. Different degradation type will define whether the data should be modified for analysis of linear regression.

Normally, the relation of a linear, quadratic, or cubic function can be represented in arithmetic or logarithmic scale. For making sure to be a better advantage for all batches and combined batches, static method should be applied which is supposed to provide degradation as line or curve.

Statement/labeling The labeling of the storage statement should be set up according to the need for national or regional requirements. The labeling of the drug product is based on the evaluation of stability studies. For drug that cannot tolerate freezing, there should be special instruction provided in the statement. Terminologies such as "ambient condition" or "room temperature" should not be mentioned. It is necessary to make a direct relationship between the level storage statements in the established stability of the drug product. Labeling of expiry date on the outside container is mandatory (Pawar and Khandelwal, 2019).

Q1B: Photostability Testing: This document is an extension of the principle stability program and contributes direction regarding fundamental analysis convention needed in assessing the photosensitivity and steadiness of original drugs and products.

This document represents enforced degradation stability studies, for degrading samples intentionally. These investigations, which might be attempted for improvement stage, ordinarily arranged for the drug substances, utilized for assessing the complete photosensitivity of material plus method development determinations/potentially for degradation path interpretation.

The confirmation examinations are set up for photostability analysis under standardized situations. The investigations used to distinguish prudent steps required in manufacturing/formulation in addition to light-resistant packing and/or extraordinary labeling remains expected for moderate exposure to light. In case of corroborative, the batches must be carefully chosen accordingly for long-term and accelerated studies as depicted in the Parent Guideline (ICH Q1B, 1996).

"Q1C: Stability Testing for New Dosage Forms" (ICH Q1C, 1996): It is an extension of principle stability recommendations for a novel formulation that has formerly approved medications, as well as characterizes those conditions in which reduced stability information examinations can be known. It also suggests documents/items required to be submitted regarding stability of novel dosage form, along with initial submission for original drug substances and products. The documents are to be submitted through the proprietor of the original application.

New dosage form: The definition of new dosage form defines the Pharmaceutical formulation form; it is a dissimilar pharmaceutical product category, but comprises of similar active substances as included in the current drug product accepted by relevant governing authorities (ICH Q1C, 1996).

"Q1D: Bracketing and Matrixing Designs for Stability Testing of Drug Substances and Product" (ICH Q1D, 2002): The document reports proposals for use of bracketing and matrixing of stability studies, focused in accord with ethics defined in the key stability guideline (ICH Q1A(R) Harmonized Tripartite rule off Stability Testing of New Drug Substances and Products).

Bracketing: It is referenced in the dictionary of the original recommendations and is a stability plan such as only samples from end-limits of design factors which remain verified constantly at all intervals as in full design. The plan admits that the steadiness of any intermediary stages is designated by the stability of the limit of extremes evaluated.

Matrixing: It is also referenced in the lexicon of original recommendations; matrixing is a stability plan such that specific partition of the entire quantity of potential samples for entire factor blends is confirmed at stated intervals. Thus, at a progressive interval, a different subclass of samples for all aspects would be confirmed. The design accepts that the steadiness of every subgroup of samples signifies steadiness of entire samples on any point of time. The dissimilarities within samples for similar drug products ought to be distinguished using dissimilar batches, dissimilar strengths, dissimilar sizes of related container closure systems, and occasional dissimilar container closure systems (ICH Q1D, 2002).

Q1E: Evaluation of Stability Data: The text expands the principle stability parameter by clarifying potential circumstances wherever prediction of reexamine periods or shelf lives outside the real-time records might be suitable. Moreover, it yields instances of statistical methods for stability data investigation. This guideline defines that at what time and in what way the further prediction can be viewed, whereas recommending a reexamine period for a drug substance or a shelf life for drug products which ranges outside the period. This recommendation is based on extension providing the directions introduced in the assessment sections of the parent guideline (ICH Q1E, 2003).

Q1F: Stability Data Package for Registration Application in Climatic Zones III and IV: Steering Committee of ICH supported the removal of the Q1F Guideline in June 2006 (Yokohama meeting), and carefully chosen to quit description of storage environments in Climatic Zones III and IV toward the respective particular regions and WHO. Currently, the status of this direction is withdrawn (ICH: Quality guidelines, no date).

3.2.1.2 "Q2 (R1): Validation of Analytical Procedures: Text and Methodology"

This article grants conversation that highlights the considerations during validation of analytical processes which include a module of registration applications acquiesced to the European countries, Japan, and the United States (ICH Q2 (R1), 1995). This text does not cover the tests that might be necessary for registering or export to different parts of the world. Moreover, the text presents a collection of terms and their descriptions, and it is not planned how to accomplish validation in the guidance. The summation in table format incorporates the attributes appropriate for recognition, management of contaminants, and assay processes. Other analytical procedures might be studied in the forthcoming period as augmentations to this article (ICH Q2 (R1), 1995).

3.2.1.3 Q3 Guidelines

"Q3A (R2): Impurities in New Drug Substances" (ICH Q3A (R2), 2006): The regulation is regarding registration submissions of the content and prerequisites of contaminations in a novel drug material made by chemical synthesis and not recently enrolled in a region. The subsequent drug materials such as biological/biotechnological, peptide, oligonucleotide, radiopharmaceutical, fermentation items, and semisynthetic items extracted from herbal products or crude products of animal and plant source are not covered under this recommendation.

Contaminants in novel drug materials are addressed and have two specific viewpoints:

1. Chemistry viewpoint includes characterization and description of contaminations, their particulars, a catalog of contaminants in detail, and a concise conversation of analytical methods.
2. Safety viewpoints incorporate explicit instructions for qualifying impurities that were available or not available at essentially reduced stages, in lots of other drug substances utilized in safety and clinical investigations (ICH Q3A (R2), 2006).

Q3B (R2): Impurities in New Drug Products: The guideline is applied for registration applications for content and eligibility of contaminant in novel drug products obtained from chemically produced novel drug substances which are not recently enlisted in a region. This recommendation reports about those contaminations in novel drug substances which are named as degraded outcomes of the drug material or reaction yields of the drug material with an additive-like excipient and/or immediate container closure system (mutually stated as "degradation products" in this recommendation). This document does not cover the contaminants which are increased due to added adjuvants existing in the new drug product or separated or leaked from the container closure system. This guideline likewise does not have any significant bearing on new drug products or outcomes utilized during the experimental/clinical research phases of progress. There are a few kinds of products that are not incorporated in this recommendation: peptide, radiopharmaceuticals, biological/biotechnological products, oligonucleotides, fermentation products, and semisynthetic products which are obtained from herbal products and crude products of plant or animal. Similarly, the guideline barred: (1) the unnecessary impurities that would never exist in novel drug products and it more suitably addresses the matters related to GMP, (2) polymorphic forms, and (3) enantiomeric impurities (ICH Q3B (R2), 2006).

Q3C (R5): Impurities—Guideline for Residual Solvents: This guideline recommends tolerable amounts for remaining/residual solvents in pharmaceuticals, for patient security. It also suggests the utilization of fewer harmful solvents and portrays stages viewed as toxicologically suitable for some remaining solvents.

In pharmaceuticals, remaining solvents are said as organic volatile substances that will be utilized or formed during the manufacturing of drug substances or excipients (adjuvants), or the formation of drug products. The solvents are not taken out by practical manufacturing approaches. This guideline neither addresses solvents purposely utilized as excipients nor addresses as solvates. In any case, the number of solvents in such products should be measured and acceptable.

3.2.1.4 Q4: Pharmacopeia

The ICH Q4 guideline is commonly answered to be as the effective ICH Quality Guideline. ICH Q4 has been partitioned into Q4A (Pharmacopeial Harmonisation) and Q4B (Evaluation and Recommendation of Pharmacopeial Texts for use in the ICH regions). Q4A and Q4B are utilized reciprocally. The target of the guideline is to create replaceable methods or prerequisites as shown in Fig. 3.8.

Q4B document portrays a cycle for the assessment and suggestion by the Q4B EWG to choose pharmacopeia editions to encourage their response by administrative experts for use as tradable in the ICH districts of provincial pharmacopeial monographs, as expressed in Fig. 3.8 of ICH Q4B Annexure. The current pharmacopeial methodology is for controlling inorganic contaminations, aligned with residues on ignition/sulfated ash test and other wet chemistry tests (ICH Q4B, 2007).

3.2.1.5 Q5 Guidelines

"Q5A (R1): Viral Safety Evaluation of Biotechnology Products Derived from Cell Lines of Human or Animal Origin" (ICH Q5A (R1), 1997): The guideline is related to analyzing and assessing biotechnology products from viruses, resulting due to defined cell lines of human or animal origin. It sets the evidences to be submitted during the submission of compiled application/registration. However, the term virus in the document excludes unique infectious agents, such as those linked with Bovine Spongiform Encephalopathy and scrape.

The purpose behind this content is to offer a universal outline for virus testing, experimentations for evaluation of viral clearance, and planning of studies for these. The data is represented as supplements and designated descriptions are given in the glossary (ICH Q5A (R1), 1997).

"Q5B: Quality of Biotechnological Products: Analysis of the Expression Construct in Cells Used for Production of R-DNA Derived Protein Product" (ICH Q5B, 1996): The guideline represents expression construct for the creation of recombinant DNA protein products in eukaryotic and prokaryotic cells. The text of this report provides data that are viewed as significant while evaluating the organization of the expression construct used to produce recombinant DNA—derived proteins. The report is not expected to conceal the entire quality part of rDNA resultant medicinal products (ICH Q5B, 1996).

"Q5C: Quality of Biotechnological Products: Stability Testing of Biotechnological/Biological Products" (ICH Q5C, 1996): The text indicated in this supplementary document describes how proteins and polypeptides, their byproducts and products from them, and peptide isolates are delivered utilizing rDNA technology. The origination and proposal of stability data for products, such as cytokines (interferons, interleukins, colony-stimulating factors, and tumor necrosis factors), erythropoietin, plasminogen activators, blood plasma factors, growth hormones and growth factors, insulin, monoclonal antibodies, and vaccines comprising peptides are covered in this guidance. This document does not shield

Q4A - PHARMACOPOEIAL HARMONIZATION

REGARDING EVALUATION AND RECOMMENDATION OF PHARMACOPOEIAL TEXTS FOR USE IN:

Q4 B - THE ICH REGIONS

Q4B ANNEX 1(R1) - THE ICH REGIONS ON RESIDUE ON IGNITION/SULPHATED ASH

Q4B ANNEX (R1) - THE ICH REGIONS ON TEST FOR EXTRACTABLE VOLUME OF PARENTERAL PREPARATIONS

Q4B ANNEX 3 (R1) - THE ICH REGIONS ON TEST FOR PARTICULATE CONTAMINATION: SUB-VISIBLE PARTICLES

Q4B ANNEX 4A(R1) - THE ICH REGIONS ON MICROBIOLOGICAL EXAMINATION OF NON-STERILEPRODUCTS: MICROBIAL ENUMERATIONS TESTS

Q4B ANNEX 4B(R1) - THE ICH REGIONS ON MICROBIOLzGICAL EXAMINATION OF NON-STERILEPRODUCTS: TEST FOR SPECIFIED MICRO-ORGANISMS

Q4B ANNEX 4C(R1) - THE ICH REGIONS ON MICROBIOLOGICAL EXAMINATION OF NON-STERILEPRODUCTS: ACCEPTANCE CRITERIA FOR PHARMACEUTICAL PREPARATIONS A; ND SUBSTANCES FOR PHARMACEUTICAL USE

Q4B ANNEX 5 (R1) - THE ICH REGIONS ON DISINTEGRATION TEST

Q4B ANNEX 6(R1) - THE ICH REGIONS ON UNIFORMITY OF DOSAGE UNITS

Q4B ANNEX 7 (R2) - THE ICH REGIONS ON DISSOLUTION TEST

Q4B ANNEX 8(R1) - THE ICH REGIONS ON STERILITY TEST

Q4B ANNEX 9(R1) - THE ICH REGIONS ON TABLET FRIABILITY

Q4B ANNEX10(R1) - THE ICH REGIONS ON POLYACRYLAMIDE GEL ELECTROPHORESIS

Q4B ANNEX 11 - THE ICH REGIONS ON CAPILLARY ELECTROPHORESIS

Q4B ANNEX 12 - THE ICH REGIONS ON ANALYTICAL SIEVING

Q4B ANNEX 13 - THE ICH REGIONS ON BULK DENSITY AND TAPPED DENSITY OF POWDERS

Q4B ANNEX 14 - THE ICH REGIONS ON BACTERIAL ENDOTOXINS TEST

FIGURE 3.8 Guidelines Q4 Pharmacopeias (Andrew et al., 2017)

antibiotics, and vaccines comprising peptides are covered in this guidance. This document does not cover antibiotics, allergenic extracts, heparins, vitamins, whole blood, or cellular blood components (ICH Q5C, 1996).

"Q5D: Derivation and Characterisation of Cell Substrates Used for Production of Biotechnological/Biological Products" (ICH Q5D, 1996): In this regulation, cell substrates which have a cell banking framework are covered. The text portrays "cell substrate," which discusses microscopic cells or cell lines developed from human or animal origins. The cells should have a maximum capacity for the genesis of anticipated biotechnological processes/products for human in vivo or ex vivo usage. The reactive chemicals for in vitro investigative usage are not in the scope of this regulation. Equally continuous cell lines of unspecified in vitro life expectancy and diploid cells of limited in vitro life expectancy are incorporated (ICH Q5D, 1996).

"Q5E: Comparability of Biotechnological/Biological Products Subject to Changes in their Manufacturing Process" (ICH Q5E, 2005): This guideline discloses standards for evaluating the comparability of biotechnological/biological products; formerly and afterward by making variations in the manufacturing procedure for the drug substance or drug product. Along these lines, the document is proposed for an assortment of applicable technical data that may indicate that the manufacturing process would not adversely affect the QSE of the drug product. The document does not recommend a specific analytical, nonclinical, or clinical approach. The main importance within the guideline is on quality characteristics (ICH Q5E, 2005).

3.2.1.6   Q6 Guidelines

"Q6A: Specifications: Test Procedures and Acceptance Criteria for New Drug Substances and New Drug Products" (ICH Q6A, 2000): The guideline conveys the background and explanation of acceptance measures, including determination of investigative processes for novel drug materials having chemical synthesis during derivation or source and novel drug products, which have not been listed formerly in the United States, the European Union, or Japan.

The text reports the marketing consent of novel drug products (comprising combination products) and where relevant it is likewise accomplished for the novel drug substances. The guidance does not report the usage of drug substances or drug products through the clinical research phases of drug development. This guideline also addresses the specification for test processes and recognition norms for biotechnological/biological products. The document of this recommendation does not include radiopharmaceuticals, products of fermentation, oligonucleotides, herbal products, and crude products of animal or plant origin (ICH Q6A, 2000).

"Q6B: Specifications: Test Procedures and Acceptance Criteria for Biotechnological/Biological Product" (ICH Q6B, 1999): This guideline depicts the proteins and polypeptides, their subsidiaries, and products made using them (e.g., conjugates). The manufacturing of these polypeptides is from recombinant or nonrecombinant cell-culture expression arrangement and can be exceptionally refined and used for a suitable set of investigative practices. This document may likewise apply to additional product categories, for example, proteins and polypeptides from body tissues and liquids. Hence for determining appropriateness, manufacturers are required to have access to suitable regulatory authorities.

Antibiotics, heparins, synthetic peptides and polypeptides, cell metabolites, vitamins, DNA products, allergenic extracts, cells, conservative vaccines, whole blood and cellular blood components are not included in this guideline. There is a distinct ICH Guideline for "Specifications: Test Procedures and Acceptance Criteria for New Drugs Substances and New Drug Products: Chemical Substances" which reports conditions and other criteria for chemical substances (ICH Q6B, 1999).

3.2.1.7   "Q7: Good Manufacturing Practice Guide for Active Pharmaceutical Ingredients"

The guideline deals with GMP for the manufacturing of active pharmaceutical ingredients (APIs) under a suitable guidance system for supervising prominence (ICH Q7, 2000). In this Guidance "manufacturing" is characterized to incorporate all processes for material receiving, production, packaging, repackaging, labeling, relabeling, quality control, release, storage, and distribution of APIs and the related controls. The guideline is not expected to characterize registration/filing necessities or transform pharmacopoeia requirements (ICH Q7, 2000).

3.2.1.8   "Q8 (R2): Pharmaceutical Development"

The recommendation is designed to give directions for the content of Section 3.2.P.2 (pharmaceutical development) for drug products as characterized within the recommendation, also present in Module 3 of the CTD (ICH M4) (ICH Q8 (R2), 2017). This recommendation does not relate to the contents of records for drug products during the clinical research phases during drug development. The standards within this rule are imperative for replication during those stages too. This specific rule may similarly be appropriate for dissimilar kinds of items (ICH Q8 (R2), 2017).

3.2.1.9 "Q9: Quality Risk Management"

The recommendation conveys ideologies and illustrations for quality risk managing that can be helpful for various sections of drug quality (ICH Q9, 2015). This includes the highlights concerning development, manufacturing, distribution, examination, and compliance/review measures all through the life span of drug substances, drug (medicinal) products, and biological and biotechnological products (along with the usage of raw ingredients, adjuvants added as excipients, solvents, packaging, and labeling of materials) (ICH Q9, 2015).

3.2.1.10 "Q10: Pharmaceutical Quality System"

This guideline appropriately supports the advancements and manufacturing of drug substances, drug products, including biotechnology and biological products, all through their life span (ICH Q10, no date; ICH: Quality guidelines, no date). The components for ICH Q10 ought to be useful, such that it remains suitable and balanced to each of the product life span phases (ICH Q10: Pharmaceutical quality system (PQS), no date). The guidance includes the following methodological happenings for new and prevailing products related to the life cycle of a product:

1. Pharmaceutical progress and development;
2. Technology transfer and handover;
3. Commercial manufacturing;
4. Product termination.

3.2.1.11 "Q11: Development and Manufacture of Drug Substances (Chemical Entities and Biotechnological/Biological Entities)"

The guideline talks about features of progress and manufacturing that identify with drug substance, including steps intended to eliminate contamination (ICH Q11, 2011). ICH Q11 also gives an explanation of the philosophies and models assigned in ICH Guidelines on Pharmaceutical Development (Q8), Quality Risk Management (Q9), and Pharmaceutical Quality System (PQS, Q10), which are related to the growth and production of a drug substance.

The guidance is relevant to drug substances that are distinct in the limits of ICH Guidelines Q6A and Q6B. The guideline does not have any significant content of suggestions in the course of clinical research phases of drug development. The guideline will not cover regional prerequisites for postapproval changes (ICH Q11, 2011).

3.2.1.12 "Q12: Technical and Regulatory Considerations for Pharmaceutical Product Lifecycle Management"

The recommendation is related to the cost of structure for simplifying the organization of postapproval Chemistry, Manufacturing, and Control (CMC) variations in an accomplished process (ICH Q12, 2017). It is planned to establish a system, where the increased flow of product and process information will reduce the number of regulatory submissions. This document will augment the industry's capacity to accomplish numerous CMC changes successfully below the association's PQS with fewer requirements for widespread supervisory omissions before final operation (ICH Q12, 2017).

3.2.1.13 "Q13: Continuous Manufacturing of Drug Substances and Drug Products"

This is another ICH guideline that builds up to establish harmonized, scientific, and technical requirements needed for fulfillment of regulators' expectations for usage and appraisal of Continuous Manufacturing (CM) to expand admittance to medicines (ICH Q13, 2018). Here the ICH guidance would encourage international harmonization and decrease probable obstructions for implementation of CM expertise (ICH Q13, 2018).

3.2.1.14 "Q14: Analytical Procedure Development"

It is a new recommendation, involving harmonizing of scientific methodologies for analytical procedure development (ICH Q14, 2018). The document offers standards detecting with the details of the Analytical Procedure Development process. The guidance has some proposals to improve regulatory interaction between industry and regulators; and support some proficient, scientific, and risk-based consent just as postapproval modification for managing analytical procedures (ICH Q14, 2018).

3.2.2   Safety guidelines

A broad set of safety guidelines have been created by the ICH to reveal possible risks, such as genotoxicity, carcinogenicity, and reprotoxicity (ICH: Safety guidelines, no date). Safety guidelines are tabulated in Fig. 3.9.

3.2.2.1   S1 Guidelines

The guideline is for Rodent Carcinogenicity Studies for Human Pharmaceuticals: Current S1 safety guidelines on rodent carcinogenicity testing are recommended for presenting a more complete and unified method that reports the hazard of human carcinogenicity due to pharmaceuticals.

"S1A: Need for Carcinogenicity Studies of Pharmaceuticals" (ICH: Safety guidelines, no date): The guideline gives reliable meaning of conditions beneath which it is important, for embracing carcinogenicity studies on novel drugs. This document suggests the identified risk factors as well as proposed signs, symptoms, and extent of contact. Outcomes from toxicokinetics, genotoxicity studies, and mechanistic studies would be regularly applied in preclinical safety assessment.

"S1B: Testing for Carcinogenicity of Pharmaceuticals": The guideline is needed for performing carcinogenicity studies in both rats and mice, and it additionally provides substitute testing strategies that might be applied without risking safety.

"S1C (R2): Dose Selection for Carcinogenicity Studies of Pharmaceuticals" (ICH: Safety guidelines, no date): This specific guidance is related to the conditions required for the determination of high-dose usage in carcinogenicity studies on novel medicinal agents to synchronize with present practices and develop the plan of studies.

3.2.2.2   "S2 (R1): Guidance on Genotoxicity Testing and Data Interpretation for Pharmaceuticals Intended for Human Use"

"S2A: Guidance on Specific Aspects of Regulatory Genotoxicity Tests for Pharmaceuticals"(ICH: Safety guidelines, no date): It explicitly gives directions and suggestions for in vitro and in vivo tests and on assessment of obtained outcomes. A supplement of terms has been incorporated for the identification of genotoxicity-based evaluations to increase uniformity in submissions.

S1	S1A - GUIDELINE ON THE NEED FOR CARCINOGENICITY STUDIES OF PHARMACEUTICALS
	S1B - TESTING FOR CARCINOGENICITY OF PHARMACEUTICALS
	S1C(R2) - DOSE SELECTION FOR CARCINOGENICITY STUDIES OF PHARMACEUTICALS
S2	S2(R1) - GUIDANCE ON GENOTOXICITY TESTING AND DATA INTERPRETATION FOR PHARMACEUTICALS INTENDED FOR HUMAN USE
S3	S3A - NOTE FOR GUIDANCE ON TOXICOKINETICS: THE ASSESSMENT OF SYSTEMIC EXPOSURE IN TOXICITY STUDIES
	S3B - PHARMACOKINETICS:GUIDANCE FOR REPEATED DOSE TISSUE DISTRIBUTION STUDIES
S4	S4 - DURATION OF CHRONIC TOXICITY TESTING IN ANIMALS (RODENT AND NON RODENT TOXICITY TESTING)
S5	S5(R2) - DETECTION OF TOXICITY TO REPRODUCTION FOR MEDICINAL PRODUCTS & TOXICITY TO MALE FERTILITY
S6	S6(R1) - ADDENDUM TO ICH S6: PRECLINICAL SAFETY EVALUATION OF BIOTECHNOLOGY-DERIVED PHARMACEUTICALS
S7	S7A - SAFETY PHARMACOLOGY STUDIES FOR HUMAN PHARMACEUTICALS
	S7B - THE NON-CLINICAL EVALUATION OF THE POTENTIAL FOR DELAYED VENTRICULAR REPOLARIZATION (QT INTERVAL PROLONGATION) BY HUMAN PHARMACEUTICALS
S8	S8 - IMMUNOTOXICITY STUDIES FOR HUMAN PHARMACEUTICALS
S9	S9 - NONCLINICAL EVALUATION FOR ANTICANCER PHARMACEUTICALS
S10	S10 - PHOTOSAFETY EVALUATION OF PHARMACEUTICALS

FIGURE 3.9   International Council for Harmonisation (ICH) "Safety guidelines" (ICH: Safety guidelines, no date).

"S2B: Genotoxicity: A Standard Battery for Genotoxicity Testing for Pharmaceuticals" (ICH: Safety guidelines, no date): The documentation of a typical group of assays has to be led for enrollment and degree of positive investigation in a specific genotoxicity assay in the usual sequence.

3.2.2.3 S3 Guidelines

"S3A: Note for Guidance on Toxicokinetics: The Assessment of Systemic Exposure in Toxicity Studies" (ICH: Safety guidelines, no date): This guideline is generated to test strategies in toxicokinetics and for requirement to integrate pharmacokinetics into toxicity evaluation, for assisting in the translation of the toxicology outcomes as well as for promoting rational study design development. Toxicokinetics is considered a part of conducting nonclinical toxicity studies or exceptionally planning supportive studies.

"S3B: Pharmacokinetics: Guidance for Repeated Dose Tissue Distribution Studies" (ICH: Safety guidelines, no date): S3B is for pharmacokinetics guidance obligatory when suitable data cannot be obtained from further origins. This provides complete information on absorption, distribution, metabolism, and elimination of a compound which is significant for the explanation of pharmacology and toxicology studies. This is a valuable guideline for planning toxicology and pharmacology studies.

3.2.2.4 "S4: Duration of Chronic Toxicity Testing in Animals (Rodent and Non-Rodent Toxicity Testing)"

The goal of this guideline is the safety assessment of medicinal products for their progress of medicinal products, except for those efficiently shielded by ICH Guideline on safety studies for biotechnological products, for example monoclonal antibodies and recombinant DNA proteins (Gayasuddin, 2013; ICH: Safety guidelines, no date).

3.2.2.5 "S5-R2: Detection of Toxicity to Reproduction for Medicinal Products and Toxicity to Male Fertility"

The guideline makes available directions to test reproductive toxicity (ICH: Safety guidelines, no date; Gayasuddin, 2013). It also characterizes the times of treatment to be utilized in animals which reflect human vulnerability to medical products and permits greater precise recognizable proof of phases at hazard.

3.2.2.6 "S6: Addendum to ICH S6: Preclinical Safety Evaluation of Biotechnology-Derived Pharmaceuticals"

The Supplement is proposed to complement and provide explanation and updates over topics of ICH S6 guidelines, such as choice of species, study planning, immunogenicity, and reproductive and development toxicity (ICH: Safety guidelines, no date). This recommendation should simplify the appropriate manner of clinical trials, lessen the usage of animals in agreement with the 3Rs (reduce/refine/replace) ethics and also lessen the usage of extra drug development resources. This addendum does not modify the possibility of the original ICH S6 guidance (Gayasuddin, 2013).

3.2.2.7 S7 Guidelines

"S7A: Safety Pharmacology Studies for Human Pharmaceuticals" (ICH: Safety guidelines, no date): This guidance talks about the objective, description, and possibility of safety in pharmacology studies; it reports which studies are required before the beginning of Phase 1 clinical studies as there is a requirement of data for marketing (Gayasuddin, 2013).

"S7B: Non-Clinical Evaluation of the Probable for Delayed Ventricular Repolarization (Qt Interval Prolongation) by Human Pharmaceuticals" (ICH: Safety guidelines, no date): S7B guideline represents a nonclinical evaluation procedure for evaluating the capability of a test substance to postpone ventricular repolarization. It commonly comprises nonclinical assays and unified risk assessments.

3.2.2.8 "S8: Immunotoxicity Studies for Human Pharmaceuticals"

This guidance is about suggestions required for nonclinical evaluation of immunosuppression induced by low−molecular weight drugs (nonbiologicals) and also performing studies of immunotoxicity (ICH: Safety guidelines, no date). It is applied to novel pharmaceuticals planned for human use, in addition to marketed drug products with various signs or dissimilar deviations from the existing product marker. The deviation reported could affect unreported and important toxicological matters.

3.2.2.9 "S9: Nonclinical Evaluation for Anticancer Pharmaceuticals"

The guideline is for pharmaceuticals that are simply planned for the treatment of malignant growth in patients with late-stage or progressed ailment irrespective of the course of administration, comprising both small molecule and biotechnology-derived pharmaceuticals (ICH: Safety guidelines, no date). It depicts the category and timing of nonclinical studies corresponding to the advancement of anticancer pharmaceuticals and references.

3.2.2.10 "S10: Photosafety Evaluation of Pharmaceuticals"

The S10 guideline is on photo safety evaluation plans for pharmaceuticals (ICH: Safety guidelines, no date). It pertains to novel APIs, novel adjuvants as excipients in clinical formulations for dermal usage, and photodynamic therapy products.

3.2.3 Efficacy guidelines

Efficacy guidelines of ICH are related to design, conduct, safety, and reporting of clinical trials as shown in Fig. 3.10. They cover innovative kinds of medications developed from biotechnological measures and utilization of pharmacogenetics/genomics methods to yield enhanced targeted medicines (ICH: Efficacy guidelines, no date).

The guideline from E1 to E2F reports on clinical safety is described as follows and also shown in Fig. 3.10.

E1 - THE EXTENT OF POPULATION EXPOSURE TO ASSESS CLINICAL SAFETY
E2A - CLINICAL SAFETY DATA MANAGEMENT
E2B(R2) - MAINTENANCE OF THE ICH GUIDELINE ON CLINICAL SAFETY DATA MANAGEMENT
E2C(R1) - CLINICAL SAFETY DATA MANAGEMENT: PERIODIC SAFETY UPDATE REPORTS FOR MARKETED DRUGS
E2D - POST-APPROVAL SAFETY DATA MANAGEMENT: DEFINITIONS AND STANDARDS FOR EXPEDITED REPORTING
E2E - PHARMACOVIGILANCE PLANNING
E2F - DEVELOPMENT SAFETY UPDATE REPORT
E3 - STRUCTURE AND CONTENT OF CLINICAL STUDY REPORTS
E4 - DOSE-RESPONSE INFORMATION TO SUPPORT DRUG REGISTRATION
E5(R1) - ETHNIC FACTORS IN THE ACCEPTABILITY OF FOREIGN CLINICAL DATA
E6(R1) - GUIDELINE FOR GOOD CLINICAL PRACTICE
E7 - STUDIES IN SUPPORT OF SPECIAL POPULATIONS:GERIATRICS
E8 - GENERAL CONSIDERATIONS FOR CLINICAL TRIALS
E9 - STATISTICAL PRINCIPLES FOR CLINICAL TRIALS
E10 - CHOICE OF CONTROL GROUP AND RELATED ISSUES IN CLINICAL TRIALS
E11 - CLINICAL INVESTIGATION OF MEDICINAL PRODUCTS IN THE PEDIATRIC POPULATION
E12 - PRINCIPLES FOR CLINICAL EVALUATION OF NEW ANTIHYPERTENSIVE DRUGS
E14 - THE CLINICAL EVALUATION OF QT/QTC INTERVAL PROLONGATION AND PROARRHYTHMIC POTENTIAL FOR NON-ANTIARRHYTHMIC DRUGS
E15 - DEFINITIONS FOR GENOMIC BIOMARKERS, PHARMACOGENOMICS, PHARMACOGENETICS, GENOMIC DATA AND SAMPLE CODING CATEGORIES
E16 - GENOMIC BIOMARKERS RELATED TO DRUG RESPONSE: CONTEXT, STRUCTURE AND FORMAT OF QUALIFICATION SUBMISSIONS

FIGURE 3.10 International Council for Harmonisation (ICH) "Efficacy guidelines" (ICH: Efficacy guidelines, no date).

3.2.3.1 "E1: The Extent of Population Exposure to Assess Clinical Safety"

This document is for drugs utilized for prolonged management of less hazardous situations (ICH E1, 1994). The tripartite harmonized ICH Recommendations were concluded under Step 4 in 1994 (October). This deed provides proposals on patient's statistics and extent of contact for safety assessment of drugs, planned for prolonged management of less hazardous conditions. Occasions where the rate of incidence varies throughout a more extended timeframe are to be considered, based on severity and prominence to the risk–benefit evaluation of the drug. The safety assessment during clinical drug development is not required to describe adverse events, for instance, those happening in less than 1 in 1000 patients (ICH E1, 1994).

3.2.3.2 E2 Guidelines

"E2A: Clinical Safety Data Management" (ICH E2A, 1994; Gayasuddin, 2013): The descriptions and principles which have quickened the reporting of E2A include two matters inside the broad subject of clinical safety data management that are suitable for harmonization:

1. The progress of typical descriptions and terminology for key parts of clinical safety commentary.
2. The suitable process for managing accelerated (rapid) documentation, in the preapproval phase.

E2B (R2): Maintenance of the ICH Guideline on Clinical Safety Data Management: This document portrays the data elements for communication of discrete individual-based case safety description in E2B (R2) and regulates the data elements for communication of individual case safety reports (ICSRs) by distinguishing. These were important by characterizing the data elements for communication of all categories of specific case safety reports, irrespective of origin and its terminus (Gayasuddin, 2013).

E2C (R1): Clinical Safety Data Management: Periodic Safety Update Reports for Marketed Drugs: This recommendation is for the arrangement and content of well-being updates, which is required at intermissions by regulatory experts after marketing of products. The guideline is proposed to guarantee that overall safety reports should be given to experts at distinct periods, for products marketed with best proficiency and preventing the authorities from exertion due to duplication. The revision of E2C (R2) was made by the Steering Committee in 2010 (December). It will assess the ICH Pharmacovigilance certification, conduct a break and evaluate for probable enhancement of ICH E2C, E2E, E2F, and draft ICH E2C R2 casing periodic benefit–risk valuation writing (Gayasuddin, 2013).

E2D: Post-Approval Safety Data Management: *Definitions and Standards for Expedited Reporting*—This document gives a normalized method for postapproval safety data supervision, including assisted summarizing to the applicable regulatory specialists. The description of terms and concepts related to the postapproval phase is also specified (Gayasuddin, 2013).

E2E: Pharmacovigilance Planning: The preparation of pharmacovigilance events, particularly in arrangement for the early postmarketing phase of a novel drug, includes chemical entities, biotech-derived products, and vaccines. The primary emphasis is on safety requirements and pharmacovigilance plan, to be surrendered during stages of license submission (Gayasuddin, 2013).

E2F: Development Safety Update Report (DSUR): The chief emphasis of the DSUR is on the information from interventional clinical trials of investigational drugs containing biologicals, with or devoid of marketing approval, regardless of whether joined by profit-making or noncommercial sponsors. It has been planned for periodic reporting of drugs under development (including marketed drugs under exploration) among the ICH regions (Gayasuddin, 2013).

3.2.3.3 "E3: Structure and Content of Clinical Study Reports"

This document is an "integrated" full description of a specific investigation of any therapeutic, prophylactic, or diagnostic agent (discussed as drug or treatment) that appeared in patients, in which the clinical and statistical depiction, presentations, and examinations are incorporated within a solitary report, consolidating tables and figures along with primary content of the report, or toward the end of the transcript, with appendices comprising the processes, sample case description forms, investigator-associated evidence, and *data associated to the examined drugs/investigational products comprising active control/comparators, technical statistical documents, associated publications, patient data listings, and technical statistical particulars* (ICH E3, 1995).

3.2.3.4 "E4: Dose–Response Information to Support Drug Registration"

This guideline gives information on the connections among dose, drug concentration in blood, and clinical reaction which is significant for safe and effective usage of drugs in distinct patients (ICH: Efficacy guidelines, no date;

Gayasuddin, 2013). The conceptions of minimum effective dose and maximum valuable dose do not effectively interpret for specific differences and do not permit an assessment, at different doses, of both useful and unwanted effects. Some random dose gives an amalgamation of necessary and unnecessary effects, with no single dose fundamentally optimum for all patients (ICH: Efficacy guidelines, no date).

3.2.3.5 "E5 (R1): Ethnic Factors in the Acceptability of Foreign Clinical Data"

This article talks about the essential qualities of drug receiver and extraneous qualities, related to surroundings and values which could influence the after effects of clinical studies passed in regions (ICH: Efficacy guidelines, no date; Gayasuddin, 2013). It depicts the idea of the "bridging study" that a new region may demand to decide whether information from an additional area is appropriate to its population.

3.2.3.6 "E6 (R1): Guideline for Good Clinical Practice"

This guideline of efficacy portrays the duties and opportunities of all participants in the conduct of clinical trials, including investigators, monitors, sponsors, and Institutional Review Boards (ICH: Efficacy guidelines, no date; Gayasuddin, 2013). Good Clinical Practices comprises monitoring, reporting, and archiving of clinical trials and including Supplements in basic archives and on the Investigator's Brochure which concurred before the ICH process.

3.2.3.7 "E7: Studies in Support of Special Populations: Geriatrics"

This guideline conveys suggestions on the exceptional concerns which apply in the planning and conduct of clinical trials which are probably going to have noteworthy usage in the old people (ICH: Efficacy guidelines, no date; Gayasuddin, 2013). It necessitates special deliberation because of the continuous event of existing diseases, simultaneous drug therapy, and the effect of drug interaction.

3.2.3.8 "E8: General Considerations for Clinical Trials"

This article gives the overall technical principles for conduct, performance, and control of clinical trials (ICH: Efficacy guidelines, no date; Gayasuddin, 2013). The article tends to a broad scope of issues in the design and performance of clinical trials.

3.2.3.9 "E9: Statistical Principles for Clinical Trials"

This document is a biostatistical recommendation that portrays fundamental contemplations on the plan and investigation of clinical trials, particularly the "confirmatory" (hypothesis-testing) trials that are motives for showing capability (ICH: Efficacy guidelines, no date; Gayasuddin, 2013). The record will help the technical specialists accused of getting ready application synopses or evaluating indications of efficacy and safety, basically from clinical trials in advanced stages of growth.

3.2.3.10 "E10: Choice of Control Group and Related Issues in Clinical Trials"

This article inclines toward the decision of control groups in clinical trials keeping in view the moral and derivable characteristics and drawbacks of various types of control groups (ICH: Efficacy guidelines, no date). It brings up the assay sensitivity issues in the active control equivalence/noninferiority trials that limit the helpfulness of the trial plan in various situations (Gayasuddin, 2013).

3.2.3.11 "E11: Clinical Investigation of Medicinal Products in the Pediatric Population"

This article inclines toward conducting clinical trials in pediatric populations (ICH: Efficacy guidelines, no date). It will encourage the advancement of safe and active usage of therapeutic agents in pediatrics (Gayasuddin, 2013).

3.2.3.12 "E12: Principles for Clinical Evaluation of New Antihypertensive Drugs"

This guideline provides a bunch of "Principles" on which there is an overall arrangement among every one of the three ICH regions, including endpoints and trial designs (ICH: Efficacy guidelines, no date). It would not be dependent on typical techniques by creating a complete harmonized document (Gayasuddin, 2013).

3.2.3.13 "E14: The Clinical Evaluation of Qt/Qtc Interval Prolongation and Proarrhythmic Potential for Non-Antiarrhythmic Drugs"

This article conveys proposals for supporting the concerned during design, conduct, analysis, and understanding of clinical studies, which are to be surveyed for the capability of a drug to postpone cardiac repolarization (ICH: Efficacy guidelines, no date). This evaluation ought to remember evaluating impacts of new agents for the QT/QTc interval as well as the gathering of an adverse effect related to the cardiovascular system. The experimental approach utilized for a specific drug ought to be customized, reliant upon the pharmacodynamics, pharmacokinetics, and safety attributes of the product, as well as on its suggested clinical usage. The evaluation of the impacts of drugs on cardiac repolarization is a matter of dynamic examination. At the point when extra information (nonclinical and clinical) is gathered, later on, this document might be reconsidered and updated (Gayasuddin, 2013).

3.2.3.14 "E15: Definitions for Genomic Biomarkers, Pharmaco-Genomics, Pharmacogenetics, Genomic Data and Sample Coding Categories"

The recommendation discusses the pharmacogenomics and pharmacogenetics which can enhance the discovery, development, and utilization of pharmaceuticals (ICH: Efficacy guidelines, no date; Gayasuddin, 2013).

3.2.3.15 "E16: Biomarkers Related to Drug or Biotechnology Product Development"

The recommendation depicts suggestions related to the situation, structure, and layout of governing submissions for the capability of genomic biomarkers, as characterized in ICH E15 (ICH: Efficacy guidelines, no date; Gayasuddin, 2013).

3.2.3.16 "E17: General Principles of Planning and Design of Multi-Regional Clinical Trials"

This guideline delivers direction on all-purpose principles of Multiregional Clinical Trial (MRCT) (ICH: Efficacy guidelines, no date). In ICH regions and further beyond them, drug development has been proliferated and MRCT for controlling submissions is performed. This guideline complements the leadership on MRCTs provided in ICH E5 (R1) Guideline and enables MRCT data recognition and receiving by multiple regulatory agencies.

3.2.3.17 "E18: Genomic Sampling and Management of Genomic Data"

This recommendation will ease the execution of genomic studies by permitting a mutual agreement of vital factors toward impartial gathering, storage, and ideal use of genomic samples and data (ICH: Efficacy guidelines, no date). It is envisioned to nurture communications between several stakeholders and to enhance genomic research inside clinical studies.

3.2.3.18 "E19: Optimization of Safety Data Collection"

This new guideline is projected for synchronized direction, and a directed methodology for collecting safety data during late-stage pre- or postmarketing studies, and a method of implementation (ICH: Efficacy guidelines, no date). Identifying that safety of patient well-being is critically important during drug development program; hence the collection of needless data may be troublesome to patients and develops hindrance for participating in clinical research. The planned guideline would be reliable with risk-based methods and quality-by-design principles.

3.2.3.19 "E20: Adaptive Clinical Trials"

The E20 EWG is working on the progress of a new E20 Guideline on "Adaptive Clinical Trials" on the strategy development, conduct, examination, and explanation of adaptive clinical trials (ICH: Efficacy guidelines, no date). The guideline provides an obvious and coordinated set of principles for regulatory evaluation of these studies (Adaptive clinical trials) in a universal drug development program. These principles should also provide freedom to assess the deliberate advanced methods to clinical trial design during the development process.

3.2.4 Multidisciplinary guidelines

These guidelines represent highly significant issues that are not included in QSE classifications. However, these guidelines comprised the Common Technical Documents (CTDs), MedDRA for ICH as well as the progress of Electronic Standards for the Transfer of Regulatory Information (ESTRI). The classification of guideline is shown in Fig. 3.11 (ICH Multidisciplinary guidelines, no date).

M1 - Med DRA TERMINOLOGY
M1 - PtC WG Med DRA POINTS TO CONSIDER
M2 - ICH M2: ELECTRONIC STANDARDS
M2 - ELECTRONIC COMMON TECHNICAL DOCUMENT (ECTD) - FILE FORMAT CRITERIA M2 (R2) - ELECTRONIC TRANSMISSION OF INDIVIDUAL CASE SAFETY REPORTS MESSAGE SPECIFICATION
M3 - NONCLINICAL SAFETY STUDIES
M3(R2) - GUIDANCE ON NONCLINICAL SAFETY STUDIES FOR THE CONDUCT OF HUMAN CLINICAL TRIALS AND MARKETING AUTHORIZATION FOR PHARMACEUTICALS
M4 - THE COMMON TECHNICAL DOCUMENT
M4Q(R1) - THE CTD ON QUALITY M4E(R1) - THE CTD ON EFFICACY M4S(R2) - THE CTD ON SAFETY M4 (R4) - ORGANISATION INCLUDING THE GRANULARITY DOCUMENT THAT PROVIDES GUIDANCE ON DOCUMENT LOCATION AND PAGINATIONS
M5 - DATA ELEMENTS AND STANDARDS FOR DRUG DICTIONARIES
M6 - VIRUS AND GENE THERAPY VECTOR SHEDDING AND TRANSMISSION
M7 - MUTAGENIC IMPURITIES
M7(R1) - ASSESSMENT AND CONTROL OF DNA REACTIVE (MUTAGENIC) IMPURITIES IN PHARMACEUTICALS TO LIMIT POTENTIAL CARCINOGENIC RISK M7(R2) - MAINTENANCE EWG/IWG ASSESSMENT AND CONTROL OF DNA REACTIVE (MUTAGENIC) IMPURITIES IN PHARMACEUTICALS TO LIMIT POTENTIAL CARCINOGENIC RISK
M8 - ELECTRONIC COMMON TECHNICAL DOCUMENT (ECTD)
M9 - BIOPHARMACEUTICS CLASSIFICATION SYSTEM-BASED BIOWAIVERS
M10 - BIOANALYTICAL METHOD VALIDATION
M11 - CLINICAL ELECTRONIC STRUCTURED HARMONISED PROTOCOL (CESHARP)
M12 - DRUG INTERACTION STUDIES

FIGURE 3.11 International Council for Harmonisation (ICH) "Multidisciplinary guidelines" (ICH: Multidisciplinary guidelines, no date).

3.2.4.1 M1: Medical Dictionary for Regulatory Activities

The requirement of a MedDRA was noted by the ICH Steering Committee in the 1990s. However, the nomenclature was introduced in 1999. All evidence and data regarding MedDRA, including the considerable opinions for each MedDRA version (Revision), are accessible through the MedDRA page of the ICH guideline.

M1 PtC WG MedDRA Points to Consider:

The MedDRA (with nomenclature in 1999) use was supported with M1 PtC (point to consider) WG (working group) updates with each MedDRA release documents on *MedDRA Term Selection* and *MedDRA Data Retrieval and Presentation*, which is available in English and Japanese, as well as condensed versions available in all MedDRA languages. These documents delivered a detailed direction from cases and opinions, including queries and their solutions on several issues focused on regulatory importance such as data quality, medication errors, and product quality issues (ICH MedDRA, 2016).

The terminologies are an important part of the regulatory processes, reporting of medical history, result investigations, and presentations. Some of the payment computer tools available to support MedDRA and extract maximum information from it are Standardized MedDRA Queries; MedDRA Web Browsers; MedDRA Version Analysis Tool; and Mapping tools. The structure of MedDRA is shown in Fig. 3.12.

3.2.4.2 M2: Electronic standards

"M2 EWG Electronic Standards for the Transfer of Regulatory Information" (ICH M2, 1994):

ICH M2 Electronic Working Group was created in 1994 by the ICH Navigating Committee, for facilitating the exchange of electronic exchange of information as ESTRI. This was for completing the necessities of pharmaceutical companies and regulators. The group has been assigned the task of transmitting logical large volumes of information to regulatory authorities through electronic means. ICH M2 Working Group has been involved in Endorsements for International Criteria; Electronic message for E2B ICH Guideline, and ICH M4 guideline for CTD through Standards Development Organization (SDO) process. In 2010, it was decided by the Working Group that efforts with respect to electronic CTD will be under the ICH M8 Working Group. Thus, due to extreme work under M2 working groups, subgroups M5 and E2B (R3) have been created (ICH M2, 1994). Hence, M2 would be responsible to provide a basic framework for the establishment of E2B (R3) and M5 groups, but would not be involved directly in their working. Thus, M2 Working Group shares a concern for SDO association management.

3.2.4.3 M3: Nonclinical Safety Studies

"M3 (R2) Guidance on Nonclinical Safety Studies for the Conduct of Human Clinical Trials and Marketing Authorization for Pharmaceuticals" (ICH M3 (R2), 2009):

The current guidelines represent a contract related to the category and duration of nonclinical safety studies and its timing, for supporting performance of human clinical trials and its marketing approval for pharmaceuticals.

This guidance facilitates the timely conduct of clinical trials and lessens animal usage, as per the 3Rs the (REDUCE/REFINE/REPLACE) principles and also lessens the use of other drug development resources. The guidelines focus on policy for allowing usage of in vitro methods for assessing safety and efficacy of chemicals and Pharmaceutical dosages (ICH M3 (R2), 2009). The guideline suggests that developed and validated methods can replace existing testing protocols used during evaluation.

Marketing approval for pharmaceutically important drugs requires strong data on Pharmacological studies; general toxicity studies; toxicokinetics and nonclinical pharmacokinetic studies; reproduction toxicity studies; genotoxicity studies; carcinogenicity studies for drugs proposed to be administered for longer duration; phototoxicity; immunotoxicity and abuse liability. In cases, where appropriate strategies are available for estimating the safety of products

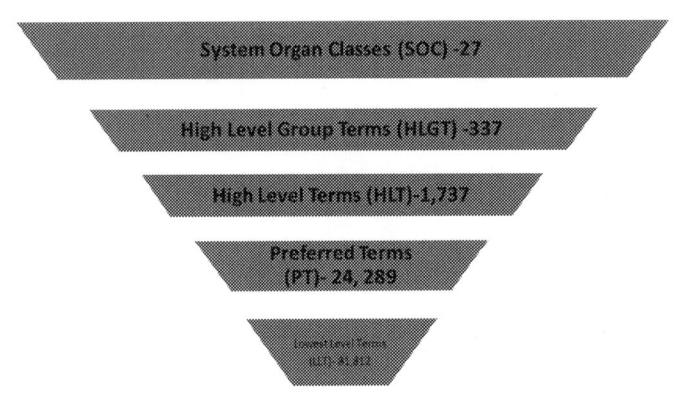

FIGURE 3.12 Structure of Medical Dictionary for Regulatory Affairs.

(such as biotechnology-derived products), the ICH M3 guidelines regulate the timing of nonclinical studies concerning clinical advances. The guidelines also control and optimize the pharmaceutical developments in life-threatening disorders such as cancer, resistant viral infections, and hereditary diseases.

The principle behind the development of ICH M3 recommendations is to estimate potential adverse effects, dose necessity, and maximum safe dose for the human population. Hence, the data is required for supporting and initiating the clinical studies.

3.2.4.4 M4: Common Technical Document

This guideline discourses about the CTD, which was decided by ICH Navigating Committee in November 2000. The guideline brings a plan of data arrangement or presentation that should be followed before the submission of data to Regulatory Authorities. This is very much necessary for a better and thoughtful understanding of results and data evaluation. The reviewer will quickly adapt to the application of subjects and matters in it. The agreement to accumulate all informational data in a custom scheme has transformed the regulatory evaluation procedures and synchronized electronic submission enabling proper execution of good review practices. For the businesses industries, it caused an exclusion of the vitality to restructure the information and evidence for compliance to different ICH regulators.

The CTD is structured in five Modules, where Module 1 is precise for a region, while Modules 2, 3, 4, and 5 are mutual among all regions. However, in 2003 CTD became a compulsory layout for New Drug Applications in European Union and Japan, with a strong suggested format for FDA, United States.

1. Module1 provides executive and recommending data along with evidences. It contains documents precise regionally; for example, Submission forms or the planned markings to be used regionally (label).
2. Module 2 reviews an overview of drugs, including their pharmacological class, mechanism, and planned clinical use. It delivers the general compendium of the "quality" data given, the nonclinical and clinical overview, as well as the nonclinical printed synopses and the organized synopses.
3. Module 3 provides data/evidences on quality matters.
4. Module 4 includes the nonclinical study reports.
5. Module 5 comprises the clinical study reports.

The Granularity Paper in Annexure (Annex) was involved in 2002 and further modified in 2003 and 2004 (ICH M4Q (R1), 2002; ICH: Multidisciplinary guidelines, no date; ICH M4E (R2), 2016; ICH M4, 2016)

3.2.4.5 "M5: Data Elements and Standards for Drug Dictionaries"

The ICH Committee, in November 2003, recommended a concept for the guideline M5 and subsequently formed M5 EWG for the standardization of medicinal product identifiers and associated terminology (ICH: Multidisciplinary guidelines, no date). Particularly there is a necessity, to be recognized for harmonizing product data for enabling electronic exchange of ICSRs within and across ICH regions using the ICH E2B layout in postmarketing pharmacovigilance.

The drafted guideline was updated for public feedback and submitted to the International Organization for Standardization (ISO) for the growth of electronic messaging specifications in 2007 (February). Thus, five Standards (International) for Identification of Medicinal Products (IDMP) were published by ISO in 2012. These criteria maintained electronic interchange of ICSRs for maintenance of postmarketing consequence of drug and augment its persistence. Thus, after completion of finalized Criteria for IDMP, ICH working groups came to an agreement on stopping the M5 Working group. A new E2B IWG for electronic information exchange of ICSR has been developed. This includes five ISO IDMP standards (ISO11238:2012, ISO11239:2012, ISO11240:2012, ISO11615:2012, and ISO11616:2012) for electronic exchange of safety reports (ICH M6, 2009).

3.2.4.6 "M6: Virus and Gene Therapy Vector Shedding and Transmission"

In September 2009, the ICH Navigating Committee suggested the conclusion by the ICH GTDG of the ICH Consideration document which states "General Principles to Address Virus and Vector Shedding," the ICH Navigating Committee suggested expansion of ICH Guideline on this subject with the motive of delivering more detailed data/evidence to improve Harmonization between the ICH regions (ICH M6, 2009).

The guideline will help regulators to harmonize information on the virus and vector identification, by removing unproductive and nonuseful data. It is important to note that vectors in gene therapy may be wild; persisting for prolonged periods in human cells and shedding through excreta may promote their transmission leading to adverse situations. Harmonization would help to appropriately evaluate data from clinical or nonclinical studies, collecting information for pharmacovigilance and which may ease marketing authorization (ICH Considerations, 2009).

3.2.4.7 "M7: Mutagenic Impurities (Assessment and Control of DNA Reactive (Mutagenic) Impurities in Pharmaceuticals to Limit Potential Carcinogenic Risk)"

The ICH M7 Standard was established in 2014 and suggested for the examination of Structure Activity Relationships with respect to genotoxicity (ICH M7 (R1), 2017). The guideline is aimed to focus on genotoxic impurities. Some available guidelines Q3A; Q3B focuses on the identification of genotoxic impurities, but there is no available guidance on acceptable limits (AIs). The guideline balances the results of Q3A; Q3B; and M2 documents. The focus is to restrict genotoxic impurities, which possess carcinogenic probability.

It is envisioned to decide queries such as whether impurities with a similar prospective mechanism of action must not be shared in calculating a Threshold of Toxicological Concern (TTC) and whether TTC may vary based on changes during accepted period of practice. The ICH M7 Guideline has a Supplement, finalized in 2017 to review identified mutagenic impurities involved during drug synthesis. The Supplement offers valuable information concerning the satisfactory limits of known mutagenic impurities/carcinogenic and supporting monographs.

There is a preservation process that includes tolerable limits (Acceptable Intakes, AIs) for new DNA reactive (mutagenic) contaminants and revising tolerable limits for contaminants previously recorded in Addendum, along with new data (ICH M7, 2009). The M7 (R2) guideline reports the maintenance EWG/IWG which is reviewing and working on M7 (R1) for the integration of acceptable limits (AIs) or Permitted Daily Exposures for new DNA reactive (mutagenic) contaminants. The outcome will be a future ICH M7 (R2) version (ICH M7 (R1), 2017).

3.2.4.8 "M8: Electronic Common Technical Document (ECTD)"

The guideline was formed under the supervision of ICH M2 working group. The working group manages and produces the application habitat for the next release of eCTD (ICH M8, 2010). However, support of the guideline to ICH eCTD v3.2.2 and STF (Study Tagging Files) v2.6.1 will continue as an IWG. This guidance acts as a facilitator for the electronic interchange of regulatory data. The activities under guidelines comprise the following:

- Development of eCTD in ICH;
- Cooperation with HL7 for more necessities;
- Steering of the draft standard;
- Evaluation of analytical results;
- Development of an application document from ICH;
- Regulatory standard through ISO.

The role and task addressed in the document are as follows:

1. Providing support for the development of the next major release of ICH eCTD (ICH M8, 2010).
   a. Should coordinate for business and technical sources.
   b. Should maintain relations with SDO for technical upgradation of eCTDs. They must preserve the reliability of ICH Global and ICH Regional requirements through SDOs.
   c. Creating test plans and methods for evaluating ICH Global and ICH Regional requirements for better harmonization.
2. Providing support for the current version of ICH eCTD and STF specifications as:
   a. Should make available the changes for global alterations to specifications in the description and working.
3. Provide technical evaluation of subject matters from the procedure of ICH M4 CTD guidelines within the situation of eCTD (ICH M8, 2010).
   a. Identification of problems arising due to the use of CTD /eCTD should be noted and brought in to review. Hence, it becomes their duty for providing technical solutions along with scientific solutions concerning CTD for QSE guidelines also.
   b. Should connect with experts in the working group of QSE guidelines for clarifying questions related to eCTD (ICH M8: Electronic Common Technical Document, no date).

3.2.4.9 "M9: Biopharmaceutics Classification System-Based Biowaivers"

The guideline was endorsed by the ICH Assembly in October 2016. The guideline aims to classify compounds with a similar in vitro release (ICH: Multidisciplinary guidelines, no date). Hence, two products (with the same drug) are said to be bioequivalent, if their bioavailability is within AIs after administration of a similar molar dose. In vivo studies evaluate the degree and magnitude of absorption by the drug. Hence, Biopharmaceutics Classification System (BCS) reduces prerequisites for in vivo studies, based on outcomes of in vitro studies. Thus, BCS is based on the hydrophilicity possessed by the drug and its intestinal absorptivity. This new multidisciplinary directional approach reports the BCS-based biowaivers. BCS-based biowaivers may be appropriate to BCS Class I (High Solubility, High Permeability) and Class III (High Solubility, Low Permeability) drugs, but BCS-based biowaivers for mentioned classes are not considered globally. This means that pharmaceutical businesses have to track dissimilar methods in diverse regions. This guideline supports biopharmaceutics classification of medicinal products and the waiver of bioequivalence studies. Thus this harmonizes existing regional regulation, by supporting efficient global drug development (Biopharmaceutics Classification System-Based Biowaivers M9, 2019).

3.2.4.10   "M10: Bioanalytical Method Validation"

This paper by the ICH Management Committee was recommended in 2016 (October) (ICH: Multidisciplinary guidelines, no date). It is a latest versatile guideline, for application toward authentication of bioanalytical approaches, and analysis of study samples for clinical and nonclinical studies. The guideline is planned for harmonizing and streamlining the comprehensive drug development process. The data obtained through an authenticated and certified approach is important for the evaluation of the marketing authorization application.

The guideline discusses the validation method and regulatory requirements essential for different types of analytical studies essential for the estimation of an analyte. The guideline covers measurable analysis using ligand-binding assays and chromatographic methods (liquid or gas chromatography) used in conjunction with mass spectroscopy. The studies conducted as per Good Laboratory Practices or Good Clinical Practices should conform to their necessities. However, the guideline does not cover the bioanalysis of biomarkers and methods for evaluating immunogenicity. A harmonized guideline will endorse the rapid, balanced, and actual nonclinical and clinical studies, thus proceeding with operations of the ICH (Bioanalytical Method Validation M10, 2019).

3.2.4.11   "M11: Clinical Electronic Structured Harmonised Protocol (CESHARP)"

This guideline was recommended by the ICH Management Committee in November 2018 (ICH: Multidisciplinary guidelines, no date). The proposal is given by the ICH working groups to describe the procedure for analysis of the clinical study. The planned document is required to provide a pattern to support sponsors for exchanging procedures. The guideline will aim to work on two approaches in the beginning:

1. Template with predefined identification criteria for headers, shared scripts, and terminologies creating a better environment for sharing of datasets.
2. A method discussing description using an open-ended electronic format for exchange of the clinical information.

The proposed guideline is designed to improve the efficiency of the study and connect them for cross-discussions. This will lead to wider acceptability among regulators and industry. Hence, a multidisciplinary group has been constituted for further initiatives with a draft technical document for submission in June 2020 (ICH M11, 2018).

3.2.4.12   "M12: Drug Interaction Studies"

The guidance was recommended by the ICH Assembly in June 2018 (ICH: Multidisciplinary guidelines, no date). The M12 EWG is working on the development of a new M12 Guideline on "Drug Interaction Studies" intending to provide a reliable method in designing, conducting, and interpreting drug−drug interaction studies during therapeutic product development (ICH M12, 2019).

The harmonized strategies bring the expertise, skill, potentials, and opportunities of regulators to a common stage for developing common consensus on drug−drug interaction. However, drug−drug interactions are affected by parameters, such as species and region. Regional differences in populations may delay patient access to drugs from other areas. Thus, an increase in the operation of resources would be enabled by the harmonization of guidelines. Some problems to be addressed with synchronization by ICH are as follows:

1. In vitro studies—The unavailability of harmonization led to a difference in endorsements for molecules under study by different regulatory agencies. Hence, the assessment of the worldwide potential for the molecule becomes difficult. The degrading metabolites in regional populations may differ but a compilation of data will give wider scope for research.
2. Clinical drug interaction studies—Consensus on clinical studies will help in evaluating the clinical effects of a drug in various populations. Hence, reporting of results can be easier for further support to marketing applications. Thus,

the progress in a universally settled list of substrates, enzymes used, inducers, and transporters is required for better results and population data for drug interaction studies (ICH M12, 2019).

3.3 Conclusion

ICH has expanded the global participation of all regulators, by forming QSE as crucial components in multidimensional approaches for safeguarding the patient safety and integrity of data in all forms. This chapter defines the role of ICH and its methods in making recommendations for achieving greater harmonization of processes relating to interpretation, implementation of scientific guidelines, and prerequisites for product registration. Hence, the ICH guidelines also reduce the expense of preparing registration dossiers, by finally improving the marketed products. These initiatives taken by ICH are the exceptional value additions for drug developers and regulatory authorities. Thus improving the access to essential medicines results in providing benefits to the public health in the developing countries.

References

Andrew, T., David, E., Raymond, W.N., 2017. ICH quality guidelines: an implementation guide. John Wiley & Sons, Inc., pp. 281–310. Available from: https://onlinelibrary.wiley.com/doi/abs/10.1002/9781118971147.ch9.

Biopharmaceutics Classification System-Based Biowaivers M9, 2019. Available from: <https://database.ich.org/sites/default/files/M9_Guideline_Step4_2019_1116.pdf> (accessed 21.03.20.).

Bioanalytical Method Validation M10, 2019. Available from: <https://database.ich.org/sites/default/files/M10_EWG_Draft_Guideline.pdf> (accessed 21.03.20.).

Chinchole, A.S., Poul, B., Panchal, C.V., Chavan, D.V., 2014. A review on stability guidelines by ICH and USFDA guidelines for new formulation and dosage form. PharmaTutor 2 (8), 32–53.

Coordinators, no date. Available from: <https://www.ich.org/page/coordinators> (accessed 25.12.19.).

Fernand, S., 1996. The Story of ICH, European Pharmaceutical Law Notebooks on ICH, vol. 2. CEDEF, Madrid, N° 4.

Gupta, A., Goel, R., Jain, S., Saini, V., 2014. A review on impact of ICH and its harmonisation on human health care and pharmaceuticals. JPRCP 4 (2), 1–9.

Gayasuddin, M., 2013. ICH guidelines on safety and efficacy [online]. Available from: <https://www.slideshare.net/mdgayas70/ich-guidelines-seminar> (accessed 10.03.20.).

Huynh, B.K., 2010. Pharmaceutical stability testing to support global market: Pharm asp. Springer Science + Business Media.

ICH Association annual report 2018. Available from: <https://admin.ich.org/sites/default/files/inline-files/2018_ich-annualreport_2019_0506.pdf>.

ICH Introduction organization and guidelines—a precise insight, no date. Available from: <https://www.slideshare.net/rxvichu/ich-introduction-objectives-guidelines-a-brief-insight> (accessed 24.12.19.).

ICH Q1A (R2): Stability testing of new drug substances and products. | European Medicine Agency, 1996. Available from: <https://www.ema.europa.eu/en/documents/scientific-guideline/ich-q-1-r2-stability-testing-new-drug-substances-products-step-5_en.pdf> (accessed 01.03.20.).

ICH Q1B: Stability testing: photo stability testing of new drug substances and product | European Medicine Agency, 1996. Available from: <https://database.ich.org/sites/default/files/Q1B%20Guideline.pdf> (accessed 01.03.20.).

ICH Q1C: Stability testing for new dosage forms | European Medicine Agency, 1996. Available from: <https://database.ich.org/sites/default/files/Q1C%20Guideline.pdf> (accessed 01.03.20.).

ICH Q1D: Bracketing and matrixing design for stability testing of new drug substances and products | European Medicine Agency, 2002. Available from: <https://www.ema.europa.eu/en/documents/scientific-guideline/ich-q-1-d-bracketing-matrixing-designs-stability-testing-drug-substances-drug-products-step-5_en.pdf> (accessed 01.03.20.).

ICH Q1E: Evaluation of stability data | European Medicine Agency, 2003. Available from: <https://www.ema.europa.eu/en/documents/scientific-guideline/ich-q-1-e-evaluation-stability-data-step-5_en.pdf> (accessed 01.03.20.).

ICH Q2 (R1): Validation of analytical procedures: text and methodology | European Medicine Agency, 1995. Available from: <https://www.ema.europa.eu/en/documents/scientific-guideline/ich-q-2-r1-validation-analytical-procedures-text-methodology-step-5_en.pdf> (accessed 24.03.20.).

ICH Q3A (R2): Impurities in new drug substances | European Medicine Agency, 2006. Available from: <https://www.ema.europa.eu/en/documents/scientific-guideline/ich-q-3-r2-impurities-new-drug-substances-step-5_en.pdf> (accessed 24.03.20.).

ICH Q3B (R2): Impurities in new drug products | European Medicine Agency, 2006. Available from: <https://www.ema.europa.eu/en/documents/scientific-guideline/ich-q-3-b-r2-impurities-new-drug-products-step-5_en.pdf> (accessed 24.03.20.).

ICH Q4B: Evaluation and recommendation of pharmacopoeial texts for use in the ICH regions | European Medicine Agency, 2007. Available from: <https://www.ema.europa.eu/en/documents/scientific-guideline/ich-q-4-b-note-evaluation-recommendation-pharmacopoeial-texts-use-ich-regions-step-5_en.pdf> (accessed 24.03.20.).

ICH Q5A (R1): Viral safety evaluation of biotechnology products derived from cell lines of human or animal origin | European Medicine Agency, 1997. Available from: <https://www.ema.europa.eu/en/documents/scientific-guideline/ich-q-5-r1-viral-safetyevaluation-biotechnology-products-derived-cell-lines-human-animal-origin_en.pdf> (accessed 24.03.20.).

ICH Q5B: Analysis of the expression construct in cells used for production of R-DNA derived protein products | European Medicine Agency, 1996. Available from: <https://www.ema.europa.eu/en/documents/scientific-guideline/ich-q-5-b-analysis-expression-construct-cell-lines-used-production-r-dna-derived-protein-products_en.pdf/> (accessed 24.03.20.).

ICH Q5C: Stability testing of biotechnological/biological products. | European Medicine Agency, 1996. Available from: <https://www.ema.europa.eu/en/documents/scientific-guideline/ich-topic-q-5-c-quality-biotechnological-products-stability-testingbiotechnological/biological-products_en.pdf> (accessed 26.03.20.).

ICH Q5D: Derivation and characterization of cell subtracts used for production of biotechnological / biological products | European Medicine Agency, 1996. Available from: <https://www.ema.europa.eu/en/documents/scientific-guideline/ich-q-5-d-derivation-characterisation-cell-substrates-used-production-biotechnological/biological-products-step-5_en.pdf> (accessed 26.03.20.).

ICH Q5E: Comparability of biotechnological/biological products subject to changes in their manufacturing process| European Medicine Agency, 2005. Available from: <https://www.ema.europa.eu/en/documents/scientific-guideline/ich-q-5-e-comparabilitybiotechnological/biological-products-step-5_en.pdf> (accessed 26.03.20.).

ICH Q6A: Specifications: test procedure and acceptance criteria for new drug substances and new drug products: chemical substances | European Medicine Agency, 2000. Available from: <https://www.ema.europa.eu/en/documents/scientific-guideline/ich-q-6-test-procedures-acceptance-criteria-new-drug-substances-new-drug-products-chemical_en.pdf> (accessed 26.03.20.).

ICH Q6B: Specification: test procedures and acceptance criteria for biotechnological/biological products | European Medicine Agency, 1999. Available from: <https://www.ema.europa.eu/en/documents/scientific-guideline/ich-q-6-b-test-procedures-acceptance-criteria-biotechnological/biological-products-step-5_en.pdf> (accessed 26.03.20.).

ICH Q7: Good manufacturing practice guide for active pharmaceutical ingredients | European Medicine Agency, 2000. Available from: <https://www.ema.europa.eu/en/documents/scientific-guideline/ich-q-7-good-manufacturing-practice-active-pharmaceutical-ingredients-step-5_en.pdf> (accessed 04.04.20.).

ICH Q8 (R2): Pharmaceutical development | European Medicine Agency, 2017. Available from: <https://www.ema.europa.eu/en/documents/scientific-guideline/international-conference-harmonisation-technical-requirements-registration-pharmaceuticals-human-use_en-11.pdf> (accessed 04.04.20.).

ICH Q9: Quality risk management | European Medicine Agency, 2015. Available from: <https://www.ema.europa.eu/en/documents/scientific-guideline/international-conference-harmonisation-technical-requirements-registration-pharmaceuticals-human-use_en-3.pdf> (accessed 04.04.20.).

ICH Q10: Pharmaceutical quality system (PQS), no date. Available from: <https://database.ich.org/sites/default/files/Q10_Presentation.pdf> (accessed 08.04.20.).

ICH Q11: Development and manufacture of drug substances (chemical entities and bio technological/biological entities) | European Medicine Agency, 2011. Available from: <https://www.ema.europa.eu/en/documents/scientific-guideline/draft-ich-guideline-q11-development-manufacture-drug-substances-chemical-entities-biotechnological/biological-entities_en.pdf> (accessed 08.04.20.).

ICH Q12: Technical and regulatory considerations for pharmaceutical product life cycle management | European Medicine Agency, 2017. Available from: <https://www.ema.europa.eu/en/documents/scientific-guideline/draft-ich-guideline-q12-technical-regulatory-considerations-pharmaceutical-product-lifecycle_en.pdf> (accessed 08.04.20.).

ICH Q13: Continuous manufacturing of drug substances and drug products, 2018. Available from: <https://database.ich.org/sites/default/files/Q13%20Concept%20Paper.pdf> (accessed 02.03.20.).

ICH Q14: Analytical procedure development and revision of Q2 (R1) analytical validation, 2018. Available from: <https://database.ich.org/sites/default/files/Q2R2-Q14_EWG_Concept_Paper.pdf> (accessed 02.03.20.).

ICH: Efficacy guidelines, no date. Available from: <https://www.ich.org/page/efficacy-guidelines> (accessed 18.04.20.).

ICH E1: The extent of population exposure to assess clinical safety for drugs intended for long-term treatment of non-life-threatening conditions, 1994. Available from: <https://database.ich.org/sites/default/files/E1_Guideline.pdf> (accessed 18.04.20.).

ICH E2A: Clinical safety data management: definitions and standards for Expedited reporting, 1994. Available from: <https://database.ich.org/sites/default/files/E2A_Guideline.pdf> (accessed 18.04.20.).

ICH E3: Structure and content of clinical study reports, 1995. Available from: <https://database.ich.org/sites/default/files/E3_Guideline.pdf> (accessed 18.04.20.).

ICH: Multidisciplinary guidelines, no date. Available from: <https://www.ich.org/page/multidisciplinary-guidelines> (accessed 09.03.20.).

ICH: Safety guidelines, no date. Available from: <https://www.ich.org/page/safety-guidelines> (accessed 02.03.20.).

ICH: Quality guidelines, no date. Available from: <https://www.ich.org/page/quality-guidelines> (accessed 01.03.20.).

ICH M2: Electronic standards for the transfer of regulatory information, 1994. Available from: <https://database.ich.org/sites/default/files/M2_EWG_Concept_Paper.pdf> (accessed 21.03.20.).

ICH M3 (R2): Guidance on nonclinical safety studies for the conduct of human clinical trials and marketing authorization for pharmaceuticals, 2009. Available from: <https://database.ich.org/sites/default/files/M3_R2__Guideline.pdf> (accessed 21.03.20.).

ICH MedDRA: Extension of the remit for the points to consider working group (M1 PtC) to develop and maintain a companion document to the PtC documents, 2016. Available from: <https://database.ich.org/sites/default/files/M1_PtC_WG_Concept_Paper.pdf> (accessed 21.03.20.).

ICH M4Q (R1): The common technical document for the registration of pharmaceuticals for human use: quality, 2002. Available from: <https://database.ich.org/sites/default/files/M4Q_R1_Guideline.pdf> (accessed 21.03.20.).

ICH M4E (R2): Revision of M4E guideline on enhancing the format and structure of benefit-risk information in ICH efficacy, 2016. Available from: <https://database.ich.org/sites/default/files/M4E_R2_Guideline.pdf> (accessed 21.03.20.).

ICH M4: Organisation of the common technical document for the registration of pharmaceuticals for human use, 2016. Available from: <https://database.ich.org/sites/default/files/M4_R4__Guideline.pdf> (accessed 21.03.20.).

ICH M6: Guideline on virus and gene therapy vector shedding and transmission, 2009. Available from: <https://database.ich.org/sites/default/files/M6_Concept_Paper.pdf> (accessed 21.03.20.).

ICH Considerations: General principles to address virus and vector shedding, 2009. Available from: <https://database.ich.org/sites/default/files/M6_Appendix1.pdf> (accessed 21.03.20.).

ICH M7: Assessment and control of DNA reactive (mutagenic) impurities in pharmaceuticals to limit potential carcinogenic risk, 2009. Available from: <https://database.ich.org/sites/default/files/M7_R1_Concept_Paper.pdf> (accessed 21.03.20.).

ICH M7 (R1): Assessment and control of dna reactive (mutagenic) impurities in pharmaceuticals to limit potential carcinogenic risk, 2017. Available from: <https://database.ich.org/sites/default/files/M7_R1_Guideline.pdf> (accessed 21.03.20.).

ICH M8: Electronic common technical document, 2010. Available from: <https://database.ich.org/sites/default/files/M8_EWG_IWG_Concept_Paper.pdf> (accessed 21.03.20.).

ICH M8: Electronic common technical document, no date. Available from: <https://database.ich.org/sites/default/files/M8_EWG_IWG_REVISED_Concept_Paper.pdf> (accessed 21.03.20.).

ICH M11: Clinical electronic structured harmonised protocol (CeSHarP), 2018. Available from: <https://database.ich.org/sites/default/files/M11_EWG_Concept_Paper.pdf> (accessed 21.03.20.).

ICH M12: Drug interaction studies, 2019. Available from: <https://database.ich.org/sites/default/files/M12_FinalConceptPaper_2019_1117.pdf> (accessed 21.03.20.).

ICH: Stability testing of new drug substances and products Q1A (R2), 2003. Available from: <https://database.ich.org/sites/default/files/Q1A%28R2%29%20Step4.pdf> (accessed 01.03.20.).

Khagga, B., Kaitha, M.V., Dammu, R., Mogili, S., 2019. ICH guidelines—"Q" series (quality guidelines)—a review. GSC Biol. Pharm. Sci. 6 (03), 089–106.

Overview of ICH, 2019. Available from: <https://admin.ich.org/sites/default/files/2019-11/OverviewOfICH_2019_1128_0.pdf

Pawar, A.K., Khandelwal, H.R., 2019. An overview—international conference on harmonisation and ICH (Q1) stability testing guideline for pharmaceutical development. IJRASET 7 (12), 1042–1052.

Somvanshi, Y., Satbha, I.P., 2015. ICH guidelines and main focus on Stability Guidelines for new formulation and dosage forms. World J. Pharm. Res. 4 (10), 561–578.

Ur-Rahman, A., 2017. List of current ICH quality guidelines. Available from: <https://www.scribd.com/document/357604700/List-of-Current-ICH-Quality-Guidelines-Pharmaceutical> (accessed 22.12.19.).

Zachary, B., 2015. ICH makes organizational changes. Regulatory Affairs Professionals Society. Available from: <https://www.raps.org/regulatory-focus%E2%84%A2/news-articles/2015/10/ich-makes-organizational-changes> (accessed 27.02.21.).

Chapter 4

Regulatory affairs for chemistry, manufacturing, and controls

Sonal Gupta[1], Sanjula Baboota[2], Javed Ali[2] and Shweta Dang[1]

[1]*Department of Biotechnology, Jaypee Institute of Information Technology, Noida, India,* [2]*Department of Pharmaceutics, School of Pharmaceutical Education and Research, Jamia Hamdard, New Delhi, India*

4.1 Introduction

Regulatory approvals are required to ensure the safety, efficacy, and consistency of a health product, whether it is a drug or biological product, a medical device or a combination product (CP). Besides the preclinical and clinical investigations, chemistry, manufacturing, and controls (CMC) section plays a vital role in approvals (Schmuff and Lin, 2014). CMC section of a dossier includes detailed characterization, stability studies of drug substance and drug product, manufacturing processes and controls, qualification of the manufacturing sites, analytical methods and their validation, and equipment and personnel involved (Balasubramanian et al., 2018). The scope of the CMC section includes various applications submitted for regulatory approvals, such as investigational new drug (IND)/clinical trial application, new drug application (NDA)/ market authorization application (MAA), abbreviated new drug application (ANDA) and biological licensing application (BLA).

Depending on the type of medicinal product, that is, small molecules (drugs) or large molecules, such as monoclonal antibodies, peptides, or other biologics, the requirements for CMC section also change.

The "quality" section [module 3 in Common Technical Document (ICH M4Q)] gives a standardized structure of registration dossier for describing CMC information. It also elaborates on the ideal manufacturing conditions for the product, maintaining the consistency in quality parameters for each batch (Steinmetz and Spack, 2009).

Chemistry section of CMC primarily focuses on characterization of the drug substance, that is, active pharmaceutical ingredient (API), or new molecular entity or the biologic. For example, for a drug substance the chemistry section would include a detailed description to ascertain identity; physical and chemical properties, such as solubility, particle size, polymorphic form, assay procedures, stability, impurities, and microbial levels. All these tests/procedures should have specifications and acceptance criteria as defined in pharmacopoeias (Bhavyasri et al., 2019).

Manufacturing section of CMC includes analytical procedures and manufacturing operations involved. It includes the procedures to manufacture the drug substance, preformulation, and formulation methods and strategies for the drug product, and processes to characterize the product via various analytical procedures.

Controls section of CMC requires the manufacturers to give details of the kind of process controls they have on their drug products to ensure product quality and stability. In-process quality control (IPQC) tests, specifications of the drug substance and product, and acceptance criteria are some of the essential components of this section (Fabio et al., 2019). Approval agencies also require a gist of stability tests performed, procedures followed, and the resulting data from the studies. "The International Conference on Harmonisation of Technical Requirements for Registration of Pharmaceuticals for Human Use (*ICH*) guidance on stability studies is outlined in ICH Q1A, Q1B, Q1C, Q1D, and Q1E and guidance for biotechnology products is outlined in ICH Q5C.5" (ICH, 2003). The goal of stability testing is to emphasize on how different environmental factors (light, temperature, and humidity) affect the quality of a drug substance and product over a period of its shelf life. It further reestablishes the stability (conditions of temperature and humidity at which the product is to be stored during shelf life) of the product (Bajaj et al., 2012). These guidelines address the information that is required to be submitted for new molecular entities and related drugs in registration applications.

Regulatory Affairs in the Pharmaceutical Industry. DOI: https://doi.org/10.1016/B978-0-12-822211-9.00003-4
© 2022 Elsevier Inc. All rights reserved.

CMC section is related to quality of drug products to be used in preclinical and clinical components and, therefore, this section is different from other parts of the dossier [Chemistry, Manufacturing, and Control (CMC), 2020]. Furthermore, CMC is graded in nature as the applicant is required to submit additional information when the drug development process progresses and enters from preclinical to the clinical stage and later to commercial batches (Akshatha et al., 2019).

Some of the advantages of well-planned CMC are that it can reduce cost, avoid compliance issues, and avert product recalls and revenue losses. Also, CMC accomplishments can add to the product portfolio, thereby increasing the manufacturing capability of a company (Hansen, 2014).

CMC Regulatory Affairs (RA) has the crucial responsibility for providing the approach that is required to achieve speedy regulatory approvals. It plays a key role in the development, licensing, manufacturing, and marketing of pharmaceutical products (Gad, 2008; Yousefi et al., 2017). It also strategically collaborates with technical, scientific, quality, and commercial areas within a firm and with extramural contract manufacturing organizations (CMOs). Therefore, CMC RA has a crucial role to play in the expansion, authorization, production, and ongoing commercialization of medical products (Vijay et al., 2017), as shown in Fig. 4.1.

This chapter focuses on CMC regulatory requirements at different stages (IND and NDA), postapproval changes and their reporting categories as defined by the U.S. Food and Drug Administration (US FDA), ICH Q8 guidelines, regulations of CPs, and medical devices.

4.2 Chemistry, manufacturing, and controls submission at investigational new drug (IND) stage

IND refers to an application submitted to the regulatory authorities for a new therapeutic drug or bioactive compound which is to be investigated in humans via a clinical test. IND can also be submitted for a previously authorized product in the market for exploring a new clinical indication (Guidelines for Investigational New Drugs (IND) Requirements, 2010).

The key features of CMC in IND include the initial characterization, chemistry, synthesis, or manufacturing of the drug substance and drug product. The purpose of this section is to ensure via detailed characterization, process controls, and IPQC tests to provide for a safe product for participants of clinical trials and later to a larger population. Detailed information has to be submitted in each phase of the investigation to guarantee the correct identification, features, purity, and potency of the prospective product. As the investigation progresses, modifications in the new drug preparation protocols and changes in the dosage form are expected, and these need to be reported to the authorities (US FDA 21 CFR Part 312, 2018a).

Following the submission and approval of an IND application, the sponsor can initiate the clinical trials. The following section describes different phases of these trials (Davy et al., 2019).

Phase 0 studies: Some of the clinical studies initiate drug trials in humans with phase 0 trials. Largely the purpose of this phase 0 trial is to find out the most suitable drug candidate out of the 4—5 lead molecules. Microdoses are administered to human volunteers just to assess the pharmacokinetic parameters and elucidate the mechanism of action.

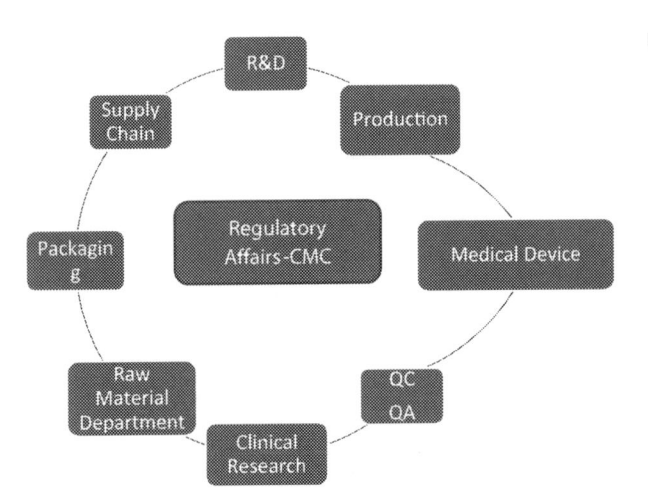

FIGURE 4.1 CMC Regulatory Affairs: "Heart" of regulatory approvals.

This is specially planned when the sponsor has few molecules which look promising and screening is done using this trial. In FDA, an exploratory IND needs to be submitted before this trial and the sponsor has to conduct phase 1 trial following the completion of this trial.

Phase 1 studies: The purpose of phase 1 studies is to assess the safety of the drug product. The doses are generally divided by a safety factor and doses are escalated under a plan so that no volunteer is exposed to an unseen risk or adverse effect. Another purpose of this trial is to assess the dose-limiting toxicities, that is the dose where the drug starts to exhibit adverse effects. To proceed for Phase 2 studies, enough data on the pharmacological and pharmacokinetics course of the drug should be established during Phase 1 studies. The total number of healthy subjects included in Phase 1 clinical trial can depend on the type of product being investigated (20−80 volunteers). The CMC section pertaining to Phase 1 for a drug substance includes identification, brief description about physicochemical properties, purity and strength, stability data, brief manufacturing process with a list of reagents, and the raw material being used.

Phase 2 studies: Involves the controlled clinical studies to assess the drug efficacy for certain specific symptom(s) in patients with the diseased condition under investigation and to assess the side effects and risks related to the drug. These investigations are generally well ordered, carefully supervised, and performed on a comparatively small population of patients (EMA, 2019).

Before progressing to Phase 3 clinical studies, a crucial end of phase 2 (EOP-2) meeting is planned to discuss the progression into Phase 3 trials; there are many verticals to this meeting, but from the point of view of CMC section, this meeting can be planned to discuss CMC-only issues with the authorities. The purpose of EOP-2 meetings for CMC vertical is to finalize and agree upon the raw material, analytical methods, impurity profiling, specifications, stability, dosage form, dissolution methods, and so forth.

Phase 3 studies: These are conducted after the initial confirmation of the proposed efficacy of the drug has been attained and the overall benefit−risk relationship of the drugs (information on efficacy and safety) is established to provide a reasonable basis for physician labeling. Phase 3 studies are generally performed on several hundred to several thousand subjects (Guidelines for Investigational New Drugs IND Requirements, 2010). From the CMC point of view, the applicant at this stage has to prepare for the NDA, and accordingly, the CMC section should be nearing optimization.

4.3 Chemistry, manufacturing, and controls submission at new drug application (NDA) stage

As the drug product progresses into various phases of clinical trials, the applicant must ensure that the manufacturing protocols are optimized and controlled in a way so that they can be representative of the commercial-level batches. CMC regulatory submissions at NDA stage are not limited to information associated with the API and finished dosage form (Van Buskirk et al., 2014). It also contains information on different levels starting from basic drug product characterization, analytical methodology, production methods and process controls, dissolution methods, the stability of the product per se, packaging details, training of personnel, and so on. Setting up the specifications is also one of the important cornerstones of CMC submissions. Broadly, the following sections are required for the CMC submission for a drug product.

1. *Common information*
   a. Classification: including *collection name, chemical name, company code, other non-proprietary name(s), and CAS number*;
   b. Structure: including *structural formula, molecular formula, and molecular mass*;
   c. Overall characteristics such as *physical description, physical form (polymorphic form, solvate, hydrate), solubility, pH, and pKa.*
2. *Production*
   a. Name and address of the units used for the production of clinical lots of drug products;
   b. Details of the Production Method and Controls, including flow schema and documented depiction of the production;
   c. Quality control of resources: drug-related data from their origins at the risk of transmitting encephalopathies like bovine spongiform encephalopathy (BSE)/transmissible spongiform encephalopathies(TSE).
3. *Classification of API*
   a. Proof of structure (e.g., infrared(IR) spectrocopy, ultraviolet (UV) spectrocopy, nuclear magnetic resonance (NMR), mass spectrometry (MS), elemental analysis).

    b. Open argument on the possibility for isomerism and testifying the stereochemistry,

    c. Abstract on polymorphic forms, and

    d. Abstract on the studies of the particle size distribution.

4. *Adulteration*

    a. Drug-associated adulterations, such as "chemical name, structure, and origin";

    b. Procedure-associated adulterations, such as "solvents and reagents";

    c. Actual levels of adulterations found in clinical lots.

5. *Regulation of drug*

    a. Stipulations, including assessment of investigative processes and approval benchmarks;

    b. Lot investigation: elucidation of lots to be used in the analysis (lot number, size of lot, date and site of manufacture) and abstract of findings.

6. *Vessel closing system*

    a. Description of the vessel closing system(s) for the storage and delivery of the drug substance.

7. *Strength*

    a. Strength information: Abstract and findings (abstract to support clinical testing);

    b. Submission procedure: In the absence of long-term information, submit the interim stability data (Lionberger et al., 2008).

4.4 CMC changes and maintaining the CMC regulatory compliance

Once the product is approved for market launch, CMC may have to be modified because of modifications or alterations in the manufacturing practices, QC, machinery, laboratories, accountable staff, or cataloging, it is necessary to report the regulatory authorities about the particulars of these modifications. The sponsor is required to confirm that no safety and efficacy apprehension arises by making any production process modification. Therefore, quality information in the form of comparability protocols to compare before and after production changes must be submitted to the approving organization (Mantus and Pisano, 2014).

The following are report documentation classes of the postauthorization modifications provided by "Section 506A of the Federal Food, Drugs and Cosmetics Act and 21 CFR 314.70" (Guidance for Industry, 2004), which are as follows:

1. *Main modification*: Main modifications have an extensive possibility to have an impact on the "identity, power, quality, purity, or strength" of the pharmaceutical product because these features may affect the safety or efficiency of the drug product. It is a prerequisite to get prior approval by submitting a Supplement to the FDA before this kind of change can be implemented. These Supplements are called and should be clearly labeled as a Prior Approval Supplement (PAS).

2. *Moderate modification:* Modifications that can have a reasonable probability of antagonistic impact on the "identity, strength, quality, purity, or potency" of the pharmaceutical product are called moderate change. The moderate modifications can be of two types:

    a. Supplement modifications come to effect in 30 days, also known as changes being effected-30 (CBE-30);

    b. Supplement modification made to be effected or changes being effected (CBE).

3. *Minor modification:* A minor modification is an alteration having marginal probability to cause any antagonistic impact on the "identity, strength, quality, purity, or potency" of the pharmaceutical product as these factors can affect the safety or efficiency of the drug product (Guidance for Industry: Changes to an Approved NDA or ANDA, 2004).

Based on the type of CMC modification the reporting categories of the said CMC change can be reported to FDA under the following four categories: (1) Annual report, (2) Change Being Effected, (3) Change Being Effected-30, and (4) PAS, as shown in Fig. 4.2; minor changes being part of annual report and major changes requiring prior approval.

Annual Report (AR): An AR (minor changes) is given annually within 6−12 months of the date of sanction of the NDA/BLA, slight changes in CMC after the acceptance of the manufacturing method in the production process, QC, and machinery/testing site are described. These updates/changes pose a negligible impact on the quality and safety of a product.

Change Being Effected (CBE): CBE (moderate changes) includes CMC modifications after acceptance in the manufacturing technique, QC, machinery, or testing laboratories are detailed. These variations do not pose any

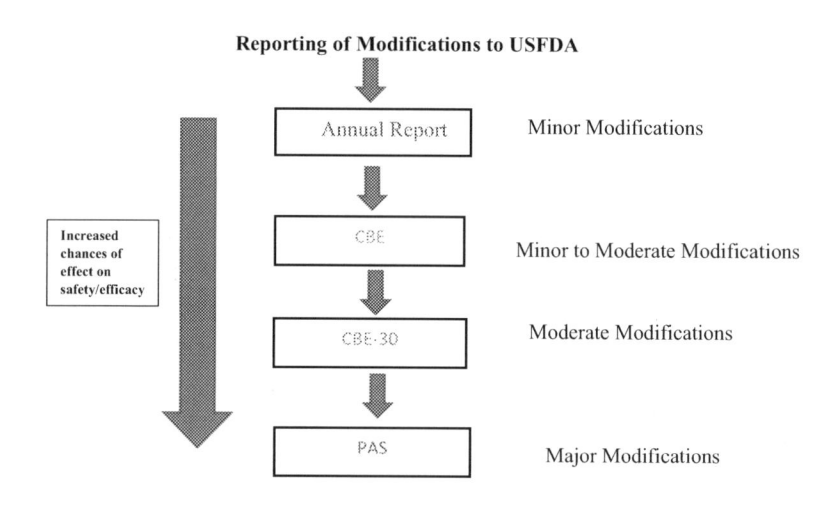

Reporting of Modifications to USFDA

Annual Report — Minor Modifications

CBE — Minor to Moderate Modifications

CBE-30 — Moderate Modifications

PAS — Major Modifications

Increased chances of effect on safety/efficacy

FIGURE 4.2 Reporting categories of the chemistry, manufacturing, and control change.

significant effects on the quality of a drug product. A CBE appendage is enclosed to the sanctioning organization prior or simultaneously with the marketing of the product modified according to the variations.

Change Being Effected-30 (CBE-30): CBE-30 includes a moderate change but has to be reported 30 days before the change is implemented and the product is distributed with a modified procedure.

PAS: In a PAS, changes in the manufacturing technique, QC, machinery, or testing laboratory are described. It needs the submission to the FDA followed by feedback and acceptance sanctioned by the monitoring organization beforehand and an approval is required from FDA before the production with new modifications can be adopted. In few circumstances, it may be inadequate to describe and evaluate prospective impacts of a CMC amendment based on product quality information. The impact of the new modification is required to be analyzed in nonclinical or clinical studies to indicate that there is no undesirable impact on the safety or efficacy of the drug or on its pharmacology (e.g., pharmacodynamics) and pharmacokinetics.

These modifications may have a significant effect on the quality of drug product, its efficiency, and strength and therefore are put under the category of PAS, that is, prior approval is required before the distribution of the drug product is done with the modified process.

Some of the examples of the minor and major modifications are as follows:

1. *Constituents and composition*:
   a. Qualitative or quantitative modifications in the production, comprising *inactive ingredients*, according to the sanctioned use is considered the main change that necessitates a supplement before sanction, excluding exempted by regulatory agencies.
   b. Small changes such as removal or decrease of a constituent affecting color of drug can be reported in an annual report (Changes to an Approved NDA or ANDA, 2004).
2. *Manufacturing sites*:
   a. Major change: If the manufacturing place is shifted to a different site or a production unit is resumed that was not operational for more than 2 years, and had never been inspected is considered as a major change. If the site is used to manufacture or process a drug intermediate, it will not come under the major change.
   b. Moderate change: If the modification is in the form of oral solid dosage, it is considered as a moderate change. Shifting to a different site for processing of the ultimate intermediate will fall under moderate change.
   c. Minor change: If shifting to a new site is only for the secondary packaging, it will be considered as a minor change (Changes to an Approved NDA or ANDA, 2004).
3. *Manufacturing process*:
   a. Major change: Any change in the dose delivered to the patient, such as release type or other features, comprising the addition or removal of a code inscription by stamping, debossing, or imprinting on a "modified-release solid oral dosage form" is regarded as a major change.
   b. Moderate change: Redefining an intermediate (except the final material) for drug substance is considered as a moderate change. A modification in the techniques or controls that offers reassurance that the drug product will have the characteristics of identity, power, quality, purity, or effectiveness that it signifies to retain.

   c. Minor change: A small modification in the current code imprint for a dosage form is known as minor change (Changes to an Approved NDA or ANDA, 2004).

4. *Specifications:*

   a. Major change: Creating a fresh supervisory, investigative scheme comprising a description of a substitute investigative method as a supervisory process.

   b. Moderate change: Comforting an approval standard or avoiding a test to abide by an authorized agency that agrees with FDA legislative and supervisory needs. Besides specification, better guarantee that the drug product will exhibit the features of identity, potency, quality, purity, or effectiveness that it claims or is signified to retain.

   c. Minor change: Contraction of approval standards (Changes to an Approved NDA or ANDA, 2004).

5. *Container closure system*:

   a. Major change: A variation in the parts of preliminary packing of any drug product when its parts regulate the dose delivery.

   b. Moderate change: Changes in dimensions of a container for a sterile drug substance. A change in desiccant by either addition or deletion will be considered as a moderate change.

   c. Minor change: A nonsterilized solid dosage form exhibiting a change in the size and/or shape of a container will be regarded as a minor change.

6. *Labeling*:

   a. Major change: When there are changes according to the postmarketing study results, and cataloging variations related to the new symptoms and applications are considered as a major change.

   b. Moderate change: Adding an antagonistic effect because of data provided to the candidate or an organization.

   c. Minor change: Variations in the labeling to comply with an official compendium (Changes to an Approved NDA or ANDA, 2004).

7. *Miscellaneous changes*

   a. Major change: Addition of a few protocols, such as stability protocol or comparability protocol.

   b. Moderate change: To give guarantee of the *"identity, strength, quality, purity, or potency"* of the drug product, reduction of the expiration-dating period is also regarded as a moderate change. In case of the delay in expiration date, that has been reduced earlier under this establishment, also have to be presented in a CBE-in-30-days supplement; however, postponement of expiration date dependent on the information acquired through the procedure accepted in the submission.

   c. Minor change: On the basis of complete shelf life information on manufactured lots acquired through the procedure accepted in the submission, the expiration-dating period can be extended.

8. *Multiple related changes*:

Centre for Drug Evaluation and Research (CDER) of USFDA acclaims that application must be in harmony with the most restraining of the types suggested for the specific modifications for *multiple related changes* where the suggested documented classes for specific modifications vary. When the several associated modifications have the unchanged suggested documented class, CDER suggests that the submission must be in agreement with the documented class for the specific modifications (Guidance for Industry, 2004).

Before applying these modifications to the process or product, the sponsor must establish that there are negligible effects of the above changes on the quality of a drug product. In a few of the instances, re-verification of the investigations, and batch release examination may be enough, but some type of changes could also need a process/analytical method and/or lot release testing, and exhaustive comparability tests (before and after modifications) (Changes to an Approved NDA or ANDA, 2004). Comparability protocol is a documented plan to be submitted by a manufacturer in case of postapproval changes to be made to the drug products, and this applies to NDA/ANDA/BLA. The purpose of the comparability protocol is to let the regulatory authorities know about the plan of the manufacturer to assess the effect of the proposed change on the safety and efficacy of the drug molecule. ICH Q8 guidelines also talk about the development of a design space around the product; so that any changes that take place post approvals are taken care of in advance. Implementation of such plans ensures smooth approvals for postproduction changes. The following section on ICH Q8 guidelines focuses on the development of a *process analytical technology (PAT), CGMPs, Quality by Design (QbD), continuous manufacturing, and six sigma pharmaceutical quality* (Patil and Pethe, 2013).

ICH (Q8) targets to propose an eminent product with superior characteristics and its production technique to unfailingly provide the anticipated quality drug product. The data and facts drawn from medical advancement revisions and production experience offer technical knowledge to upkeep the setting up of the project site, stipulations, and production panels. Information from drug development investigation can be a base for quality damage control. Drug development segment should comprise of the information:

1. Suitability of the selected dosage form for the indicated application;
2. Adequate information in every section to support an understanding of the drug product development and its production method;
3. Abstract including tabular and graphical presentation;
4. Features of drugs, such as *substances, excipients, container closure systems, and production technique*, that are crucial for the quality product should be assessed and regulatory policies complied with;
5. Essential preparation characteristics and procedure considerations have to be recognized through the evaluation of the degree to which their discrepancy can affect the quality of the drug product (ICH guideline, 2009).

To apprehend this flexibility, the contender should establish an enriched understanding of product competence for various material characteristics, production methods, and practice considerations. This knowledge can be extended by using an official investigational proposal, PAT, literature review. Drug development should at least comprise:

1. *Quality target product profile (QTPP)*: QTPP lays the foundation for the scheme of drug development. QTPP is associated with the anticipated application, quality, safety, and efficiency, also the mode of delivery, administration, dosage form, bioavailability, stability, vessel closure, and strength (ICH guideline, 2009).
2. *Identifying potential critical quality attributes (CQAs)*: CQAs need to be identified so that the aspects related to the safety of the drug product can be addressed in time. A CQA is a *physical, chemical, biological, or microbiological property* that should lie within an apt range to guarantee the product of required quality. CQAs of *solid oral dosage forms* are generally those features that impact the levels of purity/impurity, stability, rate of release of drug. CQAs for other dosage forms can further comprise product aspects explicitly, such as *aerodynamic properties for inhaled products, sterility for parenteral, and adhesion properties for transdermal patches*. Prospective drug product CQAs resulting from the quality objective product portfolio and prior information is used to monitor the product and procedure improvement (ICH guideline, 2009).
3. *Design space*: This is a space where the guidelines specify that the variability in the processes is taken care of by drawing a space around the process technology. The purpose of creating a design space is to ensure enough experiments on optimization of processes is done and any manufacturing changes done postapproval are well taken care of, leading to a lesser dependency of getting these changes approved again via comparability protocols. The correlation between the procedure inputs *material attributes and process parameters* and the crucial quality characteristics in a design space can be explained as:
   a. Selection of variables: To understand the process in more detail, all independent and dependent variables should be identified and studied for their possible impact on the quality of the product.
   b. Describing a design space in a submission: A design space can be defined as an optimization space where all the variables of the process have been tested and impact of any change is studied. A well-designed space around the manufacturing process can obviate the need for postapproval changes and delay in regulatory approvals.
   c. Unit operation design space(s): The applicant can select to decide liberated design spaces for one or more facility tasks or to determine a single design space that extends to various processes.
   d. Relationship of design space to scale and equipment: The applicant should defend the significance of a design space established at a *small or pilot scale* to the suggested industrial-scale production technique and confer the probable stakes in the *scale-up operation*.
4. *Control strategy*: A control strategy is planned to assure that a quality product will be manufactured in a controlled manner that is having appropriate process controls in place to get a product with satisfactory quality. The components of the control strategy should explain and validate how *in-process controls and the controls of input materials (drug substance and excipients), intermediates (in-process materials), container closure system, and drug products contribute to the final product quality* (ICH guideline, 2009).

4.5 Combination product regulations

According to the "21 CFR 3.2(e)," a CP is a drug made up of two or more controlled parts, such as *medicine/device, biologic/device, drug/biologic, or drug/device/biologic*, that may be combined *physically/chemically* or blended to form a single entity or single package/unit comprising two or more separate products packaged together, such as *drug and device, device and biological products, or biological and drug products* or a *drug, device, or biological product*, which is packed discretely conferring to its original design with recommended labeling and is proposed for usage only with an accepted single, specific *drug, device, or biological product*. Both of them must attain the proposed usage and symptom and after acceptance of the proposed product, the labeling of the accepted drug product will be required to be modified "to reflect a change in intended use, dosage form, strength, route of administration, or considerable change in dose." A list of CPs is tabulated in Table 4.1 (Vihar et al., 2014).

The FDA's Office of Combination Products (OCPs) was founded in 2002, and the main objective of this office was to address the requirements and regulations on CPs. OCP has got a vast range of responsibilities by the laws covering the regulatory life cycle of CPs (Vihar et al., 2014). Fig. 4.3 gives a depiction of the scope of CPs.

CPs do not have a single approach of action because it is composed of two or more approved products and every component has its contribution in its mode of action. According to the FDA, the definition of the primary mode of action (PMOA) is "the single mode of action of a CP that provides the most important therapeutic action of the CP." Most crucial curative effect means the effect which produces a major impact on the overall outcome of the drug product (Vihar et al., 2014).

Characteristically, CPs with a PMOA credited to the drug constituents is assigned to the "CDER, a Device PMOA to the CDRH, and a biologic PMOA to the CBER (21 CFR 3.4)." The allocated center can discuss or work together

TABLE 4.1 Nine different types for combination products (USFDA, Combination Product Definition, Combination Product Types, 2018b).

Type	Description	Common example(s)
1	Drug/biological product combination	Antibody—drug conjugates, progenitor cells combined with a drug to promote homing
2	Device coated/impregnated/otherwise combined with drugDevice has an additional function in addition to delivering the drug	Drug pills embedded with sensors, contact lens coated with a drug, drug-eluting stents, drug-eluting leads, condoms with spermicide, dental floss with fluoride, antimicrobial-coated catheters/sutures, bone cement with antibiotics
3	Prefilled biological product delivery device/systemBiological product is filled into or otherwise combined with the device and the sole purpose of the device is to deliver biological product	Vaccine or other biological product in a prefilled syringe, auto-injector, nasal spray, transdermal systems, or microneedle patch preloaded with biological product
4	Prefilled drug delivery device/systemDrug is filled into or otherwise combined with the device and the sole purpose of the device is to deliver drug	Prefilled drug syringe, auto-injectors, metered-dose inhalers, dry powder inhalers, nasal spray, pumps, transdermal systems, prefilled iontophoresis system or microneedle "patch"
5	Convenience kit or copackageDrug and device are provided as individual constituent parts within the same package	Drug or biological product vials packaged with device(s) or accessory kits (empty syringes, auto-injectors, transfer sets), first aid or surgical kits containing devices and drugs
6	Device coated or otherwise combined with a biological productDevice has an additional function in addition to delivering the drug	Live cells seeded on or in a device scaffold, extracorporeal column with column-bound protein
7	Other type of Part 3 combination product (e.g., drug/device/biological product)Combination product not otherwise described	All three articles are combined in a single product (e.g., a prefilled syringe containing an antibody—drug conjugate), device to manufacture a biological product also includes a drug or biological product in the kit, or the product contains two different combination product types (e.g., Type 1 and Type 2 are provided together
8	Separate products requiring cross labeling	Light-activated drugs or biological products not copackaged but labeled for use with a specific light source device
9	Possible combination based on cross labeling of separate products	Drug/biological product under development utilizes a device, but unclear whether the final product will require that the two be cross-labeled

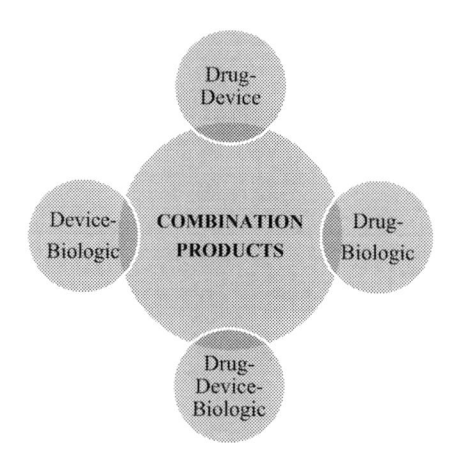

FIGURE 4.3 Combination products: scope.

with the other centers for the assessment of the CP. The CP should follow the center's submission category for assessment before marketing upon allocation to a principal center (Vihar et al., 2014).

According to the Medical Device User Fee and Modernization Act (MDUFMA) of 2002, the responsibilities of the OCP are to allocate an FDA center to have a principal investigator for the screening of CP; assure efficient and regular market report of CPs before commercialization, by monitoring the analyses comprising more than one approval authority organization; validate the uniformity and aptness of the after-market directive; resolve disagreements concerning the regularity of premarket review; appraise the contracts, administration records, or processes particular to the project of CPs; and submit yearly records on the accomplishments of agency and influence to Congress (Eunjoo and Susan, 2018).

The *Combination Products Policy Council* offers a broader platform to set up CP policy across the FDA and make sure that the guiding principle is executed in a reliable way all over the Agency.

4.5.1 Premarket review process

- For an efficient review, a single application is generally suitable for CPs. Cross-center collaboration is the key because these innovative products are a combination of a drug, device, and/or biological product. The FDA will apply a dependable, risk-based method to deal with supervisory queries, which includes technical problems, using significant knowledge from the principal and referred center (Holbein, 2009).
- FDA is printing the regulation draft as a share of its responsibilities in the application of the *"21st Century Cures Act"* and supports the organization's promises to provide clarity, effectiveness, and supervisory reliability in enabling accelerated growth of safe and efficient CPs (Guidance for Industry and FDA Staff, 2019).

The FDA proposes that every time a component of the drug is moved into Class II devices (first time), the CP might not be found to be considerably corresponding to the base device due to the technical advancements and updated usage. Similar consequences happen for following suggestions after a CP is clear if the guarantor wants to considerably update the statements for the portion of a drug component or to modify the drug portion by swapping an active ingredient from another. In both instances, the guarantor would have to ask for fresh cataloging or submit a premarket approval (PMA) for the novel CP (Guidance for Industry and FDA Staff, 2019).

Regulations for CPs has been depicted in Fig. 4.4

4.5.2 Marketing application

The type of marketing application (single or separate) will depend on the kind of CP and agreement, authorization can be attained by submitting an individual advertising claim or by different advertising claims for the single component of a CP. Usually, an individual advertising claim is enough for CP's authorization or agreement. Although, sometimes, a candidate can acquiesce two advertising claims while a single application would be enough to get some advantage that increases only from approval under a submission such as *new drug product exclusivity, orphan status, or proprietary data protection when two firms are involved* (Guidance for Industry and FDA Staff, 2019).

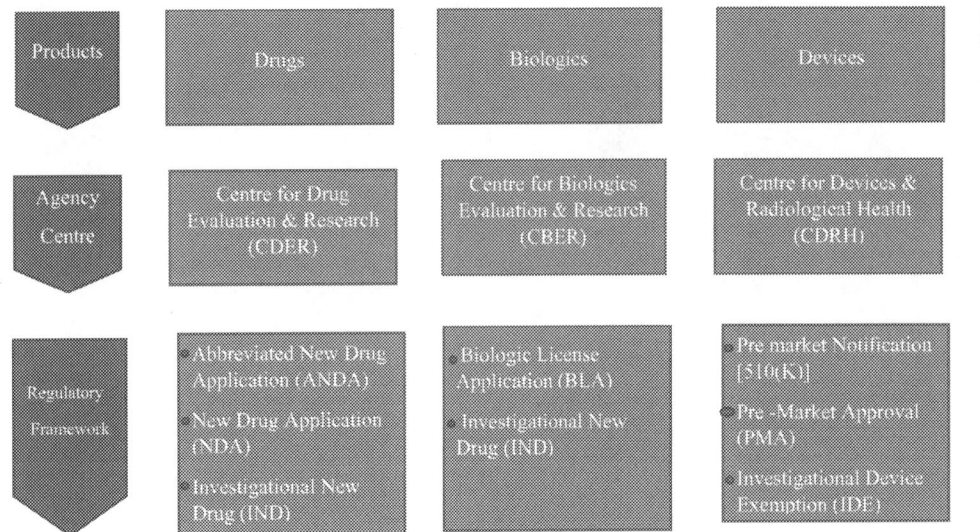

FIGURE 4.4 Regulation of combination products.

The FDA can decide that two advertising claims are required if:

- One of the single component of a CP is previously permitted for alternative usage.
- Different classification is required to indicate its novel envisioned usage in the CP.
- Classification of previously permitted product is the matter of legal ramifications distinct from those that will relate to the CP (Guidance for Industry and FDA Staff, 2019).

4.6 Medical devices regulations

"An instrument, apparatus, implement, machine, contrivance, implant, in vitro reagent, or other similar or related article, including a part, or accessory is known as a medical device" (Shindell, 1983) and it is:

- Recognized in the formal "National Formulary or the United States Pharmacopoeia" or any complement to them.
- Suggested for application in the screening of illness or additional disorders or in the therapy, alleviation, healing, or deterrence of illness in human beings/animals.
- Anticipated to impact the arrangement or functioning in human beings/animals and that does not attain its prime proposed use through chemical action within or in human beings/animals and which is not dependent on metabolism for the attainment of its principal envisioned uses.

Food, Drug, and Cosmetic (FD&C) Act gives standard guidelines for all medical devices (Class I, II, and III) to control. "1700 different generic types of devices are classified and grouped into 16 medical specialties referred to as panels by FDA." All the standard varieties of devices are allocated to one of the given supervisory classes based on the level of control essential to assure the safety and efficiency of the device (Guidance for Industry and FDA Staff, 2014).

Following are the three classes and the requirements:

1. Class I "General Controls":
   a. With exceptions;
   b. Without exceptions;
2. Class II "General Controls and Special Controls":
   a. With exceptions;
   b. Without exceptions;
3. Class III "General Controls and PMA" (Guidance for Industry and FDA Staff, 2014).

The type of PMA submission necessary for FDA sanction for commercialization is dependent on the class to which a device is assigned, as described in Table 4.2. If a device is grouped under Class I or II and if it is not exempted, a 510 (k) will be needed for commercialization. All the devices categorized as exceptions are subject to the boundaries

TABLE 4.2 Examples of medical devices categorized according to the risk levels.

Medical devices	Risk class	Risk level
Implantable defibrillator/heart valves	D	High risk
Longue depressor/surgical retractors	A	Low risk
Bone fixation plate/lung ventilator	C	Moderate to high risk
Hypodermic needles	B	Low to moderate risk

on exemptions. PMA application will be required for Class III devices unless the device is a preamendments device (Johnson, 2016).

The classification of the device depends on its intended use and usage indications. A subdivision of envisioned usage comes up once a more particular symptom is mentioned in the device's labeling, such as "for making incisions in the cornea." Suggestions for consumption can be conveyed either orally or by device's labeling. Furthermore, the grouping is on the basis of risk, implying that the risk the device can cause to the patient is the main factor in the class it is allocated. Class I comprises devices with the minimum risk and Class III comprises those with the maximum risk (Guidance for Industry and FDA Staff, 2014).

The basic compliance necessities that producers of medical devices must comply (Altayyar, 2020):

1. *Establishment Registration*: Producers and suppliers of medical devices must record their establishment with the FDA. Detailed registration information must be validated annually between October 1 and December 31. Besides registering, overseas producers must also entitle a representative (Guidance for Industry and FDA Staff, 2014).
2. *Medical Device Listing*: Major requirement that is mandatory to record with the FDA is to enlist the devices, the establishment and the functions conducted on those devices. If a device needs notice prior to commercialization in the United States or PMA, then the proprietor should also submit the FDA "premarket submission number." Registering and citation give the site of medical device manufacturing and the devices manufactured at those facilities to the FDA (Mori et al., 2014).
3. *Premarket Notification Letter*: The FDA decides if a PMA is appropriate for filing by appraising the submitted data necessary for "FD&C Act, the PMA regulations (21 CFR 814)." The filing of a claim infers that the FDA has incepted that the claim is satisfactorily comprehensive to initiate an exhaustive appraisal. On receipt of the PMA, FDA will inform the candidate (within 45 days) if the request has been filed. This communication will have the date on which FDA filed the PMA and PMA reference number. Accelerated appraisal status may be updated at this time. The "date of filing" is the date on which a PMA (accepted for filing) was received by the agency. The 180-day period for assessment of a PMA commences from the "date of filing" (Guidance for Industry and FDA Staff, 2014).
4. *PMA*: It is an FDA procedure for regulatory and scientific assessment to assess the effectiveness and safety of Class III medical devices. Class III includes those medical devices that are of considerable significance in averting damage to human health or that may pose a risk of disease or damage and provide sustained support to human life. The FDA has established that common and specific controls are inadequate to ensure the effectiveness and safety of Class III devices due to risks associated with them. Therefore, to attain a marketing approval, "a PMA application under section 515 of the FD&C Act" is required for these Class III devices (Guidance for Industry and FDA Staff, 2019).
5. *Investigational device exception (IDE)*: An IDE allows the use of a medical investigational device in a clinical study so that data on effectiveness and safety can be collected. Clinical studies are regularly performed to upkeep a PMA. Investigational use implicates clinical assessment of some specific reforms and novel envisioned applications of authorized marketed devices. All clinical assessments of investigational devices (unless exempt) must have an approved IDE before the study is commenced.
6. *Quality system regulation (QC)/GMP*: To assure that their products unfailingly follow the specifications and necessities, manufacturers must follow and establish the quality system regulation. The quality standards for products (food, drugs, biologics, and devices) regulated by the FDA are called CGMPs. CGMP requirements for devices in part 820 (21 CFR part 820) were approved by "section 520(f) of the Federal Food, Drug, and Cosmetic Act."
7. *Labeling*: The guidelines in "21 CFR Part 801, Labeling; Part 809, In Vitro Diagnostic Products for Human Use; and Part 812," IDEs are envisioned to govern the information of labeling. Similarly, "21 CFR Part 807, Premarket Notification; and Part 814, Premarket Approval and 820.30," Design controls assist in regulating the information of

labeling by design and premarket compliances. The FD&C Act and the intent of regulations is for producers to have a labeling regulatory program so that their labeling is always in agreement with the guidelines and meet the user's requirements. During the design phase, concise and clear software generated and/or printed labeling is written and reviewed by a formal process under quality system followed by the development of the "ink substrate" and attachment techniques for printed labeling. Subsequently, if the manufacturer's quality system are in place, it assures the application of the right label and the right attachment of labels to meet regulatory and customer requirements (Guidance for Industry and FDA Staff, 2019).

8. *Medical device reporting:* This guidance document describes and explains the FDA's present-day regulation that states record-keeping and reporting necessities relevant to medical device manufacturers for device-associated adverse effects and glitches. These guidelines are enclosed in "Title 21 under Medical Device Reporting (MDR) regulation, Code of Federal Regulations (CFR), Part 803, as authorized by section 519 of the Federal Food, Drug, and Cosmetic Act (FD&C Act)" (Guidance for Industry and FDA Staff, 2014).

4.7 Conclusion

The regulatory guidelines and ever-evolving pharmaceutical market present some grim CMC challenges that include recommendations for a survey of latent technological methodologies in the sustenance of monitoring policy progress from an industrial point of view. Similarly, manufacturing CPs and medical devices have unique challenges that must be addressed to cover different aspects of these products. Several existing guidelines have very specific necessities involving molecular size and delivery methods that vary by region. There is a necessity for a reliable system of guidelines that can be standardized, and experiments involving CMC can dole out explicitly using the apt technology and statistical methods. Nonetheless, these methods are comprehended in present ICH regulatory brochures. The particulars of pertinence to intricate, innovative techniques may result in different supervisory recommendations and consequences. The upcoming goalmouths for efficient regulation of novel technologies and modalities could be assisted by further guideline education, monitoring harmonization, and industrial collaboration via associations, empowering business to provide crucial information to supervisory body in a precise and clear way and developing commonly implied stake-profit scrutiny to manufacture products of suitable quality characteristics, efficiency, and safety.

References

Akshatha, G., Anoop Narayanan, V., Sandeep, D.S., Narayana Charyulu, R., 2019. Chemistry, manufacturing and control (CMC) evaluations of ANDA submission in the USA. Ind. J. Pharm. Educ. Res. 53 (3), 414–420.

Altayyar, S.S., 2020. The essential principles of safety and effectiveness for medical devices and role of standards. Med. Devices (Auckl.) 13, 49–55.

Bajaj, S., Singla, D., Sakhuja, N., 2012. Stability testing of pharmaceutical products. J. Appl. Pharm. Sci. 02 (03), 129–138.

Balasubramanian, J., Varma, C.T., Babu, E., Ram, S.H., Vinoth, 2018. Influence of (QbR) question based review to revamp CMC submission review. World J. Pharm. Med. Res. 4 (4), 100–106.

Bhavyasri, K., Manisha Vishnumurthy, K., Rambabu, D., Sumakanth, M., 2019. ICH guidelines – "Q" series (quality guidelines)—a review. GSC Biol. Pharm. Sci. 6 (3), 89–106.

Chemistry, Manufacturing, and Control (CMC) Information for human gene therapy investigational new drug applications (INDs) guidance for industry. U.S. Department of Health and Human Services, Food and Drug Administration Centre for Biologics Evaluation and Research, 2020. <https://www.fda.gov/media/113760/download> (accessed 11.01.20.).

Davy, C., Erica, M.C., Anita, V.E., Erica, K., Sarah, H.L., 2019. Regulatory Affairs 101: introduction to investigational new drug applications and clinical trial applications. Clin. Transl. Sci. 12, 334–342.

EMA/338312/2016 Rev. 3. European Medicine Agency, 2019. <https://www.ema.europa.eu/en/documents/other/about-us-european-medicines-agency-ema_en.pdf> (accessed 09.02.20.).

Eunjoo, P., Susan, B., 2018. Drugs. An Overview of FDA Regulated Products—From Drugs and Cosmetics to Food and Tobacco. Academic PressPage v, ISBN 9780128111550. Available from: https://doi.org/10.1016/B978-0-12-811155-0.00018-1.

Fabio, P., Alessandro, C., Stefania, S., Iolanda, G., Elena, M., Aldo, C., 2019. The requirements for manufacturing highly active or sensitizing drugs comparing good manufacturing practices. Acta Biomed. 90 (2), 288–299.

Gad, S.C., 2008. Quality in the Manufacture of Medicine and Other Healthcare Products. Pharmaceutical Press, pp. 29–41, Chapter 3.

Guidance for Industry: Changes to an approved NDA or ANDA, Revision 1., April 2004. <http://www.fda.gov/downloads/Drugs/GuidanceComplianceRegulatoryInformation/Guidances/pdf (accessed 15.01.20.).

Guidance for Industry and FDA Staff, 2014. The 510(k) Program: evaluating substantial equivalence in premarket notifications [510(k)]. <https://www.fda.gov/media/82395/download> (accessed 20.01.20.).

Guidance for Industry and FDA Staff: Principles of premarket pathways for combination products, 2019. <https://www.fda.gov/media/119958/download> (accessed 22.01.20.).

Guidelines for Investigational New Drugs (IND) Requirements, 2010. <https://www.sfda.gov.sa/sites/default/files/2020-09/Guidelinesfor InvestigationalNewDrug_IND__v11.pdf> (accessed 11.01.20.).

Hansen, K.R.N., 2014. New Product Introduction in the Pharmaceutical Industry. DTU Management Engineering.

Holbein, M.E.B., 2009. Understanding fda regulatory requirements for investigational new drug applications for sponsor-investigators. J. Investig. Med. 57 (6), 688−694.

ICH harmonised tripartite guideline, 2003. Stability testing of new drug substances and products Q1a(R2).

ICH harmonised tripartite guideline, 2009. Pharmaceutical development Q8(R2).

Johnson, J.A., September 14, 2016. FDA regulation of medical devices. Specialist in biomedical policy.

Lionberger, A.R., Lee, L.S., Lee, L., Raw, A., Yu, X.L., 2008. Quality by design: concepts for ANDAs. AAPS J. 10, 2.

Mantus, D., Pisano, D.J., 2014. FDA Regulatory Affairs, third ed. CRC Press, Boca Raton, FL, pp. 218−219.

Mori, K., Watanabe, M., Horiuchi, N., Tamura, A., Kutsumi, H., 2014. The role of the pharmaceuticals and medical devices agency and healthcare professionals in post-marketing safety. Clin. J. Gastroenterol. 7, 103−107.

Patil, A.S., Pethe, A.M., 2013. Quality by design (QbD): a new concept for development of quality pharmaceuticals. Int. J. Pharm. Qual. Assur. 4 (2), 13−19.

Schmuff, N.R., Lin, D.T., 2014. Chemistry, manufacturing and controls (CMC). In: Wiley StatsRef: Statistics Reference Online. <https://doi.org/10.1002/9781118445112.stat07152> (accessed 28.01.20.).

Shindell, D.S., 1983. Effect of the medical device legislation on automation in medicine. In: Nair, S., Prakash, O., Imbruce, R.P. (Eds.), Computers in Critical Care and Pulmonary Medicine. Springer, Boston, MA.

Steinmetz, K.L., Spack, E.G., 2009. The basics of preclinical drug development for neurodegenerative disease indications. BMC Neurol. 9, S2.

USFDA, 2018a. 21 CFR part 312 investigational new drug application. <https://www.accessdata.fda.gov/scripts/cdrh/cfdocs/cfcfr/CFRSearch.cfm?fr=312.23> (accessed 12.02.20.).

USFDA, 2018b. Combination product definition, combination product types. <https://www.fda.gov/combination-products/about-combination-products/combination-product-definition-combination-product-types> (accessed 22.01.20.).

Van Buskirk, G.A., Asotra, S., Balducci, C., et al., 2014. Best practices for the development, scale-up, and post-approval change control of IR and MR dosage forms in the current quality-by-design paradigm. AAPS PharmSciTech 15, 665−693.

Vihar, K., Prabahar, E., Nadendla, R.R., Srinivasarao, D.B., 2014. Regulatory strategy for registration of combination products to us-FDA. Int. J. Drug. Reg. Aff. 2 (3), 27−42.

Vijay, K., Meenu, B., Purva, D., 2017. Correlation of regulatory affairs officer with different department of pharmaceutical industry in India and impact of GST. World. J. Pharm. Res. 6 (9), 147−153.

Yousefi, N., Mehralian, G., Rasekh, H.R., Yousefi, M., 2017. New product development in the pharmaceutical industry: evidence from a generic market. Iran. J. Pharm. Res. 16 (2), 834−846.

Chapter 5

Global submissions for drug approvals

Shrestha Sharma[1], Syed Arman Rabbani[2] and Rajesh Sharma[1]

[1]Department of Pharmaceutics, School of Medical and Allied Sciences, K.R. Mangalam University, Gurgaon, India, [2]Department of Clinical Pharmacy and Pharmacology, RAK College of Pharmaceutical Sciences, RAK Medical and Health Sciences University, Ras Al-Khaimah, United Arab Emirates

5.1 Global submissions

5.1.1 Introduction

To ascertain various concerns linked with efficacy and safety of drugs, all countries need to establish regulatory agencies which could supervise the new drug development process and provide marketing authorization (MA) to new drug products and medical devices as almost all drugs are associated with some amount of risk or occurrence of an adverse event. There have been number of unfortunate incidences in the past in which drugs have instigated serious side effects and adverse events, which could be due to the drug itself or the excipients used or from the toxic impurities present in drug products. Due to these concerns, stringent drug regulation policy is needed to safeguard the safety and efficacy of drugs for the general public in every country (Jin, 2014). New drug approval procedure is defined as a stepwise method provided by regulatory agencies of each country that set guidelines for a drug manufacturer or a sponsor who wishes to seek MA in a specific country. The drug approval process includes various stages starting from new drug discovery, preclinical investigations on animal models, clinical phase trials in humans to seek MA and postsurveillance investigations (Fig. 5.1).

Currently different countries stick to their own regulatory requirements as prescribed by the governing bodies for new drug approval since it is very difficult to have single regulatory entity for providing MA in all countries. Single administrative methodology all through the world is beyond the realm of imagination in light of the fact that in every nation, administrative offices are represented by nation's own laws. Therefore, it is essential to have understanding

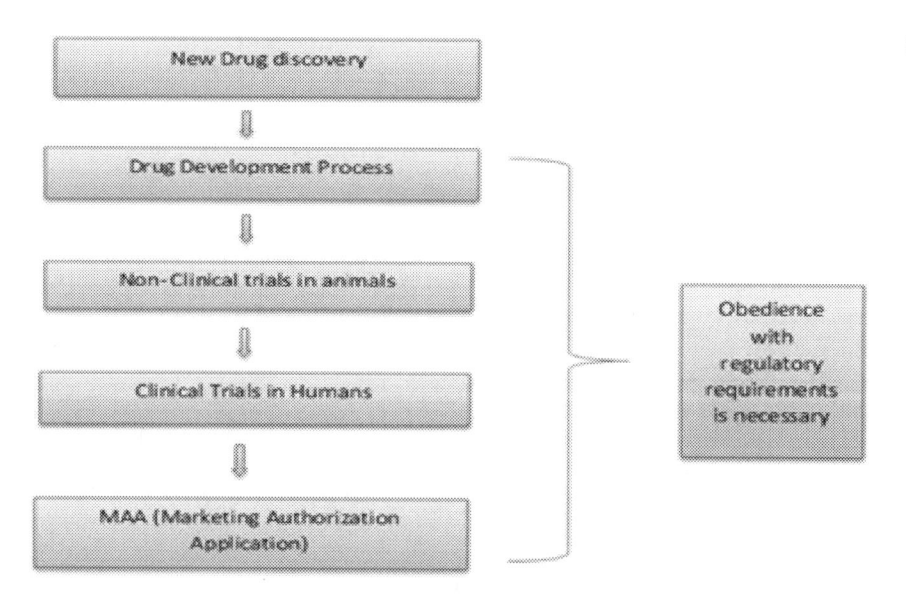

FIGURE 5.1 Steps in a regulatory process.

Regulatory Affairs in the Pharmaceutical Industry. DOI: https://doi.org/10.1016/B978-0-12-822211-9.00005-8
© 2022 Elsevier Inc. All rights reserved.

about regulatory requirements for MAA of various countries. Since, the United States and European Union have been the budding markets for developed new drug products around the world; therefore, various pharmaceutical companies follow their regulatory guidelines for drug approval process. However, the International Conference on Harmonization (ICH) has revolutionized regulatory review processes throughout the world by assembling all Quality, Safety, and Efficacy data in a common format known as common technical document (CTD) (Gelman, 2006). It is widely accepted by various countries to submit their required data in an electronic form which is termed as electronic CTD (eCTD) (Inpharma Weekly, 2003). CTD has eradicated the need of formatting and reformatting of the submissions according to country-specific guidelines in which the applicant needs to have market authorization for his drug. This chapter highlights the regulatory processes of the United States, European Union, India, the United Kingdom, Japan, and Australia along with CTD, Investigational Medicinal Products Dossier (IMPD), and Investigator's Brochure (IB).

5.1.2 Drug approval in the United States

The United States has set the world's most rigorous standards for the approval of new drugs. Due to which, these standards are taken into consideration by many countries. The regulating agency for drug approval in the United States is the Food and Drug Administration (FDA). The role of FDA in the new drug development process starts when the drug's applicant has already done the pharmacological screening for the new drug and performed acute toxicity studies in animals and now wishes to evaluate its pharmacological efficacy in humans. The FDA Center for Drug Evaluation and Research (CDER) is the chief regulator for drugs and medical devices seeking approval for use in the United States. Before the CDER starts drug assessment, drug organizations should perform a drug's preclinical and clinical examinations and archive the outcomes portraying the security and viability of the medication. The outcomes are then delivered to CDER which forms groups of individuals that comprise experienced people from different foundations, including specialists, scientific experts, pharmacologists, and different researchers who survey the submitted report. The whole process takes around 10 years for a new entity to enter into the market (Jin, 2014; Gieringer, 1985; Van Norman, 2016a,b).

5.1.2.1 Drug development process

The new drug development process consists of preclinical and clinical phases. It begins from investigational new drug (IND) which is characterized under 21 CFR 312.3b as another medication or a natural compound that is utilized in clinical examination. After doing preclinical studies on animal models and assuring safety and efficacy of drug for human use, IND application is submitted to the FDA for conducting clinical trials. When IND has been affirmed, different periods of clinical preliminaries start which for the most part take around 1—3 years to finish keeping in view the security of the volunteers engaged with the investigation (Holbein, 2009). After conclusion of Phase III clinical studies, the applicant files new drug application (NDA) to the FDA for further processing. NDA acts as a medium by which the drug applicants officially suggest FDA to affirm the new medication available to be purchased and advertising after Phase IIIA preliminaries (Kashyap et al., 2018; Prajapati et al., 2014). The advisory committee assesses the reports put together by the support and gives their assent after suggestion from its individuals (Sweet et al., 2011). If the FDA approves the NDA then additional postmarketing studies need to be performed. Periodic safety update report (PSUR)/ periodic benefit—risk evaluation report are documents that are periodically submitted to the regulatory bodies by the pharmacovigilance team to provide a risk—benefit assessment of the authorized medicinal drug. The aim of PSUR is to report new and emerging safety information. For sales and marketing of generic drugs, "Abbreviated New Drug Application (ANDA)" is submitted to the FDA. After the endorsement of ANDA, the candidate can fabricate and advertise the generic drugs for protected, successful, and minimal effort option of the pioneer drug. The generic drugs are termed as "Abbreviated" as they do not require to include preclinical and clinical data subsequent to providing in vivo—in vitro correlation with the reference medication to exhibit its safety and efficacy. The entire cycle includes time-frame between 8 and 12 years (Sweet et al., 2011).

5.1.2.2 Investigational new drug application

After preclinical studies, if the new drug is found to be safe in animals the sponsor can submit IND application to the FDA to begin clinical trials in humans. Before submission, the sponsor should have all preclinical data and relevant information which is crucial to confirm that the said drug will not cause any harm or risks to patients when intended preliminary clinical trials. The IND application is submitted by the firm or the Institution (Van Norman, 2016a,b; Rawat and Gupta, 2011; US Food and Drug Administration, 2021).

IND application is categorized into three types:

1. *Investigator IND*: Investigator IND is put forward by the doctor who has done research on an unapproved drug or for another indication/use of an already approved drug. He is exclusively answerable for commencement and conduction of examination work.
2. *Emergency Use IND*: The need of this application may happen in a crisis condition when there is no ideal opportunity for accommodation of an IND. In quite a specific case, the FDA can allow the shipment of the test drug ahead of time of the IND accommodation. It is required when the planned subject neglects to meet the standards of a current investigation convention, or if an affirmed study convention does not exist. In such case, the typical strategy is to cooperate with the maker and to know whether the medication or biological product can be accessible at the time of crisis under the organization's IND (CFR Title 21 Part 312).
3. *Treatment IND*: This particular application is for those experimental drugs that have shown promising results in clinical investigation for curing serious or life-threatening diseases. However, the clinical trials are started only after the FDA review process.

Furthermore, IND applications are classified as commercial IND and research IND based on their purpose. Commercial IND is provided by the sponsor to commercialize its drug product by applying for MA. In another case, FDA can also name an IND application as commercial in case the applicant wishes that his new drug product is to be commercialized in future. Whereas a research IND (also known as noncommercial IND) is submitted when the applicant (either individual investigator, academic institution, or nonprofit entity) does not plan to commercialize its new drug product. These types of INDs are meant mainly for research purpose and are approved quickly compared with commercial IND and in most cases also publish its results in reputed journals (Van Norman, 2016a,b; Rawat and Gupta, 2011).

CDER's Pre-IND counsel program assists on the following issues to the applicant (Rawat and Gupta, 2011):

1. Gathering information on science, assembling, and control of the IND;
2. The plan for preclinical investigations to be performed on animals;
3. Designing of the clinical examinations convention to be performed on human volunteers for leading the clinical preliminaries.

Once the sponsor has submitted the IND, he has to wait for at least 30 days before starting the clinical trials. During this period, the FDA can review the submitted IND application to assure safety of the research subjects. The whole process of IND application is given as a flow chart in Fig. 5.2.

5.1.2.2.1 Contents of investigational new drug

There are three main areas that are included in an IND application:

- *Animal pharmacology and toxicology studies*: These studies provide safety information about the preclinical studies done on animals and these studies provide assessment about the drug product whether or not it is safe to be tested on human beings.
- *Manufacturing information*: This section talks about the product composition, details of the manufacturer, stability data, and various in-process quality controls used in production of the drug product.
- *Clinical protocol and investigator information*: This section gives details about the study protocol and informed consent of the research subjects involved in the study. Institutional Review Board (IRB) reviews the study protocol and lay down regulatory guidelines that are to be followed strictly by the manufacturer.

5.1.2.3 New drug application

The NDA application is the medium by which drug applicants officially request that the FDA may commend a new drug for sales and marketing in the United States. NDA application speaks the complete description of the drug (Kashyap et al., 2013). Its main aim is to confirm that the new drug is quite safe and efficacious for its proposed use in the study population. The drug applicant or sponsor should have all the information related to the drug starting from preclinical animal studies data to Phase 3 clinical trial data (US Food and Drug Administration, 2021). NDA is submitted to the FDA in application form number 356h, which contains all the basic identification information. The gathered information for nonclinical pharmacology and toxicological discoveries that incorporates different studies, for example, pharmacological studies, acute toxicity studies, multidose toxicity studies, mutagenicity, and reproductive studies should

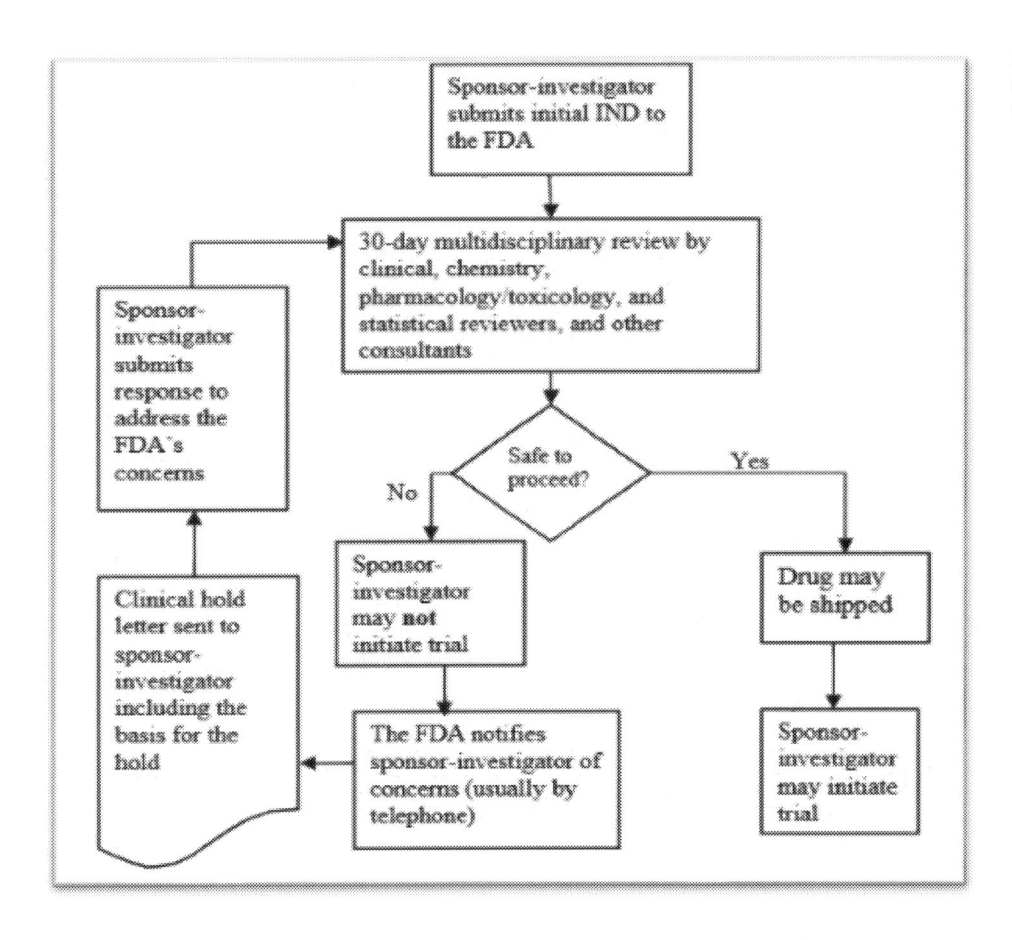

FIGURE 5.2 Investigational new drug process for drug approval in the United States.

be submitted along with the application. The summary of clinical information, including insights concerning clinical preliminaries and antagonistic medication occasions ought to be similarly provided (Gupta et al., 2013).

The submission of NDA is done using three types of applications that are explained below:

Archival copy: Archival copy is used as a reference copy, which is followed by the FDA reviewers and it consists of all the information in the application. It also has information that is not provided in other applications.

Review copy: It comprises the NDA's technical section along with the cover letter, form FDA-365h, NDA index, labeling section, and application summary.

Field copy: This kind of application is needed by the FDA inspectors when they are inspecting and approving pre-approval facilities.

5.1.2.3.1 Food and Drug Administration review

After the submission of an NDA, the FDA reviews whether it is thorough in all aspects. If the NDA is incomplete with respect to all necessary documents, the team reviewing the application can reject to file the NDA (Kashyap et al., 2013). If the FDA finds it complete in all aspects, the review team takes 6—10 months to decide regarding approval of the drug. The process includes FDA approval (Fig. 5.3) (Gupta et al., 2013).

5.1.2.3.2 Food and Drug Administration approval

After reviewing NDA, once the FDA draws conclusion after seeing drug's safety and efficacy data for its prescribed use, the applicant needs to draft and refine the prescribed information. This is referred to as "labeling." "Labeling accurately and objectively describes the basis for approval and how best to use the drug" (Food and Drug administration, 2015).

Before marketing and approval of the drug, all issues and queries must be fixed. At this stage, the applicant or developer can take a decision whether or not to continue further development (Sweet et al., 2011; Kashyap et al., 2013).

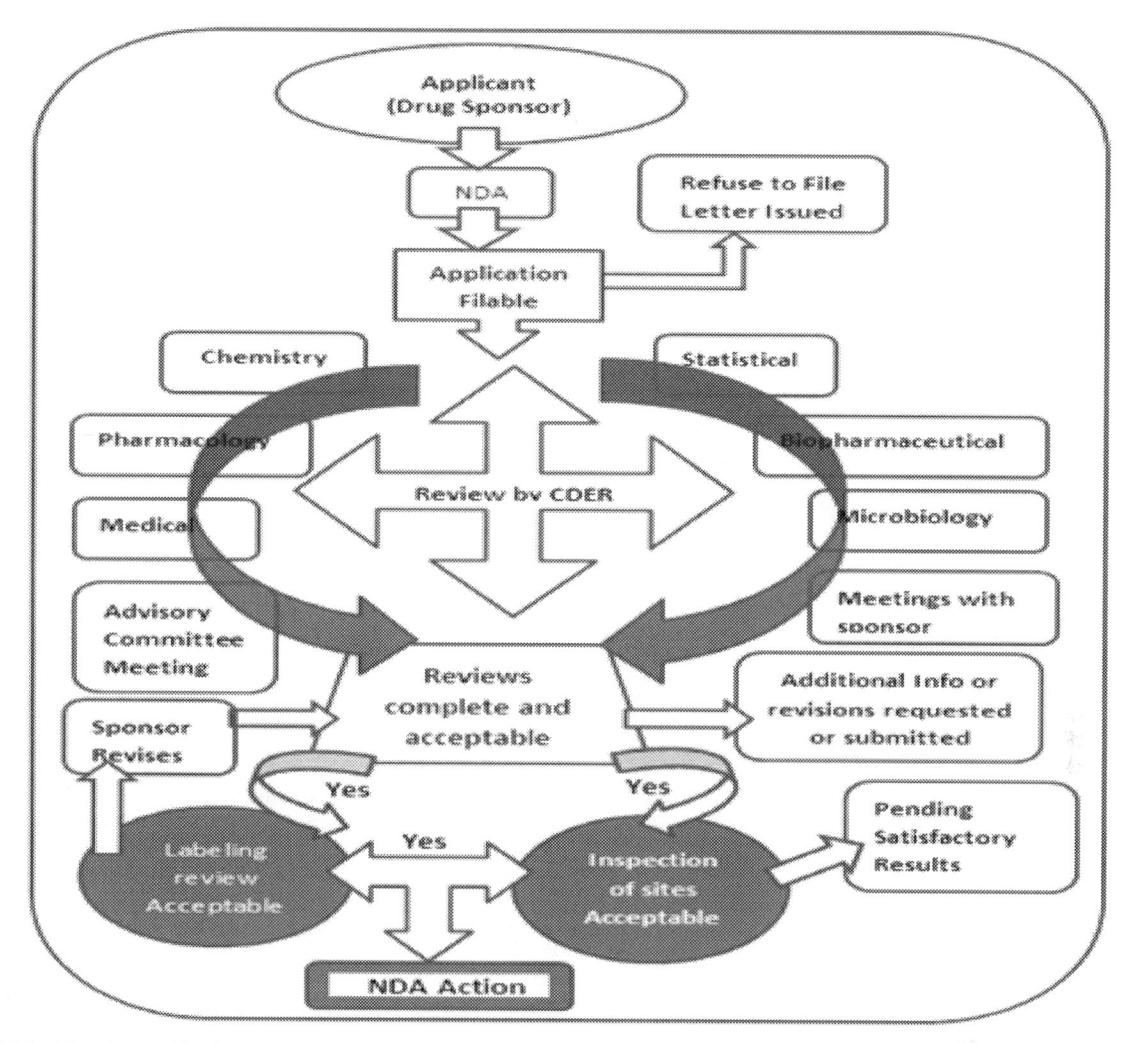

FIGURE 5.3   New drug application process for approval in the United States.

5.1.2.4   Abbreviated new drug application

Abbreviated new drug application (ANDA) consists of data which has been submitted to the FDA for review process and potential approval for the generic drug product (Informa, 2018). Once the ANDA has been approved, the sponsor can manufacture or market the generic drug product in order to deliver a safe, effective, and low-cost substitute to the branded drug to which it is being referred. *Such generic drug applications are called "abbreviated" since there is no requirement to incorporate preclinical and clinical data for establishing safety and effectiveness of drug* (US Food and Drug Administration, *New Drug Application, 2021*) But the manufacturers producing generic drugs should prove that the said generic product is having bioequivalence similar to the branded product available in the market (Fig. 5.4).

5.1.3   Drug approval in Europe and United Kingdom

In the United Kingdom, regulation of drugs, medical devices, and products is governed by the Medicines and Healthcare Products Regulatory Agency (MHRA). The drugs that are intended to be marketed in the United Kingdom will require taking a license from the UK drug regulatory agency, MHRA, on the basis of results of clinical trials, which have been performed on thousands of people. Based on the safety data, permission for the marketing of the drug in the United Kingdom is granted (IPA Pharma Times, 2018).

The European Medicines Regulatory System consists of 50 regulatory bodies from 31 European economic area countries (28 EU Member States plus Iceland, Liechtenstein, and Norway), the European Commission (EC), and the European Medicines Agency (EMA). All these regulatory authorities meet up and share their mastery in the evaluation

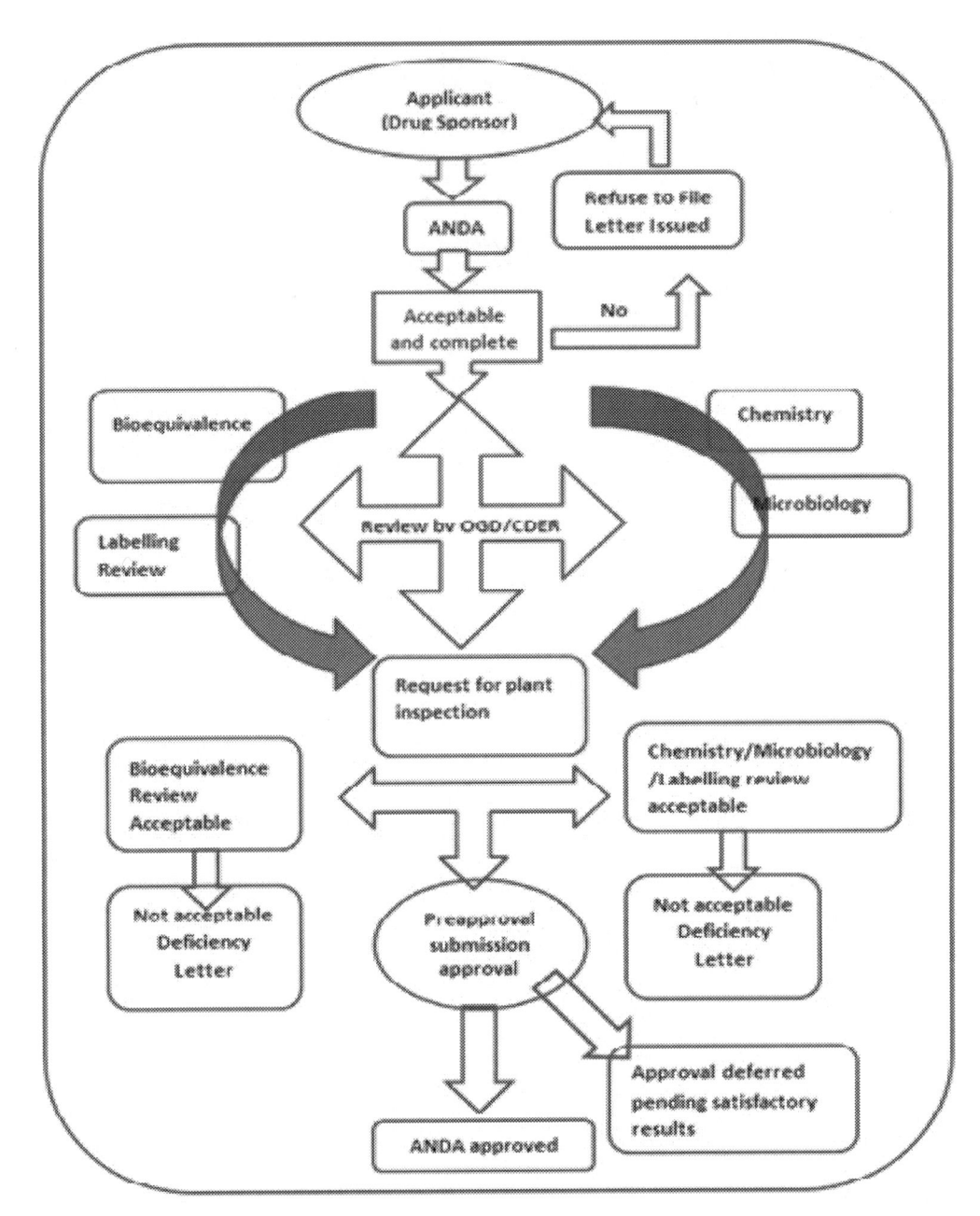

FIGURE 5.4 ANDA process of drug approval in the United States.

of new medicines and their security profile. There are two regulatory steps in the drug approval process in Europe before a drug enters the market. These steps include clinical trial application (CTA) and MA application (Kanti et al., 2019). CTA is submitted to the regulatory bodies in Europe for taking clinical preliminary approval, which is then looked into by the Research Ethics Committee. MA application is submitted together by a drug manufacturer looking for authorization to bring a medicinal product (for instance, another medication or generic drugs) into the European market (Kanti et al., 2019; Kramer et al., 2012). *The major difference between these applications is that the Clinical Trial Applications are approved at the Member State level, whereas marketing authorization applications are approved at both the Member State level and centralized level* (Ghalamkarpour, 2009; European Medicine Agency, 2018; Van Norman, 2016a,b).

The marketing license can be obtained in the United Kingdom by different procedures that are quite similar to the E.U. procedures. They are discussed in the following sections.

5.1.3.1 Centralized procedure

In this procedure, marketing of a new drug is done based on a single evaluation, which is applicable across the Europe, and its marketing approval is effective throughout the EU. The sponsor needs to apply for a single authorization to the EMA which is then evaluated by the *Committee for Medicinal Products for Human Use (CHMP)* or *Committee for Medicinal Products for Veterinary Use (CVMP)* to recommend EC whether or not to grant a MA (Ghalamkarpour, 2009).

The whole procedure for evaluation takes around 210 days, which can be extended further if required. Within 15 days, EMA has to send its recommendation to the EC to initiate the decision-making phase. Once the license is issued by the EC, the centralized marketing approval is effective throughout all EU Member States. In the next 15 days, a draft implementing decision is conveyed by the EC to the Standing Committee on *Medicinal Products for Human Use*, permitting for its analysis by the EU countries. The comments must be reverted back in 15 days. *Once the committee approves, the draft decision is adopted via an empowerment procedure. The adoption of the decision should take place within 67 days of the opinion of the EMA. The Commission's Secretariat-General then notifies the decision to the marketing authorization holder. The decision is subsequently published in the Community Register* (Kashyap et al., 2013). The whole centralized procedure is described in a flow chart form in Fig. 5.5.

MAs in the European Union are primarily valid for a period of five years. For further renewal, applications are submitted to the EMA to extend for a period of six months before the expiry of the five-year period (European Medicines Agency, 2018; Chakraborty, 2019). The adoption of the centralized procedure is necessary in case of innovative new drugs, which include drugs for the treatment of rare diseases. It is compulsory for treatment of cancer, HIV/AIDS, and medicines obtained from biotechnology processes, such as genetic engineering.

5.1.3.2 Mutual recognition procedure

The mutual recognition procedure should be followed if the new drug is already given the MA for one Member State and when the drug applicant desires to get MA for the same drug product in other Member States. The Member State that has been previously given MA for the drug product is termed as the *Reference Member State (RMS)*. In order to obtain MA in another state, the sponsor or applicant must submit an identical dossier as RMS in the concerned Member State if they want to market their product (Chakraborty, 2019; Vijay, 2014). The complete procedure is described in a flow chart form in Fig. 5.6. The RMS submits the product evaluation to other Member State/s, which are called as *Concerned Member States (CMS). The CMS is requested to jointly recognize the MA of the RMS. In case, the drug applicant is successful to obtain MA, the CMS will then issue a MA for that product permitting the marketing of that*

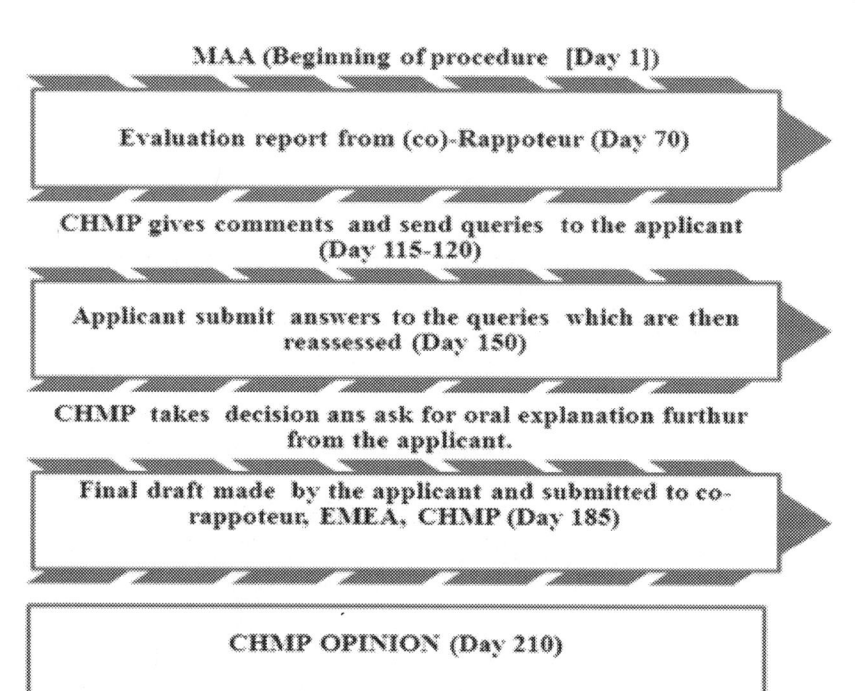

MAA (Beginning of procedure [Day 1])

Evaluation report from (co)-Rappoteur (Day 70)

CHMP gives comments and send queries to the applicant (Day 115-120)

Applicant submit answers to the queries which are then reassessed (Day 150)

CHMP takes decision ans ask for oral explanation furthur from the applicant.

Final draft made by the applicant and submitted to co-rappoteur, EMEA, CHMP (Day 185)

CHMP OPINION (Day 210)

FIGURE 5.5 Flow chart for a centralized procedure.

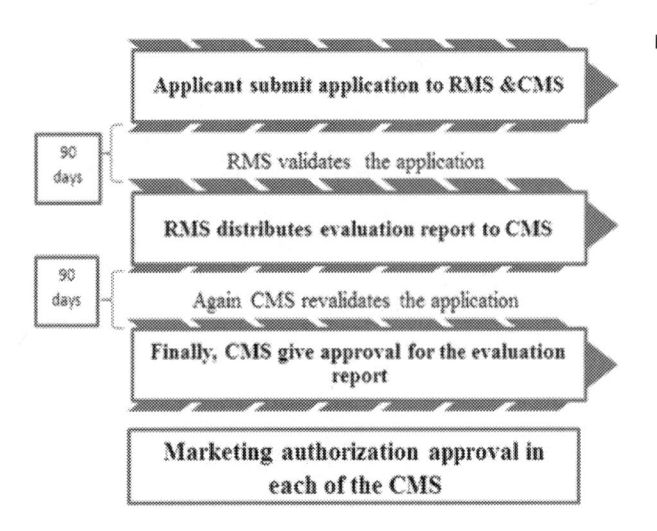

FIGURE 5.6 Flow chart for mutual recognition procedure.

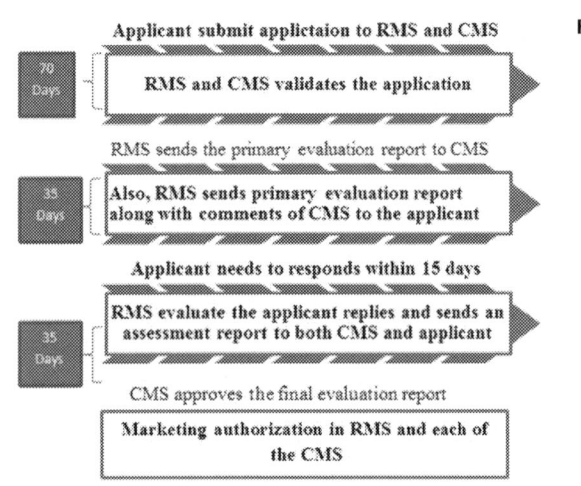

FIGURE 5.7 Flow chart for decentralized procedure.

product in their country. This mutual recognition process takes around 390 days' time (European Medicine Agency, 2018). The whole mutual recognition procedure is described in a flow chart form in Fig. 5.6.

5.1.3.3 Nationalized/centralized procedure

In the nationalized/centralized procedure of drug approval in European states, MA is obtained for single member state only and the drug sponsor or the company submits MA application in the concerned state only. Under this process, new active drug substances that do not come under the centralized procedure can get MA by this procedure. The time limit for the nationalized process is 210 days (Chakraborty, 2019).

5.1.3.4 Decentralized procedure

In the decentralized process, the manufacturing company or sponsor can simultaneously apply for product authorization in the RMS and the CMS for new drugs which are yet to be approved in any E.U. country and principally does not lie within the centralized procedure's essential drugs list. On the basis of the evaluation done by RMS, CMS may raise queries. In the decentralized procedure, the MA could be sanctioned as per the decision made by the RMS and CMS. The time taken for the whole procedure is 210 days. The later steps are quite identical to the mutual recognition procedure (European Medicine Agency, 2018). The whole procedure is described in a flow chart form in Fig. 5.7.

Application process: Electronic common technical documentation method (eCTD) is commonly used for submission of the application. If the applicant is not able to submit by eCTD, he can submit through nonelectronic submission process (IPA Pharma Times, 2018; LOC, Approval Of Medical Devices, 2020).

The clinical trials directive has been made available by the EC, which is implemented in the EU for harmonizing laws, regulations, and administration necessities of the member state regarding enactment of Good Clinical Practice (GCP) guidelines for conducting clinical trials on medicinal products for human consumption. In the E.U. countries and countries that follow the E.U. Directives, the equivalent information that is required for a new product application is an effective **IMPD**. In the European Union, before conducting human clinical trials, the sponsor should receive approval to start clinical trials by a submission process called the CTA. IMPD is prepared for obtaining the CTA for Investigational Medicinal Products (IMPs) and it should contain all the information related to the reference products and placebo. It is the main basis which is required for taking approval for initiation of clinical trials by the regulatory authorities in the European Union (Clinical Trials for Medicines: Apply for Authorisation in the UK, 2014; Cordis. europa.eu, 2013).

5.1.4   Investigational medicinal product dossier

Investigational medicinal product dossier (IMPD) consists of scientific documents of the new drug product to evaluate the performance of drug based on clinical trial outcomes. The main objective of IMPD is to set harmonized requirements for the documentation, which have to be submitted throughout the European community. This dossier comprises complete data with regard to quality, manufacture, control of an IMP (including reference product and placebo), and compiled data obtained from preclinical and clinical studies. The data provided should ascertain the drug quality, efficacy, and safety as mentioned by the EMA for its intended use in addition to the administrative documents, samples of finished product or related substances and reagents required for performing analysis of the finished product (DeAngelis et al., 2005).

Despite providing whole information regarding IMP, it is preferable to represent data in dossier in the form of a table along with very brief description focusing on important points. IMPD should not be a huge or bulky document. The IMPD seems to be equivalent to IND application in the United States.

The major goals of the dossiers are:

- To deliver sufficient information regarding safety and efficacy of the drug,
- To ascertain that the advantages of the drug prevail over the side effects,
- To ensure proper labeling of the drug with appropriate package insert, and
- To confirm whether the techniques used in manufacturing of the drug are adequate and in-process quality control is maintained throughout.

The whole process is in compliance with GMP. In the following two cases no documentation is required:

- If the IMP is produced in the European Union and is unmodified and holds MA in the European Union or in an ICH country;
- If the IMP is not produced inside the EU and is unmodified, but still holds the MA in the European Union.

However, when the IMP does not have MA in the European Union or in an ICH country and is not produced inside the EU, additional documents are required:

- One copy of import authorization.
- Manufacturing compliance certificate by the qualified person in the European Union.

5.1.4.1   Types of Investigational Medicinal Products Dossier

The European Union has classified IMPD into two categories, "**full IMPD**" and "**simplified IMPD**" based on the description of the drug product in the CTA or MAA. When a sponsor wants to apply for a CTA, a full IMPD is needed in case there is little or no information available for the IMP previously or in case it is not feasible to cross-refer to data if submitted by some another drug sponsor and/or if there is no previous MA in the community. It comprises the summaries of detailed information relating to quality, manufacture, and control parameters of the IMP in addition to preclinical and clinical data that include animal pharmacology and toxicology studies (Clinical Trials for Medicines: Apply For Authorisation In The UK, 2014). The dossier also contains earlier reports of clinical trials as well as user acceptance with the product and overall risks—benefit evaluation. A simplified IMPD is needed if some data related to quality, safety, and efficacy are available previously as part of the MA or a clinical trial with the competent authority and where the data can be cross referred to other documents (Honorio, 2020).

5.1.4.2 Components of Investigational Medicinal Products Dossier

The IMPD contains the detailed information under various headings that includes Quality (chemistry, manufacturing and controls) data, Non-clinical pharmacology and toxicology data, previous clinical trials and human experience data, overall risk and benefit assessment (IMPD Guidance, 2010; Nugent, et al., 2017). They are discussed in detail below:

1. Quality data

The sponsor or the company needs to provide a short description of data relating to chemical, pharmaceutical, and biological characteristics of the IMP. As per the regulatory directive, sponsors have to provide IMPs for a clinical trial that are manufactured according to the principles of GMP.

For this purpose, the applicant needs to provide the following information:

- If IMP is produced in the European Union and it is not holding MA in European Union then only one copy of the manufacturing authorization is needed along with details about the authorization.
- If IMP is not produced in the EU and also not holding MA in the EU then additional documents are required:
  - Certification by the Qualified Personnel that confirms that the production site works in accordance to GMP,
  - GMP compliance for active biological substance, and
  - Importer's authorization copy.

Wherever appropriate, the transmissible spongiform encephalopathy (TSE) certificate, certificate of investigation, and viral security information need to be submitted which guarantees the stability and nature of the product (IMPD Guidance, 2010).

IMP Quality Data comprises various components that are essential for establishing the quality of an IMP. General information related to the drug substance or API, such as nomenclature, structure should be incorporated along with its detailed physicochemical properties (Nugent et al., 2017; Kumar et al., 2013). It should also contain residential details of the manufacturers and details of the formulation procedure, validation, and process controls. Information regarding quality control of various excipients should also be included along with regulation of important steps and intermediates produced in the production phase. Information related to identification of the drug by various techniques and determination of impurities should also be given. The analytical procedures should be developed and validated as per the specifications. This section should also contain reference standards or materials, container closure system, and stability data. Details about the formulation should be provided that mainly includes the drug product, excipients, formulation preparation, calculation of overages, and the physicochemical and biological properties.

2. Nonclinical pharmacology and toxicology data

The applicant needs to submit a short description of animal pharmacology and toxicology studies, which have been done earlier for any IMP to be utilized in the clinical trials. In case of absence of such data, proper justification is required. The sponsor also needs to send a list of proper references along with it. These incorporate different pharmacodynamic, pharmacokinetic, and toxicological investigations (Fig. 5.8).

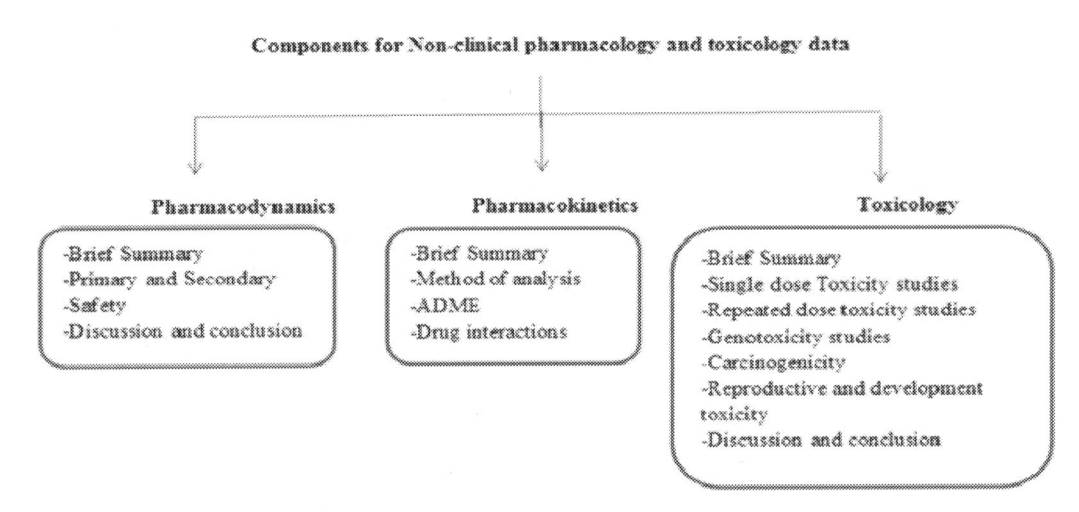

FIGURE 5.8 Components for nonclinical pharmacology and toxicology data.

It is always preferred to represent data in the form of a table with brief description highlighting the salient points. These summaries permit evaluation of the relevance of the study and if the clinical trials protocols are followed precisely throughout the study. All Good Laboratory Practice guidelines must be met (IMPD Guidance, 2010). If any deviations occur from the laid guidelines, then proper justification from the sponsor is required. The test material to be used for toxicity studies must be in accordance and analyzed with respect to qualitative and quantitative impurity profiles. The test compound is prepared using appropriate controls (IMPD Guidance, 2010).

3. Previous clinical trial data

In this section, previous clinical trial data of the IMP is summarized. The clinical trials must be conducted as per the principles of GCP (Fig. 5.9). The same can be ascertained by the drug sponsor in a declaration of the GCP status (Nugent et al., 2017).

4. Overall risk and benefit assessment

This section is very important as it represents compiled summary, which co-relates between nonclinical and clinical data with the likely side effects and benefits for the mentioned clinical trial. If the clinical study is terminated prematurely, proper justification must be provided. Moreover, the assessment of risks and potential benefits done on minors or disabled adults must be properly documented. The major aim of pharmacological and toxicological studies is to determine the serious side effects of the new medicinal product. The sponsor can utilize the related pharmacology, toxicology, and kinetic results to identify likely risks to humans. After integrating the available data and analyzing it, possible mechanisms of drug action should be described; depending on the time of exposure to achieve the pharmacological response. Wherever appropriate, safety margins need to be expressed in terms of AUC and C_{max} data in place of initial rather than in terms of the initial dose. The clinical significance of results obtained animal studies and clinical trials along with prescribed suggestions for examining of beneficial and harmful side effects are also addressed (Nugent et al., 2017).

Referring to the IB

- The sponsor or applicant can either submit a separate IMPD or he can refer to IB for various preclinical and clinical sections of IMPD. In second situation, summarized preclinical and clinical data in tabular form should be provided so that the evaluators can decide regarding significant side effects of the IMP and its safe usage (Clinical Trials for Medicines: Apply For Authorisation In The UK, 2014).
- If some expert examinations are required for some preclinical or clinical data, then the applicant has to provide the preclinical and clinical data as part of the IMPD (Cordis.europa.eu, 2013; DeAngelis et al., 2005).

Referring to the SmPC (summary of product characteristics),

- The applicant can refer to SmPC for IMPD if the new drug product IMP has got a MA in any one of the Member States or in any of the ICH country. Following conditions should be followed:

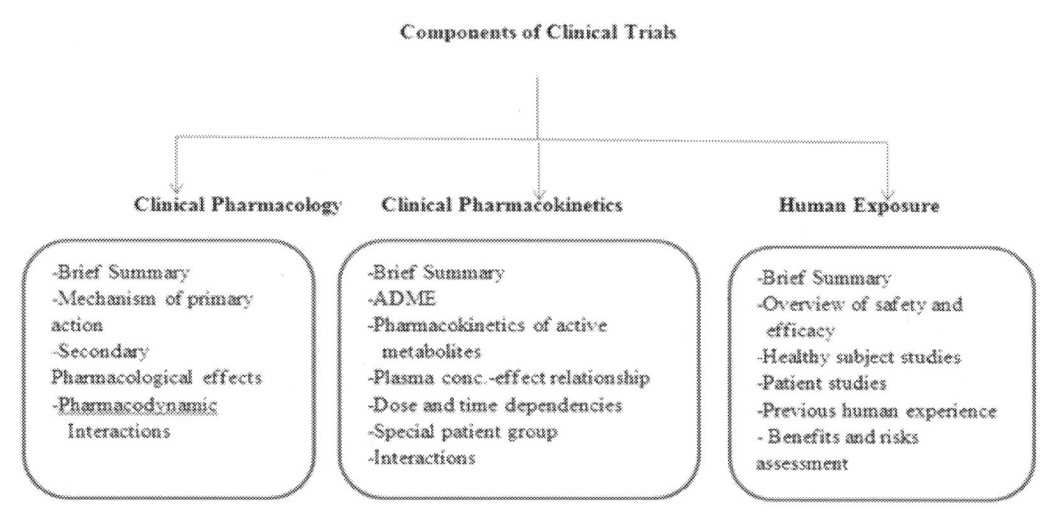

FIGURE 5.9 Various components of clinical trials.

* The IMPD has been presented before by the same drug sponsor or some other applicant and monitored by regulatory authority. In such cases, applicants can cross-refer to the previous submission.
* If IMPD is submitted by other sponsor, an authorization letter from that sponsor is required by regulatory agency to cross-refer to that data. The detailed requisites are given below.

IMPD in case of placebo: In case the drug product is a placebo containing no drug, the following requirements should be met:

* All data related to IMP along with chemical and pharmaceutical quality documentation regarding IMP clinical trials are submitted. In this case there is no requirement to submit animal and human trials data.
* If the placebo is having the same composition as that of the IMP and made by the same company and it is not sterile, then no quality data, nonclinical, or clinical data are required.
* If IMP is a placebo and presented previously in the CTA in the related member state, then no quality, nonclinical, and clinical data need to be produced.

IMPD in case of marketed products:

* The sponsor or the applicant can provide the latest version of the SmPC in form of IMPD if the IMP has got the MA in any of the Member State in the European Union and is utilized in similar form, for the similar indications.
* In case the drug sponsor is the MA holder and has submitted an application to vary the SmPC, that are not authorized, the type of the variation and its reason must be specified in the cover letter.
* If the IMP which is going to be used in the clinical trial has got a MA in the concerned Member State (CMS) but the procedure permits that any brand of the IMP with a MA in that member state may be given to the trial subjects.

5.1.4.3 Substantial modifications and amendments

The European Medicines Agency (EMA) gives the detailed guidance for notification to the competent authorities relating to the changes in the IMP's Product Specification File as the development of the product proceeds (Clinical Trials for Medicines: Apply For Authorisation In The UK, 2014).

In this particular guidance, the EMEA provides various cases for changes to IMP quality data which are observed as *substantial* but they still have a profound effect on one or more of the below mentioned criteria (Fig. 5.10).

5.1.5 Drug approval process in Australia

In Australia, Therapeutic Goods Administration (TGA) is the drug monitoring agency for regulating production, import, and sale of drugs and medical devices and comes under Australian Government Department of Health and Ageing

FIGURE 5.10 List of substantial changes.

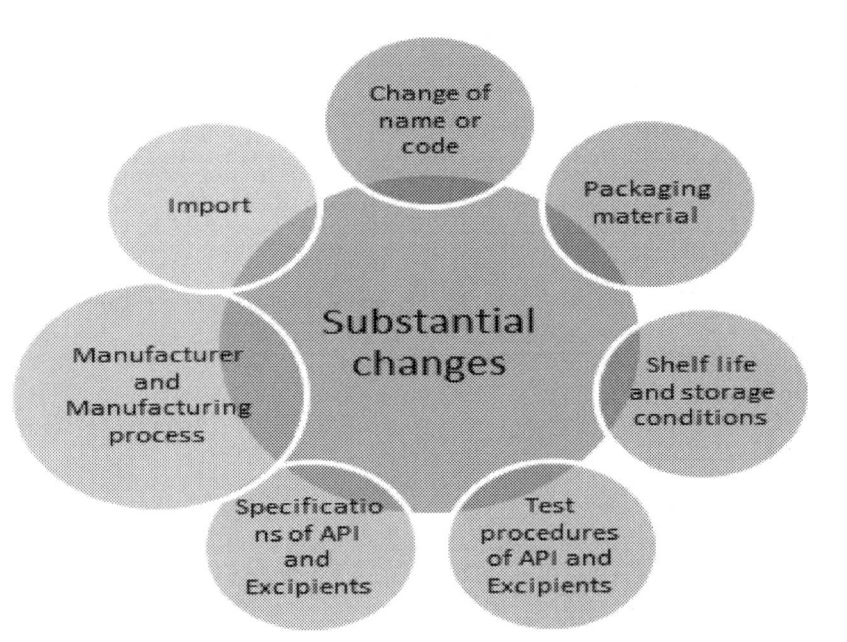

(Therapeutic Goods Administration, 2017). *The regulation of drugs by TGA is done by three steps premarket assessment, postmarket monitoring and enforcement of standards and licensing of Australian manufacturers and verifying overseas manufacturers compliance with the same standards as their Australian counterparts (Therapeutic Goods Administration, 2017).*

A prescription medicine comes under the category of registered medicines and evaluated by TGA for safety, quality, and effectiveness. There are basically three categories of applications that are submitted to the TGA for therapeutic goods registration (Therapeutic Goods Administration, 2017). *Category 1 application*: In this category applications are provided for new medicines, new dosage forms, new strengths, and new generics. Also, if there are more than one drug indications or some changes in drug product information it is included under Category 1 application.

Category 2 application: These types of applications are used to register a prescription medicine with the same formulation, dosage, and indications as in two acceptable countries and for which two independent evaluation reports are there (Therapeutic Goods Administration, 2017).

Category 3 application: Such applications are submitted if any kind of change has been made to quality information of registered medicines provided or medicines included in ARTG which may or may not render medicines separate and distinct (separate registration is needed). In this category, the application does not require any clinical, preclinical, or bioequivalence data (Therapeutic Goods Administration, 2017).

5.1.5.1 New drug approval process

The new drug approval process is divided into several stages. They are discussed in the following sections.

5.1.5.1.1 Presubmission

The presubmission process starts with the filling of presubmission planning form (PPF). Supporting data is also provided which contains scope, scale, and the complexity of the proposed dossier Therapeutic Goods Administration (TGA) (Therapeutic Goods Administration, Market authorization, 2014).

5.1.5.1.2 Submission

After presubmission, full submission is required which comprises the following key elements (Therapeutic Goods Administration, Prescription Medicines Registration Process, 2013).

1. Expected date by which complete dossier is submitted must be confirmed.
2. The fixed application fees should be paid along with application.
3. Plan of work and its administration details.
4. Evaluation of the application form with regard to TGA regulatory requirement.
5. Notification letter is issued which also includes notice of evaluation and fee payable, if applicable.

5.1.5.1.3 First-round assessment

In this stage, the data presented in the dossier is examined by the evaluators. After evaluation, consolidated section 31 request is sent from all evaluation areas by TGA to the applicant by the date as specified in the planning letter (Therapeutic Goods Administration, *Phase 3: First Round Assessment*, 2020).

5.1.5.1.4 Consolidated section 31 request response

This section allows the applicant time to consider the TGA's consolidated section 31 *request for information or documents, and make a response and revert it back to the TGA* (Therapeutic Goods Administration, *Phase 4: Consolidated Section 31 Request Response*, 2020).

5.1.5.1.5 Second-round assessment

The evaluators will assess the response submitted by the applicant against section 31r *equest (if applicable) and finish the evaluation of the submitted data* (Therapeutic Goods Administration (TGA). 2021. Phase 5: Second Round Assessment, 2020).

5.1.5.1.6 Expert advisory review

The evaluation reports are thoroughly examined by some delegate appointed by TGA. He may ask for independent advice on various queries raised on application. The chief advisory group for prescription medicines is the Advisory Committee on Prescription Medicines (ACPM). Some specific issues are referred to the Pharmaceutical Subcommittee of the ACPM, or to the Advisory Committee on the Safety of Medicines (ACSOM) (Therapeutic Goods Administration, *Phase 6: Expert Advisory Review*, 2020).

5.1.5.1.7 Decision

The TGA delegate will then decide whether the application evaluated should be approved or rejected (Therapeutic Goods Administration, *Phase 7: Decision*, 2020).

5.1.5.1.8 Postdecision

After approval of application, all administrative and regulatory activities are finished. The outstanding payments if remaining are then completed (if applicable) and the ARTG entry is finalized (Therapeutic Goods Administration, *Phase 8, 2020)*.

The whole process of drug approval takes around one-year time. Dossier is compiled according to the European CTD format. According to that format, data are divided into five modules.

5.1.6 Drug approval in Japan

The governing agencies that serve to review and approve drugs in Japan are Pharmaceuticals and Medical Devices Agency (PMDA) and *Ministry of Health, Labour,* and *Welfare (MHLW)* (Smith, Japan Pharma Market Review, 2019). The drug approval procedure starts with submission of IND followed by NDA. In Japan, the regulatory authorities recommend the submission of IND Application in the CTD format (Information on Japanese Regulatory Affairs, 2018). The applicant or sponsor may fix a pre-IND submission meeting with PMDA, before formally sending the application for IND to the PMDA, to safeguard perfect and efficient processing of the IND approval. After submitting the application, PMDA examines it in detail (*Purdie Pascoe, Post Marketing Clinical Follow-up, 2018*) Purdie Pascoe.

This might take a maximum time of 30 days for evaluating initial IND and another 14 days for assessing second and consecutive INDs. The questions raised by PMDA have to be replied by the drug applicant. When the review process by the PMDA is over, the IND application is forwarded to the IRB for further evaluation. IRB takes approximately 1−4 weeks of time to review. When IRB gives a positive response for the submitted IND application, clinical trials can be started. After completion of the clinical trials, the sponsor must submit the NDA to the PMDA (Freyr Global Regulatory Solutions and Services Company, 2017). PMDA then examines the application and discusses various issues in a scheduled meeting with the drug applicant. In case there are major concerns, PMDA arranges a meeting between the external expert and PMDA reviewer. PMDA reviewers then prepare a summary report and discuss it in detail with the applicant in a face-to-face meeting. After the application has been reviewed and evaluated by PMDA, it puts its recommendation for approval to the MHLW. After its examination, the MHLW either grants approval or reject the NDAs. *After getting drug approval from MHLW, it enters into the NHI list for negotiation of the prices. The complete drug review process takes around 12 months, while the priority review takes nine months* (Purdie Pascoe, 2018; Freyr Global Regulatory Solutions and Services Company, 2017).

5.1.7 Approval of new drug in India

The Drugs and Cosmetic Act 1940 and Rules 1945 were approved by the Indian parliament to monitor the import, manufacture, distribution, and sale of drugs and cosmetics. Schedule Y of Drugs & Cosmetics (D&C) act lay down the rules and specific requirements for the conduction of clinical trials. Amendments in this act were done in the year 2005. Under the D&C Act, the Central Drugs Standard Control Organization (CDSCO) is accountable for drug approval process; conduction of Clinical Trials for new drug; and putting stringent guidelines for manufacture, quality, and sale of all drugs. It also coordinates the actions of State Drug Control Organizations by giving expert guidance with a vision of keeping uniformity in the enactment of the Drugs and Cosmetics Act (*Databases For Research & Education Gale, 2017*). In case any company desires to formulate a new drug in India, it requires to seek approval from the licensing authority of India, that is, Drug Controller General of India (DCGI). The manufacturer needs to apply for grant of permission by filling Form no. 44 and submitting the required data which includes clinical trial protocol, investigator's brochures, and informed consent documents to the licensing authority [India and Industry, I, 2021. *Pharma Industry In India: Pharma Sector Overview, Market Size, Analysis. (India and Industry, Pharma Industry In India: Pharma Sector Overview, Market Size, 2018).* One copy of the application form needs to be submitted to the ethical committee, and commencement of clinical trials is done only after approval by both DCGI and ethical committee (Kem, 2013; CDSCO, 2015). All clinical studies must ensure safety and efficacy of the investigated new drug molecule in the Indian population as per the guidelines laid down in Schedule Y and reports of clinical studies are submitted in the prescribed format (CDSCO, 2015). The whole procedure for drug approval process in India is shown in Fig. 5.11.

Some important highlights are as under:

- There is a provision under Rule—122A of the *Drugs and Cosmetics Act 1940 and Rules 1945 to waive clinical trials in India* when the licensing authority finds that the new drug is of public health interest or permission can be granted to import new drugs based on the clinical trials performed in other countries (Kem, 2013).
- *Under* section 2.4 *(a) of Schedule Y of Drugs and Cosmetics Act 1940 and Rules 1945, the new drug substances that are discovered in India mandatorily require all phases of clinical trials* (Kashyap et al., 2018).
- When the new drug moiety is discovered outside India, the applicant needs to submit the available data from the clinical studies. The licensing authority thus reviews the data and recommends either to repeat clinical trials in India or directly allow the applicant to conduct Phase III clinical studies.
- *The section 2.8 of Schedule Y of Drugs and Cosmetics Act 1940 and Rules 1945* tells about the requirement for the conduction of plasma studies and bioequivalence studies in order to reveal that the statistics obtained in the Indian population are equivalent to the records obtained outside the country and then allow the applicant to conduct Phase III trials marketing. Nundy et al., 2005.

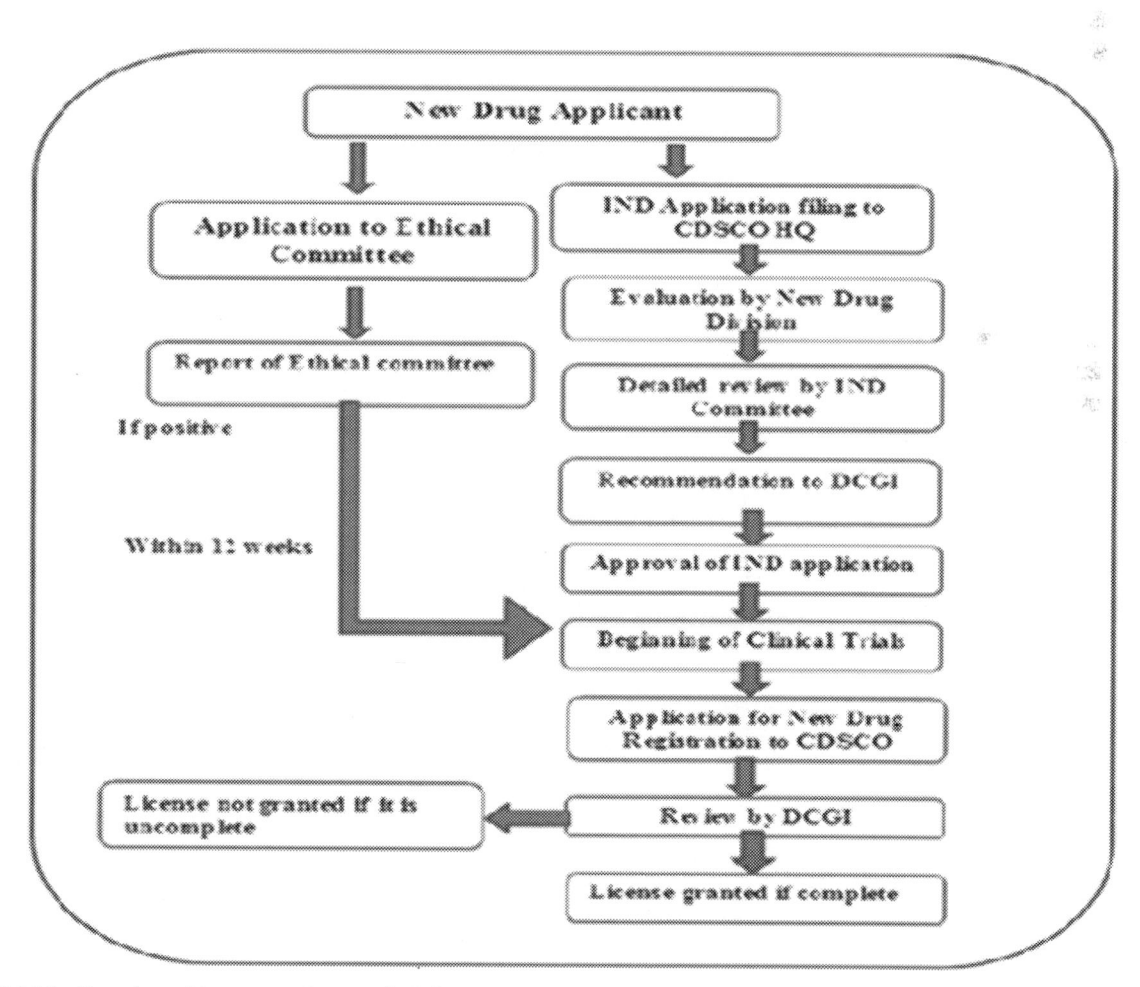

FIGURE 5.11   Flow chart of drug approval process in India.

In short, more precise requirements for clinical trials may vary from person to person, which further depends on the limit by which the licensing authority is worried about the well-being and adequacy of study volunteers. The drug approval procedure in India is a very complex process and it should comply with all the necessary requirements starting from IND, NDA, to ANDA. There are certain differences in the drug approval processes among India, the United States, and Europe. They are listed in Table 5.1 (Van Norman, 2016a,b).

The registration for the new drug is done under Form number 44 along with detailed preclinical and clinical testing data. Besides providing safety and efficacy data of the drug, the data regarding marketing status in other countries is also required (Suresh et al., 2021, CDSCO, 2015 a,b). *The necessary details such as prescriptions, samples and testing protocols, product monograph, labels, and packaging details also needs to be submitted* (Sawant et al., 2018). The NDA is thoroughly examined for approximately 12−18 months. Once the NDA is approved, the company is permitted to do sales and marketing of the new drug product. Post marketing surveillance is to monitor long-term side effects (Prajapati et al., 2014). The main differences in drug registration process among the United States, the European Union, India, Japan, and the United Kingdom are summarized in Table 5.1.

TABLE 5.1 Principal differences in registration processes for new drugs among the United States, European Union, India, Japan, and the United Kingdom (Prajapati et al., 2014; Sawant et al., 2018; Ghooi, 2010).

Requirements	United States	European Union	India	Japan	United Kingdom
Approving body	USFDA	Three bodies • EMEA • CHMP • NHA	DCGI	• PMDA • MHLW	MHRA
Application	NDA/ANDA	MAA	MAA	NDA	MAA
Approval timeline	∼ 18 months	∼12 months	12−18 months	∼12 months	390 days
Presentation	eCTD and paper	eCTD	Paper	Paper	eCTD
Registration process	Single registration process	Multiple registration process: • Centralized procedure • Decentralized procedure • Mutual recognition procedure • Nationalized procedure	Single registration process	Single registration process	Single registration process
TSE/BSE study data	Not required	Required	Required	Not required	Required
Braille code	Not required for labeling	Required for labeling	Not required for labeling	Required for labeling	Required for labeling
Postapproval changes	• Minor • Moderate • Major	• Type IA variation • Type IB variation • Type II variation	• Major quality changes • Moderate quality changes	• Partial change application • Minor change Notification • Low or nonapproved matters	• Major changes • Moderate changes • Minor changes

ANDA, Abbreviated new drug application; *BSE*, Bovine Spongiform Encephalopathy; *EMEA*, Europe, Middle East, and Africa; *MAA*, Marketing Authorisation Application; *NHA*, National Healthcareer Association; *CHMP*, Committee for Medicinal Products for Human Use; *DCGI*, Drug Controller General of India; *eCTD*, electronic common technical document; *MHLW*, Ministry of Health, Labour, and Welfare; *MHRA*, Medicines and Healthcare Products Regulatory Agency; *NDA*, new drug application; *PMDA*, Pharmaceuticals and Medical Devices Agency; *TSE*, transmissible spongiform encephalopathy; *USFDA*, U.S. Food and Drug Administration.

5.2 Common technical document

Common technical document (CTD) is an internationally accepted "well-structured common format" and consists of various specifications for preparing a dossier that is required for the registration of new drugs and medical devices in the Europe, Japan, and the United States (Molzon, 2003). *It was prepared by the joint effort of European Medicines Agency (EMA, Europe), the Food and Drug Administration (FDA, United States), and the Ministry of Health, Labour and Welfare (Japan). The CTD is maintained by the International Conference on Harmonisation of Technical Requirements for Registration of Pharmaceuticals for Human Use (ICH)* [Freyr—Global Regulatory Solutions and Services Company, 2021 (*IND And NDA Regulatory Submissions In Japan- Decoded, 2016*).

In July 2003, the CTD has become the common and mandatory document for registration of NDAs in the Europe, the United States, and Japan (Jordan, 2014). Later this format was accepted by many other countries that include Australia, Canada, and Switzerland. In India, CDSCO followed CTD guidelines for meeting technical requirements for registration of biological products in the year 2009.

The primary objective of ICH to prepare CTD is to evade repetitive preclinical and clinical data and to develop a mutual understanding of the technical necessities to back the registration procedure in all regions. All such objectives are attained by following harmonized guidelines, which could benefit preclinical and clinical studies and avoids unnecessary delays in drug development process across the world with simultaneously following quality, safety, and efficacy and also the regulatory guidelines to safeguard public health (Molzon, 2003; Jordan, 2014).

eCTD has eliminated the need for formatting and reformatting of the submissions according to the different guidelines of different regulatory bodies of various nations in which the applicant wishes to gain market authorization for his drug. It has improved the application submission proficiencies and the reviewer efficacy. eCTD is in the process of implementation in Singapore, Republic of South Korea, China, Chinese Taipei, Brazil. The paper submission in CTD is replaced by eCTD by electronic submission. The file formats used in eCTD are in the form of PDF and XML. In case of graphs and figures, other formats such as JPEG, PNG, and GIF are used (Inpharma Weekly, 2003; Freyr - Global Regulatory Solutions and Services Company, 2015).

The CTD is organized into five modules each containing specific data. Module 1 is region specific and Modules 2, 3, 4, and 5 are intended to be common for all regions (Jordan, 2014).

1. *Administrative and prescribing information*
2. *Overview and summary of modules 3−5*
3. *Quality (pharmaceutical documentation)*
4. *Preclinical (Pharmacology/Toxicology)*
5. *Clinical-efficacy and safety (Clinical Trials).*

5.2.1 Module 1: general information

This module is region specific, not harmonized, and different for each country. It consists of administrative and prescribing data about the company and legal documents. It also contains general information on the drug product, summary of testing procedure for quality control along with a complete impurity profile, and regulatory status in other countries (Molzon, 2003).

5.2.2 Module 2: CTD summaries

This module contains overall summaries of quality, nonclinical, and clinical data under various sections (Table 5.2). The quality overall summary is an outline of the data mentioned in Module 3. It summarizes the information on drug substance and excipients and their stability and quality aspects. The nonclinical overview section briefly mentions pharmacological, pharmacokinetic, and toxicological evaluation of the drug. The clinical overview section talks about summary and analysis of the clinical data (Jordan, 2014).

5.2.3 Module 3: quality

This module of CTD provides harmonized structure of quality aspects of the intended drug or medicinal product. It contains general information of the drug, such as chemical structure, general properties, manufacture of drug substance, manufacturing process, control of critical steps, process validation, and quality control tests. It also included information

TABLE 5.2 Description of subsections in common technical document (CTD) summaries (Jordan, 2014).

Module	Content
2.1	CTD table of contents (modules 2–5)
2.2	CTD Introduction
2.3	Quality overall summary
2.4	Nonclinical overview
2.5	Clinical overview
2.6	Nonclinical summaries
2.7	Clinical summaries

Source: Jordan, D., 2014. An overview of the common technical document (CTD) regulatory dossier. Med. Writ., 23(2), pp. 101–105.

related to stability and container closure system (Jordan, 2014; Freyr - Global Regulatory Solutions and Services Company, 2015).

5.2.4 Module 4: nonclinical study reports

This module describes the format and organization of the nonclinical (pharmacotoxicological) data relevant to the application. It includes various study reports of pharmacological, pharmacokinetic, and toxicological studies (Inpharma Weekly, 2003).

5.2.5 Module 5: clinical study reports

This module defines the format and organization of clinical data significant to the application. It includes detailed reports of biopharmaceutical, human pharmacokinetic, and pharmacodynamic studies. It also incorporates reports of safety, efficacy studies, and postmarketing experience (Jordan, 2014).

5.3 Investigator's brochure

The Investigator's Brochure (IB) comprises of clinical and nonclinical data on the investigational product which is relevant to the study of the products on human volunteers. It is a comprehensive document summarizing all the relevant information on the new investigational drug (ICH GCP, Fiebig, 2014). As per the legal framework, the information contained in the IB must be brief, simplified, balanced, and nonpromotional. It is significant to make sure that the investigator easily comprehends the whole document and can produce an informed and unbiased benefit—risk evaluation in relation to the aptness of the trial (Fiebig, 2014).

5.3.1 General considerations

- IB is a vital document that is prepared not only for IND but it is also required to be shown to the clinical investigators and finally presented in front of the IRB.
- It should be given to every clinical investigator and the IRB at each of the clinical sites.
- The IB must be provided in the form of summary containing the nonclinical (safety), clinical, and CMC (quality) data, which is required for the said clinical trial.
- It offers basic data to the investigators and other volunteers who are included in the study about the rationale of the study and also talks about various key features required for compliance of the protocol.
- A well-qualified personnel having good knowledge and experience can take part in the improvement of an IB for clinical trial, but the contents of the IB must be accepted by various disciplines that creates the prescribed data.
- In case it is allowed by the regulatory agencies, a basic product information brochure, package leaflet, or labeling may be an appropriate alternative, provided that it includes current, comprehensive, and detailed information on all aspects of the investigational product that might be of importance to the investigator.
- If a marketed product is being studied for a new use, an IB specific to that new use has to be prepared.

5.3.2   Purpose of an Investigator's Brochure

- It is predominantly written to allow investigators performing clinical studies to evaluate the hazards and profits related to the new drug.
- It provides better and clear information in short, simple, and concise manner.
- It helps in clinical trial management for the given study subjects throughout the clinical trial process.
- *It also provides complete information to the investigators and subjects regarding dose, dosing frequency, dosing interval, methods of administration, and safe monitoring procedures* (Fiebig, 2014).

5.3.3   Aims of an Investigator's Brochure

- To give the principal investigator a clear and better knowledge of the likely risk—benefits which have to be specified in all observations and precautions that are required for performing the clinical trials.
- To provide summaries of the clinical and nonclinical data, which serve as a roadmap and provide guidance to the investigator.
- To provide current up-to-date scientific information on investigational product to the investigator (Robert, 2016).

5.3.4   Revision of an Investigator's Brochure

- It should be reviewed annually and revised or updated in accordance with the sponsor's prescribed procedure, stage of development, and production of the relevant new information.
- The revised version must be included in the IND/NDA annual report for providing evidence during scale-up and postapproval changes.
- *In compliance with GCP guidelines, related new information is very important and after discussion & it has be told to the principal investigators and possibly to the IRBs & Regulatory Authorities (FDA) before it is incorporated in a revised and updated IB* (Trilogy Writing & Consulting GmbH, 2015).
- The sponsor is accountable for warranting that the recent IB must be presented to the investigators, and the investigators are accountable for giving the latest IB to the respective IRBs.

5.3.5   Contents of Investigator's Brochure

The IB must be well distributed into various sections, which includes Table of contents, Summary, Introduction, Physicochemical properties of product, and Nonclinical and clinical studies ([ICH GCP, *INVESTIGATOR'S BROCHURE*; Fiebig, 2014). The summary of IB should not be more than two pages, which highlights the major points relevant to the clinical development of the investigational product. The Introduction section should contain information regarding all active ingredients, rationale, and primary objectives of the work along with prophylactic, therapeutic, or diagnostic indications.

In the next section, a detailed information must be provided for the investigational product substances (which include chemical and/or structural formula) along with a brief summary, including physical, chemical, and pharmaceutical properties of the IMP. Moreover, detailed information regarding formulation should be included along proper justification of all the excipients involved in it. The instructions required for storage and handling of the dosage forms must be included. The section dealing with nonclinical studies focuses on chief outcomes of all relevant nonclinical pharmacology, toxicology, pharmacokinetic, and product metabolism studies and divided further into these subsections. A summary sheet is required in this section that mainly includes the methodology used along with results and discussion. It should also address the relevance of the findings to the investigated therapeutic and the possible unfavorable and unintended effects in humans. The information in the summary sheet shall also include description of the species of animals used, number of animals used in each group, effective dose, therapeutic index, and a detailed study protocol. The comparison among various animal models should be done in terms of blood/tissue levels.

5.3.5.1   Nonclinical pharmacology

It comprises a detailed description of the pharmacological aspects of the investigational product and its significant metabolites studied in various animal models. It must include various studies that could evaluate the pharmacological activity of IMP in terms of efficacy models, receptor binding, and specificity, keeping in view the safety of animal species involved in the study.

5.3.5.2 Pharmacokinetics and product metabolism in animals

This subsection includes summary of the pharmacokinetics of absorption, distribution, metabolism and excretion (ADME) of the Investigational Medicinal Product (IMP) performed in all animal models. It should also mention local and systemic bioavailability of the IMP and its metabolites, and to establish their relationship with pharmacodynamics in animal species.

5.3.5.3 Toxicology

Various toxicological studies should be performed and well documented in IB. They are carried out in various animal species and classified into single-dose toxicity studies, repeated-dose toxicity studies, carcinogenicity studies, reproductive toxicity studies, genotoxicity (mutagenicity) studies, and special studies related to irritancy and sensitization.

The IB should include a section on clinical studies that are performed on human volunteers. These studies include various pharmacokinetics, pharmacodynamics, drug metabolism, dose response safety, efficacy, and other pharmacological activities on humans (ICH GCP, 2021; Thsti.res.in 2021) binding, distribution, elimination, and bioavailability (absolute and relative) studies. For these studies volunteers are divided into *various* subgroups on the basis of gender, age, and diseased condition. Various interactions and effects of food are also studied. A brief description of information needs to be supplied for the product and its metabolites dealing with safety, pharmacodynamics, efficacy, and dose response which are received from previous trials in humans (healthy volunteers and/or patients). All adverse drug reactions observed in clinical trials are summarized along with variations in occurrence of these adverse reactions in different subjects. The IB should also mention countries where the investigational product has been previously marketed or approved. Any significant information arising from the marketed use should be summarized (e.g., formulations, dosages, routes of administration, and adverse product reactions). It should also make remarks on the countries where the investigational product did not receive any approval/registration for marketing or was withdrawn from marketing/registration.

5.3.6 Summary of data and guidance for the investigator

This section should summarize the preclinical and clinical data and also give proper interpretation. All these results help to anticipate the adverse drug effects and other related side effects.

The major objective of this section was to give the investigator a clear understanding of the likely risks and benefits, particular observations, and precautions which are required for a clinical trial. This whole information must be based on the available physical, chemical, pharmaceutical, pharmacological, toxicological, and clinical data on the investigational product. Proper guidelines must be given for recognition and handling of possible overdose and adverse drug reactions.

5.3.7 Regulation of Investigator's Brochure

Section 7 of ICH E6 gives information on the contents of IB and the information it must contain. Regulatory authorities, such as the EMA and national competent authorities, need a recent IB for any medicine being studied. The IB is provided to the regulatory authorities along with the CTA, which is then explored by the administrative specialists to confirm that it is exact, finished, and unprejudiced (Thaker et al., 2019).

If the IND product has got a MA and its pharmacology is largely understood by the medical practitioners, an extensive IB may not be required. In such cases, the Summary of Product Characteristics (SmPC) or a package leaflet or labeling should be utilized in its place as a suitable alternative to an IB (Fiebig, 2014).

5.4 Conclusion

Development of a new drug needs tremendous amount of research work in the field of chemistry, manufacturing, controls, preclinical science, and clinical trials. Drug reviewers in regulatory agencies across the world have the responsibility of assessing whether the submitted data support the safety, efficacy, and quality control of a new drug product in order to safeguard the public health. At present different countries have different regulatory guidelines for approval of a new drug. The regulatory processes in different countries are under a constant state of examination to identify methods of simplifying approval processes (while not compromising) with safety and efficacy. There is a great need to formulate international standards for regulatory requirements so that the information generated from a specific region could be mutually accepted by other regions. This necessity has been recognized by both regulatory authorities and the pharmaceutical industries. As a result, the ICH which consists of the European Community, the United States, and Japan came into existence to examine and make harmonized regulatory guidelines in the form of CTD for sales and marketing registration of pharmaceuticals for human use across the world.

References

CDSCO, 2015a. [online] Available from: <https://cdsco.gov.in/opencms/export/sites/CDSCO_WEB/Pdf-documents/acts_rules/2016DrugsandCosmeticsAct1940Rules1945.pdf> (accessed 17.01.21.).

CDSCO, 2015b. Approved new drugs. [online] Available from: <https://cdsco.gov.in/opencms/opencms/en/Approval_new/Approved-New-Drugs/> (accessed 17.01.21.).

CFR Title 21 Part 312. Investigational New Drug Application. Available from: <https://www.accessdata.fda.gov/scripts/cdrh/cfdocs/cfcfr/CFRSearch.cfm?CFRPart=312&showFR=1> (assessed 17.01.21).

Clinical Trials for Medicines: Apply for Authorisation in the UK, 2014. [online] Available from: <https://www.gov.uk/guidance/clinical-trials-for-medicines-apply-for-authorisation-in-the-uk> (accessed 17.01.21.).

Chakraborty, K., 2019. A new drug approval process in Europe: a review. Int. J. Drug. Regul. Aff. 7 (3), 21–29.

Cordis.europa.eu, 2013. CORDIS. European Commission. [online] Available from: <https://cordis.europa.eu/project/id/602893/reporting> (accessed 17.01.21.).

DeAngelis, C., Drazen, J., Frizelle, F., Haug, C., Hoey, J., Horton, R., et al., 2005. Clinical trial registration. Arch. Dermatol. 141 (1).

Databases For Research & Education Gale, 2017. [online] Available from: <https://www.gale.com/databases> (accessed 17.01.21.).

European Medicine Agency, 2018. [online] Available from: <https://www.ema.europa.eu/en/documents/leaflet/european-regulatory-system-medicines-european-medicines-agency-consistent-approach-medicines_en.pdf> (accessed 17.01.21.).

Fiebig, D., 2014. The Investigator's Brochure: A Multidisciplinary Document. [online] Available from: <https://journal.emwa.org/regulatory-writing-basics/the-investigators-brochure-a-multidisciplinary-document/> (accessed 17.01.21.).

Food and Drug Administration, 2015. [online] Available from: <https://www.fda.gov/home> (accessed 30.12.20.).

Freyr Global Regulatory Solutions and Services Company, 2015. What is eCTD? [online] Available from: <https://www.freyrsolutions.com/what-is-ectd> (accessed 17.01.21.).

Freyr Global Regulatory Solutions and Services Company, 2017. IND and NDA Regulatory Submissions in Japan – Decoded. [online] Available from: <https://www.freyrsolutions.com/blog/ind-nda-regulatory-submissions-japan> (accessed 17.01.21.).

Gelman, R., 2006. International marketing applications according to the ICH CTD format: comparison of structure and document requirements. Qual. Assur. J. 10 (2), 111–120.

Ghalamkarpour, 2009. [online] Available from: <https://www.sgsgroup.fr/~/media/Global/Documents/Technical%20Documents/SGS-Clinical-Marketing-Authorization-EN-09.pdf> (accessed 17.01.21.).

Ghooi, R.B., 2010. Trials and tribulations of clinical research teaching and training. Perspect. Clin. Res. 1, 139–142.

Gieringer, D.H., 1985. The safety and efficacy of new drug approval. Cato J. 5 (1), 177–201. PMID:11616801.

Gupta et al., 2013. [online] Available from: <https://www.globalresearchonline.net/journalcontents/v13-2/004.pdf> (accessed 17.01.21.).

Holbein, M., 2009. Understanding FDA regulatory requirements for investigational new drug applications for sponsor-investigators. J. Investig. Med. 57 (6), 688–694.

Honorio, S., Phases of drug development: good practices in clinical research [Internet]. Available from: <http://www.hstelearning.mit.edu> (cited July 26, 2020).

Informa, 2018. [online] Available from: <https://www.mhsource.com/resource/process.html> (accessed 17.01.21.).

Information on Japanese Regulatory Affairs, 2018. [online] Available from: <https://www.jpma.or.jp/english/parj/pdf/2018.pdf> (accessed 17.01.21.).

Inpharma Weekly, 2003. The United States FDA has published the final requirements for submission of labeling for human prescription drugs and biologics in electronic format rule. &NA;(1418), p. 3.

ICH GCP, 2021. Investigator's Brochure. [online] Available from: <https://ichgcp.net/7-investigators-brochure> (accessed 17.01.21.).

IMPD Guidance, 2010. IMP Dossier IMPD Guidance. [online] Available from: <https://www.imp-dossier.eu/imdp_guidance/> (accessed 17.01.21.).

IND and NDA Regulatory Submissions In Japan- Decoded, 2016. [online] Available from: <https://www.freyrsolutions.com/blog/ind-nda-regulatory-submissions-japan> (accessed 17.01.21.).

India and Industry, Pharma Industry In India: Pharma Sector Overview, Market Size, 2018. [online] Available from: <https://www.ibef.org/industry/pharmaceutical-india.aspx> (accessed 17.01.21.).

IPA Pharma Times, 2018. [online] Available from: <https://ipapharma622693298.files.wordpress.com/2019/02/aug2018.pdf> (accessed 17.01.21.).

Jin, J., 2014. FDA approval of new drugs. JAMA 311 (9), 978.

Jordan, D., 2014. An overview of the common technical document (CTD) regulatory dossier. Med. Writ. 23 (2), 101–105.

Kanti, S.P.Y., Csoka, I, Chandra, A., Shukla, V.K., 2019. Drug approval process in India and Europe. Int. J. Drug. Regul. Aff. 7 (1), 34–40. Available from: https://doi.org/10.22270/ijdra.v7i1.304.

Kashyap, et al., 2013. [online] Available from: <https://ijdra.com/index.php/journal/article/download/107/31> (accessed 17.01.21.).

Kem, 2013. [online] Available from: <https://www.kem.edu/wp-content/uploads/2019/12/Schedule-Yammended-version-CDSCO-Compensation.pdf> (accessed 17.01.21.).

Kashyap, P., Duggal, E., Budhwaar, V., Nanda, D., Badjatya, J., 2018. Drug approval process: a contrastive approach. Int. J. Drug. Regul. Aff. 1 (2), 11–19.

Kramer, D., Xu, S., Kesselheim, A., 2012. Regulation of medical devices in the United States and European Union. N. Engl. J. Med. 366 (9), 848–855.

Kumar, S., Panwar, R., Singh, U., 2013. Regulatory affairs in the pharmacy curriculum. Int. J. Res. Dev. Pharm. Life Sci. 2 (6), 690–698. Available from: https://ijrdpl.com/index.php/ijrdpl/article/view/330 (accessed 17.01.21.).

LOC, Approval of Medical Devices, 2020. Law Library of Congress. [online] Available from: <https://www.loc.gov/law/help/medical-devices/foreign.php> (accessed 17.01.21.).

Molzon, J., 2003. The common technical document: the changing face of the new drug application. Nat. Rev. Drug. Discov. 2 (1), 71–74.

New Drug Application, 2021. [online] Available from: <https://www.fda.gov/drugs/types-applications/new-drug-application-nda> (accessed 17.01.21.).

Nundy S., M.Chir. M., and Gulhati C.M., 2005. A New Colonialism? – Conducting Clinical Trials in India. April 21, 2005 N Engl J Med 2005; 352:1633–1636 https://www.nejm.org/toc/nejm/352/16?query=article_issue_link https://doi.org/10.1056/NEJMp048361.

Nugent, et al., 2017. [online]. Available from: <https://www.researchgate.net/publication/312005138_Preparation_of_a_Preclinical_Dossier_to_Support_an_Investigational_New_Drug_IND_Application_and_First-In-Human_Clinical_Trial> (accessed 17.01.21.).

Prajapati, V., Goswami, R., Makvana, P., Badjatya, J.K., 2014. A review on drug approval process for United States, Europe and India. Int. J. Drug. Regul. Aff. 2 (1), 1–11. Available from: https://doi.org/10.22270/ijdra.v2i1.7.

Purdie Pascoe, 2018. Post Marketing Clinical Follow-Up (PMCF)—Purdie Pascoe. [online] Available from: <https://www.purdiepascoe.com/post-marketing-clinical-followup-pmcf> (accessed 17.01.21.).

Rawat, S.R. Gupta, A., 2011. Regulatory requirements for drug development and approval in United States: a review. 1, 01–06.

Robert, 2016. [online] Available from: <https://od.lk/d/N18xNzgzMjgyNjZf/%28Drugs%20and%20the%20Pharmaceutical%20Sciences%29%20R.%20Berry%20Ira%20Robert%20P.%20Martin%20-%20The%20Pharmaceutical%20Regulatory%20Process-Informa%20Health.pdf> (accessed 17.01.21.).

Sawant, A.M., Mall, D.P., Bhagwat, D.A., 2018. Regulatory requirements and drug approval process in India, Europe and United States. Pharm. Regul. Aff. 7 (2), 1000210.

Smith, Japan Pharma Market Review, 2019. [online] Thepharmaletter.com. Available from: <https://www.thepharmaletter.com/article/japan-pharma-market-review> (accessed 17.01.21.).

Suresh, S., Puranik, S., Patel, P., 2021. An overview of regulatory process for pharmaceutical sector in India. [online]. Available from: <https://www.rroij.com/open-access/an-overview-of-regulatory-process-for-pharmaceutical-sector-in-india.php?aid = 34904> (accessed 17.01.21.).

Sweet, B., Schwemm, A., Parsons, D., 2011. Review of the processes for FDA oversight of drugs, medical devices, and combination products. J. Manag. Care Pharm. 17 (1), 40–50.

Thsti.res.in, 2021. [online] Available from: <https://thsti.res.in/pdf/ICMR_Ethical_Guidelines_2017.pdf> (accessed 17.01.21.).

Thaker, Z., Jethva, K., Bhatt, D., Zaveri, M., Deshpande, S., 2019. Int. J. Pharm. Sci. Res. 10 (2).

Therapeutic Goods Administration, Market authorization, 2014. [online] Available from: <https://www.tga.gov.au/book-page/1-market-authorisation> (accessed 17.01.21.).

Therapeutic Goods Administration, 2017. [online] Available from: <https://www.tga.gov.au/> (accessed 30.12.20.).

Therapeutic Goods Administration (TGA), 2020. Phase 3: first round assessment. [online] Available from: <https://www.tga.gov.au/book-page/phase-3-first-round-assessment> (accessed 17.01.21.).

Therapeutic Goods Administration (TGA), 2020. Phase 4: consolidated section 31 request response. [online] Available from: <https://www.tga.gov.au/book-page/phase-4-consolidated-section-31-request-response> (accessed 17.01.21.).

Therapeutic Goods Administration (TGA), 2020. Phase 5: second round assessment. [online] Available from: <https://www.tga.gov.au/book-page/phase-5-second-round-assessment> (accessed 17.01.21.).

Therapeutic Goods Administration (TGA), 2020. Phase 6: expert advisory review. [online] Available from: <https://www.tga.gov.au/book-page/phase-6-expert-advisory-review> (accessed 17.01.21.).

Therapeutic Goods Administration (TGA), 2020. Phase 7: decision. [online] Available from: <https://www.tga.gov.au/book-page/phase-7-decision> (accessed 17.01.21.).

Therapeutic Goods Administration, Prescription Medicines Registration Process, 2013. [online] Available at: <https://www.tga.gov.au/prescription-medicines-registration-process> (accessed 17.01.21.).

Trilogy Writing & Consulting GmbH, 2015. The Investigator's Brochure—a multidisciplinary document—trilogy writing & consulting GmbH. [online] Available from: <https://www.trilogywriting.com/publications/investigators-brochure-multidisciplinary-document/> (accessed 17.01.21.).

Therapeutic Goods Administration (TGA), 2020. Phase 8: post-decision. [online] Available from: <https://www.tga.gov.au/book-page/phase-8-post-decision> (accessed 17.01.21.).

United States Food and Drug Administration, 2021. Investigational new drug (IND) application. [online] Available from: <https://www.fda.gov/drugs/types-applications/investigational-new-drug-ind-application> (accessed 17.01.21.).

US Food and Drug Administration, 2021. Novel Drug Approvals for 2020. [online] Available from: <https://https://www.fda.gov/drugs/new-drugs-fda-cders-new-molecular-entities-and-new-therapeutic-biological-products/novel-drug-approvals-2020> (accessed 17.01.21.).

Van Norman, G., 2016a. Drugs and devices. JACC Basic Transl. Sci. 1 (5), 399–412.

Van Norman, G., 2016b. Drugs, devices, and the FDA: part 1. JACC Basic Transl. Sci. 1 (3), 170–179.

Vijay, 2014. [online] Available from: <https://www.pharmabiz.com/NewsDetails.aspx?aid=83047&sid=1> (accessed 12.01.21.).

Chapter 6

Regulatory requirements of regulated market

Sandesh Lodha, Hetal Patel, Shrikant Joshi, Gajanan Kalyankar and Ashish Mishra

Maliba Pharmacy College, Uka Tarsadia University, Bardoli, Surat, India

6.1 Introduction

With the fewer restrictions in the trade worldwide, the governments need to ensure the efficacy, safety, and quality of the drugs and their products, and that is why there are regulations in place (Handoo et al., 2012). The pharma market is governed by the United States, the European Union (EU), and Japan. Each of them has a specific regulatory agency for marketing authorization process in their country. In a nutshell, marketing authorization of a product means availing regulatory approval as deemed necessary, by the law of the land, to sell it in a country or a region in the territory. For purposes of clarity, let us take an example of the United States and Europe: (1) "marketing authorization" in the United States denotes the final approval of a new drug applications (NDA), supplemental new drug application (sNDA), or biological licensing authority (BLA), allowing promoting and selling of such product for interstate trade in the United States and (2) whereas in Europe, it means approving to market such a product either by a Regulatory Authority in any constituent country within the EU or by the European Medicines Agency (EMA) according to the Council Directive 2001/83/EC or Council Regulation 2309/93/EEC (Law Insider, web reference).

The name of regulating body and time frame for marketing authorization is listed in Table 6.1.

This chapter deals with the marketing authorization of pharmaceuticals in Europe, the United States, Japan, Australia, and India.

6.2 Marketing authorization of pharmaceuticals in the EU

6.2.1 Introduction

The EU includes 27 member states and at present offers three different ways for submitting a drug product for obtaining marketing authorization. These processes of drug review and marketing approval are intended to streamline and improve the healthcare system (Ghalamkarpour, 2009).

The European Commission consults the relevant bodies of the participant states, the European Medicines Agency (EMA), and other parties seeking benefits. The three procedures that are currently applicable are:

1. Mutual Recognition Procedure (MRP)
2. Decentralized Procedure (DCP)
3. Centralized Procedure (CP)

https://www.ema.europa.eu/en.

It must be noted that the marketing approval process is always dynamic and the product dossier must be frequently updated to confirm that scientific advancement and new regulatory necessities are respected.

The European Medicines Agency (EMA) is given the task of conducting appropriate appraisal of submissions for central marketing approvals in the European Union. (https://www.ema.europa.eu/en).

Regulatory Affairs in the Pharmaceutical Industry. DOI: https://doi.org/10.1016/B978-0-12-822211-9.00004-6
© 2022 Elsevier Inc. All rights reserved.

TABLE 6.1 Country wise regulating body and time frame for the evaluation of application.

Country name	Regulatory body name	Time required for evaluation of marketing authorization application
India	CDSCO	150 days
European Union	EMA	210 days
United States	USFDA	180 days
Canada	Health Canada	210 days
Japan	PMDA	160–180 days
Brazil	ANVISA	180 days
Australia	TGA	255 (working days)
Russia	Roszdravnadzor	120 days
Moldova	AM	160 days
Singapore	Health Science Authority	90–240 days
Malaysia	National Pharmaceutical Control Bureau	80–210 days
Philippines	FDA	180 days
Myanmar	FDA	365 days
Thailand	TFDA	70–110 days (working days)
Cambodia	Department of Drugs and Food	365 days
Indonesia	National Agency for Drug and Food Control	100–150 days (working days)
Vietnam	Ministry of Health	365 days

AM, Agentia Medicamentului; *ANVISA*, Agencia Nacional de Vigilancia Sanitaria; *CDSCO*, Central Drugs Standard Control Organization; *EMA*, European Medicines Agency; *FDA*, Food and Drug Administration; *PMDA*, Pharmaceuticals and Medical Devices Agency; *TFDA*, Thailand Food and Drug Administration; *TGA*, Therapeutic Goods Administration; *USFDA*, US Food and Drug Administration.

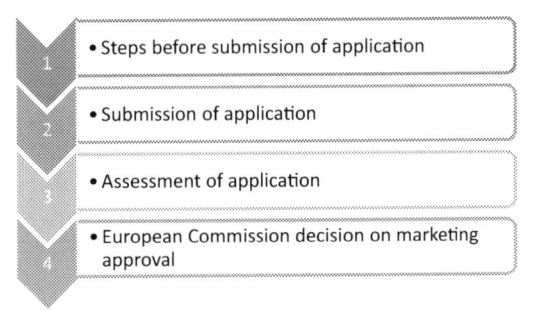

1 • Steps before submission of application

2 • Submission of application

3 • Assessment of application

4 • European Commission decision on marketing approval

FIGURE 6.1 Steps involved in centralized procedure.

This approval procedure lets the pharmaceutical companies tender a solitary application to EMA for marketing the drug product. It also ensures the product's availability throughout the European Economic Area (EEA) with a single marketing approval (European Medicines Agency, web reference). The centralized procedure is compulsory for the medicinal agents used to treat viral infection or AIDS; neoplastic disorders; diabetes mellitus; neurodegenerative and autoimmune disorders; drug products that are derived biotechnologically such as by genetic engineering, somatic cell therapy, or tissue-engineered processes; and orphan medicines and veterinary medicines that are used as growth or yield enhancers. It is not applicable to drugs containing new active pharmaceutical ingredients (API) for purposes other than those indicated above; that are a major therapeutic or technological innovation; and whose approval would be beneficial to the public or animal health at the EU level. In order to be sold in the EU, the vast majority of therapeutic novelties must first go through the centralized approval process. There are four steps involved which are depicted in Fig. 6.1.

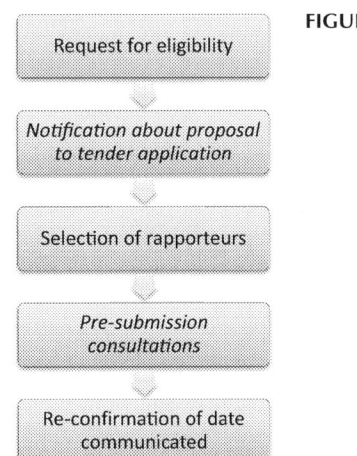

FIGURE 6.2   Stepwise presubmission process.

6.2.2   Steps before submission of application (EMA/821278/2015)

Presubmission application process is depicted in Fig. 6.2.

6.2.2.1   Submission of request for eligibility

To see whether a product qualifies for the centralized procedure's evaluation, the applicant needs to submit an eligibility request in a specific form along with the justification. It needs to be submitted 7−18 months before applying for marketing approval.

6.2.2.2   Notification about the proposal to tender application

Applicants need to decide the date of submission carefully using published guides for better prediction meeting or adhering deadlines of submissions/responses. This will allow both the industry and the regulatory agencies to plan workload and resourcing of related procedures better to ensure patients timely access to new drug products. The statement of intent should be tendered 7 months before submitting the marketing approval application.

6.2.2.3   Selection of rapporteurs

Committee for Medicinal Products for Human Use (CHMP) and Pharmacovigilance Risk Assessment Committee (PRAC) employs co-rapporteurs to carry out the technical evaluation. For drug applications intended for advanced treatment, co-rapporteurs are also employed from among the associates of Committee for Advanced Therapies (CAT), who head assessors (https://www.ema.europa.eu/en).

6.2.2.4   Presubmission consultations

The applicants can avail advice on regulatory and procedural matters from the agency through "marketing authorization application (MAA) presubmission meeting request form." This form summarizes the most important subjects discussed in the application for initial marketing approval and which are likely to come up in MAA presubmission consultation. It, however, must be understood that this presubmission meeting is in no way a measure of the outcome of assessment of submitted draft documents. The consultation usually takes place 6−7 months before submitting application for marketing approval.

6.2.2.5   Reconfirmation of date decided for submission

Applicants need to confirm again the date agreed earlier with EMA, or inform them of alterations or terminations by sending the form to pa-bus@ema.europa.eu, picking "notification of change" in the "scope of the request" column and mentioning the changed date in the corresponding field. This needs to be finished 2 to 3 months before submitting application for marketing approvals   (https://www.ema.europa.eu/en/human-regulatory/marketing-authorisation/obtaining-eu-marketing-authorisation-step-step).

6.2.3 Submission of the application

6.2.3.1 Submission

Applicants should submit the application via eSubmission gateway or web client using electronic common technical document (eCTD) format. If EMA needs any extra information to validate the application, it may give a new deadline. The eSubmission has to be done separately for human (Human eSubmission) as well as for veterinary (VET eSubmission) studies.

The Human Harmonization Group (HHG) develops standards and guidance documents for eSubmission as per the European approval protocols for human drug products. The documents need to be granted approval by the eSubmission expert group before becoming public. The Veterinary eSubmission is also undertaken likewise.

eCTD has been the only accepted electronic format for applications and submissions in centralized process since January 1, 2016 (e.g., fresh applications, disparities, and renewal requests). Other digital presentation, including non-eCTD electronic submissions (NeeS), is frequently rejected, and the submission goes unnoticed. Furthermore, the submission is also excluded if the eCTD submission shows Technical Validation as invalid.

A new or consolidated eCTD sequence has to be made available if applications are revised during the assessment process, for example, while responding to a query or a withdrawal, in order to preserve the eCTD life cycle. Standby arrangements for an eCTD application that has already been submitted (e.g., after rectifications) are not approved. Any modification to an eCTD application necessitates the creation of a new eCTD sequence.

The centralized procedure has mandated the use of electronic application forms (eAFs) since July 1, 2015. Even when the submission is for different strengths/dosage form, the EMA strongly recommends using a common eAF for each submission.

6.2.3.2 Validating application

EMA carries out a technical authentication of the applications that has been sent to ascertain if regulatory requirements for technical evaluation have been met in the application before the procedure is initiated. If EMA believes that it is necessary, then the applicant has to provide the requested information within the stipulated time. Once the application is submitted to EMA in the prescribed format, it will conduct a scientific validation. The applicant is immediately informed about the result of this assessment in case of eSubmission Gateway/web client.

If the report is not found valid upon assessment and the extra sequence is also not submitted within the time limit, it gets routinely deferred to the next month. Active substance master file (ASMF) proposals are also treated similarly. The agency has the responsibility of informing the applicant about various stages of content validation.

A validation supplementary information (VSI) can be sought from the applicant if any issue arises during validation. The applicant's response, termed as a new sequence, to resolve the validation issues should reach the agency before the start of the procedure. If the validation results are positive then the scientific evaluation will begin on the next available date in the agency timetable with the applicant being charged with the requisite fee. However a negative result necessitates the submission of a newer application and repayment of the validation fee.

There will be four possible outcomes while validating initial MAA:

1. *Outcome one (deemed valid the very first time, with no further queries)*:
   According to the EMA schedule, the scientific assessment will begin on the next available start date.
2. *Outcome two (some additional information needed)*:
   The agency may seek more information, clarifications, or corrections from the applicant.
3. *Outcome three (deferral of validation)*:
   The agency may request more information, clarifications, or corrections from the applicant. If the desired request is not submitted within the stipulated time, then the validation is held up by giving the applicant up to 2 months from the date of first VSI application.
4. *Outcome four (negative validation)*:
   A negative validation letter is issued with fees to be charged if the issues are not resolved within 2 months of first VSI application.

Only applications received on or before the deadline set by the agency are validated. A positive outcome of validation is must for the agency to initiate the process on the next available date.

6.2.4   Evaluation of the application

6.2.4.1   Scientific assessment

Committee for Medicinal Products for Human Use (CHMP) assesses the submissions taking suggestions from Pharmacovigilance Risk Assessment Committee (PRAC) on risk-management issues and Committee for Advanced Therapies (CAT) on advanced therapy. This may require about 210 working days. The committees has members from EU States, Iceland and Norway, with co-opted members from specific scientific domain (https://www.ema.europa.eu/en/human-regulatory/marketing-authorisation/obtaining-eu-marketing-authorisation-step-step).

Section 5 ensures that EMA receives the judgment of the Committee for Medicinal Products for Human Use (CHMP) within 210 days as per the following timetable (Table 6.2), which in rare cases can be further compressed.

After receiving the responses, the CHMP prepares a timetable for their assessment in the following manner (Table 6.3):

Applications can opt for accelerated assessment if the CHMP considers that the drug product could be offered as most important in public health and is a therapeutic breakthrough. Upon requesting and providing necessary validation, the CHMP can bring down the time frame to 150 days. The accelerated assessment request needs to be made within 60−90 days before submitting the MAA. For this request, applicants may seek the advice from the EMA procedure manager. The EMA strongly recommends a presubmission consultation to the applicant 6−7 months before submitting the application for accelerated assessment, where the proposal for accelerated assessment can be taken up with EMA and CHMP and other committees are also involved.

Under the PRIME arrangement offered since March 2016, the applicants can opt for eligibility under accelerated assessment during the clinical development if their product shows the promise.

6.2.4.2   CHMP scientific opinion

After completing the assessment, the CHMP releases the scientific review of the product's approvability. The European Commission accepts the EMA's recommendation and grants marketing approval. After that the EMA makes its decision publicly.

TABLE 6.2 Timeline for the judgment of the CHMP.

Day	Action
1[a]	Process starts.
80	Assessment Report(s) received by EMA.Report sent to the applicant stating these are preliminary inferences and not conclusion of CHMP.
94	PRAC rapporteur distributes within members the RMP evaluation report, EMA communicates this to the applicant.
100	Corapporteurs, other Committee affiliates, peer reviewers and EMA give remarks.
101−104	PRAC accepts PRAC RMP evaluation report and suggestions for D120 LoQ.
107	Updated version of PRAC RMP AR and LoQ is shared with the constituent members and EMA.
115	Receipt of raised questions, outline and suggestions of CHMP members and EMA.
120	CHMP accepts LoQ and conclusions communicated to the applicant by the EMA. Clock stops. CHMP accepts the request for GMP/GLP/GCP scrutiny, if needed.
121[a]	Tendering responses and revised SmPC, labeling and packaging details. Clock starts again.

AR, Assessment report; *GCP*, good clinical practice; *GLP*, good laboratory practice; *GMP*, good manufacturing practice; *LoQ*, list of question; *RMP*, risk management plan; *SmPC*, summary of product characteristics.
[a]*Dates for the tendering replies are displayed on the EMA website.*
Source: https://www.ema.europa.eu/en/human-regulatory/marketing-authorisation/obtaining-eu-marketing-authorisation-step-step.

TABLE 6.3 Timeline for assessment.

Day	Action
157	Joint Response Assessment Report is acknowledged by CHMP, PRAC, and EMA. EMA sends this Report to the applicant and can call a meeting with applicant around day 165 involving QRD subgroup.
160	PRAC, CHMP, and EMA communicate comments on RMP assessment.
166	PRAC after liaison with RMP and then with CHMP accepts PRAC RMP Assessment Overview and Advice for D180 LoOl.
170	The CHMP Rapporteur incorporates several contributions and opinions in the draft LoOls.
180	CHMP adopts LoOl, other conclusions and assessment report to be communicated to applicant by EMA. Clock stops.
181	Submission of response or oral explanation. Clock restarts.
194	Assessment of the applicant's responses by CHMP and PRAC.
200	PRAC, CHMP, and EMA comment on the review report.
204	Updated report is sent to PRAC, CHMP, and EMA.
By 210	CHMP Opinion and Assessment Report is accepted. Preparation of a schedule for translating product information.

LoOl, list of outstanding issue; *QRD*, quality review of documents.
Source: https://www.ema.europa.eu/en/human-regulatory/marketing-authorisation/obtaining-eu-marketing-authorisation-step-step.

TABLE 6.4 Timeline for publishing annexures.

Day	Action
215	Applicant sends the product information and Annex A in the 25 languages to the EMA and the "QRD Form 1" via Eudralink.[a]
229	EU States send comments to the applicant and EMA along with QRD Form 1
235	Applicant sends translated versions of SmPC, Annex II, labeling and packaging flyers, and Annexes IV and 127a if needed (+ "QRD Form 2" and "PDF checklist") via Eudralink.
237	Communication of views and annexes in all languages of EU to applicant, the commission and all member states.
239–261	Draft commission verdict, standing committee discussion.
By 277	Finalization of EPAR in discussion with CHMP and applicant.
277	Final commission verdict.

QRD, Quality review of documents; *SmPC*, summary of product characteristics.
[a]By email: qrd@ema.europa.eu.
Source: https://www.ema.europa.eu/en/human-regulatory/marketing-authorisation/obtaining-eu-marketing-authorisation-step-step.

6.2.5 Decision on marketing approval

6.2.5.1 Decision

The European Commission is the central authority to approve products upon EMA's endorsement which are legally binding. The marketing authorization is legal in all EU member countries and the EEA, that is, Iceland, Liechtenstein, and Norway. EC decisions are made public in the Community Register. EMA also records an European public assessment report (EPAR) for each drug preparation. If the application is rejected, EMA publishes a refusal EPAR along with evaluation statement. This will be done within 67 days after accepting CHMP view. The following timetable is used to enlist the annexures (Table 6.4).

6.2.5.2   Reexamination

As per the Article 9(2) of Regulation (EC) No 726/2004, the applicant can ask for reassessment within 15 days of receiving CHMP judgment. The rationale for this has to be communicated to EMA within 60 days of receiving CHMP judgment. The applicant can also ask for the consultations of Scientific Advisory Group (SAG) during reevaluation. The CHMP has the task of appointing CHMP corapporteurs for coordination of the reevaluation. For drug products of higher treatment, different CAT corapporteurs can be appointed and a new PRAC rapporteur will be chosen if PRAC is involved. The CHAP has to decide on the matter within 60 days. If desired an oral presentation may also be conducted within this period.

6.2.6   Assigning new marketing approval number and product information requirements

6.2.6.1   Assigning number

The EU main marketing authorization number is assigned by the European Commission. The agency mediates with the European Commission for including the EU subnumbers for each component in the Annex A of the drug product. These subnumbers have to be included in each linguistic version of the Annex A and be communicated to the applicant.

6.2.6.2   Product information requirement

The EMA offers direction to applicants with suggestion on how to incorporate product information such as product features, labeling and packaging flyers, normal titles, statements, and terms in all EU languages and outlines the setup and design for the product information.

In January 2020, EMA, Heads of Medicines Agencies, and EC stated that better access of patients and healthcare experts to information on drug products are the main principles guiding progress and practice of electronic product information.

6.2.6.3   Pharmacovigilance

Applicants are needed to incorporate a risk management strategy in their MAA. This portrays the latest information on the product safety and imminent pharmacovigilance (PhV) actions planned to monitor the product's safety. Patient registries are a kind of system which employ observational means (word is not correct) and can be used to carry out PhV. Companies should mention a risk management plan (RMP) while seeking marketing approval. For products without an RMP, safety concerns are needed to be attended. All RMPs are needed to provide a summary, which presents the document in a layman format. For centrally approved products, the EMA publishes this brief along with the public review account. RMPs are regularly revised all over the product's lifetime when new information comes in public domain.

6.2.6.4   Compliance

Marketing approval holders are required to ensure that they or their parties working on their behalf should meet the standards set out in the EU regulation and guidelines. Compliance warrants the dependability and integrity of data which give credence to authorization and their efficacy, safety, and quality. The EMA harmonizes these standards at the EU level. Its scientific committees may ask for the samples of medicines to be examined in an official laboratory. PhV examination and sampling and testing are the parts of compliance.

6.2.6.4.1   Pharmacovigilance inspections

These inspections are carried out to confirm that the need for monitoring the safety of medicinal products is being satisfied. This responsibility rests with the competent establishments of the nation.

6.2.6.4.2   Sampling and testing

The primary goal of the sampling and testing program is to find out the compliance of products after marketing against the standard provisions. This comprises the following:

- monitoring the quality of final products all through the official shelf life and distribution network;
- confirming that the regulating procedures are acceptable;
- inspecting alleged quality flaws (if needed);
- supporting with the testing of falsified drug products (if needed). The process flow from submission to decision of marketing authorization application is depicted in Fig. 6.3.

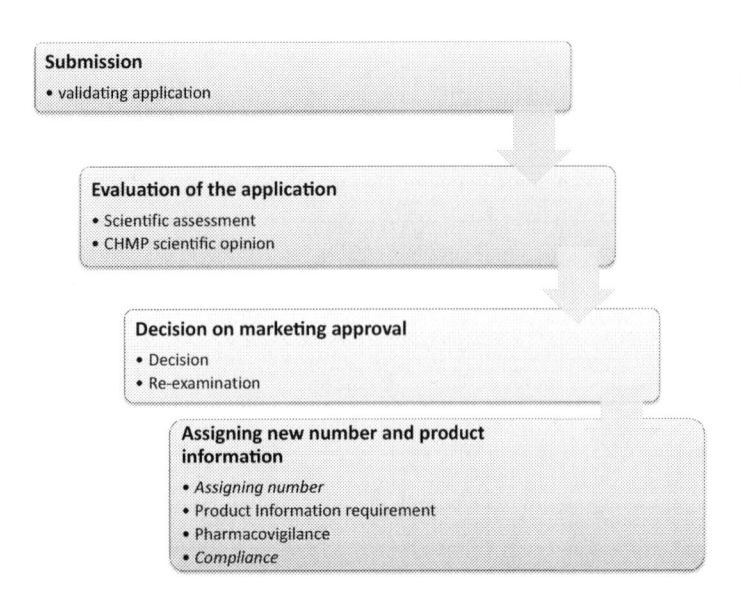

FIGURE 6.3 Summary of process in marketing authorization from submission to decision.

6.2.7 Withdrawal of MAA

If the applicant wants to withdraw his MAA during assessment, he/she has to produce a letter, conveying that the applicant withdraws his application, to the Product Lead. He should state whether the withdrawal is complete or partial giving motives behind withdrawal. It must be signed by the agent officiating for the applicant. The MAA withdrawal letter is also posted on the EMA's website for applicants to see (after providing the due protection to personal data). The withdrawal request can be taken up at any stage during the assessment (from validation of the MAA to acceptance of the final CHMP judgment). However the agency still levies the fee for the application right from the start regardless of its conclusion and published information in them.

6.2.8 Marketing approval: biosimilar medicines

The drug molecule, which is very similar to an existing one whose marketing approval has expired, is termed as biosimilar in the EU. EMA evaluates the applications to market biosimilar drug products before granting them approval for marketing in the EU. The category also includes "monoclonal antibodies, recombinant proteins, blood products, plasma products and immunological products." The legal necessities and measures for applying for biosimilars can be traced from Article 6 of Regulation (EC) 726/2004 and Article 10(4) of Directive 2001/83/EC. One important requirement is that the reference product should have exhausted its protection period.

Applicant needs to establish through comparative studies that:

- his product and reference product are very similar in spite of naturally inherent variations among biologicals;
- his product and reference product do not have any major differences in their clinical efficacy, safety, and quality;
- comparability study is unique for each product. Data obtained from initial studies govern the level; and
- preclinical and clinical studies are needed for further drug development.

For "biosimilars," the following centralized procedure can be adopted:

1. *Mandatory scope*: According to Article 3(1) of Regulation (EC) No 726/2004, for medicines developed through biotechnology as defined in the Annex (point 1) of Regulation (EC). The reference can be a product approved in a National/MRP or Centralized Procedure (https://ec.europa.eu/health/sites/health/files/files/eudralex/vol-1/reg_2004_726/reg_2004_726_en.pdf).

2. *Optional scope*: When the product is outside mandatory scope, as described previously, for example,
   a. Similar biological product approved via the centralized procedure with direct entry under Article 3(3) of Regulation (EC) No 726/2004.

b. Similar biological product of a National/MRP/DCP category not included in mandatory scope but can be accepted under Article 3(2)(b), if it can be established that the product is:

    i. a therapeutic or technical novelty or

    ii. the granting of approval is in public interest (https://www.ema.europa.eu/en/human-regulatory/marketing-authorisation/biosimilar-medicines-marketing-authorisation).

An "eligibility request" needs to be tendered in the prescribed form with the explanation of suitability for assessment under centralized procedure. The request is to be sent to cpeligibility@ema.europa.eu. Also, EMA is to be informed of intention preferably 6–18 months in advance through "letter of intent (LoI) to submit."

The selection process of rapporteur/corapporteur and the review team is taken in hand about 7 months ahead of MAA submission date. PRAC (co-)rapporteurs are also appointed alongside. The process follows the guidelines laid down in Section 4.2 of the paper "CHMP Rapporteur/Co-Rapporteur appointment: principles, objective criteria and methodology" shall be applied. After receiving application, the EMA begins validating which is to be finished by the scheduled procedure start date. Meanwhile the applicants should be ready with the replies to the queries raised so far. Once this validation procedure is over and rapporteur team has the dossier with them, the EMA starts the evaluation procedure on the date mentioned on the website. For the biosimilars which are centrally approved with the positive validation, the procedure will begin that month. For biosimilar approved through a National/MRP/DCP, the EMA starts evaluation after verifying with the Member State. The evaluation procedure begins only if all the related data have been received.

The applicant needs to provide whatever part is asked by the CHMP members within a month of beginning of evaluation process; otherwise, the EMA holds the process till the query has been resolved. Applicant needs to tender the MAA as per the EMA calendar. The agency makes it sure that the CHMP submits its report within 210 days (excluding clock stops) as per the timetable (Table 6.5).

The applicant needs to submit samples of packaging along with the leaflet to the agency for assessment, before marketing the product.

Provision for Postapproval Marketing/Cessation: If the biosimilar is not commercialized after receiving marketing approval, a 3-year period sans marketing begins after the expiry of protection period, namely, 6 or 10 years, of the reference product as per previous legislation.

The new data protection guidelines (8 + 2 + 1) are applicable to the reference products whose MAA has been tendered after formation of the EU Regulation, namely, after October 30, 2005, for National/MRP/DCP and November 20, 2005, for the CP.

Marketing Authorization Holder (MAH) is also instructed to notify the EMA, in 60 days of giving marketing approval, regarding other related expiry dates to be considered. The fate of an exemption request depends on this information.

6.2.9 Marketing approval: generic and hybrid applications

6.2.9.1 Generic/hybrid centrally authorized product

The applicant needs to mention in his 'LoI to submit' that he has ready access to the CP under Article 3(3)of Regulation (EC) No 726/2004. He should inform the EMA 6–18 months before submitting the dossier, that it is a generic/hybrid application of a product approved via CP. EMA then apprises the applicant about the result of the eligibility.

6.2.9.2 Generic/hybrid medicinal application of a national/MRP/DCP product

Generic/hybrid approved via the national/MRP/DCP procedure can be considered for CP, if the product can be proven as:
- a therapeutic or technical novelty, or
- the granting of approval is for public good

        https://www.ema.europa.eu/en/human-regulatory/marketing-authorisation/generic-medicines/generic-hybrid-applications.

The product is considered a scientific or technical innovation if:

- it offers a new option in treatment, prevention, or diagnosis of a disease, or
- its development or production is based on new scientific facts or novel technology or their application.

TABLE 6.5 Timeline for submitting CHMP report with clock stops.

Day	Action
1[a]	Process begins.
80	EMA receives CHMP rapporteur and forwards it to the applicant for information purpose only.
87	RMP review and suggested RMP LoQ are circulated by PRAC rapporteur.
90	GxP examination appeal is accepted.
100	Comments are received from agency's and rapporteurs' end.
101–104	RMP review and D120 LoQ advice are adopted by PRAC.
115	All the above reviews, endorsement, and advice are received by CHMP members and if appropriate, by EMA.
120	CHMP assessment statement is adopted but for "gross" oppositions, a GxP review problem is taken up. A timeline for translations is prepared.
121[a]	Replies, reviewed SmPC, labeling, and packaging in English are submitted. Clock restarts.
150	RMP review and suggested LoOI distributed by PRAC.
157	EMA sends combined review to the applicant just for his information.
167	PRAC RMP review and D180 LoOI are accepted.
170	CHMP members will provide their comments
180	CHMP debate and verdict on need to discuss "unresolved topics" and/or an verbal clarification by the applicant. Clock stops for verbal clarification. Final review submission by assessors by day 180.
181	Clock restarts. Verbal clarification (if needed), distribution of final GxP review.
183	RMP review distributed by PRAC rapporteur.
197	Final PRAC RMP review and suggestions are accepted by PRAC.
By day 210	Acceptance of CHMP View and evaluation. Acceptance of a timeline for providing translations.

LoQ, List of question; *LoOI*, list of outstanding issues; *SmPC*, summaries of product characteristic.
[a]*After receiving the replies, the EMA prepares a timetable for assessing these replies.*

As far as "interest of patients" is concerned, a product, which tackles a specific health concern or offers a different contribution to health care in the EU, can be considered.

The applicant should inform the EMA of their intention to apply, 6–18 months before the submission justifying the eligibility of the product for the CP within provision(s) of Regulation (EC) No 726/2004. EMA then apprises the applicant about the outcome of the eligibility.

One important requirement is that the reference product should have exhausted its protection period.

6.2.9.2.1 Generic medicinal product

As per Article 10 (1) of Directive 2001/83/EC the pre-clinical and clinical data need not be submitted if it can be established that reference product is approved under Article 6 of the same Directive for at least 8 years anywhere in EU.

A generic is termed as a medicinal product if it has vis-à-vis the reference product:

- the same composition, qualitatively and quantitatively, of API(s),
- the same dosage form,
- and which is proven to be bioequivalent using recommended bioavailability procedures.

6.2.9.2.2 Hybrid medicinal product

Under Article 10(3) of Directive 2001/83/EC hybrid product are generic ones with requirements of pre-clinical and clinical studies in conditions:

- which do not fulfill the strict description of a "generic" product;
- whose bioavailability does not correlate well with bioequivalence;
- if there are alterations in the API(s), clinical use, dosage form, drug amount, or route of administration
  https://www.ema.europa.eu/en/human-regulatory/marketing-authorisation/generic-medicines/generic-hybrid-applications.

The results of tests carried out meet the standards mentioned in the Annex to the Directive 2001/83/EC as amended by Directive 2003/63/EC. Some directions on additional studies to be carried out are given in Annex IV of the Chapter 1 of the Notice to Applicants.

For this type of applications, marketing approval is granted in accordance with Articles 8(3), 10a, 10b, or 10c of Directive 2001/83/EC.

6.2.9.3 Appointment of rapporteur/corapporteur

For generic applications the selection begins at a CHMP meeting 3–7 months before MAA submissive date, to give them about 2–6 months time. During the same period, PRAC rapporteur and PhV rapporteur are also nominated. For hybrid applications, the time periods are 7 and 6 months for appointment and assessment, respectively, prior to MAA submission date. Everything else remains the same.

6.2.9.4 Reassessment of a CHMP judgment on a generic/hybrid product

CHMP views can be subjected to a review as per Article 62(1) of Regulation (EC) No 726/2004 of March 31, 2004. The details are outlined in Section 5.1.

6.2.9.5 MAA format

The applications are to be done in CTD format, like any other MAA. Some specific requirements are as follows:

6.2.9.5.1 Module 1

- Applicants, in Module 1.5.2, need to furnish rationale and evidence to establish their product is:
- A "generic" of a reference product (Art 10.1). This brief includes particulars of the product, composition in API(s), dosage form, safety, and efficacy of the API(s) with respect to that of the reference product and bioavailability data, if needed.
- A "hybrid" of a reference product (Art 10.3). This brief includes particulars of the product, composition in API(s), dosage form, dosage, clinical use, route of administration with respect to that of the reference product and bioavailability data.
- EU RMP.

6.2.9.5.2 Module 2

Module 2 provides the quality summary along with nonclinical and clinical study outline which are only required if any additional studies are included. The module focuses on:

- Impurity profiling of the API(s) wherever decomposition occurs during storage;
- Assessment of BABE studies or a rationale for not performing them, whenever needed;
- Published articles related to the product and its use;
- Any novel claim emerging from product characteristics [supplementary protection certificate (SPC)] and its therapeutics substantiated by research published;
- If different salts, isomers, ethers, esters, or complexes of the API of the reference product are used, evidence establishing that their efficacy and safety do not differ much from reference product should be provided.

6.2.9.5.3 Module 3

The applicant should specify in Table A that their product is devoid of transmission risk of animal spongiform encephalopathy as per Module 3.2. R regional information, if relevant or not applicable, if otherwise.

6.2.9.5.4 Modules 4 and 5

- A "generic" as per Article 10.1 need not provide toxicological, pharmacological, or clinical data. However BABE data where apt should be given in Section 5.3.1 of eCTD. For newer salts, isomers, ethers, esters, or complexes of the API of the reference product used, evidence establishing that their efficacy and safety do not differ much from reference product should be provided as per CTD format.
- A "hybrid" as per Article 10.3 needs to incorporate suitable preclinical and clinical data as asked in notice to applicants.

For application other than these, meeting quality requirements in the submission is responsibility of the applicant and is central to the complete process.

6.2.9.6 Protection period of reference product

While submitting generic/hybrid application, one important requirement is that the reference product should have exhausted its protection period so as to ensure availability of the reference product dossier to the applicant.

For generic/hybrid application given via CP, when referring to:

- a CP reference product, 8- or 10-year protection duration, as appropriate, needs to be over and the eligibility established;
- a nationally authorized reference product, the 6- or 10-year protection duration depending on Member State granting marketing approval or 8-year protection duration, as appropriate, needs to be over and the eligibility established.

6.2.9.7 Evaluation of generic/hybrid application

The process is nearly identical to that of MA for biosimilars. While EMA validates the application, the applicants prepare the answers to the queries raised. Thereafter rapporteur team takes over the dossier for evaluation. The verification of the Member State is needed in case of products which are not centrally approved.

The timeline of generic/hybrid products is nearly identical to the one for biosimilars. The marketing authorization also follows the rights, limitations, and exemptions as applicable to biosimilars.

6.2.10 Marketing approval: pediatrics

For seeking marketing approvals of those drug products which are not approved in the EU on July 26, 2008, the MAA needs to furnish data of studies performed under pediatric investigation plan (PIP) or provide evidence for PIP deferment or waiver. The Regulation (EC) No 1901/2006 (the "Pediatric Regulation") describes requirements, returns, and enticements for bringing in market a pediatric preparation. This makes sure that drug products used in pediatric patients are developed ethically, meet quality standards and are properly approved for use in children, and have sufficient data for safer use in all kinds of patients not more than 18 years of age.

As per Article 7 of the Pediatric Regulation, an unapproved drug product, as of July 26, 2008, needs to provide:

- results of all studies completed and detail data complying with the agreed PIP;
- PIP verdict including the deferment granted;
- EMA decision giving class waiver;
- while tendering results, the applicant needs to provide justification of proposed variations in product information.

Showcasing results of studies conducted complying with the agreed PIP is a precondition to derive benefits from the pediatric reward (Article 36(1) of Regulation (EC) No 1901/2006).

The applicant also has to fulfill "PIP compliance check." It verifies meeting requirements as stated in the PIP verdict such as schedules of the studies conducted and the data collected. Applicants are suggested to undergo compliance check before tendering MAA so as to finish validation on time. Other particulars such as composition of PIP or waiver, time limit for tendering PIP or waiver applications, Disparity/Postponement applications, and compliance check with an accepted PIP are also given with EMA guidelines.

6.2.11   Pediatric-use marketing authorizations

The pediatric-use marketing authorization (PUMA) covers the clinical uses and suitable formulation(s) meant for pediatric patients. It covers the drug products which are:

- already approved;
- no more protected by SPC.

    The development of a PUMA is as per PIP, sanctioned by Pediatric Committee (PDCO).

6.2.11.1   Incentives

- Automatic access to the CP;
- 8 + 2 years of data protection;
- Retention of name and brand containing the same API, if the MAH is same;
- Partial fee concessions under CP for MA and postapproval activities for a year.

6.2.11.2   Applying for a PUMA

The PUMA applicant needs to tender a presubmission form to cpeligibility@ema.europa.eu prior to (font change) submitting request confirmation of eligibility. Requirement of data submission for PUMA applications is similar to other MAA. The cross-references to dossiers of other products can be used if the data protection period of the reference product is over as per Article 14(11) of Regulation (EC) No. 726/2004 or Article 10 of Directive 2001/83/EC).

- Data of all studies conducted and collected complying with PIP;
- PDCO view and EMA verdict on compliance or the applicant's compliance statement (in Module 1.10);
- A risk managing proposal describing ways to make sure the continuation of efficacy and probable adverse effects in the pediatric utilization.

6.3   Marketing authorization of pharmaceuticals in the United Kingdom

6.3.1   Application process

All national applications for the United Kingdom and Great Britain (England, Scotland, and Wales) must be submitted via the MHRA Submissions Portal. Queries regarding submission portal must be directed to email ID submissions@mhra.gov.uk. The application must be submitted using eCTD. To assist the application, presubmission checklist can be used. The eAF and cover letter tools can be utilized to figure out what details need to be included in the application. The application will not be validated if the provided details are not correct. The MHRA advocates using a validation tool to verify your request, since they would use the Extedo Eurs is Yours validation tool to ensure that NeeS and eCTD submissions are technically correct. Any concerns in regard to submitting an application need to contact at IPUenquiries@mhra.gov.uk.

6.3.2   Product license number

Before submitting an application for a United Kingdom, Great Britain, or Northern Ireland license, you must obtain a product license (PL) number from the MHRA Portal or by emailing PLNumberAllocation@mhra.gov.uk.

6.3.3   Active substance master files

The MHRA needs active substance master file (ASMF) holders to submit a dossier. The applicant is responsible for ensuring that the ASMF is submitted either before or at the same time as the application would be invalid without it.

    The ASMF holder must use MHRA submissions to submit a new ASMF and any modifications to an existing ASMF. Any concern regarding MHRA submission can be sent to an email submissions@mhra.gov.uk. Guidance is available on the website for submitting ASMFs. In support of UK and GB national authorizations, certificates of suitability (CEPs) are still accepted.

6.3.4 Summary of product characteristics

The SPC prototype should be used to apply for the summary of product characteristics (SmPC) to the MHRA in the correct format. Your application will be refused if you do not use this template. Other than adding the relevant information, these models should not be altered in any way.

6.3.5 Providing a name for your medicine

The MHRA examines each product name application to ensure that the proposed name will enable the medication to be taken safely and correctly. More information is available in naming of medicines guidance document.

6.3.6 Fast track your marketing authorization

If there is clear proof of gain in a public health emergency or if there is a shortage of an appropriate drug that has been checked by the Department of Health and Social Care (DHSC), applications will be expedited.

To request that your marketing authorization be expedited, you may send an email to RIS.NA@mhra.gov.uk with a letter of not more than three pages. The following things should be included in the letter:

- the reason for fast tracking;
- a brief overview of the product's major clinical properties;
- evidence demonstrating the product's purported benefits for the proposed indication(s).

If you need to expedite your application due to a supply shortage, please contact the DHSC by emailing DHSCmedicinesupplyteam@dhsc.gov.uk. There is no extra charge for applications that are fast-tracked.

6.3.7 Payments

After your application has been validated, you will be sent an invoice with guidance about how to pay the balance owed. All invoices must be paid in full when they are sent. Nonpayment can result in the penalty fees. The penalties are defined in detail in fees regulations.

Nonpayment can result in the revocation of any license or authorization, as well as legal action can be taken to recover any unpaid sums owed to the Crown.

6.3.8 Rejection

Any submission that does not conform to the standards will be rejected. If applicant's submission is rejected, MHRA will send an email explaining the reason for the rejection. After that applicant must resend the whole submission with the errors fixed. Applicant does not need to email the corrected deficiencies.

If the application is denied due to technical problems, applicant will not be charged. If applicant believes that the application was incorrectly denied, then he/she may contact via email IPUenquiries@mhra.gov.uk.

6.4 Marketing authorization of pharmaceuticals in the United States

6.4.1 Introduction

Since there are fewer restrictions in the global trade, each nation has its own set of regulations, and governments have to ensure the safety, efficacy, and quality of the products. Since each country's regulatory requirements vary from one another, the applicant must ensure that his product is produced in accordance with the regulatory needs of the country in which he approaches for marketing authorization (Handoo et al., 2012; Agarwal and Karwa, 2018).

Pharmaceutical regulations detail administrative, legal, and technical actions put in place by the governments to control pharmaceutical trade. The pharmaceutical market, in terms of value, is governed by three geographical entities, the United States, the EU, and Japan (Fayad, 2003).

The pharmaceutical industry's expansion boosted the US economy. The American government has the strictest drug approval criteria in the world. The regulatory body of the United States is responsible for developing, processing, supplying, and selling safe and effective drug products and devices within the country.

It makes sure that new and effective drugs reach to the market rapidly but concurrently it has to check for testing and safety of the products. The US administrative agency evaluates applications to ensure that the drug is safe for patients. However it was criticized also due to delaying in the process of approvals so-called "drug lag" and expensive complex procedure (Jawahar and Lakshmi, 2017; Van Norman, 2016).

6.4.1.1 Authorities or Body and act of the United States for marketing authorization of pharmaceuticals

The authority regulating the promotion and sale of drug products in the United States is the United States Food and Drug Administration (USFDA) (Van Norman, 2016). Code of Federal Regulations (CFR) section 21 covers the maximum regulations of the food and drugs (USFDA, 2018a).

6.4.1.2 Types of applications

Marketing authorization exercises control over the following five types of applications (USFDA, 2014):

1. Investigational new drug (IND) applications;
2. New drug applications (NDA);
3. Abbreviated new drug applications (ANDA);
4. Biological licensing authority (BLA);
5. Over-the-counter drugs (OTC).

6.4.1.2.1 Investigational new drug application

To distribute or transport API or medicines across the United States, marketing approval is needed as per the federal law of the United States. Possession of IND provides an exemption from this law. The IND is filed by the applicant to USFDA to seek permission for conducting clinical trials only if drug candidate is found safe in preclinical investigations. The fees charged for IND application can be referred from USFDA websites (USFDA, 2019d).

IND applications are accepted in two different categories:

1. *Commercial*: applications submitted by companies referred to as sponsors by USFDA.
2. *Research*: These applications are submitted for noncommercial research and include Investigator IND, Treatment IND, and Emergency Use IND:
   a. An Investigator IND is applied by a medical practitioner. He will do the investigation and the investigational drug is used under his supervision.
   b. Treatment IND is applied for investigational drugs which found promising in the clinical trials for serious conditions but whose final clinical work and USFDA review are still on.
   c. Emergency Use IND includes USFDA authorized usage of an investigational new drug in an emergency due to a lack of time in submitting a complete IND application (Van Norman, 2016).

The following steps are needed to be followed for IND submissions:

1. Before submitting IND, the applicant can plan pre-IND meeting with USFDA. This discussion will assist the applicant to streamline animal study, clinical trials, and collection and processing of the data. The USFDA's Center for Drug Evaluation and Research (CDER) runs the Pre-IND Consultation Program to encourage early contact between applicants and reviewer team in order to direct for collection of the necessary data for IND submission.
2. To file an IND, one needs to fill three sets of forms: Form 1571 which deals with study design and protocol; Form 1572 which deals with declaration of the principal investigator; and Form 3674 which certifies that the study is registered as per 42 U.S.C. Section 282(j)(5)(B) and performed as per ClinicalTrials.gov Data Bank (USFDA). There is a need to submit Form USFDA 1572 for each investigator taking part in the study. Three main areas that need to be discussed in IND applications are pharmacology and toxicology studies on animals, way of manufacturing of drug, and protocol for clinical trials and applicant's detail.
3. After submitting the IND application, the applicants need to wait for 30 days before conducting any clinical trials. USFDA can ask for extra information or can keep the study on "clinical hold" position (USFDA, 2020a; Holbein, 2009).

6.4.1.2.2 New drug applications

Since 1938, the manufacturer (sponsor, as termed by USFDA) has to submit NDA to seek permission for marketing authorization of any drug in the United States. NDA gives a complete picture of a drug as the investigator needs to provide data from a preclinical study to phase 3 clinical trials (Umscheid et al., 2011).

6.4.1.2.2.1 Types of NDA filing

NDA filing is of two types: (1) 505(b)(1) and (2) 505(b)(2).

1.505(b)(1): It is meant for a new drug which has not been studied earlier or received approval. The sponsor is needed to carry out all studies which can adequately prove the efficacy, safety, and quality of the API. It includes comprehensive reportage of chemistry, preclinical pharmacology/toxicology, clinical pharmacology, and other clinical investigations, manufacturing, and controls.

2.505(b)(2): The Hatch—Waxman Amendments 1984 as applied in the 505(b)(2) are intended to avoid the repetition of already-existing studies. This filing is used for studies such as change in dosage form (e.g., tablets to topical gel), strengths (larger or smaller), route of administration (oral to nasal or iontophoretic delivery), immediate release to controlled release, dosing regimen (once daily to once weekly) and/or modification in API (newer salt, ester, complex, enantiomer, racemate, combinations, etc.), the substitution of an API in a combination product, adding new indications, prescription/OTC status changes, new combination with two or more already-approved APIs individually, drug—device combination products, etc. Hence, 505(b)(2) drug product is easier to develop with less risk and cost involved or time consumed than a 505(b)(1) product (Camargo, 2018; USFDA, 2020b; CDER, 2017).

The NDA approval process is shown in Fig. 6.4.

Three types of forms are needed to be filled for the NDA application:

1. Form 356h is an application for marketing a new drug, a biologic product or an antibiotic for human use. This form includes the date of submission; applicant details; produce/production process details source, production methods, and regulation, design, contamination/crosscontamination data, capacity, environment evaluation, etc.); application information such as application type (NDA/ANDA/BLA); if an NDA, to be indicated whether 505b(1) or 505b(2); if product is a BLA, to be indicated whether 351(a) or 351(k); for ANDA or 505(b)(2) type of application—Patent and product details of innovator; establishment information; chemistry; preclinical observations; clinical observations; labeling; and safety data and data analysis with statistics.
2. User fee cover sheet (form FDA-3397):

    The Office of Financial Management (OFM) performs a task of managing the finances of the user fee programs. The process for creating a cover sheet procures the information just enough to determine the necessity of the fee, to determine the quantum of the fee, and to allow USFDA to track the status of payments. User fee programs directly link the following to generate and make payment for the cover sheets:

    a. Prescription Drug User Fee Amendments (PDUFA)
    b. Generic Drug User Fee Amendments (GDUFA)

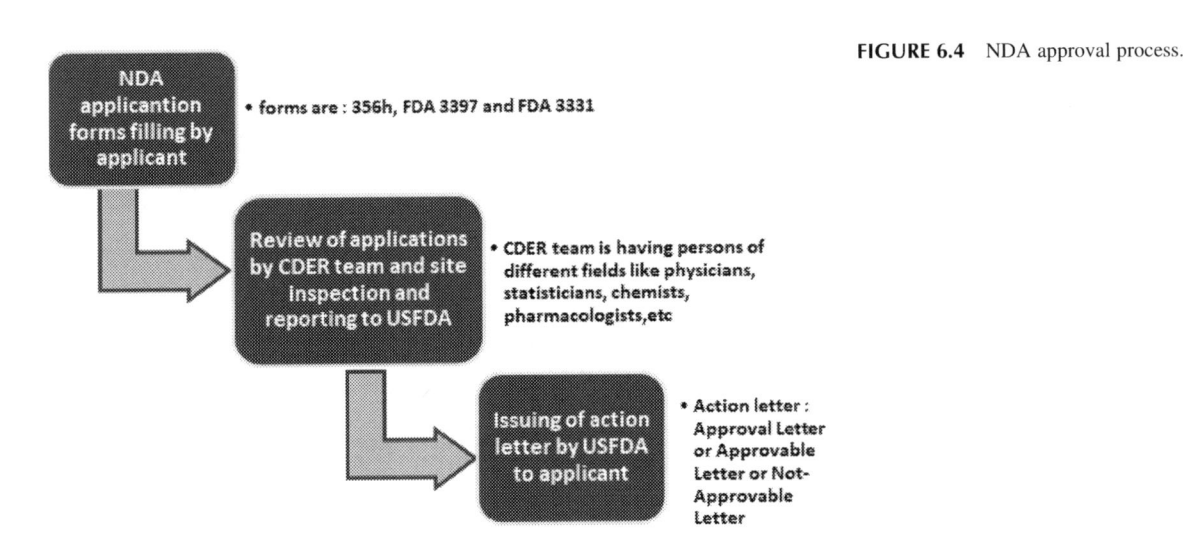

FIGURE 6.4 NDA approval process.

    c. Medical Device User Fee Amendments (MDUFA)

    d. Biosimilar User Fee Act (BsUFA)

       https://www.fda.gov/.

3. Form FDA 3331 (Field Report of the New Drug Application):

    In case of any substantial quality issues found with the product, the NDA/ANDA applicant needs to present a FAR to USFDA within 3 days from the occurrence of the issues. This Form 3331 includes firm name and address where the issue(s) was/were reported; product detail; date of first reporting of the problem to the applicant; how was the problem discovered; description of the problem(s); description of the main reason(s) of the reported problem(s); and description of corrective measures for the reported problems (USFDA, 2019a).

After the submission of the application, it will take 60 days for the USFDA to decide whether to examine the application or to reject it on account of missing information if any. If the NDA application is found complete, then CDER team composed of experts in physics, statistics, chemistry, pharmacology, and other scientists reviews the data. As per specialization, every member of the team reviews their own relevant part of the application critically. For example, the medicine expert and the statistician analyze the clinical portion; a pharmacology expert scrutinizes the preclinical study data. A supervisory examination is undertaken in addition to evaluations by each professional discipline that makes up the team. Each reviewer needs to write his evaluation containing inferences and endorsements about the application (USFDA, 2015a).

The USFDA's Division of Scientific Investigations (DSI) inspect clinical trial sites to verify the reliability of reported clinical study results. The team scans the reports of the institutional review committees at the site. It matches the actual study with the plan and checks for adverse event reporting systems. It confirms whether inclusion or exclusion criteria for the subjects are followed as per protocol or not. The USFDA also visits the production unit for inspection and ensures that facilities available are capable of manufacturing the drug as per current good manufacturing practices (cGMPs).

The project manager compiles reports of each team member and prepares an "action package" which is a record for the USFDA review. A recommendation is proposed by the team but the final decision is always taken by a senior USFDA official. The timeline for the NDA application is shown in Fig. 6.5 (Scarola, 2012; Vishal et al., 2014; USFDA, 2018b).

Once the USFDA has finished reviewing the NDA, it releases one of the following three action letters:

1. *Approval letter*: Indicating that the drug has been granted approval.

2. *Approvable letter*: Indicating that the drug will eventually be granted approval, but needs some rectifications, for the inadequacies, such as changes in the labeling.

3. *Not-approvable letter*: Indicating that the drug is not fit for approval with a list of justifications in support.

USFDA can stop any further consideration in the NDA approval process if the sponsor does not reply within the specified period. The sponsor has the option of withdrawing the application at any time during the review process, even before the USFDA has made a filing decision. Such withdrawals are done "without prejudice to refilling" and do not impede any future resubmissions to USFDA. The developer can formally appeal if he disagrees with any of the USFDA

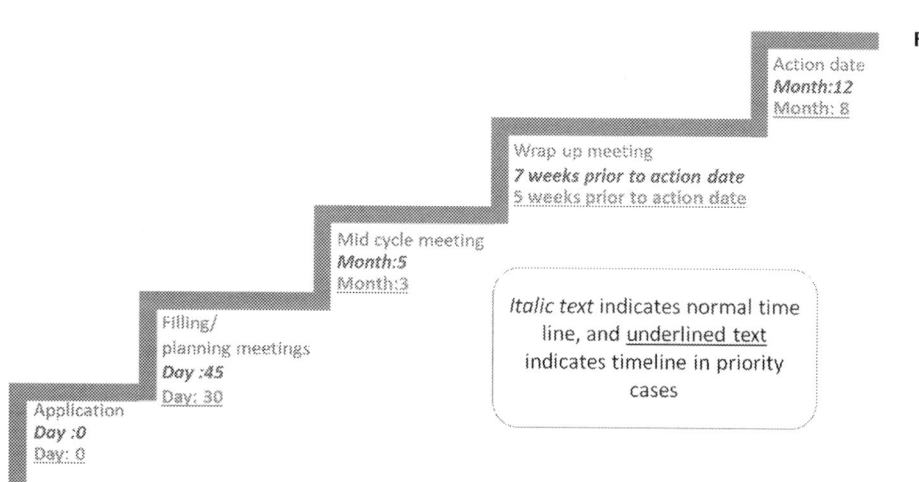

FIGURE 6.5 NDA review timeline.

decision. The reviewers are trained to maintain consistency in drug reviews; the USFDA gives the highest priority to good review practices. Occasionally, though, few questions need additional consideration which can be addressed by the meeting of USFDA with its Advisory Committee. The accelerated approvals are provided for the drugs used in serious illness in which existing treatment is not satisfactory. The USFDA can withdraw the approval if further studies do not support the claimed performance (USFDA, 2020c).

6.4.1.2.3 Abbreviated new drug application

For the past few decades, the generic industry has been rising at an exponential rate, and it is expected to continue to do so. The ANDA is a set of data submitted for the review by the USFDA and subsequent approval of the generic product (Boehm et al., 2013).

The generic product is similar to the innovator product in the dosage form, dose, route of administration, quality attributes, and proposed performance and purpose. The *Orange Book* of USFDA contains both official innovator and generic products.

Generic applications are called "abbreviated" as they do not include preclinical and clinical study data. The generic product needs to establish scientifically that its performance is similar to the innovator product. They need to demonstrate "bioequivalence" with the innovator product. To obtain USFDA approval, the generic product should be able to deliver the same amount of drug in a similar time-period into a patient's bloodstream as the innovator product. However news of an ANDA filing can be detrimental to the finances of the brand name holder as this may lead to a huge drop in its share price and a steep climb in the share price of a generic drug maker (USFDA, 2019b).

6.4.1.2.3.1 Applications of ANDA
Paper ANDA submissions are no longer accepted by the USFDA. USFDA accepts all ANDA submissions in eCTD format. The following forms need to be filled for ANDA:

1. Form 356h is an "Application for the Marketing of a New Drug, a Biologic or an Antibiotic Drug meant for human Use".
2. Form 3674 certifies that the study is registered as per 42 U.S.C. Section 282(j)(5)(B) and performed as per ClinicalTrials.gov Data Bank.
3. DMFs are submissions to USFDA meant to enlist confidential, detailed information of facilities, procedures, and utilities of production, dispensation, packaging, and storage of the applied product.
4. Form FDA 3794.

The form is Generic Drug User Fee Amendments (GDUFA) cover sheet. It covers industry user fees so that the review of generic drug applications is done on time and is reliable and predictable. After fee payment as per GDUFA, the applicant can submit a complete set of dossiers along with all other required datasets and application forms (CDER and CBER, 2014; USFDA, 2019c).

"Refuse to file" letter is issued to the applicant in case of incomplete application. The applicant can do modifications in the applications and apply again with corrections. The complete application without any deficiency is forwarded to the OGD or Center for Drug Evaluation and Research (CDER) review team for the assessment. The review team assesses bioequivalence and if bioequivalence reviews are not acceptable, then a bioequivalence deficiency letter is issued. If any discrepancy is found in the application for microbiology, chemistry, and labeling then a not-approvable letter is issued. Preapproval plant inspection is done after acceptance from bioequivalence, microbiology, chemistry, and labeling check. If plant inspection is acceptable, then ANDA approval is granted by the USFDA and if it is not acceptable then the application is under status "Approval deferred pending satisfactory results." MAPP is a Manual of Policies and Procedures provided by the USFDA and is used by the Division of Filing Review (DFR), Office of Regulatory Operations (ORO) in the Office of Generic Drugs (OGD) for the filing review of an ANDA (Rafi et al., 2018; Khatun et al., 2018).

6.4.1.2.3.2 Types of ANDA filling
Para I: ANDA applicant needs to verify that there is no listed patent.
Para II: The patent has already expired.
Para I or Para II ANDA is granted immediately if it fulfills all relevant regulatory and technical (efficacy, safety, and bioequivalence) requirements.
Para III: This certification is applied when the ANDA applicant is planning to sell the generic drug only after the expiry of the patent of that drug.

Para IV: It is applied when the applicant is sure that its product or the commercialization of its product does not infringe upon the innovator's patent(s) or the applicant is certain that innovator's patent(s) is/are not valid.

After Para IV submission by the applicant, USFDA needs to notify the patentee about this ANDA submission. The patentee can file a suit of infringement against ANDA applicant in 45 days of the notice. The patentee gets a 30-month window to fight in a court. ANDA is approved if the court finds the patent to be invalid or that the ANDA applicant is not infringing.

As per Hatch—Waxman Act, the first company to apply for an ANDA gets 180 days marketing exclusivity meaning that the generic product can be marketed for 180 days even before the expiry of the patent. During this period, a duopoly exists for the product in the market. The first generic company makes huge profits with a minor investment during these 180 days. CDER and CBER of USFDA have drafted guidance to the industry to answer the queries on180-day exclusivity. Although ANDA satisfies all the functional requirements, USFDA may grant tentative approval due to unexpired patents or drug exclusivities issues. In this situation, the product cannot be marketed until the final approval (USFDA, 2019d; Hemphill and Lemley, 2010; Khatun et al., 2018).

6.4.1.2.4 Biologics license application

The BLA seeks consent to present biological or those delivering them such as blood, allergenic, gene manipulation, monoclonal antibodies, immunomodulators, growth factors, cytokines, peptides, medical device, cell and tissue product, vaccines, xenotransplantation products, etc. for trade purpose in the United States. The applicant is needed to file Form 356h for seeking approvals under BLA. If follows the same review timeline as that of the NDA process.

Though BLA and NDA have the same review process, the BLA has its peculiarities like the Center for Drug Evaluation and Research (CDER) and the Center for Biologics Evaluation and Research (CBER) and both will jointly monitor the BLAs. As there is greater variation in biological products, the USFDA may need a closer examination of the production process and capability. The BLA is asked to incorporate broad details on all studies such as patient profiles and lists, statistical analysis protocol (SAP), and investigative study (USFDA, 2015b).

6.4.1.2.5 Over-the-counter drugs

CDER's division for nonprescription drugs oversees approval of OTC (nonprescription) drug products. Nonprescription Drug Advisory Committee meets on a regular basis to help the FDA for solving issues regarding OTC applications (USFDA, 2020d).

Because there are nearly 3000 OTC products, the USFDA classifies them into 80 therapeutic classes (such as analgesics and antacids) and reviews the application based on class not individually.

Each category of OTC drug a monograph is developed and published in Federal Register. An OTC monograph is defined as a "rule book for each therapeutic category establishing conditions, such as API, use, dose, labelling, and testing, under which an OTC drug is generally recognized as safe and effective (GRASE) and can be marketed without an NDA and FDA premarket approval (USFDA, 2020e).

Without going through the FDA approval process, new products that meet the final monograph can be sold. Drugs that do not match the final monograph must go through the NDA application process (USFDA, 2020d).

6.4.2 Marketing of veterinary products in the United States

Organizations manufacturing or repacking animal medicines for supply in the United States need to register under the Center for Veterinary Medicine (CVM) of USFDA. All veterinary products presented for import in the United States must be approved by New Animal Drug Application (NADA), and alternatively one can obtain conditional approval or index listing (for minor species). For veterinary products of generic type Abbreviated New Animal Drug Application is applicable. If needed, the USFDA verifies the stated NADA, conditional approval or index listing by equating the submission with the USFDA's reference dataset. If the submission is not provided or is not complete or correct, then the evaluation gets delayed. If the information is adequate, then the submission is verified; in case of a deficiency, the USFDA may ask the applicant to provide additional data or may hold up the product. If the product needs and does not possess NADA, conditional approval, or index information, the approval may not be granted (USFDA, 2018c).

Following data are needed in the NADA submissions:

1. *Chemistry, manufacturing process and controls*: This portion provides the details of the manufacturing process of new animal API. It also provides details on staff, amenities, vessels, components and composition, industrial process, and GMP compliance.
2. *Efficacy*: This portion includes the studies carried out to establish the efficacy of API. Dose justification and estimation are the parts in the application.
3. *Safety*: The studies on the toxicity of API and limits of its safe use in the targeted animal make up this portion. The safety of persons coming into contact with API while delivering the drug is also studied.
4. *Human food safety*: The portion includes both short- and long-duration toxicities and metabolic studies, analytical method development and validation, and residual depletion from tissues. The study is essential for dairy animals to find whether and what amount of the drug is found in the food or if it is causing undesired consequences.
5. *Labeling*: The NADA applicant should also provide the labeling.
6. *Environmental review*: The environmental evidence should conform the National Environmental Policy Act (NEPA). The review is done to find out the environmental impact statements (EIS) or is used to establish a finding of no significant impact (FONSI).
7. *Freedom of information (FOI) summary (food-producing animal species)*: This portion deals with the studies for authorization of API and a brief of the environmental evaluation. This has to be made public after approval is granted (CVM, 2018; USFDA, 2021).

6.5 Marketing authorization process for Japan

Pharmaceuticals and Medical Devices Agency (PMDA), the regulatory agency of Japan, works in tandem with Ministry of Health, Labour and Welfare (MHLW) for the protection of public health by assuring quality, efficacy, and safety of pharmaceuticals and medical devices. The applicants can seek marketing authorization for a new drug/device/generic drug/orphan drug/OTC drug/"behind-the-counter (BTC)" drug (a drug which requires pharmacists' counsel and that can be bought from a pharmacy without physician's prescription) and quasidrugs in Japan (PMDA; Hori, 2006; PMDA-profile of services).

6.5.1 New drug application

The applicants need to submit NDA dossier to PMDA for marketing of NDA in Japan. The dossier contains documents on development; use and authorizations abroad; production procedures, references, and tests; structure elucidation and physicochemical characterization, stability data, pharmacology of drug, absorption-distribution-metabolism-elimination pattern, toxicity profile, and clinical study data. Regulatory bodies in Japan require application documents in CTD format. PMDA accepts applications only in Japanese as Japan's Pharmaceutical Affairs Law mandates all marketing applications to be prepared in Japanese. NDA approval process is shown in Fig. 6.6.

The NDA application is evaluated by PMDA reviewer team whose members are from the fields of pharmaceutical science, physical science, biostatistics, medicine, veterinary, etc. The team evaluates the drug product for its quality,

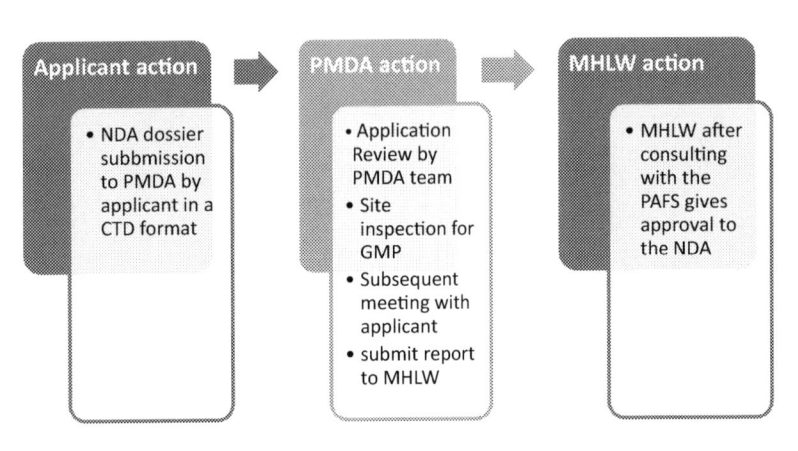

FIGURE 6.6 Submission and approval of NDA in Japan.

pharmacology, toxicology, pharmacokinetics, and clinical use. After meeting with applicant in person, the reviewer gives him questions for him to answer. GMP inspection of the manufacturing locations is then carried out. In order to impart effectiveness of the review process, reviewers can also seek assistance from external field experts.

The PMDA reviewer, after seeking suggestions from the external expert, summarizes the key observations and holds discussions, twice if needed, with the applicant.

The results of the review as well as that of GMP compliance reports are submitted by PMDA reviewer to the MHLW. MHLW after consulting with the Pharmaceutical Affairs and Food Sanitation Council (PAFS) gives approval for NDA and the new drug is published in the government gazette. The deliverance of approval certificate is done by the Evaluation and Licensing Division after the approval date.

To perform clinical studies for new drug manufacturing and marketing, applicant should submit study protocol well in advance to MHLW. In past, clinical study on Japanese population was must; hence separate clinical study was expected to obtain marketing authorization in Japan. To match with the international requirements, NDA application guideline was modified and two new notifications are issued to accept the foreign clinical data:

Handling of Data on Clinical trials on Drugs Performed in Foreign Countries
Ethnic Factors to be considered for Accepting Foreign Clinical Trial Data

https://www.pmda.go.jp/english.

As per these notifications, whenever an NDA utilizes data generated from clinical studies performed in foreign countries, it is first evaluated to ensure that it stands to the legal necessities of Japan. The NDA is then evaluated for its aptness of ethnic factors, intrinsic or extrinsic. If required, a bridging study is conducted to establish that the outcomes of clinical study conducted elsewhere can be extrapolated to the Japanese population, and those clinical data are accepted. The applicant needs to take advice from PMDA to conduct bridging studies. The pharmacokinetic studies are to be mandatorily conducted in Japanese people for bridging study. To encourage clinical trials globally, so as to make drug development more rapid and efficient and to do away with drug lag where the new drug approval takes several years, global concepts of clinical trials are employed. Additionally, the notice "Basic Principles on Global Clinical Trials (Reference Cases)" has been circulated to facilitate mutual cooperation and knowledge sharing in the area of international clinical trials for Japan, China, and South Korea.

If authorization is rejected, applicants have the right to plea under the Administrative Appeal Act to MHLW. Alternatively, the applicant can also appeal for a judicial review of the decision-making process of PMDA at the Japanese courts. "Points to consider in applications for decreasing the PMDA review period for new drugs" has been circulated in 2010. It included issues from applicant's perspective to accomplish the PMDA review period target of 12 months in a regular review process and 9 months for priority cases in 2013 (PMDA Reviews; APEC, 2015; JPMA, 2020).

Special Approval for Emergency (SAE) has also been explained in pharmaceuticals and medical devices. SAE can be applied for those drugs which need to be used to prevent harm to the health by the spread of diseases in emergency situation; there is no other existing product to manage such emergency situation and a product has been approved in other country having similar regulated system as in Japan. Saint-Raymond et al. (2020) compared the first regulatory approvals for Remdesivir, drug used for Covid situation, through emergency pathways in the United States, Japan, and the EU (Saint-Raymond et al., 2020).

6.5.2 Generic drug approval process

The reexamination period needs to be completed before the generic drug application can be filed. This is done to provide protection to branded products from patent and reexamination period. The PMDA then evaluates the provided data for: (1) stability tests, (2) specification and test methods, and (3) bioequivalence study and finds out the equivalence (efficacy, safety, and quality) between generic and innovator drug. Application for generic drug product must be given in CTD format. Data requirements to approve generic drugs are details of standards and manufacturing and test methods for ascertaining the veracity of these data, stability data, and absorption, distribution, metabolism, excretion (ADME) data to establish bioequivalence (Kuribayashi et al., 2015).

6.5.3 Orphan drug regulation in Japan

Amended Pharmaceutical Affairs Law dealt with rare diseases in 1993. The orphan drugs were designated for rare diseases (occurrence in less than 50,000 patients). This apart some more conditions need to be fulfilled like nonavailability of drug or therapy for the disease concerned; substantial increase in safety and efficacy profile, strong rationale advocated for its utility and development plan following a valid process. The regulatory bodies involved for approval of orphan drug are MHLW, PAFSC, and PMDA (O'Connor, 2013; Liu et al., 2010).

6.5.4 Biological product approval in Japan

The consultation regarding clinical trials of biotechnology products and biosimilars come under the purview of PMDA's Office of Biologicals. Requirements are different for biological product to be used as regenerative medicine product. MHLW needs to consult "Pharmaceutical Affairs and Food Sanitation Council" to term that it is a biological product (PMDA reviews). MHLW published one guidance entitled "Guideline for the quality, safety and efficacy assurance of biosimilar products" in 2009. According to the Japanese Guideline for the Development of Biosimilar Products, applicants must develop their own manufacturing process in order to elucidate quality attributes and demonstrate high similarity of these characteristics to reference products. Furthermore, data from both clinical and nonclinical studies are included to demonstrate biosimilarity (Arato, 2016).

6.6 Marketing authorization for pharmaceuticals in Australia

6.6.1 Introduction

Australia, a developed nation, has a sophisticated, rigorous system to evaluate medicinal products prior to commercialization. The regulatory control of pharmaceuticals comes under Therapeutic Goods Administration (TGA) established through Therapeutic Goods Act (1989) and Therapeutic Goods Regulations (1990) (the Regulations) by the Department of Health, Australia. To manage finances, TGA raises funds by charging fees for assessments, yearly registrations, and examinations.

Under this act, a therapeutic good is defined as a good existing in any form for therapeutic use. It can be a medication or a medical device used for diagnosing, preventing, or treating an ailment, flaw or injury; or affecting physiology; determining vulnerability to a disease; or regulating or averting conception; or finding pregnancy; or as a anatomical replacement.

The chief goal of TGA is to measure and screen all activities to make sure that the therapeutic goods accessible are of satisfactory universal standard, and that they are available within a required time for healing benefits. The TGA controls the procurement, production, and marketing of drug products in Australia (https://www.tga.gov.au/what-tga-regulates).

The TGA exercises its regulatory control over drug products in Australia via the following procedures:

- Assessment and authorization of drug products meant for use in Australia;
- Authorizing producers as per global norms under GMP;
- Postmarketing surveillance, by collecting samples, instances of adverse effects, and answering questions of community;
- Expansion, upkeep, and surveillance of the structures for registration and entry of drug products; and
- Evaluation of drugs for export.

6.6.1.1 Premarket evaluation

Before introducing any drug product in Australia, it should be listed or registered with Australian Register of Therapeutic Goods (ARTG). It is analyzed using various methods but many methods are common for both.

- For finding out if the product is registrable or listable, Schedules 4 and 5 of the TGA regulations 1990 can be referred. After acceptance of application, the applicant needs to pay the fees.
- For assessment, TGA can also seek help from external evaluators.
- The accepted application is designated either Australian Listed (AUST L) or Australian Registered (AUST R) number depending on the category.
- Upon rejection the applicant has a right of appeal under TGA rules.
- The applicant may have to provide further data to the TGA for assessment. A rejection in this may lead the applicant to an appeal to the Secretary, Department of Health and subsequently to Administrative Appeals Tribunal.

6.6.1.2 Application for listed drug products

- Listing in the TGA register requires first a successful self-evaluation as per TGA standards.
- The application can be submitted in either hard copy via Form F03 or electronically via Electronic Lodgment Facility (ELF).
- Business Management Unit (BMU) then verifies the application and ensures that the fee is paid.
- The verified document is sent to ARTG section of TGA.
- TGA releases a certificate with AUST L number and list of norms to be followed.
- In the postlisting phase, within 10 days, the document is sent to Australian Listed Drugs Unit. To make sure that product constituents are permissible, claims made are not prohibitive and cautionary declarations are contained within wherever needed.
- Upon clearing the eligibility hurdle, the applicant receives a confirmatory message and the product gets listed with ARTG (Sai Kumari et al., 2016).

6.6.2 Application for registering drug product

Category 1 application, coming under subregulations 16C(3)(b) and 16D(3)(b), is for new drug or an alteration in components or a novel dosage forms, new amount or new generic and newer clinical use and revisions in the produce information.

Category 2 application, coming under subregulations 16C(3)(a) and 16D(3)(a), is used for products already authorized in two well-regulated countries and which furnish two different assessment reports while applying. The countries where the product is already approved should meet the norms prescribed in Australia.

Category 3 application is for a product requiring change only in quality figures of already-registered product which does not require any pharmacological, clinical, and BABE data.

Application submission and evaluation take place in eight phases as shown in Fig. 6.7. All application completes their submission and evaluation phases in different timelines. Time taken for handling application of listed medicine at TGA, when applied electronically and in hard copy is 10 and 30 days, respectively. Time required for new OTC product application handling will be 71 days. TGA required 255, 175, and 45 days processing time, for application of prescription medicines for category 1, category 2 and category 3, respectively.

Presubmission phase	• Milestone1-PPF lodged before first of month • PPF Lodged Before First of Month
Submission Phase	• Milestone-2 • Processing of Accepted Dossiers at TGA
First Round Assessment Phase	• Milestone-3 • First Round of Assessment and consolidation of section 31Request
Consolidated S.31 Request Response Phase	• Milestone-4 • TGA Received Response to s.31 Request from Applicant
Second Round Assessment Phase	• Milestone-5 • Second Round Assessment Complete
Expert Advisory Review Phase	• Milestone-6 • Advisory Committee Meeting and Report Preparation
Decision Phase	• Milestone-7 • Delegate decision including PI/CMI/RMP Negotiation
Post decision Phase	• Milestone-8 • Administrative and regulatory activities complete

FIGURE 6.7 Phases for submission and evaluation of applications for registering drug products in Australia.

6.6.2.1 Phase 1: presubmission phase

In this phase the planning data must be furnished by the applicant in the presubmission planning form (PPF). This contains information about the type of application and quality requirements, as well as pharmacological and clinical data from the dossier. Thus PPF gives TGA an indication of actual resource management.

Presubmission meetings with TGA can be asked for if needed. These may be conducted any time before PPF lodgment. The PPF is to be tendered online or through eBusiness Services (eBS). PPFs are administered on first date of every month. An important part of PPF is Module 2 which provides data on the scope, measure, and intricacy of the planned dossier. If the PPF is found acceptable, TGA sends a planning letter with anticipated lodgment date and timeline for application. Upon receipt of the planning letter submission phase is deemed over. TGA may also give some more time to address any issues pertaining to PPF which is not found convincing in submission or oral hearing. This is sent by the fifteenth day of the next month in which the PPF was originally administered.

6.6.2.1.1 Orphan drug

Drugs deemed safe by USFDA or other respectable regulatory bodies are considered for TGA approval under orphan drug category. TGA generally gives fee waiver for application and evaluation of orphan drugs. Applications are to be made with TGA 8–12 weeks prior to the presubmission phase. Upon nonreceipt of orphan status, the application is treated as any other and charged as such.

6.6.2.1.2 Priority evaluations

Applicant can also opt for priority evaluation status with Director, Drug Safety Evaluation Board (DSEB) in presubmission phase if the drug is a new chemical entity (NCE)with clinical facts suggesting a lot of promise in a grave disease. The timeline of registration process of 150 days gets reduced to 60 days (Bootes et al., 2019).

6.6.2.1.3 USFDA format in TGA presubmission

A drug is proposed for use in life-threatening conditions where no other treatment options are available. In such a case, the applicant can tender application in USFDA format and differences can be deliberated with the TGA in presubmission.

6.6.2.1.4 Literature-based submission

In cases where experimental data is not found, applicant can provide literature-based data to TGA. This is true for drugs which are not introduced in Australia but widely approved elsewhere. However authorization by TGA is done selectively on merit.

The applicant must arrive at an understanding with TGA before applying under this category. This is done 90 days before presubmission. The grounds for discussion can be:

- search methodology
- databases explored
- selection of literature (TGA—literature-based submissions)

6.6.2.1.5 Fixed combination products

For these applications, before filing PPF, the applicant needs to rationalize the products with the TGA as per the EU guidelines which are acceptable in Australia. If any of the combined drugs is not registered, the applicant needs to propose filing dates for the unregistered drug also.

6.6.2.2 Phase 2: submission phase

Any application not absolutely meeting TGA regulatory stipulations is not accepted for assessment. There is no provision of redressal mechanism to address the deficiencies in TGA requirements during the submission phase. Once submission phase is over, the TGA dispatches a notification informing if application is "effective" and hence accepted for assessment or is "not effective" and therefore not accepted for assessment. Any data sent after application has been tendered should be supplied in a covering letter highlighting submission number of the relevant application.

6.6.2.2.1 Planning and tracking of applications

TGA regularly notifies the applicant of the evaluation timeline: Milestones for the different stages of regulatory mechanism are as follows:

6.6.2.2.2 Key dates

For registration of applications as an NCE, novel drug combination, comparable product of biological origin, additional clinical use, the dossier should reach the TGA by seventh of month after the planning letter has been received. For registration of application as a key or trivial diversion, new generic product, alteration in product information, the dossier should reach the TGA by 14th of month after planning letter has been received. At the end of this phase, TGA dispatches the notification letter before month ends.

6.6.2.2.3 Lodgment of application

Applicants of an NCE, novel drug combination, and new generic product need to file their application electronically via eBS before filing the hard copy to the TGA.

6.6.2.2.4 Processing the application

An application is deemed effective and thus considered for assessment if it arrives within time limit, constant with the data and meets applicable TGA regulatory conditions.

6.6.2.2.5 Evaluation fee

The full fee is paid after acceptance for assessment. The application lapses if the applicant fails to pay the evaluation fee within 60 days of notification.

6.6.2.3   Phase 3: first-round evaluation

It begins the day after sending notification letter. In case of the queries a combined section 31 request is collected and sent to the applicant within specified date. The query can be in the form of direct contact with the applicant to search for explanation or can be raised informally if it requires minor explanation. The informal query saves time as it does not change the timeline. The TGA may use the services of external experts to assess the dossier. The coordination with the applicant with respect to evaluation is done by TGA. This phase needs 4 months for generic and 5 months for other applications. Then TGA issues Milestone 3 letter to the applicant. Milestone 3 letter includes section 31 request for data (if needed) and copies of the phase 3 evaluation reports prepared by RMP and quality, pharmacological, and clinical evaluators.

6.6.2.4   Phase 4: combined section 31 request–response

The response time for section 31 is 30 or 60 days as proposed by applicant in PPF and agreed by TGA in planning letter. After reviewing phase 3 report, applicants may explain to TGA the apparent errors of fact or key oversights. Replies to the evaluation reports are included in Module 1.0.2. If there is no section 31 request, applicants need to reply by the timeline of Milestone 3. Usually 14 days, after TGA's phase 3 report is dispatched, are given in Milestone 4.

   If required applicant sends TGA, a reply regarding section 31 request, and phase 3 evaluation reports.

6.6.2.5   Phase 5: second-round assessment

The phase 5 begins as soon as phase 4 is over, even if the Milestone 4 is not yet achieved. During this phase, applicant replies to the section 31 request and evaluator finishes assessing the data. The TGA has to compile evaluation reports within 60 days for new generics and 30 days for other applications.

   If the application referred to Advisory Committee on Medicines (ACM) the applicant can request ACM for suggestions. Otherwise TGA issues completed phase 5 reports not submitted to ACM.

6.6.2.5.1 Review of evaluation reports

The DSEB report is sent to applicant and to ACM if advice is sought. If applicant finds some discrepancies, he can revert to TGA and can also suggest changes in product information. This allays the concerns early and reduces post-ACM discussions and subsequently approval time. The timeline for this period is 14 days.

6.6.2.6 Phase 6: expert advisory review

After evaluation, DSEB may refer it to ACM for suggestions. The TGA delegate reviews and requests advice from ACM including proposal to approve or not.

A copy is also sent to the applicant. This phase commences the day ACM advice is sought by the representative and the second-round evaluation reports prepared by RMP, quality, pharmacological and clinical evaluators are sent to the applicant. ACM meeting is held twenty three working days after this date.

The applicant must make sure that the pre-ACM reply and comments, errors or omissions in the second round of evaluation are received by TGA thirteen days prior to meeting date.

The phase ends when ACM suggestions are communicated to the applicant on 15th day of the month of ACM consultation. TGA informs the applicant about the suggestions received from ACM is the milestone 6.

https://www.tga.gov.au/.

6.6.2.7 Phase 7: post-ACM (decision phase)

ACM assesses the application and request issues proposed by the TGA representative and deliver its own resolve to the representative office which will give its verdict on whether to approve the application or not. The applicant is informed within 28 days about verdict being taken. While giving approval the delegate apprises the applicant of any remaining issues. Then TGA conveys the final product data and consumer medicines information (CMI) with the applicant. Upon rejection the decision letter describes the reasons for rejection and the applicant is free to appeal. In Milestone 7, a verdict is given for approval or nonapproval of the application and the decision is communicated to the applicant.

6.6.2.8 Phase 8: postapproval procedures

TGA issues a Certificate of Registration with AUST R number after final authorization. The approval holder has to pay yearly registration fees. He also has to communicate the TGA the date of launching the product in the market.

6.6.2.8.1 Scheduling

The assessment results are sent to National Drugs and Poisons Schedule Committee (NDPSC). Schedules of the product are pronounced by NDPSC and managed by TGA. If the applicant wants any change in schedule, then he should apply to NPDSC with appropriate data to support the proposal.

6.6.2.8.2 Appeal provisions

There is a complete system for appealing against administrative verdicts. Informal routes of plea can also be availed.

6.6.2.8.2.1 Informal appeal mechanisms

An informal appeal can be made at Standing Arbitration Committee for Therapeutic Goods (SAC) or the Pharmaceutical Sub-Committee (PSC) of Australian Drug Evaluation Committee (ADEC) during assessment. This also stops the clock which is not the case when TGA finds problems in the category 3 application or makes section 31 request (https://www.tga.gov.au/).

6.6.2.8.2.2 Formal appeal mechanisms These are known as section 60 appeals, for example:

- denial of registration or listing status on the ARTG,

- change or addition of requirements for registration or entry,
- termination of registration or entry, or
- withdrawal or deferral of a production license

https://www.tga.gov.au/

6.6.2.8.2.3 Administrative Appeals Tribunal To challenge section 60 appeal, the applicant can appeal at Administrative Appeals Tribunal (AAT) within 28 days of the Minister's verdict following review. If AAT suggests a merit review, any party can appeal at the federal court any time.

If TGA is unable to complete a Category 1 or Category 2 assessment within the timeline, the applicant can request to the secretary to treat application as rejected. The applicant can then appeal for review under Section 24E (ARGPM, 2020; Therapeutic Goods Act, 1989; Therapeutic Goods Regulations, 1990).

The preparation and online submission of dossiers is done in accordance with eCTD. The application provides details of information in eCTD through five different modules.

1. *Module 1*: In this module, the applicant must include administrative details such as a cover letter, the company's name and address, and the sponsors' information. The applicant also provides field copy, debarment, and financial certification papers, as well as patent information. GMP procedures, compliance meetings, references to pediatric growth, and PhV, antibiotic resistance, and overseas assessment reports are all detailed in the application.
2. *Module 2*: Module 2 contains a full table of contents as well as a concise introduction to the program. In Module 2, the applicant offers an overview of quality and nonclinical and clinical research overviews.
3. *Module 3*: Module 3 discusses the quality of drug substances and the finished product (formulation). The applicant describes the chemical structure, manufacturing process, and characteristics of the drug substance and the product in this module.
4. *Module 4*: Module 4 requires the applicant to submit study reports on main and secondary pharmacodynamics. It contains data on drug interactions, as well as all pharmacokinetic research involving absorption, delivery, metabolism, and excretion. It also provides information on different toxicity studies as well as references to related literature.
5. *Module 5*: Module 5 is for human clinical research reports. Bioavailability, bioequivalence, in vitro–in vivo associations, protein binding, hepatic metabolism, drug interactions, and other topics are covered. It includes a description of human pharmacokinetic and pharmacodynamics study. It also provides reports on effectiveness and safety research, as well as the required literature.

6.6.3   Registration of over-the- counter (OTC) medicine

Over-the-counter medicine is a separate category in the drug regulation and of three types, namely (1) pharmacy medications, (2) pharmacist only medications, and (3) general sales medications. The sale of pharmacy medications must be regulated by registered pharmacist, but the sales process can be facilitated by a nonpharmacist. Pharmacist medication sales must be controlled by pharmacist only and general sales medicines can be sold on nonpharmacy outlets (Marathe et al., 2020; Goh et al., 2009).

Verification of medicine as OTC medicine and ingredients

Applicant needs to ascertain if his product is an approved OTC product as per ARTG and if it contains any ingredient(s) needing assessment and if it is in Australian register.

If the applicant's medicinal product or ingredient is not approved by ARTG then applicant can make separate application for each or combined application (Hammett and Hunt, 2009).

6.6.3.1   Application levels for new OTC medicines

- N1 generic product which fulfills the criteria for OTC new medicine N1 applications (change in flavoring or coloring agent or fragrance of an already-approved OTC).
- N2 generic product which fulfills the criteria for specific OTC monograph and the basic foundations of OTC new medicine.
- N3 generic products which do not come under N1, N2, or N4 application and involve CTD Modules 1 and 3).
- N4 generic products which:
  - o need additional efficacy and safety data or
  - o have not been approved as OTC medicine subsequent to downscheduling or
  - o need stringent analysis being from umbrella segment.
- N5 new products which are not generics and is/has either a new:
  - o drug or combination of drugs, clinical use, dose, dosage form, instruction for use, patient profile.

6.6.3.2   Checking guidelines and mandatory requirements

While applying for OTC medicines applicants should check for specific guidelines applicable for their product and standard guidelines issued by European and The International Council for Harmonisation of Technical Requirements for Pharmaceuticals for Human Use (ICH) and adopted by Australia. Applicant has to submit mandatory information about the product to make application effective and proceed to evaluation.

6.6.3.3 Ensuring valid GMP evidence

While applying the applicant has to submit evidence that he is a certified manufacturer of therapeutic goods and follows GMP norms at each step. As a proof or evidence TGA accepts GMP certification from TGA for local manufacturers and GMP authorization from TGA for foreign manufacturers

6.6.3.4 Preparation and submission of application

6.6.3.4.1 Preparation of the dossier

Applicant should prepare dossier which contains all clerical and scientific data needed as per the level of application. It is important to check that information included in the dossier is complete and in the required format. It is essential to prepare dossier as per the guidance provided in CTD Module 1: OTC medicine guidelines and as per regulatory norms for the OTC product application. The application must have an appropriate covering letter.

6.6.3.4.2 Submission of application

Application is submitted online in CTD format. While submitting the application for OTC product appropriate choices between nonprescription single medicine and nonprescription composite pack should be made. Application level should also be mentioned as per the guidelines. Upon submission of submission, an ID number is generated which is used for future communication. The status of application can be followed via Business Services.

6.6.3.4.3 Withdrawing an application

TGA allows withdrawal of application if any decision has not been made and if application is made in writing. If it is done on grounds of safety issue then the data may have to be submitted to TGA. Fee refund provision is available if applicant withdraws the application prior to commencement of review process.

6.6.3.5 Fees

TGA charges the applicant with application fee and also evaluation fee depending on the application level. If a single applicant chooses to go for two applications for one drug at the same application level with adequate supporting data to allow concurrent assessment, he can opt to be invoiced the concurrent fees. In some cases, where application does not qualify for the concurrent fee, TGA may provide a waiver or concession on evaluation fee under Regulation 45(4) of TGR 1990.

6.6.3.6 Screening of application

TGA verifies the correctness of application level and other criteria of meeting the effectiveness while screening the application.

Application is considered effective if it fulfills the criteria under Section 23(2) of TGR 1989, which are as follows:

- Application fee is deposited;
- Correctness and effectiveness of application is established;
- Data under Section 7D of TGA (Section 23(2)(ba) of TGA) are filled up if the application is for restricted product;
- Product sample given to TGA (if needed).

The covering letter should mention critical data and level to make it easy for TGA to trace the application early. TGA accepts only the effective applications for evaluation and informs the applicant accordingly with statement for fees remaining, if any. Upon not finding the application effective, TGA informs the applicant and explains the grounds of rejection. It also refunds evaluation fees. Application is also taken down from Business Service.

6.6.3.7 Evaluation of medicine application

During evaluation, TGA analyzes the data and answers of applicant to TGA queries. It documents the conclusions.

Evaluation timelines depend on the application level which reflects the TGA's procedural time and excludes time taken by applicant to respond to data request. The clock stops whenever TGA waits for the applicant response to a request for information and restarts when the issue is addressed.

6.6.3.7.1 Requesting additional information

TGA raises requests for information with the applicant under section 31 of TGA providing a time limit to respond. If the query raised is about the content of a segment of the proposal folder, the applicant needs to respond in eCTD format. He is not required to submit supplementary data unless asked. The due date is not extended unless it can be established that the time given is not enough. If the asked information is not provided within time and many issues remain unresolved, then product will not be registered.

6.6.3.7.2 Expert advisory committee suggestions

TGA may seek guidance from advisory committee on Nonprescription Medicines (ACNM) especially when product is first of its kind. This can stretch the time limit by 90−180 days.

Applications submitted at the incorrect level

In such a case, TGA:

- conveys to the applicant that application is treated as belonging to the level considered while screening;
- evaluates the data pertinent to the considered level; and
- allows applicant to make necessary changes to fit in with the applied level.

If the desired changes are not made, product will not be registered. The applicant can reapply with data for the correct level if registration is still sought.

6.6.3.7.3 Making the OTC registration decision

Before going ahead with registration, applicant needs to verify the data incorporated during evaluation. Delegate of Health Secretary reviews all documents in the application to ascertain efficacy, safety, and quality of the product before registering the product under section 25 of TGA 1989.

Upon concluding to register the product the decision letter is sent to applicant with standard conditions to be complied with Section 28 of the TGR 1989. On failure to do so applicant's product is denied registration with ARTG under Section 30(1)(da) of TGA.

6.6.3.7.4 Patent authorization under Australia/US free-trade agreement

The applicant can have direct registration on ARTG by producing a US patent certificate of his product under subsection 26B(1) of TGR 1989.

6.6.3.7.5 Approval effect date

The authorization commences on the date mentioned in the medicine's registration certificate. Before this date the applicant can neither import nor export the medicine.

6.6.3.7.6 Decision to deny registration

In such a case the decision letter includes reason for denial of registration and information on seeking a review (Tongia, 2018; Emmerton, 2009; TGA-OTC Medicine Regulation, 2021).

6.6.4 Registration of complementary medicine

Complementary medicines are products that contain ingredients such as herbs, vitamins, minerals, and nutritional supplements and are homeopathic or aromatherapy preparations. They are regulated under the Therapeutic Goods Act (1989) in Australia.

The Therapeutic Goods Regulations of 1990 define a complementary medicine as a therapeutic good containing primarily one or more active ingredients, listed in Schedule 14 of the Regulations, who individually have a well-established identity and conventional use (Dunne and Phillips, 2010).

Complementary medicines regulated in Australia

For the regulation of all drugs, including complementary medicines, Australia uses a risk-based approach with a two-tiered framework (Pinder and Ghosh, 2019).

- Relatively safer medicines can be listed on the Australian Register of Therapeutic Goods (ARTG).
- Not so safe medicines must be registered on the ARTG.

6.6.4.1 Verification of complementary medicine and active ingredients

Applicant should first verify that whether their product is complementary medicine as per the TGA law, and if yes, then verify whether it is already registered in ARTG or not. Applicant has to verify that active ingredients present in their medicine are designated active ingredients and nothing else. If any of the components is noncomplementary then the product either will be considered an OTC or will be a prescription product and will be evaluated as such.

Applicant must have proprietary ingredients ID numbers for those constituents present in the formulation and for novel component such ID number can be generated by filling a proprietary ingredient form. If it is a new component then name of that substance is to be proposed through an appropriate mechanism. Medicinal products having similar ingredients and clinical use are subjected to similar schedules. An ingredient not yet scheduled but is present in a medicine will need to be classified by TGA while deciding on registration (Hammett and Hunt, 2009).

6.6.4.2 Checking ingredients and scheduling

The applicant must confirm that the active ingredients are as designated, and if the formulation has at least one noncomplementary active ingredient, it will not be evaluated by a common route. Applicant also needs to verify the scheduling of complementary medicines.

6.6.4.3 Good manufacturing practice

Applicant needs to prove that production of medicine follows GMP. To achieve this, the local applicant needs a GMP license from TGA and the foreign applicant needs a GMP clearance from TGA valid through evaluation timeline.

6.6.4.4 Determination of application category

Registration can be sought for five categories, from 1 to 5 in increasing order of risk which in turn is linked to increasing data requirement and assessment time.

1. *Category 1 (Registered Complementary Medicines (RCM) 1)*: For products similar to approved product except in name, color, flavor, and fragrance.
1. *Category 2 (RCM 2)*: For complementary medicinal product complying with a TGA monograph.
2. *Category 3 (RCM 3)*: For generic complementary products who demonstrate safety and efficacy and, the products assessed by a comparable regulatory organization.
3. *Category 4 (RCM 4)*: For products in which either of efficacy, safety, or quality has been ascertained. These also require compulsory submission of Modules 1 and 2 along with the one of Module 3 (quality), Module 4 (nonclinical), and Module 5 (clinical), whichever is found applicable.
4. *Category 5 (RCM 5)*: For new products needing registration on ARTG and whose efficacy, safety, and quality is yet to be analyzed. They include:
   a. newly registered product yet to be assessed, new active ingredient, and higher strength of the drug.
   b. newer dosage form, product consisting of an excipient not yet used in complementary products, and higher quantity of an excipient (Cameron, 1998).

6.6.4.5 Checking guidelines and requirements

While applying for complementary medicines applicants should check for specific guidelines applicable for their product and standard guidelines issued by European and ICH and adopted by Australia. Applicant has to submit mandatory information about the product to make application effective and proceed to evaluation.

6.6.4.6 Requesting exemption as part of application

Restricted representations can only be used in advertisements for therapeutic goods directed to consumer if TGA has permitted or approved the use of that representation. Applicant should read the detailed information and then make the application on this ground.

6.6.4.7 Presubmission meeting

Presubmission consultation with TGA is highly recommended before giving application. This helps in preparing a quality dossier. The meeting helps in finding critical matters related to applicant's proposal.

6.6.4.8 Preparation and submission of application

6.6.4.8.1 Preparation of dossier

The dossier needs to provide all clerical and scientific data depending on the application level in the desired format as per CTD Module 1 of Complementary Medicine with a suitable covering letter.

6.6.4.8.2 Submission of application

Application is to be tendered online in CTD format under suitable category. After submission a submission number is issued for all future dialog. The progress of the application can be gauged through Business Services. The clock starts as soon as the fee is paid.

6.6.4.8.3 Withdrawing an application

TGA allows withdrawal of application if any decision has not been made and if application is made in writing. If it is done on grounds of safety issue then the data may have to be submitted to TGA. There is provision for fee refund if applicant withdraws the application prior to commencement of review process.

6.6.4.9 Fees

The TGA charges both application fee and evaluation fee at the same time. The fee depends on the application level. if any additional charges are being levied applicant has to pay it within 60 days of paying the fees. TGA may provide a waiver or concession on evaluation fee under Regulation 45(4) of TGR 1990.

6.6.4.10 Screening of application

TGA verifies if the application meets both clerical and scientific necessities. Application is considered successful if it fulfills the criteria under Section 23(2) of TGR 1989, which are as follows:

- Application fee is deposited.
- Correctness and effectiveness of application are established.
- Data under Section 7D of TGA (Section 23(2)(ba) of TGA) are filled up if the application is for restricted product.
- Product sample given to TGA (if needed).

The covering letter should mention critical data and level to make it easy for TGA to trace the application early. TGA accepts only the effective applications for evaluation and informs the applicant accordingly with statement for fees remaining, if any. The evaluation is not undertaken until the evaluation fee is fully paid. Applicant is also allowed to make slight rectifications, noticed during screening. Upon not finding the application effective, TGA does not evaluate it and in writing to applicant explains the grounds of rejection. It also refunds evaluation fees. Application is also taken down from Business Service. Lapsing of application: Application lapses upon nonpayment of evaluation fee within 60 days.

6.6.4.11 Evaluation of application and request for information

While evaluating the application, TGA assesses the data on efficacy, safety, and quality of complementary product and may ask for more data under section 31 of TGA. It examines the applicants' answer to the query raised by TGA. TGA keeps a document of all its findings.

Evaluation timelines depend on the application category which reflects TGA's procedural time and excludes time taken by applicant to respond to data request. The clock stops whenever TGA waits for the applicant response to a request for information and restarts when the issue is addressed.

6.6.4.11.1 Response to requests for information

The applicant needs to provide the asked data, final and exact, within the given timeline. No additional time for submitting responses is given unless applicant is able to establish that the time expectation is unrealistic. If the asked information is not provided within time and many issues remain unresolved, then product will not be registered. The applicant is allowed to ascertain the particulars and especially any suggested changes before the delegate. Health Secretary takes a call on registration of the complementary medicinal product.

6.6.4.11.2 Review by the delegate

Before arriving at a conclusion, under section 25 of TGR 1989, to register the product on the ARTG, the Delegate of Health Secretary:

- Reviews documents related to:
  o Application and submitted dossier
  o Assessment reports
  o Applicant replies to information request
  o Suggestions of experts
  o Other suitable data
- Verifies under section 25 of TGA if the efficacy, safety, and quality of the product are ascertained.

Then a written statement is sent to the applicant. TGA can also take suggestions from experts, for example, Advisory Committee for Complementary Medicine (ACCM). TGA then notifies and allows applicant to discuss advisory committee's deliberation in a committee meeting. The committee proceedings may further extend the timeline.

6.6.4.11.3 Decision on registration

If everything is in order, TGA communicates with applicant about its decision through a letter which describes conditions for registration of his product under section 28 of TGA. If applicant is unable to fulfill with any of the conditions, his product is annulled from ARTG under Section 30(1)(da) of TGA. The applicant also has to ensure correctness of details of his product before the ARTG entry.

6.6.4.11.4 Patent authorization under Australia/US agreement

The applicant can have direct registration on ARTG by producing a US patent certificate of his product under subsection 26B(1) of TGR 1989.

6.6.4.11.5 Approval effect date

The authorization commences on the date mentioned in the medicine's registration certificate. Before this date the applicant can neither import nor export the medicine.

6.6.4.11.6 Decision to deny registration

In such a case the decision letter includes:

- reason for denial of registration
- information on seeking a review (CM, 2020; Ghosh et al., 2006; Tongia, 2018).

6.7 Marketing authorization of pharmaceuticals in India

6.7.1 Introduction

India is among the most organized and fastest emerging pharmaceutical markets globally (Aditi, 2018). Not only it is the largest manufacturer of generic drugs in the world but also has the largest pool of consumers of pharmaceuticals with diverse background in terms of purchasing power (Issa, 2020). With estimated worth of US$33 billion and expansion at a CAGR more than 15% between the years 2015 and 2020, Indian pharmaceutical industry is the third largest drug manufacturing industry globally (Dhanalakshmi, 2017). With implementation of the latest revisions in the present Foreign Direct Investment (FDI) policy along with the large pool of competent scientists, engineers, other professionals, and skilled workers locally available at affordable costs, India is bound to attract more global investment in the pharmaceutical sector.

Central Drugs Standard Control Organization (CDSCO) along with State Licensing Authority (SLA) provides approval for importing, production, distribution, and selling of drug products in Indian market under Drugs and Cosmetics Act 1940 and Rules 1945 (D&C Act and Rule, 2016). Approval for new drugs or marketing authorization for new products in India is regulated under the strict regulations of New Drugs and Clinical Trials Rules, 2019 (ND & CT Rules, 2019).

6.7.2   Regulatory framework

The production, importing, exporting, sale and clinical investigation of medicine in India are controlled by the following laws (Ahmad et al., 2017; Senthil et al., 2015; ND & CT Rules, 2019):

1. Drugs and Cosmetics Act, 1940 and Rules, 1945;
2. Drugs (Prices Control) Order 1995;
3. Indian Patent and Design Act, 1970;
4. Medicinal and Toilet Preparations (Excise Duties) Act, 1956;
5. Industries (Development and Regulation) Act, 1951;
6. Pharmacy Act, 1948;
7. Trade and Merchandise Marks Act, 1958;
8. Narcotic Drugs and Psychotropic Substances Act, 1985;
9. Drugs and Magic Remedies (Objectionable Advertisement) Act, 1954;
10. Factories Act;
11. New Drugs and Clinical Trials Rules, 2019.

6.7.3   Prohibition of importing and/or manufacturing of certain drugs or cosmetics

Substandard, misbranded, adulterated or spurious drugs or cosmetics are prohibited to be imported and/or manufactured for distribution, selling, stocking, exhibiting, or offering for sale in India under Chapter III, Section 10 and Chapter IV, Section 18 of D&C Act, 1940 (D&C Act and Rule, 2016).

6.7.4   Import and manufacture of drugs for commercial use in India

6.7.4.1   Import

Importing drugs for commercial use in India needs submission of prescribed forms and approval from licensing authority as mentioned in Table 6.6. The registration certificate issued by licensing authority in Form 41 under Rule 27A of D&C Rules, 1945 shall be submitted along with such application (D&C Act and Rule, 2016; Import Guidance, 2007). The application, for license to import or getting registration certificate, shall be made by manufacturer holding wholesale license for selling or distributing drugs in India or his legal agent in India either having license for manufacturing or holding license for selling or distributing drugs in India. The drug which is prohibited for manufacturing, selling, or distribution in country where it is originated shall not be imported in India (except in case required for examining, testing, or analyzing purpose) (D&C Act and Rule, 2016; Import Guidance, 2007).

The manufacturer himself or his legal agent in India should apply along with original copy of challan of prescribed fees paid in the designated bank under Head of Account "0210-Medical and Public Health, 04 Public Health, 104-Fees and Fines" (D&C Act and Rule, 2016). The fees can also be transferred by manufacturer from any bank in his country by Electronic Clearance System (ECS) to designated bank in the abovementioned Head of Account (D&C Act and Rule, 2016). Single application and license will suffice if multiple drugs or class of drugs are imported from single manufacturing unit. In case, same manufacturer having multiple factories situated in different places needs to apply separately for each unit (D&C Act and Rule, 2016).

For further clarification and requirements, refer Part IV, Rules 21 to 43 of D&C Rules, 1945.

6.7.4.2   Manufacture

If drugs are being manufactured on multiple sites/premises, the applicant needs to apply separately and obtain a separate license for every premise (D&C Act and Rule, 2016; Suresh et al., 2014). If the applicant does not own a facility for manufacturing and wishes to use an already-approved facility in the name of any other person, he can apply for loan license. The license for repacking of drugs can also be granted under these rules by licensing authority (D&C Act and Rule, 2016). The types of forms required and duration of license validity is summarized in Table 6.6. For further clarification and requirements, refer Part VII, Rules 68 to 84 of D&C Rules, 1945.

TABLE 6.6 List of various procedures along with required application format, fees, timelines, and other details for getting permission to import, manufacture, and sale of dug in Indian market.

Application types	Regulatory body	Application form no.	License in form	Rule(s) applicable	Duration of validity
Import license for drugs to be used commercially	DCGI	8—drugs excluded in schedule X 8A—drugs specified in schedule X 9—Undertaking by manufacturer	10—drugs excluded in schedule X10A—drugs specified in schedule X	23, 24, and 27	3 years (if not canceled or suspended sooner) If fresh application made before 3 months of expiry, can be extended
Import of drugs for examination, test or analysis	DCGI	12	11	33 and 34	
License for selling, stocking or exhibition or offering for sale, or distributing the drugs excluded from schedule X	SLA	19	20	59 (2) and 61 (1)	5 years (can be renewed for 5 years if applied before expiry or within 6 months after expiry)
License for selling, stocking or exhibition, or offering for sale or distributing the drugs included in schedule X	SLA	19C	20F (retail) 20G (wholesale)	59 (2) and 61 (3)	5 years (can be renewed for 5 years if applied before expiry or within 6 months after expiry)
License for selling, stocking or exhibition, or offering for sale or distributing the homeopathic medicine	SLA	19B	20C (retail) 20D (wholesale)	67A and 67C	5 years (can be renewed for 5 years if applied within 6 months after expiry)
Manufacturing for selling or distribution of drugs not included in schedule C, C(1) and X	SLA	24	25 (fresh) 26 (renewal)	69 and 71	5 years (can be renewed for 5 years if applied within 6 months after expiry)
Manufacturing on loan licenses for drugs not included in schedule C & C(1) and X	SLA	24A	25A (fresh) 26A (renewal)	69A and 71B	5 years (can be renewed for 5 years if applied within 6 months after expiry)
Repacking of drugs excluding those specified in schedule C, C(1), and X	SLA	24B	25B	70 and 71A	5 years (can be renewed for 5 years if applied within 6 months after expiry)
Manufacturing for selling or distribution of homeopathic drugs	SLA	24C	25C (fresh) 26C (renewal)		5 years (can be renewed for 5 years if applied within 6 months after expiry)
Manufacturing for selling of Ayurvedic (including Siddha) or Unani drugs	SLA	24D	25D (fresh) 26D (renewal)	153, 154, and 155	5 years (can be renewed for 5 years if applied before expiry or within 1 month after expiry)
Loan license for manufacturing for selling of Ayurvedic (including Siddha) or Unani drugs	SLA	24E	25E (fresh) 26E (renewal)	153A, 154A, and 155A	Up to December 31 of following (next) year (can be renewed one month after expiry but within 3 months)

(Continued)

TABLE 6.6 (Continued)

Application types	Regulatory body	Application form no.	License in form	Rule(s) applicable	Duration of validity
Manufacturing for selling or distribution of drugs not included in schedule C and C (1) but included in schedule X	SLA	24F	25F		5 years (can be renewed for 5 years if applied within 6 months after expiry)
Manufacturing of medicament (for sale and distribution) mentioned in schedule C and C(1) but not specified in schedule X	SLA	27	28 (fresh) 26 (renewal)	73, 75, 76, and 83	5 years (can be renewed for 5 years if applied within 6 months after expiry)
Manufacturing on loan licenses for drugs not included in schedule C and C (1)	SLA	27A	28A (fresh) 26A (renewal)		5 years (can be renewed for 5 years if applied within 6 months after expiry)
Manufacturing of medicament (for sale and distribution) mentioned in schedule C, C (1), and X	SLA	27B	28B (fresh) 26 (renewal)	73, 75, 76, and 83	5 years (can be renewed for 5 years if applied within 6 months after expiry)
Manufacturing of LVP/sera, vaccines and rDNA-derived drugs	SLA	27D	28 D (fresh) 26J (renewal)	75 and 76	5 years (can be renewed for 5 years if applied within 6 months after expiry)
Loan license for manufacturing of LVP/sera, vaccines and rDNA-derived drugs	SLA	27DA	28DA		
Manufacture for the purpose of examination, test, or analysis	SLA	30	29	89	1 year (can be renewed for 1 year at a time)
Cosmetics manufactured for selling and distribution in India	SLA	31	32 (fresh) 33 (renewal)	138 and 139	5 years (can be renewed for 5 years if applied before expiry or within 6 months after expiry)
Loan license for manufacturing cosmetics	SLA	31A	32A (fresh) 33A (renewal)	138A	5 years (can be renewed for 5 years if applied before expiry or within 6 months after expiry)
Registration certificate for premises intended to be used for manufacturing of drugs proposed for importing and using in India	DCGI	40	41	27A	3 years (if not canceled or suspended sooner) If fresh application made before 9 months of expiry, can be extended. (9 months)
Cosmetics imported for selling and distribution in India	DCGI	42	43	129A and 129C	3 years (if not canceled or suspended sooner) If fresh application made before 6 months of expiry, can be extended

6.7.5 Import and manufacturing of drugs for examination, testing, or analysis

Small quantities of drug can be imported (even of the drug, import of which is prohibited in India as mentioned in point 3 above) or manufactured for examination, testing, or analysis provided it should not be marketed (Import Guidance, 2007).

The types of forms required and the duration of license validity are summarized in Table 6.6.

6.7.6 Import or manufacture of novel homeopathic medicine

Novel Homeopathic Medicine means (D&C Act and Rule, 2016)

1. A medicine not listed in the Homeopathic Pharmacopoeia of India, Germany, the United States, or the United Kingdom
2. The medicine not reported in reliable homeopathic literature for its efficacy; or
3. A combination of one or more medicines neither mentioned in any of the above-said Pharmacopoeias nor mentioned in reliable homeopathic literature for its efficacy under the conditions recommended.

Applicant, accompanied with application for license required (Table 6.6) for importing or manufacturing new homeopathic medicine, needs to produce documentary and other evidence regarding therapeutic efficacy of the medicine.

6.7.7 Selling, stocking, exhibiting, offering for sale, or distributing drugs (including homeopathic) in India

Once license for import or manufacture is obtained from Central Licensing Authority, the product could be sold through chain of wholesalers, distributors, and retailers (Ahmad et al., 2017; D&C Act and Rule, 2016; Suresh et al., 2014). The details of forms required and duration of license validity for distribution and selling of drug in India are summarized in Table 6.6. A structure is already in place for the distribution and selling of medicine in India. As an importer or manufacturer, it does not need to establish a separate structure, hence this section is not emphasized here. For detail clarification and requirements in this regard, refer Part VI, Rules 59 to 66 of D&C Rules, 1945 for selling, stocking exhibiting, offering for sale, or distributing the drugs other than homeopathic drugs; and Part VIA, Rules 67A to 67H for homeopathic drugs (D&C Act and Rule, 2016).

6.7.8 Manufacturing Ayurvedic, Siddha, or Unani medicine

Ayurvedic, Siddha, or Unani medicine, for the purpose of D&C Rules, 1945, can be classified as (D&C Act and Rule, 2016):

1. The drugs manufactured according to the formulae prescribed in books of Ayurveda, Siddha, or Unani enlisted in First Schedule of D&C Act, 1940.
2. Patent or proprietary medicine
   a. Formulation not according to authoritative books but includes ingredients mentioned in authoritative books provided those should not be administered by parenteral route.
   b. Health promoter formulation, ingredients of which mentioned in authoritative books.
   c. Saundarya Prasadak (Husane afza)/Azhagh-sadhan formulations used for oral, skin, hair, and body care provided the ingredients are mentioned in authoritative books.
   d. Aushadh Ghana (dry/wet extracts obtained from plants prescribed in authoritative books).

While applying for the license, the applicant shall comply all the conditions mentioned in Rule 158(B) II to V of D&C Rules, 1945. The details of forms required and duration of license validity are summarized in Table 6.6. For further clarification and requirements, refer Part VII, Rules 68 to 84 of D&C Rules, 1945.

6.7.9 Cosmetics

Cosmetics can be:

1. imported for selling and distribution in India;
2. manufactured for selling and distribution in India.

6.7.9.1 Imported for selling and distribution in India

Any cosmetics should only be imported after getting approval from licensing authority by applying in prescribed forms along with fees prescribed (Clarification Cosmetics, 2015; D&C Act and Rule, 2016). The applicant willing to manufacture the drug himself or by his agent or by subsidiary or the person importing the product in India can file the application along with prescribed fees paid via designated bank. The fees can also be transferred by manufacturer from any bank in his country via ECS to the mentioned bank. In the latter case, original acknowledgment of payment can be submitted in place of challan. Single application and license will suffice if cosmetic products are imported from single manufacturing unit (Clarification cosmetics, 2015; D&C Act and Rule, 2016).

Some cosmetics are prohibited or considered illegal for import in India (D&C Act and Rule, 2016) which includes:

1. The manufacturing, selling or distribution of which is forbidden in the country it is originated;
2. Containing hexachlorophene;
3. Containing lead or arsenic compound;
4. Containing mercury compounds;
5. Undergone animal testing only (after the commencement of fifth amendment in Drug and Cosmetics Rules in 2014);
6. Point of entry in India other than 43A;
7. Contains dyes, colorants, and pigments, the use of which is restricted by the Bureau of Indian Standards (IS:4707 Part 1 as amended) and Schedule Q;
8. Not complying with the provision mentioned in Schedule S and Schedule Q or quality and safety standards mentioned in D&C Rules;
9. Not packed or labeled as per rules in Part XV of D&C Rules.

For further clarification and requirements, refer Part XIII, Rules 129 to 136 of D&C Rules, 1945.

6.7.9.2 Manufactured for selling and distribution in India

The cosmetics, if manufactured on one premises, single application and license will suffice (separate applications and separate licenses needed for separate premise) (D&C Act and Rule, 2016). The cosmetics can also be manufactured on loan license but the manufacturing facility involve should have license in Form 32. If in case the license of manufacturing facility has been canceled or suspended, the loan license will also considered as canceled or suspended (D&C Act and Rule, 2016).

Cosmetics prohibited or considered illegal for manufacturing if:

1. Colors used are other than those prescribed;
2. Containing hexachlorophene;
3. Containing lead or arsenic compound;
4. Containing mercury compounds.

For further clarification and requirements, refer Part XIV, Rules 137 to 145 of D&C Rules, 1945. For labeling, packing, and standards of cosmetics, please refer Part XV, Rules 146 to 150 of D&C Rules, 1945.

6.7.10 New drugs

At the advent of ND & CT, Rules, 2019, certain rules like Part XA and Schedule Y of D&C Rules, 1945, applicable for NCE and IND for human use became obsolete (refer Chapter XII, Rule 97 (ND & CT Rules, 2019). New drug in India is defined by Chapter I, Rule 2(w) of ND & CT, Rules, 2019 which includes:

1. Drugs including API or phytopharmaceutical previously not approved;
2. Approved earlier but is being claimed to be marketed with newer or revised indications, route of administration, dosage regimen, and dosage forms (including controlled release dosage form);
3. A fixed dose combination (FDC) (components of which are previously approved individually for certain claims), if used in combination which differs in drug ratio (the ratio proposed for the first time) or else if drug ratio is same but preparation proposed to differ in certain claims like newer or revised indications, route of administration, dosage regimen, and dosage forms (including controlled release dosage form);
4. Modified release/sustained release/novel drug delivery system of any drug authorized by the Central Licensing Authority;

5. Vaccines, recombinant DNA (rDNA) products, living-modified organism, monoclonal antibody, stem cell-derived product, gene therapeutic product or xenografts, intended to be used as drug, not approved by DCGI;
6. A novel drug already granted approval in the country (except mentioned in 4 and 5 above), considered new drug up to 4 years from the date of authorization or incorporation in Indian pharmacopoeia.

Following requirements are to be met to obtain marketing authorization of novel drug mentioned in the above definitions.

6.7.10.1 Clinical trials of novel drug or IND

The clinical trial of novel drug or IND shall only be conducted after approval of DCGI and sanctioning of protocol by the Ethics Committee for clinical trials (ND & CT Rules, 2019). The said Ethics Committee should be constituted as per Rule 7 of ND & CT, Rules, 2019, by the clinical trial site and registered with Central Licensing Authority by applying in form CT-01 and granted in form CT-02. (For other norms and functioning related to Ethics Committee, refer Chapter III, Rules 6 to 14 of ND & CT, Rules, 2019.) If in case own Ethics Committee is unavailable at trial site, the applicant can either initiate the procedure for approval or get the protocol sanctioned by Independent Ethics Committee available in the city or inside the radius of 50 km of site (ND & CT Rules, 2019).

Indian Council of Medical Research maintains Clinical Trial Registry of India (CTRI) (Pandey et al., 2008). The applicant needs to register with CTRI before starting the enrollment of subjects.

The fees to conduct clinical trials will be exempted if the trial is initiated by a person belonging to central government- or state government-funded institution/organization. The permission to carry out clinical trials in India can be granted in the following conditions (ND & CT Rules, 2019):

A. Novel drug or IND discovered, undergone research and development in India and will be manufactured and marketed in India.
B. Drug already approved outside India.

The procedural differences between these two categories are as follows:

1. Duration of reply from licensing authority, that is, 30 days in Case A while 90 days in Case B.
2. In Case A if response is not received in the prescribed time, the permission can be considered to be granted and just by informing the authorities in form CT-04A the trials can be commenced. In Case B, applicant has to wait for the reply and only after getting approval in form CT-06 the trial can be initiated.

The sponsor of the clinical trials upon successful completion of the trial shall provide free access of the novel drug or IND (for which clinical trials were conducted) to the patients enrolled (and successfully completed the same trials) in following conditions (ND & CT Rules, 2019):

1. Any investigator of the trial recommends the same drug to clinical trial subject after successful completion of trial and same was approved by the Ethics Committee;
2. No alternative treatment is available for the indication (for which the trial is conducted);
3. The drug tested benefitted the trial subject;
4. Trial subject or his legal heir consented in writing to use the drug after completion of trial and this is certified by investigator;
5. Trial subject or his legal heir declared in writing that the sponsor will not be liable for any loss due to the use of drug by trial subject after completion of trials.

The details of forms required, fees prescribed, and duration of license validity are summarized in Table 12. For further clarification and requirements for clinical trials, refer Chapter V, Part A, Rules 19 to 30 of ND & CT, Rules, 2019.

6.7.10.2 Bioavailability/bioequivalence studies

The bioavailability (BA) and bioequivalence (BE) studies shall only be conducted after approval of DCGI and sanctioning of protocol by the Ethics Committee formed as per Rule 7 and registered under Rule 8 of ND & CT, Rules, 2019. If in case own Ethics Committee at BA/BE study site is unavailable, the applicant can either establish it or get the protocol sanctioned by Independent Ethics Committee available in same city or inside the radius of 50 km (ND & CT Rules, 2019).

BA/BE studies for novel drug or IND shall only be conducted in centers registered with DCGI under Rule 47 of ND & CT, Rules, 2019. The applicant has to register the BA/BE studies of IND with CTRI before starting the enrollment of subjects.

Refer Table 6.7 for forms required, fees prescribed, and duration of license validity. For further clarification and requirements about BA/BE studies, refer Chapter V, Part B, Rules 31 to 38 of ND & CT, Rules, 2019.

6.7.10.3 Manufacture of NCE or IND for clinical trials, BA/BE studies, examination, test, or analysis (or unapproved API for development of formulation for said purpose)

The manufacturing of NCE and IND (or unapproved API for development of formulation) for said purpose shall only be done after approval of DCGI, in small quantities and it should not be used for selling in the market or for supply to anybody or any firm. After getting the permission under ND & CT Rules, 2019, applicant shall make an application for the same under Drugs and Cosmetics Rules, 1945, accompanying the permission obtained in form CT-11 (or in form CT-15 for unapproved API) (ND & CT Rules, 2019). For the detailed requirements about manufacturing of NCE or IND for said purpose, refer Chapter VIII, Rules 52 to 66 of ND & CT, Rules 2019.

6.7.10.4 Importing and/or manufacturing of NCE as API or pharmaceutical formulation for commercial use

This category can further be divided as follows (ND & CT Rules, 2019):

1. A new drug not authorized in India;
2. A new drug already authorized in India;
3. A drug previously granted approval by DCGI for certain claim, being proposed in new application to be marketed with newer or revised indications, route of administration, dosage regimen, and dosage forms;
4. A new drug product which is a FDC;
5. A phytopharmaceutical.

Application for importing (Form CT-18) and/or manufacturing (Form CT-21) of new drug from abovementioned categories should accompany the data and other particulars explained in Tables 6.7 and 6.8. In case of importing and/or manufacturing of new drug not approved in India, local clinical trials can be exempted in the following conditions (all the conditions except second condition applicable to manufacturing) (ND & CT Rules, 2019).

1. If the new drug has regulatory sanctions and marketing rights in countries mentioned, time to time by Central Licensing Authority of India under Rule 101 of ND & CT 2019, and is devoid of any reported major severe adverse effects; or
2. If the application for importing of a new drug for which global clinical trial is previously sanctioned by DCGI to be conducted in India and it is being conducted in India. Meanwhile if the same drug got marketing authorization in an one or more countries specified under time to time by Central Licensing Authority of India under Rule 101 of ND & CT 2019;
3. If no difference in response of enzyme or genes in Indian population for metabolic, pharmacodynamic, and safety parameters were known; and
4. If undertaking in writing about conduction of Phase IV trials (as per design prescribed) was obtained by Central Licensing Authority from the applicant for establishment of safety and effectiveness of new drug.

This condition may be relaxed in the following situations (ND & CT Rules, 2019):

1. Drug for serious/life-threatening conditions;
2. Drug specified for a disease of particular concern to the country's health scenario;
3. Drug specified for a disease which affects limited population (rare events) and hence drugs are unavailable or if available are costly or an orphan drug.

When the new drug is authorized and marketed for long period (not less than 2 years) in other countries and sufficient scientific literary evidence of safety is available for it, the data requirements related to Animal toxicology, Teratogenicity, Mutagenicity, Carcinogenicity, Reproduction studies, and Perinatal Studies can be altered or relaxed. After getting the permission under ND & CT, Rules, 2019, applicant shall make an application for the same under

TABLE 6.7 List of various procedures along with required application format, fees, timelines, and other details for marketing authorization of new drugs in India.

Application types	Regulatory body	Application form no.	License in form	Rule(s) applicable	Time frame for response from authorities	Duration of validity
Clinical trial of novel drug or IND in India	DCGI Ethics Committee for clinical trials	CT-04	CT-06	21 and 22	90 working days	Permission valid for 2 years
Clinical trial of a novel drug or IND discovered or undergone research and development in India and will be manufactured and marketed in India	DCGI Ethics Committee for clinical trials	CT-04 CT-04A (inform before initiation)	CT-06	21, 22, and 23	30 working days If no communication received from authority within said period, consider the permission to conduct trials have been granted	
Clinical trials of novel drug which are already approved outside India	DCGI Ethics Committee for clinical trials	CT-04	CT-06	21 and 22	90 working days	
Bioavailability or bioequivalence study of novel drug or IND	DCGI Ethics Committee for clinical trials	CT-05	CT-07	33 and 34	90 working days	Permission valid for 1 year
Manufacture of NCE or IND for clinical trials, BA/BE studies, examination, test or analysis	DCGI	CT-10	CT-11	52 and 53	90 working days	3 years (can be extended for 1 year in exceptional circumstances)
Manufacture of unapproved API for development of formulation for clinical trials, BA/BE studies, examination, test, or analysis	DCGI	CT-12— formulation CT-13—API	CT-14— formulation CT-15— API	59 and 60	90 working days	3 years (can be extended for 1 year in exceptional circumstances)
Importing the NCE or IND for clinical trials, BA/BE studies, examination, test, or analysis	DCGI	CT-16	CT-17	67 and 68	90 working days	3 years (can be extended for 1 year in exceptional circumstances)
a. Novel drug in the form of finished formulation which is previously not approved b. Novel drug in the form of finished formulation which is already approved in India for marketing	DCGI	CT-18	CT-19— API CT-20— formulation	75 and 76	90 working days	Not specified

(Continued)

TABLE 6.7 (Continued)

Application types	Regulatory body	Application form no.	License in form	Rule(s) applicable	Time frame for response from authorities	Duration of validity
c. Novel drug in the form of API which is previously not approved						
d. Novel drug in the form of API which is already approved in India for marketing						
e. Approved novel drug for claims like newer or revised strength, indications, route of administration, dosage regimen, and dosage forms						
a. Contains one or more NCE which are not approved	DCGI	CT-18	CT-19—API CT-20—formulation	75 and 76	90 working days	Not specified
b. Having approved ingredients						
c. Already approved for marketing						
d. For newer claim regarding strength, indication, route of administration, or dosage form						
a. Novel drug in form of finished formulation which is previously not approved	DCGI	CT-21	CT-22—API CT-23—formulation	80 and 81	90 working days	Not specified
b. Novel drug in the form of finished formulation which is already approved in India for marketing						
c. Novel drug in the form of API which is previously not approved						
d. Novel drug in the form of API which is already approved in India for marketing						
e. For newer claim regarding strength, indication, route of administration, or dosage form						

(Continued)

TABLE 6.7 (Continued)

Application types	Regulatory body	Application form no.	License in form	Rule(s) applicable	Time frame for response from authorities	Duration of validity
a. Contains one or more NCE which are not approved	DCGI	CT-21	CT-22—API CT-23—formulation	80 and 81	90 working days	Not specified
b. Having approved ingredients						
c. Already approved for marketing						
For new claim regarding strength, indication, route of administration, or dosage form						
Import or to manufacture phytopharmaceutical drugs	DCGI	CT-21	CT-22—API CT-23—formulation	80 and 81	90 working days	Not specified

Source: D&C Act and Rule, 2016. The Drugs and Cosmetics Act 1940 and Rules 1945. Ministry of Health and Family Welfare, Government of India.
Courtesy: https://cdsco.gov.in/opencms/export/sites/CDSCO_WEB/Pdf-documents/acts_rules/2016DrugsandCosmeticsAct1940Rules1945.pdf.

Drugs and Cosmetics Rules, 1945, accompanying the permission obtained in form CT-19 or CT-20 for importing and CT-22 or CT-23 for manufacturing (ND & CT Rules, 2019).

The types of forms required and duration of license validity are summarized in Table 6.7. For further clarification and requirements about importing and manufacturing of NCE as API or pharmaceutical formulation for commercial use, refer Chapter VIII, Rules 74 to 85 of ND & CT Rules (2019).

6.7.10.5 Fixed dose combinations

These are the products which contains two or more APIs for specific therapeutic use. The rationale behind fixed dose combinations (FDC) which is making it popular among product developers is the benefit which it provides regarding efficacy due to combined effect of two or more active ingredients (ND & CT Rules, 2019). This also makes FDCs as widely used treatment options in broad range of clinical conditions especially chronic conditions. The importing and manufacturing of FDCs in India is governed by Rules 75, 76 and 80, 81, respectively, in following categories (ND & CT Rules, 2019)

1. Contains one or more NCE which are not approved;
2. Having already-approved ingredients;
3. FDC already approved for marketing;
4. Already approved for certain claims but proposed for new claim regarding strength, indication, route of administration, or dosage form.

The details of forms required and duration of license validity are summarized in Table 6.7. For further clarification and requirements about importing and manufacturing FDC for commercial use, refer Chapter VIII, Rules 74 to 85 of ND & CT, Rules, 2019.

6.7.10.6 Phytopharmaceutical drugs

An applicant who proposes to import or manufacture phytopharmaceutical drugs for marketing in India shall apply in prescribed form and pay prescribed fee applicable. For further clarification and requirements about importing and manufacturing phytopharmaceutical for commercial use, refer Chapter VIII, Rules 74 to 85 of ND & CT, Rules, 2019.

TABLE 6.8 Details of particulars to be submitted to Licensing Authority in India along with various applications.

Sr. no.	Category and requirements
1	Application for conducting human trials or importing or manufacturing of novel medicament for selling in India (ND & CT Rules, 2019)

1. Introduction: Short description of active medicament and it is therapeutic class
2. Chemical information of active material and data about formulation
   2.1. Information on active ingredients
   2.2. Physicochemical data
   2.3. Molecular weight
   2.4. Analytical data
   2.5. Complete monograph specification
   2.6. Validations
   2.7. Stability studies
   2.8. Data on formulation
3. Preclinical pharmacological data
   3.1. Summary
   3.2. Specific and General pharmacology of drug
   3.3. Safety pharmacological data
   3.4. Pharmacokinetics: ADME
4. Preclinical toxicity studies
   4.1. General information
   4.2. Systemic toxicological data
   4.3. Toxicities related to reproductive system
   4.4. Local toxicologic studies
   4.5. Allergic reactions
   4.6. Toxicity related to genetic mutations
   4.7. Tendency to induce cancer
5. Clinical trials (Phases I, II, and III)
6. Special studies like BA/BE studies, studies in special population like pregnant and nursing mothers, children, and old-age people
7. Status of NCE under regulatory laws in other countries
8. Information pertaining to prescribing of finished product
9. Samples of API and final product along with procedures used for testing
10. NCE and Global clinical trial
11. If applied for manufacturing of drug intended to be sold in India, a copy of license for manufacturing obtained from SLA should be submitted

Sr. no.	Category and requirements
2	Permission for importing or manufacturing a novel drug which is previously approved in India (ND & CT Rules, 2019)

1. Introduction: Short description of active medicament and it is therapeutic class
2. Chemical information of active material and data about formulation
   2.1. Structure, chemical formula, generic name, and physicochemical properties
   2.2. Composition and specification of the final formulation prepared
   2.3. Specifications for testing and identification of active and inactive ingredients along with assay techniques
   2.4. Manufacture method of API and end product
   2.5. Stability data
3. Data regarding material used for marketing (samples of proposed label, literature, and carton for finished product)
4. Special studies like BA/BE studies or oral dosage form, subacute toxicological studies for intravenous infusions and injections

Sr. no.	Category and requirements
3	Conducting clinical trial for an approved novel drug with newer claims regarding strength, indication, route of administration, or dosage form or for importing or manufacturing such novel drug for selling or distribution (ND & CT Rules, 2019)

1. License number and date for previously sanctioned novel drug
2. Justify new claims therapeutically
3. Chemical information of active material and data about formulation
   3.1. Structure, chemical formula, generic name and physicochemical properties
   3.2. Composition and specification of the final formulation prepared
   3.3. Specifications for testing and identification of active and inactive ingredients along with assay techniques
   3.4. Manufacture method of API and end product
   3.5. Stability data
4. Preclinical pharmacology and toxicology data
5. Clinical trial data
6. Status of NCE under regulatory laws in other countries
7. Data regarding material used for marketing (samples of proposed label, literature, and carton for finished product)

Sr. no.	Category and requirements
4	Conducting human trial or importing or manufacturing of a phytopharmaceutical drug in India (D&C Act and Rule, 2016; ND & CT Rules, 2019)

(Continued)

TABLE 6.8 (Continued)

Sr. no.	Category and requirements	

	Part A
	1. Data from literature along with proper referencing (traditional medicine books or ethno medicine published results) regarding existing usage of the preparation
	  1.1. Short description of the drug in to consideration
	  1.2. Toxicology and safety pharmacological data
	  1.3. Present usage of the phytopharmaceutical drug
	2. Clinical pharmacological data available in scientific literature, PD data and monographs, if any
		Part B
		3. Methods to identify and authenticate; and information regarding herbal source used for extracting and fractionating the drug
		4. Procedure for extracting the active component and information regarding fractionation and purification
		5. Finished product of phytopharmaceutical drug
		6. Process to manufacture finished product
		7. Stability data
		8. Preclinical and clinical safety and pharmacology data
		9. Status under regulatory laws in country (India)
		10. Marketing information about product to be marketed
		11. Postmarketing surveillance
		Any other relevant information applicant wish to provide

5	Application for similar biologics (Similar Biologics Guidelines, 2016)	

	1. Preclinical submission stage
	  1.1. Data pertaining to reference biologics such as drug details, pharmacokinetic parameters (ADME), therapeutic index, dosing ranges, mechanism of action, bioequivalence data, the amount localized in tissues, toxicological data
	  1.2. Data pertaining to similar biologic like known or suggested therapeutic use, details of patients who will use the drug (age, gender, pediatric patient, pregnant or lactating mother, etc.), dosing frequency and time interval and route, finished formulation details along with contents therein, etc. Also toxicological data of all the contents, additives, etc
	  1.3. Data pertaining to product development like through details of process followed for manufacturing, details about cell bank, cells used, culture mediums, harvesting of cells, formulation-related details, process used to maintain purity of product, and details of reactions with packing material if any
		2. Preclinical study data (pharmacokinetics, pharmacodynamics, toxicological, and immune response in animals)
		3. For clinical trial application
		  1. Thorough description of the active medicament and process used for development
		  2. Crucial and chief quality-related parameters of finished product.
		  3. Controlling attributes for process of manufacture
		  4. Details of parameters pertaining to crucial processes involved
		  5. Data pertaining to shelf life and factors affecting it
		  6. Comparability of finished product synthesized for clinical use against reference biologic
		  7. Data pertaining to the batches synthesized to check consistence of product or to validate process, whichever is applicable
		4. Clinical study data like single and repeated dose comparative PK–PD studies, data of studies carried out to confirm safety and efficacy, data pertaining to immune responses, produced if any.
		5. Quality-related parameters for similar biologics
		  1. Analytical method data
		  2. Product characterization data
		  3. Stability data
		  4. Quality comparability data with reference biologic

ADME, Absorption, distribution, metabolism, excretion; *API*, active pharmaceutical ingredient; *BA/BE*, bioavailability/bioequivalence; *NCE*, new chemical entity; *PK–PD*, pharmacokinetic–pharmacodynamics.

6.7.11 Similar biologics

Biologicals are therapeutic/preventive/diagnostic preparations intended to be used in humans and obtained from living organisms which includes sera, vaccines, antigens, antitoxins, etc. (Cherish Babu, 2011; Malhotra, 2011). A similar biologic is the one which is comparable/replica of reference biological product (already sanctioned in India) in terms of efficacy, safety, and quality (Similar Biologics Guidelines, 2016). So as to establish regulatory framework for similar biologics in India, CDSCO in association with the DBT has formulated "Guidelines on Similar Biologics" in the year 2016 (Natarajan and Janani, 2019; Similar Biologics Guidelines, 2016). These regulatory principles address various issues such as quality aspects, manufacturing procedures, efficacy, and safety of similar biologics.

6.7.11.1   Regulatory framework

The regulations and guidelines which are applicable for similar biologics are as follows (Natarajan and Janani, 2019; Similar Biologics Guidelines, 2016):

1. Drugs and Cosmetics Act, 1940, and Rules, 1945;
2. Guidelines on Similar Biologics: Regulatory requirements for marketing authorization in India 2012;
3. CDSCO guidance for industry, 2008 (including Submission of Clinical Trial Application, Requirement for novel drug approval, postapproval changes, and preparation of quality information for submission);
4. Rules, 1989 (notified under Environment Protection Act, 1986);
5. Guidelines and Handbook for Institutional Biosafety Committees (IBSCs), 2011;
6. Guidelines for generating preclinical and clinical data for rDNA vaccines, diagnostics, and other Biologicals, 1999;
7. rDNA safety guidelines.

The authorities who control over all the aspects of similar biologics involved are as follows (Similar Biologics Guidelines, 2016):

1. Institutional Bio Safety Committee (IBSC): An institutional level committee which involve in reviewing, assessing, and approving the protocols of rDNA research.
2. Review Committee on Genetic Manipulation (RCGM): It looks after safety aspect of genetically engineered organism.
3. Genetic Engineering Appraisal Committee (GEAC): The committee looks after bulky use of harmful microorganisms in industries and recombinants in research.
4. CDSCO.

6.7.11.2   Reference biologic

It is the product which is already approved in India and is used to compare the similarity of product characterization data, nonhuman and human trial data with newly synthesized similar biologic (Natarajan and Janani, 2019; Similar Biologics Guidelines, 2016).

The reference biologic should be selected based on the following factors:

1. It should be approved in India or highly regulated countries on the basis of safety, efficacy, and quality;
2. If it is not available/approved in India then it can be imported from ICH countries (where it is licensed for marketing) to develop the similar biologic of same quality and same preclinical and clinical properties;
3. To compare quality, efficacy, and safety of drug product throughout the study same reference biologic should be used;
4. Reference biologic must have similar active medicament as that of similar biologic;
5. The product which itself is approved as similar biologic in India cannot be used as a reference biologic for other products;
6. The reference biologic must be administered by same route, have same dosage form, and have same strength as that of similar biologic.

6.7.11.3   Quality comparability study

CDSCO guidance for industry, 2008, demands full-quality dossier comprising of outcomes of comparability study between reference and similar biologics (Natarajan and Janani, 2019). It is the most crucial part of submission when an applicant wishes to process the similar biologic for clinical development (Similar Biologics Guidelines, 2016). While comparing similar biologic with reference biologic, one to one characterization studies were performed at drug substance as well as drug product level. Data for only drug product comparability can be allowed (with proper scientific justification) when drug substance cannot be isolated. While comparing, minor differences in quality components between similar and reference biologics can be permissible, subject to submission of appropriate data for verification of impact of these differences on safety and efficacy (Natarajan and Janani, 2019; Similar Biologics Guidelines, 2016).

Refer Tables 6.8 and 6.9 for details pertaining to data to be submitted along with application, phases of approval, forms needed, and regulatory agencies looking after the process.

TABLE 6.9 Phases of approval process for similar biologics along with agency involved and forms required for sanctioning.

Stage	Agency involved	Application form no.	Approval
License to manufacture for testing, analyzing, and examination (following receipt of NOC from CDSCO)	State FDA	30*	29*
License for importing the drug for purpose of testing, analyzing, and examination	CDSCO—zonal	12*	11*
Importing/exporting/transferring/receiving cells for cell bank	RCGM	B1/B3/B5/B7#	
To conduct research-oriented activities in the field of biologics and to develop biologic in to finish products	RCGM	C1#	
Permission to conduct nonhuman/animals studies	RCGM	C3a#	
Submission of nonhuman/animals study report	RCGM	C5a#	
Human/clinical studies	CDSCO	44*	CT permission letter
Permission for importing and selling/marketing or permission to manufacture	CDSCO	44*	45A/46A (bulk product) and 5/46 (finished product)*
License to manufacture	State FDA/CDSCO	27 D*	28 D*
Registration certificate for import	CDSCO	40 (with schedule DI and DII)/44*	41/45*
License or permit to import and to market the finished formulation in country	CDSCO	8 and 9*	10*

Notes: For more information, see *Drug and Cosmetics Rules 1945, #Indian Biosafety Knowledge Portal website. *CDSCO,* Central Drugs Standard Control Organization; *FDA,* Food and Drug Administration; *RCGM,* Review Committee on Genetic Manipulation.
Source: Similar Biologics Guidelines, 2016. Guidelines on similar biologics: regulatory requirements for marketing authorization in India. Courtesy: https://nib.gov.in/NIB-DBT2016.pdf.

6.7.12 SUGAM portal

CDSCO launched online SUGAM portal in 2015 to further simplify all drug regulatory-related submissions (SUGAM Portal, 2019). It delivers fast and reliable services to applicants. The portal made the processes, submission, review, follow up, and tracking of application, simple, efficient, and transparent. Applicant can track all applications submitted till date and documents saved for future in one portal (SUGAM User Manual, 2019). Some other features include separate icon bars for various sections, live CDSCO response timelines for application, "Postapproval Change" section, downloadable checklists and SMS alerts, etc. For more details, visit link https://cdscoonline.gov.in/CDSCO/homepage.

6.8 Conclusion

Drug approval or authorization process is one of the most regulated ones worldwide; in particular the developed nations such as the United States, Japan, Australia, and the EU have the most stringent norms. That is expected because the primary purpose of regulations is to safeguard public health and ensure that the company's manufacturing and marketing pharmaceutical products complys with the regulatory norms. This calls for pharmaceutical products to be developed, formulated, produced, evaluated, and tracked conforming to the regulatory guidelines so that they are effective and safe and the patient's well-being is not affected. However this concern for safety and quality does not come cheap and that is why NDA process in a lot of developing countries remains less regulated.

References

Aditi 2018. Top generic pharma companies in India. Pharma Adda. https://www.pharmaadda.in/top-generic-pharma-companies-in-india (accessed 10.03.20).

Agarwal, N.B., Karwa, M., 2018. Pharmaceutical regulations in India, history of drug regulation in India. In: Vohora, D., Singh, G. (Eds.), Pharmaceutical medicine and translational clinical research. Academic Press, London, pp. 215–231.

Ahmad, M.M., Puranik, S.B., Hasija, N.K., 2017. Regulatory requirements for marketing authorization of different categories of drugs in India. Int. J. Pharm. Pharm. Res. 8 (3), 276–291.

APEC, 2015. Drug approval system of Japan. Available from: https://www.nifds.go.kr/brd/m_95/down.do?brd_id = board_mfds_411&seq = 21651&data_tp = A&file_seq = 1 (accessed 11.05.20).

Arato, T., 2016. Japanese regulation of biosimilar products: past experience and current challenges. Br. J. Clin. Pharmacol. 82 (1), 30–40.

ARGPM, 2020. Australian regulatory guidelines for prescription medicines. Available at https://www.tga.gov.au/publication/australian-regulatory-guidelines-prescription-medicines-argpm#.U8SOJPmSwYE (accessed 10.03.20).

Boehm, G., Yao, L., Han, L., Zheng, Q., 2013. Development of the generic drug industry in the United States after the Hatch-Waxman Act of 1984. Acta Pharm. Sin. B 3 (5), 297–311.

Bootes, A., et al., 2019. Fast-track pathways for drug approvals: the Australian experience so far. Aust. Prescr. 42 (4), 118–119. Available from: https://doi.org/10.18773/austprescr.2019.044.

Camargo, 2018. 505(b)(1) versus 505(b)(2): they are not the same. Available from: https://camargopharma.com/resources/blog/505b1-versus-505b2 (accessed 15.04.20).

Cameron, H., 1998. The regulation of complementary medicines bythe therapeutic goods administration. Aust. Prescr. 21, 107–108.

CDER and CBER, 2014. Guidance for industry ANDA submissions—content and format of abbreviated new drug applications. Available from: https://www.fda.gov/files/drugs/published/ANDA-Submissions-%E2%80%94-Content-and-Format-of-Abbreviated-New-Drug-Applications.pdf (accessed 20.04.20).

CDER, 2017. Determining whether to submit an ANDA or a 505(b)(2) application guidance for industry. Available from: https://www.fda.gov/media/123567/download (accessed 21.04.20).

Cherish Babu, P.V., 2011. An Indian manufacturer's perspective for harmonization of guidelines for similar biotherapeutic products. Biologicals 39, 300–303.

Clarification Cosmetics, 2015. Clarification for import and registration of cosmetics in addition to existing guidelines. Available from: https://cdsco.gov.in/opencms/export/sites/CDSCO_WEB/Pdf-documents/cosmetics/Clarification_for_import_and_registration_ofcosmetics.pdf (accessed 10.03.20).

CM, 2020. Complementary medicines regulations. Australian Government, Department of Health, Therapeutic Goods Administration. Available from: https://www.tga.gov.au/complementary-medicines (accessed 15.03.20).

CVM, 2018. Administrative applications and the phased review process. Available from: https://www.fda.gov/media/70029/download (accessed 21.05.20).

D&C Act and Rule, 2016. The Drugs and Cosmetics Act 1940 and Rules 1945. Ministry of Health and Family Welfare, Government of India. Available from: https://cdsco.gov.in/opencms/export/sites/CDSCO_WEB/Pdf-documents/acts_rules/2016DrugsandCosmeticsAct1940Rules1945.pdf (accessed 01.04.20).

Dhanalakshmi, C., 2017. Growth of Indian pharmaceutical industry: an overview. Int. J. Multidiscip. Res. Hub. 4 (12), 6–12.

Directive 2001/83/EC of the European Parliament and of the Council of 6 November 2001 on the community code relating to medicinal products for human use, Official Journal, L 311, 28/11/2004, pp. 67–128 (Directive 2001/83/EC).

Directive 2003/63/EC. Community code relating to medicinal products for human use, Official Journal, L 159, 27/06/2003, pp. 46–94.

Dunne, A., Phillips, C., 2010. Complementary and alternative medicine–representations in popular magazines. Aust. Fam. Physician 39 (9), 671–674.

Emmerton, L., 2009. The third class of medications: sales and purchasing behaviour are associated with pharmacist only and pharmacy medicine classifications in Australia. J. Am. Pharm. Assoc 49, 31–37. Available from: https://doi.org/10.1331/JAPhA.2009.07117.

European Medicines Agency. Obtaining an EU marketing authorisation, step-by-step. European Medicines Agency (europa.eu) (accessed 14.02.21).

Fayad, N., 2003. Harmonizing pharmaceutical regulation among the United States, the European Union, and Japan: The ICH Initiative. Available from: https://dash.harvard.edu/handle/1/8852171 (accessed 15.04.20).

Ghalamkarpour, A., 2009. Marketing authorization procedures in the European Union–making the right choice. Life Sci. 33.

Ghosh, D., Skinner, M., Ferguson, L.R., 2006. The role of the therapeutic goods administration and the medicine and medical devices safety authority in evaluating complementary and alternative medicines in Australia and New Zealand. Toxicology 221, 88–94.

Goh, L.Y., Vitry, A.I., Semple, S.J., Estermanand, A., Luszcz, M.A., 2009. Self-medication with over-the-counter drugs and complementary medications in South Australia's elderly population. BMC Complement Altern. Med. 9 (42), 1–10. Available from: https://doi.org/10.1186/1472-6882-9-42.

Hammett, R., Hunt, L., 2009. The Australian medicines regulatory system: a risk-based approach to regulation. Therap. Innov. Regulat. Sci. 43 (1). Available from: https://doi.org/10.1177/009286150904300104.

Handoo, S., Arora, V., Khera, D., Nandi, P.K., Sahu, S.K., 2012. A comprehensive study on regulatory requirements for development and filing of generic drugs globally. Int. J. Pharm. Invest. 2 (3), 99–105. Available from: https://doi.org/10.4103/2230-973X.104392.

Hemphill, C.S., Lemley, M.A., 2010. Earning exclusivity: generic drug incentives and the Hatch-Waxman Act. Antitrust L.J. 77, 947.

Holbein, M.B., 2009. Understanding FDA regulatory requirements for investigational new drug applications for sponsor-investigators. J. Invest. Med. 57 (6), 688–694.

Hori, A., 2006. Review process of anticancer drugs in Japan. [Rinshoketsueki] Jpn. J. Clin. Hematol. 47 (7), 626–632.

Import Guidance, 2007. Guidance document on common submission format for import and registration of bulk drugs and finished formulations in India. Central Drugs Standard Control Organization Directorate General of Health Services, Ministry of Health and Family Welfare, Government of India. Available from: https://cdsco.gov.in/opencms/export/sites/CDSCO_WEB/Pdf-documents/import-registration/Import_guidance_doc.pdf (accessed 24.04.20).

Issa, J., 2020. The World's Pharmacy: India's Generic Drug Industry. Global Business Reports. Available from: https://www.gbreports.com/article/the-worlds-pharmacy-indias-generic-drug-industry (accessed 10.03.20).

Jawahar, N., Lakshmi, V.T., 2017. Regulatory requirements for the drug approval process in United States, Europe and India. J. Pharm. Sci. Res. 9 (10), 1943−1952.

JPMA, 2020. Pharmaceutical administration and regulations in Japan. Available from: http://www.jpma.or.jp/english/parj/whole.html (accessed 13.05.20).

Khatun, M.S., Katamreddy, J.D., Reddy, P.J., 2018. A review on ANDA submission requirements for generic drugs: "Paragraph IV certification" as per FDA CDER guidelines. Int. J. Drug. Regulat. Aff. 6 (3), 5−12.

Kuribayashi, R., Matsuhama, M., Mikami, K., 2015. Regulation of generic drugs in Japan: the current situation and future prospects. AAPS J. 17 (5), 1312−1316.

Law Insider. Marketing authorization definition (accessed 10.02.21).

Liu, B.C., He, L., He, G., He, Y., 2010. A cross-national comparative study of orphan drug policies in the United States, the European Union, and Japan: towards a made-in-China orphan drug policy. J. Public Health Policy 31 (4), 407−421.

Malhotra, H., 2011. Biosimilars and non-innovator biotherapeutics in India: an overview of the current situation. Biologicals 39, 321−324.

Marathe, P.A., Kamat, S.K., Tripathi, R.K., Raut, S.B., Khatri, N.P., 2020. Over the counter medicines: global perpective and Indian scenario. J. Postgrad. Med. 66, 28−34.

Natarajan, J., Janani, R., 2019. A review on regulatory guidelines for biologics in India. J. Pharm. Sci. Res. 11 (11), 3651−3654.

ND & CT Rules, 2019. New drugs and clinical trials rules. Central Drugs Standard Control Organization Directorate General of Health Services, Ministry of Health and Family Welfare, Government of India. Available from: https://cdsco.gov.in/opencms/export/sites/CDSCO_WEB/Pdf-documents/NewDrugs_CTRules_2019.pdf (accessed 24.04.20).

O'Connor, D.J., 2013. Orphan drug designation−Europe, the USA and Japan. Expert Opin. 1 (4), 255−259.

Pandey, A., Agrawal, A.R., Sheth, S.D., Maulik, M., Bano, R., Juneja, A., 2008. Clinical trial registry − India: Redefining the conduct of clinical trials. Indian J. Cancer 45 (3), 79−82.

Pinder, T.-A., Ghosh, D., 2019. Complementary medicine regulation in Australia. Nutraceutical and Functional Food Regulations in the United States and around the world, pp. 387−398. Available from: https://doi.org/10.1016/B978-0-12-816467-9.00025-3.

PMDA. Outline of PMDA. Available from: https://www.pmda.go.jp/english/about-pmda/outline/0005.html (accessed 18.05.20).

PMDA. Profile of services, Available from: https://www.pmda.go.jp/files/000221139.pdf (accessed 16.05.20).

PMDA Reviews. Available from: https://www.pmda.go.jp/english/review-services/reviews/0001.html (accessed 18.05.20).

Rafi, N., DS, S., Narayanan, A., 2018. Regulatory requirements and registration procedure for generic drugs in USA. Indian J. Pharm. Educ. Res. 52 (4), 544−549.

Sai Kumari, B., Sai Hanuja, G., Nagabhushanam, M.V., Nagarjuna Reddy, D., 2016. Current regulatory requirements for registration of medicines, compilation and submission of dossier in Australian Therapeutic Goods Administration. Int. J. Adv. Sci. Technol. Res. 6 (6), 144−157.

Saint-Raymond, A., Sato, J., Kishioka, Y., Teixeira, T., Hasslboeck, C., Kweder, S.L., 2020. Remdesivir emergency approvals: a comparison of the United States, Japanese, and EU systems. Expert. Rev. Clin. Pharmacol. 13 (10), 1095−1101.

Scarola, M., 2012, What to expect during the NDA review process. Available from: https://weinberggroup.com/blog/nda-review-fda-submission/ (accessed 12.04.20).

Senthil, V., Baviya Priyadharshini, R., Ramachandran, A., Ganesh, G.N.K., Shrivastava, A., 2015. Regulatory process for import and export of drugs in India. Int. J. Pharm. Sci. Res. 6 (12), 4989−4999.

Similar Biologics Guidelines, 2016. Guidelines on similar biologics: regulatory requirements for marketing authorization in India, 2016. Available from: https://nib.gov.in/NIB-DBT2016.pdf (accessed 26.03.20).

SUGAM Portal, 2019. Central Drugs Standard Control Organization Directorate General of Health Services, Ministry of Health and Family Welfare, Government of India. Available from: SUGAM Portal, https://cdscoonline.gov.in/CDSCO/Industry (accessed 24.04.20).

SUGAM User Manual, 2019. A user manual for e-Governance solution for CDSCO, Central Drug Standard Control Organization (CDSCO). Available from: https://cdsco.gov.in/opencms/export/sites/CDSCO_WEB/Pdf-documents/SUGAM_user_manual.pdf (accessed 10.03.20).

Suresh, S., Puranik, S.B., Patel, P., 2014. Regulatory requirements for registration of pharmaceutical to gain market access in India. Res. Rev. J. Pharm. Pharm. Sci. 3 (4), 49−54.

TGA-OTC Medicine Regulation, 2021. What the TGA regulates. Australian Government, Department of Health, Therapeutic Goods Administration. Available from: https://www.tga.gov.au/what-tga-regulates (accessed 10.03.20).

Therapeutic Goods Act, 1989. Available from: http://www.comlaw.gov.au/ComLaw/Legislation/ActCompilation1.nsf/0/72D440E51DF66177CA257375000E52B1/$file/TherapeuticGoods1989_WD02_Version2.pdf (accessed 12.03.20).

Therapeutic Goods Regulations, 1990. Available from: http://www.comlaw.gov.au/ComLaw/Legislation/LegislativeInstrumentCompilation1.nsf/0/C85AFC5800F19F8ECA257308002F4D8E/$file/TherapeuticGoodsRegs1990.pdf (accessed 12.03.20).

Tongia, A., 2018. Australian Regulatory Framework of Over-the-Counter and Complementary Medicine, Regulatory Focus. Regulatory Affairs Professional Society.

Umscheid, C.A., Margolis, D.J., Grossman, C.E., 2011. Key concepts of clinical trials: a narrative review. Postgrad. Med. 123 (5), 194−204.

USFDA, 2014, Types of applications. Available from: https://www.fda.gov/drugs/how-drugs-are-developed-and-approved/types-applications (accessed 14.05.20).

USFDA, 2015a, FDA's drug review process: continued. Available from: https://www.fda.gov/drugs/information-consumers-and-patients-drugs/fdas-drug-review-process-continued (accessed 16.04.20).

USFDA, 2015b, FAQ for therapeutic biological products. Available from: https://www.fda.gov/drugs/therapeutic-biologics-applications-bla/frequently-asked-questions-about-therapeutic-biological-products (accessed 14.05.20).

USFDA, 2018a, Code of Federal Regulations—Title 21—Food and Drugs. Available from: https://www.fda.gov/medical-devices/medical-device-data-bases/code-federal-regulations-title-21-food-and-drugs (accessed 04.04.20).

USFDA, 2018b, FDA drug review. Available from: https://www.fda.gov/patients/drug-development-process/step-4-fda-drug-review (accessed 26.04.20).

USFDA, 2018c, Animal and veterinary products. Available from: https://www.fda.gov/industry/regulated-products/animal-and-veterinary-products (accessed 26.04.20).

USFDA, 2019a, New drug applications (NDA). Available from: https://www.fda.gov/drugs/types-applications/new-drug-application-nda (accessed 28.04.20).

USFDA, 2019b, Abbreviated new drug application (ANDA). Available from: https://www.fda.gov/drugs/types-applications/abbreviated-new-drug-application-anda (accessed 30.04.20).

USFDA, 2019c, Abbreviated new drug application (ANDA) forms and submission requirements. Available from: https://www.fda.gov/drugs/abbreviated-new-drug-application-anda/abbreviated-new-drug-application-anda-forms-and-submission-requirements (accessed 15.05.19).

USFDA, 2019d, Paragraph IV drug product applications: generic drug patent challenge notifications. Available from: https://www.fda.gov/drugs/abbreviated-new-drug-application-anda/paragraph-iv-drug-product-applications-generic-drug-patent-challenge-notifications (accessed 15.05.20).

USFDA, 2020a, Investigational new drug (IND) application. Available from: https://www.fda.gov/drugs/types-applications/investigational-new-drug-ind-application (accessed 1.06.20).

USFDA, 2020b, Applications covered by section 505(b)(2). Available from: https://www.fda.gov/regulatory-information/search-fda-guidance-documents/applications-covered-section-505b2 (accessed 12.06.20).

USFDA, 2020c, CFR—Code of Federal Regulations—Title 21. Available from: https://www.accessdata.fda.gov/scripts/cdrh/cfdocs/cfcfr/CFRSearch.cfm?CFRPart = 814&showFR = 1&subpartNode = 21:8.0.1.1.11.3 (accessed 11.1120).

USFDA, 2020d, Drug applications for over-the-counter (OTC) drugs. Available from: https://www.fda.gov/drugs/types-applications/drug-applications-over-counter-otc-drugs (accessed 1.12.20).

USFDA, 2020e, Over-the-counter (OTC) drug monograph process. Available from: https://www.fda.gov/drugs/over-counter-otc-drug-monograph-process (accessed 1.12.20).

USFDA, 2021, New animal drug applications. Available from: https://www.fda.gov/animal-veterinary/development-approval-process/new-animal-drug-applications (accessed 6.02.21).

Van Norman, G.A., 2016. Drugs, devices, and the FDA: part 1: an overview of approval processes for drugs. JACC Basic Translat. Sci. 1 (3), 170−179.

Vishal, P., Rahulgiri, G., Pratik, M., Kumar, B.J., 2014. A review on drug approval process for United States, Europe and India. Int. J. Drug. Regulat. Aff. 2 (1), 1−11.

Chapter 7

Pharmaceutical regulatory requirements of nonregulated markets

G.N.K. Ganesh[1] and Suresh K. Mohankumar[2]

[1]*Department of Pharmaceutical Regulatory Affairs, JSS College of Pharmacy, JSS Academy of Higher Education & Research, Ooty, India,*
[2]*Pharmacy Program, Medical School, Faculty of Medicine, Health & Life Science, Swansea University, Swansea, Wales, United Kingdom*

7.1 Introduction

Pharmaceutical industry is one of the highly regulated industries which is governed with several rules and regulations to ensure the quality and safety of medicines for human healthcare and well-being needs (Chomsky, 1999).

The regulatory requirements of pharmaceuticals are country-specific and thus registration of pharmaceutical products in the developed countries is a complex process; however, the regulation of pharmaceutical products in rest of the world (ROW) is much more complex than the regulated market, as they are barely unified (Weiss and Jacobson, 2000). Of note, the economical implication of ROW market is growing universally.

Global regulatory statutes significantly impact healthcare companies. Furthermore, rules vary not only by country but also by product. The International Council for Harmonisation (ICH) "Technical Requirements for Pharmaceuticals for Human Use" mandates that the application dossier for product registration should integrate the quality, security, and competent reporting configurations (Follesdal et al., 2008). Thus obtaining regulatory approval has become one of the biggest hurdles faced by the pharmaceutical companies. Furthermore, the regulatory landscape is dynamic and the rules are continuously changing and therefore any misguided, misinterpreted, or misunderstood decisions can lead to substantial delays to the market and in many cases, it could prevent companies from ever entering a market. For start-ups and small-sized companies, limited budget coupled with a lack of in-house regulatory expertise amplifies the challenge to bring their products to market. Many times, it is in the best interest of these small medical device companies to identify markets with the least (regulatory) burdensome approach.

Product registration in underdeveloped countries is a challenging task like regulated countries (the United States, the EU, and Japan) as they are not harmonized. It creates a difference in regulatory environment in semiregulated countries. Enormous diversity of regulatory requirements is found in this area. This region consists mainly of the countries from Asia pacific, Latin America, Eastern Europe, Africa, and Gulf countries. Countries from Asia Pacific and Gulf have somewhat harmonized their regulatory environment through The Association of Southeast Asian Nations (ASEAN) and Gulf Cooperation Council organizations, and ROW countries yet to be harmonized regulations in their respective regions. The urgent requirement to rationalize and harmonize regulation was required by instance of rising cost of healthcare, research, and development and to meet the public requirement for safe and efficacious treatments to patient in need. ICH committee has given priority to harmonize the format of reporting data for quality, safety, and efficacy in the application dossier. The commercial significance of ROW markets is increasing globally. It is crucial that pharmaceutical companies keep up-to-date with the latest regulatory developments to ensure their place on the ROW market.

The Marketing Approval Application (MAA) means the filing, in each case about a licensed product in the Territory, for marketing approval (not including pricing or repayment approval) in a country other than the United States (Cheema et al., 2012). The MAA tenders extensive data on a drug, which allows the regulatory authorities to estimate quality, safety, and effectiveness, and determine the future of the marketing authorization holder's capacity to guarantee and monitor a viable benefit/risk ratio (Schwartzberg et al., 2017). This chapter favors the regulatory processes for gaining marketing authorization in ROW countries in terms of technical data requirement for the dossier.

Regulatory Affairs in the Pharmaceutical Industry. DOI: https://doi.org/10.1016/B978-0-12-822211-9.00002-2
© 2022 Elsevier Inc. All rights reserved.

7.2 Malaysia

The National Pharmaceutical Regulatory Division (NPRA) is an agency under the Ministry of Health (MoH) of Malaysia responsible for registering pharmaceutical products, traditional health supplements, and notification of cosmetic products that are marketed in Malaysia. NPRA, formerly known as the National Pharmaceutical Control Bureau (BPFK), operates at Jalan Universiti, Petaling Jaya, since its inception in October 1978. NPRA is responsible for ensuring that the Malaysian consumers obtain quality, effective, and safe remedies. Apart from medicine, natural (traditional) and cosmetic products in the Malaysian market are also regulated to ensure that it is safe and of sound quality.

The NPRA health product registration search application was developed in accordance with the Pharmaceutical Services Program Strategic Plan which emphasized the use of innovative technology to ensure that accurate pharmaceutical information is provided to the consumers.

Legal framework and regulations of regulatory bodies

1. MOH Malaysia;
2. DCA: DCA is the licensing authority;
3. NPCB:
   a. Daily operations of drug registration and monitoring/surveillance activities.
   b. Center for Compliance and Licensing (CCL) under NPCB, The Center for Postregistration of Products.

Regulatory law

1. Medicines (Advertisement and Sale) Act 1956 (rev. 1983);
2. Control of Drugs and Cosmetics Regulations 1984;
3. Sales of Drug Act 1952:
   a. **NPCB** of Malaysia is delegated the daily operations of drug registration and cosmetic notification, together with the attendant monitoring and surveillance activities;
   b. **DCA** is responsible for *Registration of Pharmaceutical and Cosmetic products, Licensing of premises for import, manufacturer, wholesale, monitoring the quality of product being market and adverse drug reaction in Malaysia.* (Venkateswarlu et al., 2014);
   c. Format followed: ACTD format.

Regulatory system

- The DCA accepts only Web-based online submissions via http://www.bpfk.gov.my.
- The applicant should register their product with ROB.
- The GMP inspections of manufacturers of registered products are taken by the CCL.
- Malaysian Regulatory Agency has identified five categories of drug products:
  - NCE,
  - Biotech,
  - Generics,
  - Abridged Procedure Pharmaceuticals (OTC), and
  - Traditional Products (as per NPRA).

Registration procedure for pharmaceuticals through online

1. Go to NPCB Web site (http://www.bpfk.gov.my). Become Quest member.
2. After the payment is done to the Digicert, in seven days (East Malaysia will take more time), Digicert will send the digital certificate via POSLAJU. The login id and password will be sent to the email address updated during the registration of Quest member.
3. By using the login ID and password, enter the Quest, go to registration, and register the product online. All the forms will be available in the form tray.
4. Submit the requested data.
5. Communicate with the NPCB officer if any additional data is required.
6. Products submitted to the DCA meeting (Fig. 7.1).

Requirements for generic registration checklist as per NPRA (see Table 7.1)
Labeling requirements (country-specific)—Malaysia

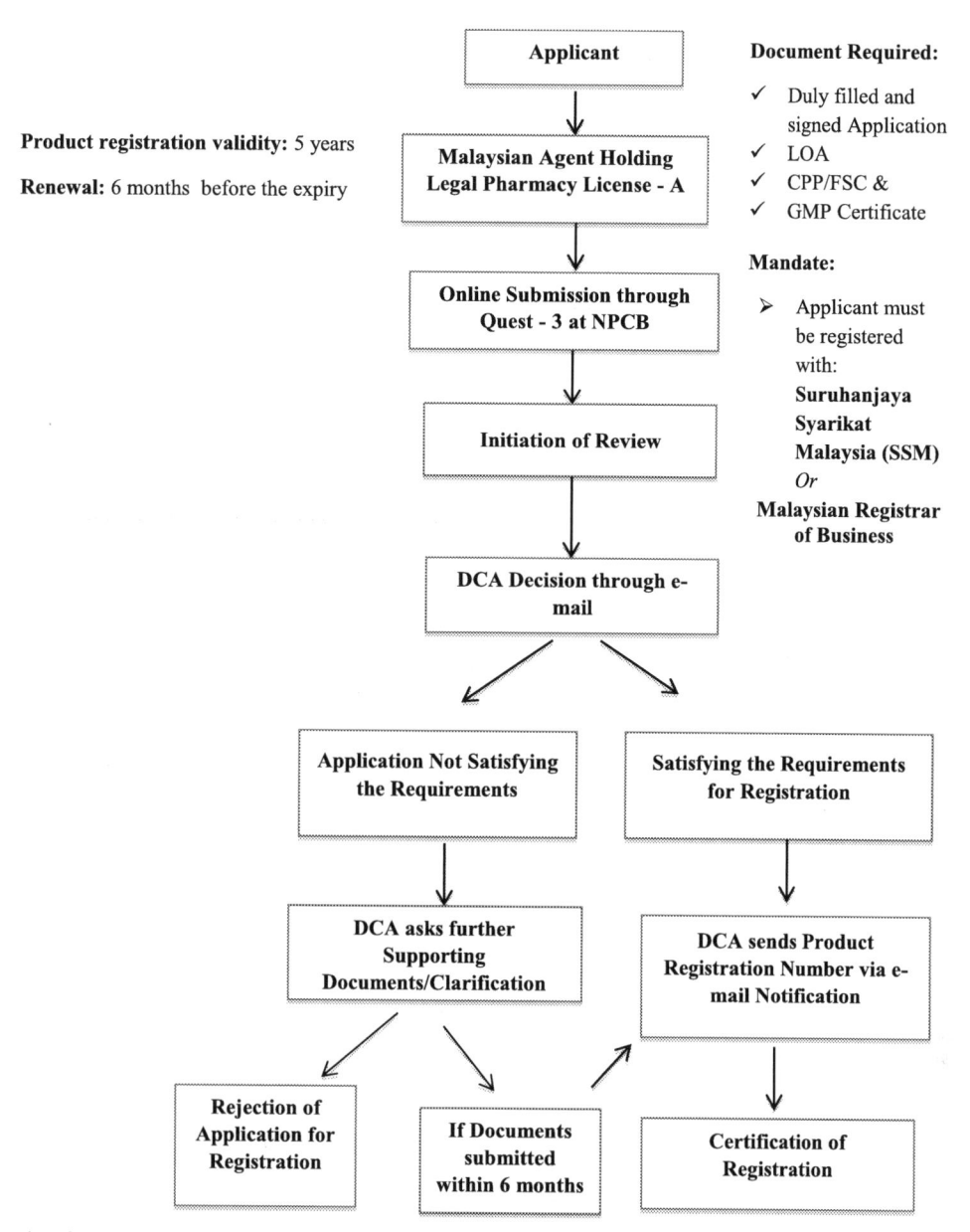

FIGURE 7.1 Flowchart for Malaysia as per National Pharmaceutical Regulatory Division.

Section D—Label (mock-up) for immediate containers, outer cartons, and proposed package inserts. The following information must be present on the label of the product (Van Dijk et al., 2014) (Table 7.2).

Malaysia BE studies

Bioequivalence is a requirement that is enforced by the DCA, MoH for generics, for ensuring the quality, safety, and efficacy of generics (Hassali et al., 2015).

Selection of the test products for bioequivalence studies in Malaysia.

WHO criteria

1. Oral immediate-release pharmaceutical products with systemic action and indicated for serious conditions requiring assured therapeutic response;
2. Narrow therapeutic window/safety margin, steep dose—response curve;
3. Pharmacokinetics (PK) complicated by variable or incomplete absorption or absorption window, nonlinear PK, and high first-pass metabolism;
4. Unfavorable physicochemical properties glow solubility, and instability.

TABLE 7.1 Requirements in Malaysia.

Section	Contents	
Part I	**Administrative data and product information**	
Section A		**Product Particular**
	A1	Name of product
	A2	Name and strength of active ingredient(s)
	A3	Dosage form
	A4	Product description
	A5.1	Pharmacodynamics/Pharmacokinetics
	A5.2	Pharmacokinetics
	A6	Indication
	A7	Recommended dose
	A8	Mode of administration
	A9	Contraindication
	A10	Warning and precautions
	A11	Interaction with other medicaments
	A12	Pregnancy and lactation
	A13	Side effects
	A14	Symptoms and treatment of overdose
	A15	Storage condition
	A16	Shelf life
	A17	Therapeutical code (if any)
		mode of action
Section B		**Product Formula**
	B1.1	Batch manufacturing formula
		Batch quantity of active substance(s)
		Batch quantity of excipient
	B1.2	Attachment of batch manufacturing formula documentation
Section C		**Particular of Packing**
	C1	Pack Size (weight, volume, quantity)
	C2	Immediate container type
		Container-type description
	C3	Barcode/Serial No.
	C4	Recommended distributor's Price
	C5	Recommended retail Price
Section D		**Mock-up, Outer Carton and Package Insert**
	D1	Label (mock-up) for immediate container
	D2	Label (mock-up) for outer carton? Y/N
	D3	Proposed package insert

(Continued)

TABLE 7.1 (Continued)

Section	Contents			
Section E		**Supplementary Documentation**		
	E1.1	Product owner (manufacturer/applicant/other)		
	E1.2	Letter of authorization from product owner		
		E2.1	Letter of appointment of contract manufacturer from product owner	
		E2.2	Letter of acceptance from contract manufacturer	
	E3	Is the active substance(s) patented in Malaysia? Y/N (if any)		
	E4	Certificate of pharmaceutical product (CPP)		
	E4.1	Certificate of pharmaceutical product (CPP) issuing body (country)		
	E4.2	Is this product licensed to be placed on the market for use in the exporting country) Y/N		
	E4.3	Is the product on the market in the exporting country? Y/N		
	E4.4	Date of issue of certificate of pharmaceutical product (CPP)		
	E4.5	Date of expiry of certificate of pharmaceutical product (CPP) (if any)		
	E5	Certificate of free sale (CFS)		
	E5.1	Certificate of free sale (CFS) issuing body (country)		
	E5.2	Date of issue of certificate of free sale (CFS)		
	E5.3	Date of expiry of certificate of free sale (CFS) (if any)		
	E6	Good manufacturing practice (GMP)		
	E6.1	Certificate of good manufacturing practice (GMP) issuing body (country)		
	E6.2	Date of issue of certificate of good manufacturing practice (GMP)		
	E6.3	Date of expiry of certificate of good manufacturing practice (GMP) (if any)		
	E7	Summary of product characteristics (Product data sheet—if any)		
	E8	Patient information leaflet (PIL)		
	E9	Attachment of protocol analysis (Finished product)		
	E10	Attachment of analytical validation		
	E11	Attachment of certificate analysis (Finished product—three recent batches)		
	E12	Other supporting document (if any)		
	E13	Manufacturer: Importer (if any)		
	E14	Other manufacturer(s) involve (if any)—GMP		
	E15	Store address (if any)		
Part II	**Quality**			
S	**Drug Substance**			
	S1	**General Information**		
		S1.1	Nomenclature	
		S1.2	Structure	
			S1.2.1	Attachment for structure
		S1.3	General properties	

(Continued)

TABLE 7.1 (Continued)

Section	Contents			
	S2	**Manufacturer**		
		S2.1	Manufacturer name	
			S2.1.1	Remarks
		S2.2	Description of manufacturing process and process controls	
		S2.3	Control of materials	
		S2.4	Control of critical steps and intermediates	
		S2.5	Process validation and/or evaluation	
		S2.6	Manufacturing process development	
	S3	**Characterization**		
		S3.1	Elucidation of structure and characteristics	
		S3.2	Impurities	
	S4	**Control of Drug Substance/Active Ingredient**		
		S4.1	Specifications, manufacturer name, and country of origin	
		S4.2	Analytical procedures/method of analysis	
		S4.3	Validation of analytical procedures (if any)	
		S4.4	Batch analysis (First batch of COA for active ingredient)	
		S4.5	Justification of specification	
	S5	**Reference Standards or Materials**		
	S6	**Container Closure System**		
	S7	**Stability Data**		
P	**Drug Product**			
	P1	**Description and Composition**		
	P2	**Pharmaceutical Development (if any)**		
		P2.1	Information on development studies	
		P2.2	Components of the drug product	
		P2.3	Finished products	
		P2.4	Manufacturing process development	
		P2.5	Container closure system (type and description)	
		P2.6	Microbiological attributes	
		P2.7	Compatibility	
	P3	**Manufacturer**		
		P3.1	Batch manufacturing formula (from product registration form)	
		P3.2	Manufacturing process and process control	
			P3.2.1	Manufacturing process flowchart (if any)
		P3.3	Control of critical steps and intermediates (in-process control)	
		P3.4	Process validation and/or evaluation	
	P4	**Control of Excipients**		
		P4.1	Specifications, manufacturer name, and country of origin	
		P4.2	Analytical procedures	

(Continued)

TABLE 7.1 (Continued)

Section	Contents		
		P4.3	Validation of analytical procedures
		P4.4	Justification of specifications
		P4.5	Excipient of Human or Animal Origin- confirmation
		P4.6	Novel Excipients
	P5	**Control of Finished Products**	
		P5.1	Specification and reference
		P5.2	Analytical procedures
		P5.3	Validation of analytical procedures
		P5.4	Batch analysis
		P5.5	Characterization of impurities
		P5.6	Justification of specification(s)
	P6	**Reference Standards or Materials**	
	P7	**Container Closure System**	
	P8	**Stability Data (Two batches)**	
	P9	**Product Interchangeability/Equivalence Evidence (if any)**	
Part III	**Nonclinical Document**		
Section A		**Table of Contents**	
Section B		**Nonclinical Overview**	
Section C		**Nonclinical Written and Tabulated Summaries**	
	1	Table of Contents	
	2	Pharmacology	
	3	Pharmacokinetics	
	4	Toxicology	
Section D		Nonclinical Study Report	
	1	Table of Contents	
	2	Pharmacology	
	3	Pharmacokinetics	
	4	Toxicology	
Part IV	**Clinical Document**		
Section A		**Table of Content**	
Section B		**Clinical Overview**	
Section C		**Clinical Summary**	
	1	Summary of Biopharmaceutics and Associated Analytical Methods	
	2	Summary of Clinical Pharmacology Studies	
	3	Summary of Clinical Efficacy	
	4	Summary of Clinical Safety	
	5	Synopses of Individual Studies	
Section D		**Tabular Listing of All Clinical Studies**	
Section E		**Clinical Study Reports**	
Section F		**List of Key Literature References**	

TABLE 7.2 Labeling requirement for Malaysia as per National Pharmaceutical Regulatory Division.

S. no.	Parameters	Unit carton	Inner labels	Blister/strips
1	Product name	√	√	√
2	Dosage form	√		
3	Name of active substance(s)	√	√	√[a]
4	Strength of active substance(s)	√	√	√[a]
5	Batch number	√	√	NA
6	Manufacturing date	√		NA
7	Expiration date	√	√	√
8	Route of administration	√	√	NA
9	Storage condition	√	√[b]	NA
10	Country's registration number	√	√[b]	NA
11	Name and address of marketing authorization (Product license) holder/ product owner	√	√[b]	Name/logo of manufacturer/product owner
12	Name and address of manufacturer	√	√[b]	NA
13	Special labeling (if applicable), for example sterile, external use, cytotoxic, alcohol content, animal origin (porcine, bovine)—to declare source of ingredients derived from animal origin, including gelatin (active, excipient, and/or capsule shell)	√	√	NA
14	Recommended daily allowance (RDA) for vitamins/multivitamins/mineral preparations used as dietary supplements	√	√	NA
15	Warnings (if applicable)	√	√[b]	NA
16	Pack sizes (unit/volume)	√	√	NA
17	Security labeling—hologram	√	√	NA
18	Name and content of preservative(s) where present	√	√	NA
19	Name and content of alcohol, where present	√	√	NA
20	The words "Keep Medicine Out of Reach of Children" or words bearing similar meaning in both B.M. and English (for EPCs only, English optional)	√	√	NA
21	Other country-specific labeling requirements (if applicable)	√	√[a]	NA

No. 17–21 of labeling requirements: Country-specific for Malaysia. *NA*, not applicable.
[a]*It is also exempted for multiingredient product with more than three ingredients. For multivitamins and minerals preparations, it is suggested to label as multivitamins and minerals.*
[b]*It is exempted for small labels like ≤ 5 mL size ampoules and vials.*

Local situation

1. Patient complaint.
2. High-volume usage in hospitals from MOH drug list (Harrison et al., 2016).

Selection of comparator products
Innovator product in the country
If the innovator product is not being identified, the comparator should be chosen in the following order:

- Approval with the ICH and associated countries such as Australia and Canada.
- WHO has to prequalify them.

7.3 Indonesia

The Indonesian Food and Drug Authority (Indonesian FDA) (Indonesian: Badan Pengawas Obat dan Makanan) or Badan POM (BPOM) is a government agency of Indonesia. BPOM is responsible for protecting public health through the control and supervision of prescription and over-the-counter pharmaceutical drugs (medications), vaccines, biopharmaceuticals, dietary supplements, food safety, traditional medicine, and cosmetics. Task and purposes of this agency are similar to USFDA

Legal framework and regulations

The following is the number of the decree issued by the head of Indonesia's national drug and food control agency: HK.00.05.3.1950 on the criteria and procedure of drug registration that enlists the country-specific requirements for Indonesia.

A new regulation that is issued by the minister, namely Regulation of the MOH in Indonesia No. 1010/MENKES/PER/XI/2008 regarding the Registration of Medicines ("Regulation 1010/2008"), lists out that a medicine that has to be distributed in Indonesia must be first registered before a Distribution License (Izin Edar) can be applied.

Format Followed as per NA-DFC ACTD

Regulatory System

Regulatory structure of Indonesia as per NA-DFC

1. The applicant must submit a drug registration to the Head of the National Agency.
2. Drug registration is categorized into:
   a. New registration
   b. Registration of drug variations

Category 1: is new drug registration with new API or newly derived component or new combination product or a biological product with a new active ingredient or with a new combination product or a new dosage form (NDF).

Category 2: is a new drug registration with the old composition in a NDF or new strength or similar biological product.

Category 3: is registration of drug or biological product with old composition with:

3.1. New indication

3.2. New posology

Category 4: is the registration of a copy drug:

4.1. Copy drug with the trade name

4.2. Copy drug with the generic name

Category 5: is registration of other preparation containing drug

*The registration of the copy drug (the generic drug) comes under the Category 4.

Drug registration

The drug registration process consists of two stages:

1. Preregistration
2. Submission of the registration dossier

Preregistration steps

The purpose of preregistration is to ascertain the application review and assessment path. One of three pathways is used by NA-DFC to review drug applications (Paths I, II, or III).

1. Path I includes drug applications for products used to treat serious or life-threatening diseases, or for essential generic drugs for public health programs.
2. New drugs which have been already approved in certain designated countries may be qualified for the Path II registration process.
3. Any drug application for products that will not qualify for Path I or Path II evaluation processes will be reviewed with the Path III process. Applications are usually reviewed within the following time frames: Path I: 100 working days.

Path II: 150 working days

Path III: 300 working days for new drugs; for all other drugs, 80 working days

Registration steps (submission of the registration documents and the evaluation process)

The registration forms and the accompanying documents can be in languages such as Bahasa Indonesian or English. Drugs which are produced only for export are not required to have any labels in Bahasa Indonesian; only English labels are required.

1. For registration of a product in Indonesia, "a complete registration form, a floppy disk, receipt of the payment of evaluation and registration fee, and the result of preregistration are attached and sent."

2. Applicant must submit a drug sample for three times of analysis and standard raw material that meets the specification and method of analysis of the active ingredient of the objective drug for quality assessment.
3. Registration dossier of copy drug with an active ingredient that has already been available in the Electronic Information Standard [Standar Informasi Elektronik (STINEL)] consists of floppy disk that has been completed in line with the data in Form A and Form B21−13, and the forms of Form A, Form B1, Form B214, Form B4, Form C1, and Form D.
4. Registration dossier of copy drug with an active ingredient that has no STINEL consists of a floppy disk that has been completed with the data in line with Form A and the forms of Form A, Form B1, Form B2, Form B3, Form C1, and Form D.
   a. Forms A—the name and the address of the person applying, the manufacturing industry, and the information related to the product;
   b. Form B1—administrative documents;
   c. Form B2—information of the product that determines the efficacy, safety, and quality;
   d. Form B3—the procedure of batch numbering system;
   e. Form B4—information of the price;
   f. Form C—contains the documents that should be attached to support the information mentioned in Form B2;
   g. Form C1—documents based on quality and technology;
   h. Form C2—preclinical documents;
   i. Form C3—clinical trial documents;
   j. Form D—list of submitted drug sample and its reference standard.

Special requirements

1. Completion of registration forms should be in Indonesian or in English.
2. Registration documents can be in Indonesian or in English.
3. Labeling of over-the-counter drug/limited over-the-counter drug must be in Indonesian.
4. Labeling of drugs for export only should at least be in English.

Other country-specific requirements which may also be included with the ACTD submission:

- Traditional medicines name;
- Package size;
- Registration number, name, and industry address (at least name of city and country);
- Composition (species name of raw ingredient);
- Effects/usefulness;
- Usage;
- Warning and contraindication (if exist);
- Production code number;
- Expiry date;
- Level of production/standard operational procedure, utility or machine;
- Source of available raw ingredients;
- Methods and test result of stability/durability;
- Efficacy and adequate safety proven through preclinical and clinical trials;
- Proof in accordance with the development of relevant scientific knowledge;
- Production process in accordance with the GMP;
- Specifications and documents of the method of analysis of all materials used in the finished product;
- Letter of attorney submitted by the applicant of imported drug (Fig. 7.2).

Labeling requirements (country-specific)—Indonesia as per NA-DFC (see Table 7.3)
Point to remember:
Once a drug is registered in Indonesia, the company has two years to relocate its facility or hire contract manufacturers to manufacture it locally.

7.4 Thailand

Thailand's pharmaceutical market will continue on a positive growth trajectory. Efforts are being made to reform regulatory processes for innovative drug registrations helping Thailand to attract greater foreign investment into its domestic

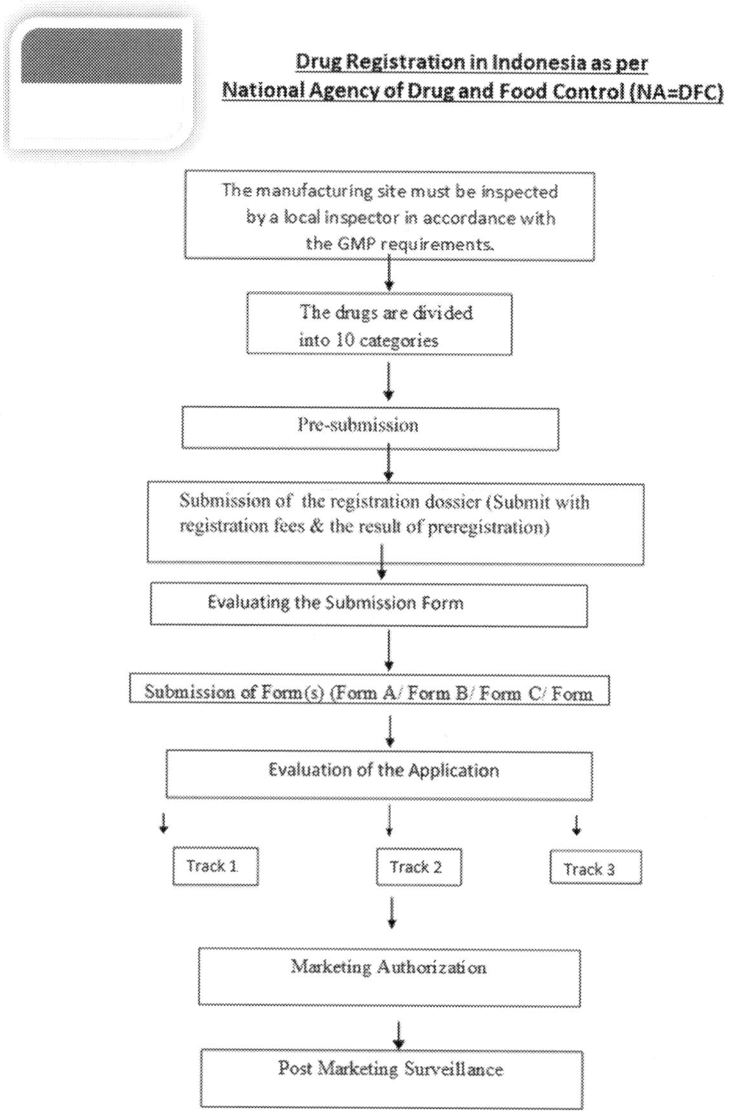

FIGURE 7.2   Indonesian drug registration process.

Drug Registration in Indonesia as per
National Agency of Drug and Food Control (NA=DFC)

The manufacturing site must be inspected
by a local inspector in accordance with
the GMP requirements.

The drugs are divided
into 10 categories

Pre-submission

Submission of the registration dossier (Submit with
registration fees & the result of preregistration)

Evaluating the Submission Form

Submission of Form(s) (Form A/ Form B/ Form C/ Form

Evaluation of the Application

Track 1   Track 2   Track 3

Marketing Authorization

Post Marketing Surveillance

pharmaceutical industry. However, comparatively because of the low levels of affordability and poor access to healthcare, the market will mainly be suited to generic producers.

Legal framework and regulations
- Covers the acts under its legal framework and regulations
- Drug Act 1987 (fifth revision)
- Food Act 1979
- Cosmetic Act 1992
- Narcotic Act 1987 (third revision)
- Psychotropic Substances Act 1992 (third revision)
- Volatile Substances Act 1990
- Medical Devices Act 1988

Medicines are classified into two groups:

- Modern drugs
- Traditional drugs

TABLE 7.3 Labeling requirements for Indonesia.

S. no.	Information to be included	Unit carton	Inner labels	Strips/ blisters	Catch covers/ envelopes	Ampoules/ vials
1	Product name	√	√	√	√	√
2	Dosage form	√	√	–	√	√
3	Package size	√	√	–	√	√
4	a. Name and strength of active ingredient(s)	√	√	√	√	√
	b. Generic name should appear under the brand name; minimal size is 80% of the brand name	√	√	√	√	√
5	*Local production:*					
	• Name of applicant	√	√	√	√	√
	• Address of applicant	√	√	–	√	√**
6	*Imported drugs:*					
	• Name of applicant and manufacturer of imported drug	√	√	√	√	√
	• Address of applicant and manufacturer of imported drug	√	√	–	√	√**
7	*Toll manufacturing:*					
	• Name of applicant and manufacturer	√	√	√	√	√
	• Address of applicant and manufacturer	√	√	–	√	√**
8	*Local production under license:*					
	• Name of applicant and licensee	√	√	√	√	√
	• Address of applicant	√	√	–	√	√**
9	Registration number	√	√	√	√	√
10	Batch number	√	√	√	√	√
11	Date of production	√	–	–	√	–
12	Expiration date	√	√	√	√	√
13	Indications	√*	*	–	√	–
14	Posology	√*	*	–	√	–
15	Contraindications	*	*	–	√	–
16	Adverse reactions	*	*	–	√	–
17	Drug interactions	*	*	–	√	–
18	Warnings—precautions	*	*	–	√	–
19	Special warnings (if any)	√	*	–	√	–
20	Storage condition	√	√	–	√	√**
21	Specific information in accordance with valid provisions (if any), for example					
	*Source of porcine	√	√	–	√	√
	*Alcohol contents	√	√	–	√	√
	• Specific information on ceiling price					

(Continued)

TABLE 7.3 (Continued)

S. no.	Information to be included	Unit carton	Inner labels	Strips/ blisters	Catch covers/ envelopes	Ampoules/ vials
22	Warning for limited over-the-counter (OTC) drug	√	√	−	√	−
23	With physician prescription only in Indonesian language (for prescription drug)	√	√	√	√	√
24	Specific round mark of prescription drug/OTC/ limited OTC	√	√	−	√	−

Notes: √, Information should be included; √*, information must be included for OTC and limited OTC (Prescription drug could refer to the brochure); √**, specifically for ampoule or vial more than 2 mL; *, Information could refer to the brochure; −, Information not necessary to be included.

The modern drugs are divided into four categories as mentioned below:

1. Household remedies sale of which does not require any license;
2. Readily packed drug products that can be sold in drug stores by nurses or any other medical professional;
3. Dangerous drugs; and
4. Specially controlled drugs.

Dangerous drugs that can be purchased without a prescription, but pharmacists must dispense them. Drugs which may tend to possess a harmful effect on health, if they are misused, will be listed in the last category for which the sales require a prescription.

Traditional drugs are those which are used in indigenous or traditional medical care as monographed in the pharmacopoeia of traditional medicines or those declared by the Minister of Public Health as traditional medicines or those permitted to be registered as traditional medicines. Less stringent control and registration of the drugs in this group are compared to that of modern drugs.

Format Followed as per FDA of Thailand: An ACTD format with certain country-based requirements.

Pharmaceutical Regulations in Thailand

Regulatory procedure

Thailand's national drug control system starts from Drug Act BE 2510 (1967) and its four amendments. The MOPH, in collaboration with the FDA's Drug Control Division, is in charge of running the system. Pharmaceutical companies that want to manufacture or export their products must first get FDA approval. To make, sell, or import pharmaceutical products into Thailand, both manufacturers and importers must obtain a license.

There are two phases to the pharmacy control system: premarketing and postmarketing. Companies must obtain a license to produce, sell, or import pharmaceuticals into Thailand during the premarketing phase, as well as to register their products in the country. Licensing is handled by the Bangkok Metropolitan Area's Drug Control Division and the surrounding provincial health offices. There are totally nine categories of licenses, including a license to produce, a license to sell, a license to act as a wholesaler of modern drugs, etc. (Fathelrahman et al., 2016).

Registration: premarketing phase

Product registration is also part of the premarketing process. Steps 1 and 3 are handled by the FDA's Drug Control Division, while Step 2 is handled by the Department of Medical Sciences. Thailand also has a regulatory process for registering new drugs.

Generally, there are three important steps for drug registration in Thailand:

1. Application for the permission to manufacture or import of drug samples (at FDA);
2. Application for the approval of quality control of drug and the analytical methods (at Department of Medical Science); and
3. Application for grant of drug registration certificate (at FDA).

Registration: postmarketing phase

Following the registration and selling of pharmaceuticals, the government's quality control mechanism appears to focus on performance, that is the final stage of the manufacturing process, rather than input/raw materials or the actual manufacturing process itself. The National Adverse Drug Reactions Monitoring Center and its 19 regional offices conduct routine inspections and pharmaceutical sampling during this process to ensure pharmaceutical quality. Outside academics are often employed to review technical papers related to drug registration. However, follow-up drug reevaluations are not routinely performed (Hettle et al., 2017).

Drug registration

The process of registration is required to ensure the quality, safety, and efficacy of the drugs being marketed in the country. Only the authorized licensees are qualified to apply for product registration. The manufacturing plants are subjected to inspection in which drug products are being manufactured.

In accordance with the new Drug Act (which is expected to be enacted within 2003) a certificate of registration for the product is valid for five years from the date of issuance.

The process of drug registration will be carried out in two channels which differ in the degrees of control and dossier submission:

1. Registration of general medicine
2. Registration of Thai traditional medicines (Garattini et al., 2007)

Because of the differences in the requirements for dossiers to be submitted for product approvals, the general medicine will be therefore defined as:

- generics whose registrations require only dossiers on product manufacturing and quality control along with product information,
- new medicines whose registrations require a complete set of product dossiers, and
- new generics whose registrations require dossiers of bioequivalence studies in addition to the required dossiers for generics submission.

Generics are pharmaceutical products which have the same active ingredient and the same dosage form as those of original products, but will be manufactured by different manufacturers (Al Ameri et al., 2012). The new medicines will include the products of new chemicals, new indications, new combinations, or any new delivery systems and NDFs. New generics are those medicines with same API, doses and dosage form as those of the new compounds that were registered after 1992 (Raw et al., 2004).

The drug registration process for general medicines is divided into five processes:

- Generic drug registration
- Traditional drug registration
- New drug registration
    - Original new drug
    - New generic drug
- Biological product registration
- Herbal medicine registration

Registration of generic drug requires the following three steps:

1. Application for permission to manufacture or import of drug samples (at FDA),
2. Application for an approval of drug quality control and analytical methods (at Department of Medical Science), and
3. Application for granting of a drug registration certificate (as per FDA).

Registration of new generic drug has the following steps:

- A protocol based upon bioequivalence study should be submitted for approval at the drug control division.
- Application seeking permission for the import or manufacture of the drug samples.
- Performance of the BE study according to the approved protocol in a specified government institute.
- Submission of the application for registration along with BE report and other useful documents.
    - The details of drug registration are listed in the official site http://www.fda.moph.go.th of the Thai FDA (Figs. 7.3 and 7.4).

Documents required for generic drug registration as per FDA of Thailand

The registration procedure of generic drugs is divided into two main steps:

Step 1: Application for the authorization to import or manufacture drug sample intended to be registered.

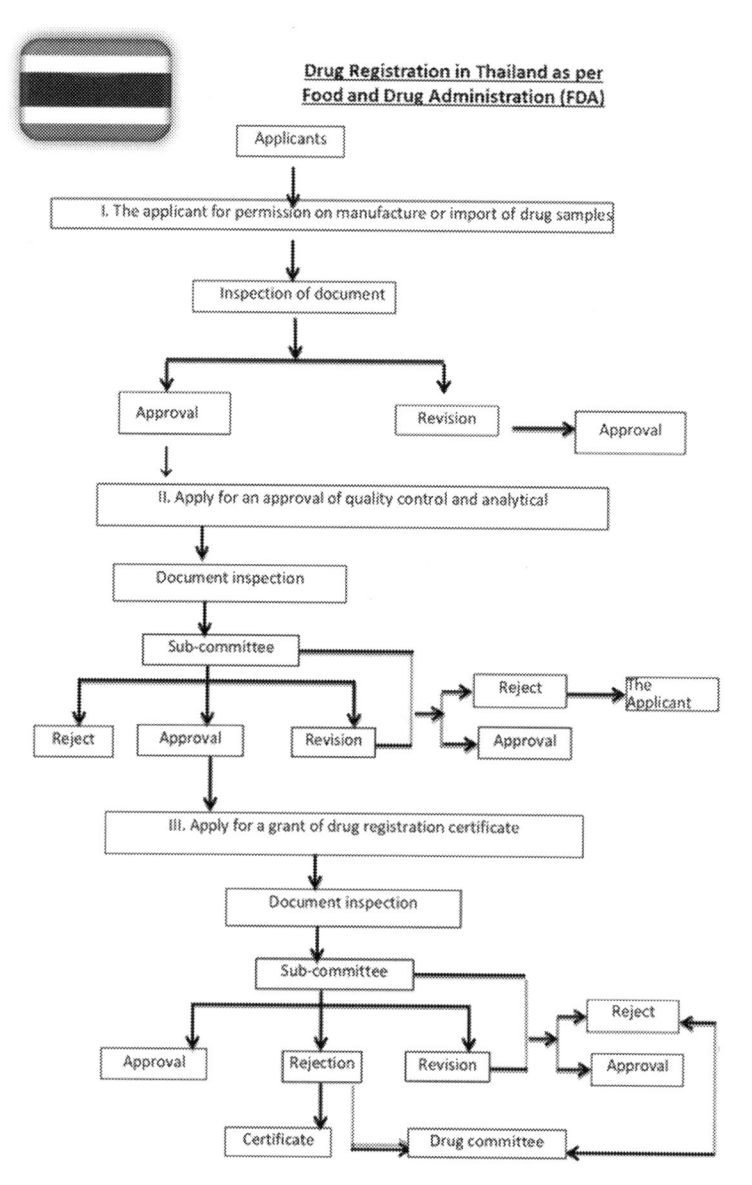

FIGURE 7.3 Drug registration in Thailand.

The following documents are required:

1. Application form to be completely filled by authorized licensee
2. Drug formula (active ingredients only)
3. Drug literature
4. Drug labeling and packaging

Step 2: Application for the approval of granted credential certificate.
The following documents are required:

1. Application form to be completely filled by authorized licensee;
2. Permit to manufacture or import drug sample;
3. Drug sample;
4. Pharmacological and toxicological study (if any);
5. Clinical trials, safety, and efficacy study (if any);
6. Complete drug formula;
7. Drug literature;

FIGURE 7.4   New drug registration as per Thailand.

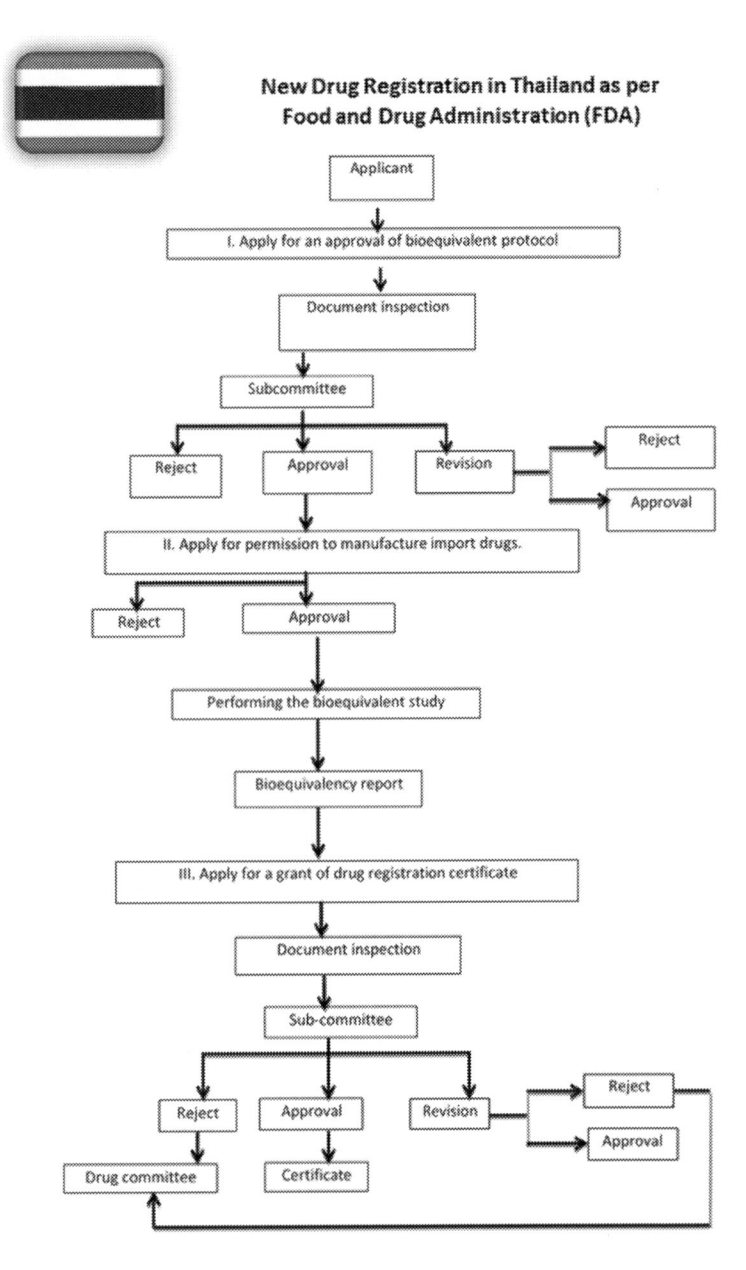

8. Labeling and packaging should consist of the drug name, registration number, drug quantity per packaging, formulas which show active ingredient and quantity of strength, lot no. batch control number, name of manufacturer and address, manufacturing date, the words "dangerous drug"/"specially controlled"/"for external use"/"for topical use" written in Thai and in red color if the drug is considered to be one of them, the word "household remedy drug" written in Thai if the drug is considered to be, the word for "veterinary use" written in Thai if the drug is considered to be, and the expire date;

9. Certificate of free sale (in case of imported drug);

10. Manufacturing method;

11. In-process control with the relevant acceptable limits;

12. Raw material specifications of active(s) and inert ingredients with the corresponding control methods in details;

13. Finished product specification with the corresponding control methods in details;

14. Certificate of analysis (CA) of active ingredient (s) (raw material) (to be required in case of that active substance dose not conform to official pharmacopoeias (USP, NF, BP, etc.));

15. Drug analytical control method;

16. Packaging;
17. Storage condition;
18. Stability studies of the finished product;
19. Certificate of GMP (in case of imported drug);

Note: Certificate of free sale should be issued by the competent authorized officer and endorsed by Thai Embassy or Thai Embassy residing in association with the country where the documents being issued.

Labeling Requirements (country-specific)—Thailand as per FDA of Thailand

According to the various drug acts, the following words have to be written in Thai;

Dangerous drug, specially controlled drug, for external use, common household remedy, topical use, and expiry date.

Thailand BE studies as per FDA of Thailand

Reference product/comparator product:

A reference product must be an innovator product, *if the innovator product is not available in the country, an alternative comparator product approved by the regulatory authority of the country can be used.*

Population:

The studies are accepted only if done on Thai population.

International BE:

Not accepted.

Guidelines followed:

Thai guidelines for the conduct of BA and BE studies adopted from "ASEAN Guidelines for the Conduct of Bioavailability and Bioequivalence Studies."

7.5 Vietnam

Legal framework and regulations

Vietnam is working to reform its legal framework in order to establish a favorable atmosphere for the growth of a multisector market economy as well as a more open and secure investment environment. Many laws and regulations have been passed in recent years to create the legal structure for the open-door policy, to comply with the integration requirements of international agreements, and, in particular, to comply with the requirements imposed by Vietnam's World Trade Organization membership (Phuong and Nguyen, 2012)

- With the improvement of the social welfare, Vietnam has made many attempts to improve the legal framework for healthcare sector. The most important laws are:
- The Pharmacy Law (2005);
- The Health Insurance Law (2008);
- The Ordinance on Private Medical and Pharmaceutical Practice 6 (2003) ("OPMPP").

Most recently, on November 23, 2009, the National Assembly of Vietnam adopted the *Law on Medical Examination and Treatment* ("LMET"). The LMET came into effect from January 1, 2011, and replaced the OPMPP (Schwartländer et al., 2011).

Regulatory system

Director and Deputy Director are appointed or terminated by the Minister of Health. The Director is responsible to the Minister of Health and the law for all activities of the department. The Deputy Director assists the Director, is responsible to the Director and to Law for the tasks assigned to him.

Organization of the department

1. Office of the department;
2. Planning and finance;
3. Department of business management and pharmacy;
4. Management and quality medicines and cosmetics;
5. Registration of drugs;
6. Department of information management, advertising drugs, and cosmetics;
7. Legislation and integration;
8. Management and drugs;

9. Units attached to the department:
   a. Journal of pharmaceutical and cosmetics;
   b. Training center, guidance comprehensive management of the quality of medicines and cosmetics;

Drug registration applications as per drug administration of Vietnam

Pharmacochemical drugs, medical bioproducts, vaccines, serum-containing antibody, bioproducts for diagnosis in vitro, traditional drugs, drugs originated from pharmaceutical materials, and medicinal raw materials shall be registered in the following types:

1. First-time registration;
2. Registration of major variations;
3. Registration of minor variations;
4. Registration renewal

Format followed: ACTD as per Drug Administration of Vietnam
Registration requirements as per drug administration of Vietnam (Table 7.4; Fig. 7.5)

Receiving drug registration dossiers

Drug registration dossiers are received at one desk by the Drug Registration Department ("DRD"). The names of the medicines and other relevant details are numbered in order and reported in the DRD's receipt diary.

Process drug registration dossiers

The DRD follows a first-in-first-out procedure while processing dossiers. After receiving input from both groups of experts, the DRD draughts letters informing applicants about the assessment results, which are signed by the Director of the Drug Administration of Vietnam (DAV) (or a Deputy Director on his behalf). Companies must send supplementary dossiers (if necessary) to the DRD's office after receiving the DRD's letters. The supplementary dossiers would then be reevaluated by DRD's experts. The narcotics would be named in the proposed drug list for awarding registration numbers at the MOH's senior board meeting if the drug registration dossiers fulfill all legal requirements. Unsuccessful supplement dossiers, as well as medications that are not suitable for visa numbers, will be notified in writing by the DRD (Buckley and Riviere, 2012).

The quality of evaluation of drug registration dossiers

There are five groups of specialists working on the evaluation: (1) legal matters, (2) quality standards, (3) manufacturing process, (4) pharmacology, and (5) clinical groups. Members of these groups must be the persons who are highly qualified, full of with substantial experience in his/her fields and usually works in research institutes, institutes of quality control, universities, national hospitals, etc. They consult with the DAV regarding the quality of the submitted dossiers. After they have commented on the drug registration dossiers, the DRD will collect, process, and conclude to present the final results and report to the MOH senior board (World Health Organization, 2017).

Timelines

The MOH will issue drug registry numbers within six months after obtaining full and correct dossiers. The MOH must respond in writing to any refusal to grant registration numbers, specifically specifying the reasons for the refusal (World Health Organization, 2017).

Validity of registration

The maximum validity of a registration number is five years from the date of signing decision on issuing registration number. In special cases, the MoH shall consider and issue specific stipulations. Within six months prior to and six months after the expiry date of the registration number for circulation, the relevant applicant may submit dossier for registration renewal. Exceeding the above duration, the applicant must resubmit dossier as for the first-time drug registration (Davies et al., 2017).

7.6 Philippine

The Philippines FDA, under the Department of Health, is the primary government agency overseeing pharmaceutical/drug registration and regulations. All imported pharmaceuticals must be registered with the Philippines FDA prior to market entry.

Foreign drug companies account for a substantial percentage of the Filipino pharmaceutical market. Furthermore, with the implementation of universal healthcare, sales growth opportunities for foreign drug companies should increase considerably.

TABLE 7.4 Registration requirements of Vietnam.

Section		Contents
Part I		**Administrative Data and Product Information**
Section A		**Product Particular**
	A1	Name of product
	A2	Name and strength of active ingredient(s)
	A3	Dosage form
	A4	Product description
	A5.1	Pharmacodynamics/Pharmacokinetics
	A5.2	Pharmacokinetics
	A6	Indication
	A7	Recommended dose
	A8	Mode of administration
	A9	Contraindication
	A10	Warning and precautions
	A11	Interaction with other medicaments
	A12	Pregnancy and lactation
	A13	Side effects
	A14	Symptoms and treatment of overdose
	A15	Storage condition
	A16	Shelf life
	A17	Therapeutical code (if any)
		mode of action
Section B		**Product Formula**
	B1.1	Batch manufacturing formula
		Batch quantity of active substance(s)
		Batch quantity of excipient
	B1.2	Attachment of batch manufacturing formula documentation
Section C		**Particular of Packing**
	C1	Pack Size (Weight, Volume, Quantity)
	C2	Immediate container type
		Container type description
	C3	Barcode/Serial No.*
	C4	Recommended distributor's Price*
	C5	Recommended retail Price*
Section D		**Mock-up, Outer Carton and Package Insert**
	D1	Label (mock-up) for immediate container
	D2	Label (mock-up) for outer carton? Y/N
	D3	Proposed package insert

(Continued)

TABLE 7.4 (Continued)

Section	Contents			
Section E		**Supplementary Documentation**		
	E1.1	Product owner (manufacturer/applicant/other)		
	E1.2	Letter of authorization from product owner		
		*E2.1	Letter of appointment of contract manufacturer from product owner	
		*E2.2	Letter of acceptance from contract manufacturer	
	E3	Is the active substance(s) patented in Malaysia? Y/N (if any)		
	E4	Certificate of pharmaceutical product (CPP)		
	E4.1	Certificate of pharmaceutical product (CPP) issuing body (country)		
	E4.2	Is this product licensed to be placed on the market for use in the exporting country) Y/N		
	E4.3	Is the product on the market in the exporting country? Y/N		
	E4.4	Date of issue of certificate of pharmaceutical product (CPP)		
	E4.5	Date of expiry of certificate of pharmaceutical product (CPP) (if any)		
	E5	Certificate of free sale (CFS)		
	E5.1	Certificate of free sale (CFS) issuing body (country)		
	E5.2	Date of issue of certificate of free sale (CFS)		
	E5.3	Date of expiry of certificate of free sale (CFS) (if any)		
	E6	Good manufacturing practice (GMP)		
	E6.1	Certificate of good manufacturing practice (GMP) issuing body(country)		
	E6.2	Date of issue of certificate of good manufacturing practice (GMP)		
	E6.3	Date of expiry of certificate of good manufacturing practice (GMP) (if any)		
	E7	Summary of product characteristics (Product data sheet—if any)		
	E8	Patient information leaflet (PIL)		
	E9	Attachment of protocol analysis (finished product)		
	E10	Attachment of analytical validation		
	E11	Attachment of certificate analysis (Finished product—three recent batches)		
	E12	Other supporting document (if any)		
	E13	Manufacturer: Importer (if any)		
	E14	Other manufacturer(s) involve (if any) GMP		
	E15	Store address (if any)		
Part II	**Quality**			
S	**Drug Substance**			
	S1	**General Information**		
		S1.1	Nomenclature	
		S1.2	Structure	
			S1.2.1	Attachment for structure
		S1.3	General properties	

(Continued)

TABLE 7.4 (Continued)

Section	Contents			
	S2	**Manufacturer**		
		S2.1	Manufacturer name	
			S2.1.1	Remarks
		S2.2	Description of manufacturing process and process Controls	
		S2.3	Control of materials	
		S2.4	Control of critical steps and intermediates	
		S2.5	Process validation and/or evaluation	
		S2.6	Manufacturing process development	
	S3	**Characterization**		
		S3.1	Elucidation of structure and characteristics	
		S3.2	Impurities	
	S4	**Control of Drug Substance/Active Ingredient**		
		S4.1	Specifications, manufacturer name and country of origin	
		S4.2	Analytical procedures/Method of analysis	
		S4.3	Validation of analytical procedures (if any)	
		S4.4	Batch analysis (1 batch of COA for active ingredient)	
		S4.5	Justification of specification	
	S5	**Reference Standards or Materials**		
	S6	**Container Closure System**		
	S7	**Stability Data**		
P	**Drug Product**			
	P1	**Description and Composition**		
	P2	**Pharmaceutical Development (if any)**		
		P2.1	Information on development studies	
		P2.2	Components of the drug product	
		P2.3	Finished products	
		P2.4	Manufacturing process development	
		P2.5	Container closure system (type and description)	
		P2.6	Microbiological attributes	
		P2.7	Compatibility	
	P3	**Manufacturer**		
		P3.1	Batch manufacturing formula (from product registration form)	
		P3.2	Manufacturing process and process control	
			P3.2.1	Manufacturing Process flowchart (if any)
		P3.3	Control of critical steps and intermediates (in-process control)	
		P3.4	Process validation and/or evaluation	
	P4	**Control of Excipients**		
		P4.1	Specifications, manufacturer name, and country of origin	
		P4.2	Analytical procedures	

(Continued)

TABLE 7.4 (Continued)

Section	Contents		
		P4.3	Validation of analytical procedures
		P4.4	Justification of specifications
		P4.5	Excipient of human or animal origin—confirmation
		P4.6	Novel excipients
	P5	**Control of Finish Products**	
		P5.1	Specification and reference
		P5.2	Analytical procedures
		P5.3	Validation of analytical procedures
		P5.4	Batch analysis
		P5.5	Characterization of impurities
		P5.6	Justification of specification(s)
	P6	**Reference Standards or Materials**	
	P7	**Container Closure System**	
	P8	**Stability Data (Two batches)**	
	P9	**Product Interchangeability/Equivalence Evidence (if any)**	
Part III	**Nonclinical Document**		
Section A		**Table of Contents**	
Section B		**Nonclinical Overview**	
Section C		**Nonclinical Written and Tabulated Summaries**	
	1	Table of Contents	
	2	Pharmacology	
	3	Pharmacokinetics	
	4	Toxicology	
Section D		**Nonclinical Study Report**	
	1	Table of Contents	
	2	Pharmacology	
	3	Pharmacokinetics	
	4	Toxicology	
Part IV	**Clinical Document**		
Section A		**Table of Content**	
Section B		**Clinical Overview**	
Section C		**Clinical Summary**	
	1	Summary of Biopharmaceutics and Associated Analytical Methods	
	2	Summary of Clinical Pharmacology Studies	
	3	Summary of Clinical Efficacy	
	4	Summary of Clinical Safety	
	5	Synopses of Individual Studies	
Section D		**Tabular Listing of All Clinical Studies**	
Section E		**Clinical Study Reports**	
Section F		**List of Key Literature References**	

New Drug Registration in Vietnam as per Drug Administration (DA)

FIGURE 7.5 New drug registration as per the drug administration of Vietnam.

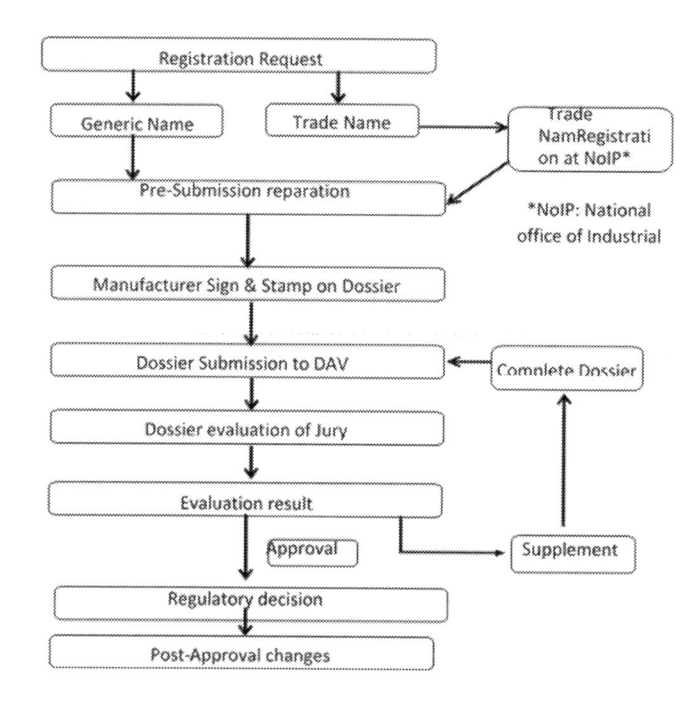

Legal framework and regulations

Republic Act (RA) 3720 of the Republic of the Philippines was amended with the passage of a new law, RA 9711—*The Food and Drug Administration (FDA) Act of 2009*. The FDA Act of 2009 created the FDA in the Department of Health (DOH) to be headed by a Director General with the rank of Undersecretary of Health.

Regulatory system

The law created four centers:

1. Center for Drug Regulation and Research (to include veterinary medicine, vaccines and biologicals);
2. Center for Food Regulation and Research;
3. Center for Cosmetics Regulation and Research (to include household hazardous/urban substances);
4. Center for Device Regulation, Radiation Health, and Research.

Format followed: country-specific

The organizational structure of FDA is as follows as per Philippine FDA 2009 and Bureau of Food and Drugs (BFAD) (Fig. 7.6).

Drug registration applications as per Philippine FDA 2009 and BFAD:

1. Initial Registration
   a. Established Drug
   b. Newly Introduced Drug
   c. Products with New Indication(S) or New Route of Administration
   d. Products with Additional Dosage or Dosage Strength
   e. Products with New Dosage Form
   f. Products with Change in
      i. Application for Initial Registration
      ii. Notification of the change in formulation including a justification for such change
      iii. Bioavailability of Bioequivalence data, as needed.

Organisational Structure of Philippine
Food & Drug Administration (FDA)

FIGURE 7.6 The organizational structure of the Food and Drug Administration, Philippine.

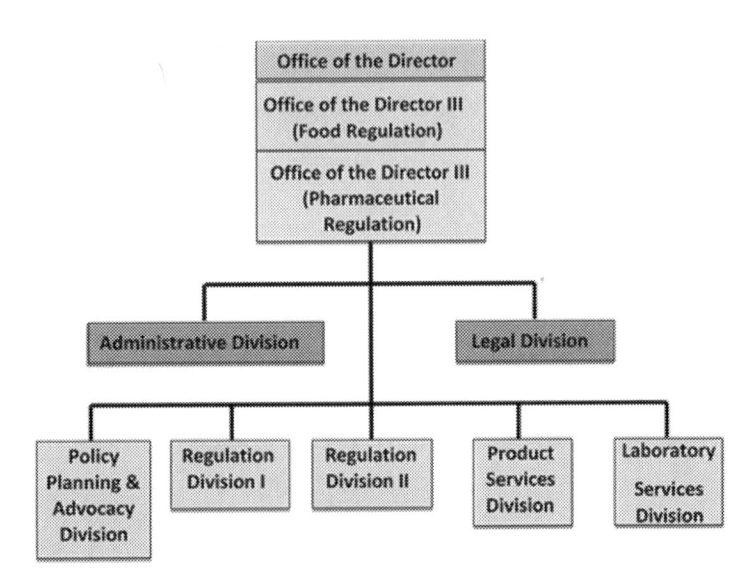

g. Products for Monitored Release Prior to Approval for General Use
h. Phase IV Clinical Trial for Products Under the Following Categories:
    i. Newly Introduced Drug
    ii. Established Drug either with new indication or new route of Administration
    iii. New Indication or New Route of Administration
    iv. Additional Dosage or Dosage Strength
2. Renewal Registration
3. Fixed-Dose Combination Drug Products
4. Products with Change of Manufacturer
5. Products with Improvement of Immediate Container or Packaging
6. Registration of Branded Version of Registered Unbranded Generic Drug Product and Generic Version of Registered Branded Drug Product

Registration requirements as per Philippine FDA 2009 and BFAD (Table 7.5)
Evaluation process (Table 7.6):[49]
The process of evaluation is as follows as per Philippine FDA 2009 and BFAD (Fig. 7.7).
Timelines
The drug registration process takes almost one year after the date of submission of the dossier.
Validity of registration
All the products which fall under the definition of drugs are required to be registered following the procedure.

If all the criteria and requirements for registration have been met all applications undergoing final evaluation are issued an approval of registration whose validity period is as follows:

1. Initial registration of drugs for general use shall be issued for either two-year or five-year validity based on the application of the company.
2. Drugs which fall under the new drug monitored release category shall be given three years registration validity.
3. Renewal registrations are valid for five years.

If any of the requirements are not met, a letter shall be sent to the company denying the application. An application for reconsideration shall no longer be allowed but the applicant may submit an application for initial registration for the same product correcting all deficiencies.

TABLE 7.5 Registration requirements of Philippines.

S. no.	Requirement	Initial	Renewal
1	Letter of application		
2	Form no. 8	Y	Y
3	Copy of valid certificate of brand name clearance.		
4	Copy of valid agreement between manufacturer and trader/distributor/importer/exporter	Y	
5	Unit dose and batch formulation	Y	Y
6	Technical specifications of all raw materials	Y	
7	Certificate of analysis of active raw material(s)	Y	
8	Certificate of analysis of finished product.	Y	Y
9	Technical specifications of finished product	Y	Y
10	Full description of the methods used, the facilities and controls in the manufacture, processing and packaging of the product	Y	
11	Details of the assay and other test procedures for product including data analysis	Y	Y
12	Detailed report of stability studies to justify claimed shelf life 1. accelerated—first batch at three elevated temp or 2. long term—three batches ($30°C/70\%RH$)	Y	
13	Sufficient samples in market or commercial presentation for laboratory analysis (as per M.C.20s. 1994) and representative sample for PSD	Y	Y
14	Unattached generic labeling materials; label, box, insert, blister/strip foil and specification	Y	Y
15	Bioavailability/bioequivalence studies (where applicable)	Y	Y
16	Comparative dissolution profile for drugs listed in list B prime	Y	Y

17	For imported drug product:
	1. Original certificate of pharmaceutical product (issued at least one year from date of filing)
	2. For countries not issuing COPP:
	   a. Certificate of free sale from country of origin
	   b. Government certificate attesting to the status of the manufacturer (Authenticated by territorial Philippine consulate)
		Y	

18	For drug product in plastic container 1. Studies done on the plastic to substantiate claim that product is safe to use 2. General information 3. Test procedures and limits 4. Empty plastic containers and closures	Y	
19	For new drug application (if applicable):		
	1. Copy of approved preclinical, clinical, and protocol for monitored release	Y	
	2. Copy of approved rationale of fixed-dose combination product (if applicable)	Y	
	3. Certificate of approval of PMS (if applicable)		Y
20	Copy of latest certificate of product registration		Y
21	Evidence of registration fee/payment (charge slip)	Y	Y

7.7 Myanmar

Myanmar is a growing country and is continuously supported by the government reforms. In the coming years, its manufacturing and construction sectors would drive the economy. Its healthcare infrastructure is gradually growing.

TABLE 7.6 Evaluation process.

Mondays	Processed food
Tuesdays and Wednesdays	Drugs, Medical Devices, Diagnostic Reagents, Drug Testing Kits, Biologicals and Vaccines, Herbal and Traditionally Used Medicines
Thursdays	Cosmetics, Household Hazardous Substances

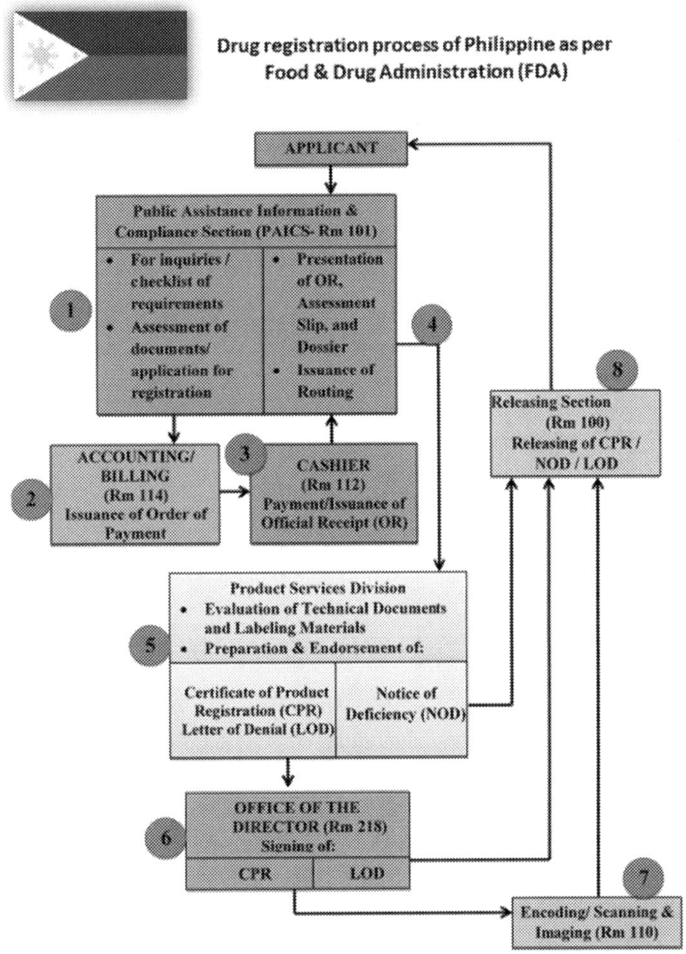

FIGURE 7.7   Drug registration process in Philippines.

Drug registration process of Philippine as per Food & Drug Administration (FDA)

Legal framework and regulations:[53]

The FDA established in 1995 and takes care of the safety and quality of food, drugs, medical devices, cosmetics, and household materials. As food and drug safety is concerned with a number of sectors in recognition of the need for integration, *Myanmar Food and Drug Board and Authority (MFDBA)* was formed in the year 2000. The Minister for Health leads the Board and members are senior officials from other related ministries. Various levels of central, district, and township Food and Drug Supervisory Committee (FDSC), Food Advisory Committee (FAC), and Drug Advisory Committee (DAC) have been formed by MFDBA in 2002.

To enable the public to have quality and safe food, efficacious drugs, medical devices, cosmetics, household materials, FDA is implementing the tasks complying with guidance from the National Health Committee, MoH and Myanmar Food and Drug Board of Authority according to National Drug Law 1992 and its provisions, National Food Law 1997 and Public Health Law 1972.

Regulatory system:[54]

- Myanmar Food and Drug Board of Authority (MFDBA) is the highest authority for the control of food and drug affairs and is chaired by the Minister for Health.
- MFDBA members come from various related departments and agencies.

For example General Administrative Dept., Myanmar Police Force, Custom, Trade, Development Affairs Dept., etc. The organization structure of MoH is shown as follows as per the MoH, Department of Health, FDA, Nay Pyi Taw.

Drug registration applications

1. Initial Application: An application for registration of drug must be submitted to the Department of Health, FDA in the original prescribed form (Form 1 Registration). Form (1) is available at one-hundred kyats each at office of the FDA.
2. Updating Changes to Registered Drugs: Updating changes to registered drugs shall be made only with the approval of FDA.
3. Renewal of Registration: Application for renewal of registration shall be submitted 90 days before the validity of the registration terminates. Failure to adhere to the 90 days requirement may result in disruption of continued validity of registration (as per MoH, Department of Health, FDA, Nay Pyi Taw).

Registration requirements

1. Administrative Documents
   a. Covering Letter
   b. Letter of Authorization (LOA)
   c. Company Profile
   d. Certificate of Pharmaceutical Product (COPP)
   e. WHO GMP Certificate
   f. Mfg. License
   g. Proforma Statement
   h. Summary Drug Information Sheet
2. Pharmaceutical Documents
   a. Name of Drug and Product Composition
   b. Pharmacopeial Reference, Qualitative and Quantitative formula

Evaluation process:

1. To apply name registration for assessment fees (It will take 10 days or 14 days).
2. After getting assessment fees documents from FDA, applicant has to remit assessment fees on Monday and Wednesday only at FDA:
   a. Monday (variation fees, assessment fees, and registration fees), and
   b. Wednesday (assessment fees and registration fees).
3. After remitting the assessment fees, applicant has to apply FDA permit (It will take 10 days).
4. After getting FDA permit, applicant has to apply FOC trade permit at Airport Trade Office. (It will take two to three days only):
   a. Need to apply trade permit if the weight of samples is too much or if the quantity of the products is too much for samples dispatching.
5. After getting FDA permit and trade permit, applicant has to inform to dispatch the samples and to submit at FDA.
6. After submitting the samples, applicant has to submit the dossiers:
   a. For dossier submission,
   b. Need to take number up to 9:30 a.m. on Tuesday for renewal and on Thursday for new product,
   c. Firstly FDA accepts the dossiers without checking details and unlimited dossier quality,
   d. Up to 3 p.m. only (renewal on Tuesday/new on Thursday),
   e. Then, after two weeks, FDA issues the preview for the complete dossier, and returns back the incomplete dossier To Whom It May Concern. Time is from 3 p.m. to 4:30 p.m.
7. Next, two weeks, laboratory test fees can be paid.
8. After laboratory test fee is paid, our product is under registration process and have to follow up and have to wait for approval.

9. After getting approval, applicant has to pay registration fees.

10. After two months, we will get DRC:

    a. After getting DRC, applicant has to apply attachment for DIAC (It will take three weeks).

Timelines

- Tentative time taken for receiving the approval (i.e., fresh registration) is 9–12 months.
- Reregistration dossier must be submitted six months before the expiry of the existing registration

Registration validity

Registration of product is valid for five years.

7.8 Sudan

Sudan's currency devaluation has led to the shortage of a number of medicines, with some products also becoming completely unavailable for sale in the country. Sudan's industry needs to import active pharmaceutical ingredients (APIs) which makes market extremely vulnerable to currency fluctuations and external headwinds. Donations are likely to play an important role in the short-to-medium term, as the industry and operational risks continue to undermine any major pharmaceutical company's activity.

Regulatory framework

"The Pharmacy and Poisons Act (2001) and its provisions established the Federal Pharmacy and Poison Board (FPPB)." All the authorities of implementation of pharmacy and poisons at were given to this board.

NMPB—Registration procedure

Procedures

Advice meeting

Prior to filing an application, NMPB will provide an opportunity to applicants to discuss their applications. A written request for such a meeting should be addressed to the director at least one month prior to the proposed date. This request should include a brief summary of the issues that are required to be discussed, so that appropriate staff necessary for the meeting can be made available. The following information is needed from the applicant before the meeting:

- A letter
- A proposed agenda with time
- A summary of issues to be discussed.

The purpose of this meeting is to discuss the data or any special requirements needed to support the application and thus to facilitate the assessment process, in case there are some potential major issues. This may also help the applicant to get feedback regarding any areas of concern from a regulatory standpoint of view. Such meetings are also useful for any priority assessment requested of life—saving drug applications, or other [such as originators (Innovators)] (as per NMPB).

Filing of application information and data

The applications with all the information and data are submitted to the receiving unit. A reference number will be assigned to the application along with the information and data received (Katsandres et al., 2002).

Screening/preevaluation and validation of the information and data

The application package will be forwarded to the screening unit, where the screening will be performed. A checklist for screening/preevaluation and validation will be used to verify that the information/material provided is complete. If any information is missing, the applicant will be notified in writing. The applicant will be given only "ONE" opportunity to complete the file within 20 working days; if the file is found to be still incomplete, the application will be rejected and the manufacturer will be required to file a new application. The performance target of NMPB (for this activity) is 10 days. If no response is received from the applicant within the performance target, the application will be returned to the applicants at their own expenses (Anciaux et al., 2016).

Solicited and unsolicited information and material

For the purpose of this guidance document, the information and material will be classified as solicited or unsolicited.

Solicited information is defined as the information and material requested by NMPB during its assessment process, including screening/preevaluation and validation.

Unsolicited information is defined as information and material which is not requested by the NMP13 during its assessment process. Unsolicited information and material considered as new information is acceptable during the screening/preevaluation and validation, but not acceptable during the assessment. Examples of unsolicited information are new biostudies, new stability data, etc. (Jacob et al., 2017).

Assessing application information

1. **Assessment of information and data**

   The assessment of the quality will be performed by NMPB scientific officers or assessors (Hansen et al., 2017).

2. **Application update**

   If it becomes evident that the application will not be completed within NMPB performance target, due to backlog of any other administrative reason, the applicant will be given an opportunity to update his application. There will be no restriction on the information and data that may be added or removed from the application. New dosage forms, new routes of administration, new strengths, and new indications may not be accepted during this process (Allen and Ansel, 2013).

3. **Application assessment**

If minor issues are identified during the assessment of information and data, these issues will be resolved through the Assessment Inquiries. Although there is no limitation of Assessment Inquires, it is expected that these issues be resolved by 2−3 Assessment Inquiries. Responses to Assessment Inquires are required within 20 days. If there are major issues which require a significant amount data or additional studies, a letter of rejection will be issued. The applicant will be given 15 days to appeal the decision. If a response is not provided within the time period, the application will be considered as withdrawn without prejudice of refiling. It should be noted that in the response to the letter of noncompliance (Table 7.7).

Labeling as per NMPB

The basic labeling, marking, and packaging regulations are provided to give a general idea of the Sudanese requirements.

- Products must be clearly marked, stamped, branded, or labeled to indicate the country of origin.
- Bilingual language (Arabic and English) labeling is advisable, particularly if the product is aimed at the mass market.
- Arabic labels must be placed on packages sold to the public.
- Information on country of origin.
- Use of English is acceptable.
- The label must be placed on the goods themselves or on the outer packaging.
- Medicines should be labeled with a batch number.
- Certain chemicals may require a CA.
- Labeling information required: (1) Placement of identification data; (2) Identification of the manufacturer; (3) Product information; (4) The name of the producer/exporter, ingredients, date of manufacturing, and date of Packing—it is recommended to pack goods securely to protect them against rough handling and pilferage.

7.9 Uganda

Legal framework and regulations

The National Drug Authority (NDA) was created as a regulatory agency in charge of the country's drug regulation. *The National Drug Policy and Authority (NDP/A) Act*, Cap. 206, created it to ensure the continuous availability of necessary, efficacious, and cost-effective drugs to Uganda's entire population as a means of providing adequate healthcare and ensuring proper drug use.

Section 3(1) of the National Drug Policy and Authority Act Cap 206 established NDA as a body corporate with perpetual succession and a common seal, and may sue or be sued in its corporate name.

NDA board

The Act refers to the Board of NDA as the Authority. It is composed of the Chairperson and 19 members from various government organizations, professions, and prominent persons (Carpenter, 2014). The Board conducts its work through the following expert Committees:

- Committee on National Formulary
- Committee on Pharmacovigilance and Clinical Trials

TABLE 7.7 Requirements for registration in Sudan.

Section	Contents			
Module 1	**Regional Administrative Information**			
1.0	Cover letter			
	1.1	Comprehensive Table of Content		
	1.2	Application Form		
	1.3	Product Information		
		1.3.1	Summary of Product Characteristics (SPC)	
			1.3.1.1	Name of the medicinal product
			1.3.1.2	Qualitative and quantitative composition
			1.3.1.3	Pharmaceutical form
			1.3.1.4	Clinical particulars
			1.3.1.5	Pharmacological properties
			1.3.1.6	Pharmaceutical properties
		1.3.2	Patient information leaflet (PIL)	
			1.3.2.1	Arabic leaflet
			1.3.2.2	Arabic Or English leaflet
				1.3.2.2.1 What *Ampicillin Sodium for Injection BP 500 mg* is and what it is used for
				1.3.2.2.2 Before you <take> <use> *Ampicillin Sodium for Injection BP 500 mg*
				1.3.2.2.3 How to <take> <use> *Ampicillin Sodium for Injection BP 500 mg*
				1.3.2.2.4 Possible side effects
				1.3.2.2.5 How to store *Ampicillin Sodium for Injection BP 500 mg*
				1.3.2.2.6 Further information
		1.3.3	Labeling	
			1.3.3.1	Particulars appearing on the <outer packaging> <and> <the immediate packaging>
			1.3.3.2	Minimum particulars to appear on blisters or strips
			1.3.3.3	Minimum particulars to appear on small immediate packaging units
		1.3.4	Artwork (Mock-ups) (two copies)	
	1.4	Samples		
	1.5	Information on the experts		
		1.5.1	Quality	
		1.5.2	Nonclinical	
		1.5.3	Clinical	
	1.6	Summary of BE		
	1.7	Environmental Risk Assessment		
		1.7.1	Nongenetically Modified Organism (Non-GMO)	
		1.7.2	GMO	

(Continued)

TABLE 7.7 (Continued)

Section	Contents			
	1.8	Pharmacovigilance		
		1.8.1	Pharmacovigilance system	
		1.8.2	Risk management plan	
	1.9	Certificates		
		1.9.1	CPP (or free sales when applicable)	
		1.9.2	GMP	
		1.9.3	Copy of registration certificate of pharmaceutical company and production line in Sudan	
		1.9.4	Certificate of analysis—Drug Substance (on a headed paper)	
		1.9.5	Certificate of analysis—Finished Product (on a headed paper)	
		1.9.6	Certificate of analysis—Excipients	
		1.9.7	Alcohol-free declaration	
		1.9.8	Pork-free declaration	
		1.9.9	Patent Information	
	1.10	Pricing		
		1.10.1	Price certificate documented by health authorities include	
		1.10.2	Other documents related to pricing list	
	1.11	Response to question		
Module 2	**Common Technical Document Summaries**			
	2.1	Table of Contents of Module 2–5		
	2.2	Introduction		
	2.3	Quality Overall Summary		
		Introduction		
		2.3.S	Drug substance	
			2.3.S.1	General Information
			2.3.S.2	Manufacture
			2.3.S.3	Characterization
			2.3.S.4	Control of Drug Substance
			2.3.S.5	Reference Standards or Materials
			2.3.S.6	Container/Closure System
			2.3.S.7	Stability
		2.3.P	Drug Product	
			2.3.P.1	Description and Composition of the Drug Product
			2.3.P.2	Pharmaceutical Development
			2.3.P.3	Manufacture
			2.3.P.4	Control of Excipients
			2.3.P.5	Control of Drug Product
			2.3.P.6	Reference Standards or Materials
			2.3.P.7	Container/Closure System
			2.3.P.8	Stability

(Continued)

TABLE 7.7 (Continued)

Section	Contents		
	2.3.A	Appendices	
		2.3.A.1	Facilities and Equipment
		2.3.A.2	Adventitious Agents Safety Evaluation
		2.3.A.3	Novel Excipients
	2.3.R	Regional Information	
2.4	Nonclinical Overview		
2.5	Clinical Overview		
	2.5.1	Product Development Rationale	
	2.5.2	Overview of Biopharmaceutics	
	2.5.3	Overview of Clinical Pharmacology	
	2.5.4	Overview of Efficacy	
	2.5.5	Overview of Safety	
	2.5.6	Benefits and Risks Conclusions	
	2.5.7	References	
2.6	Nonclinical Written and Tabulated Summaries		
	2.6.1	Introduction	
	2.6.2	Pharmacology Written Summary	
		2.6.2.1	Brief Summary
		2.6.2.2	Primary Pharmacodynamics
		2.6.2.3	Secondary Pharmacodynamics
		2.6.2.4	Safety Pharmacology
		2.6.2.5	Pharmacodynamic Drug Interactions
		2.6.2.6	Discussion and Conclusions
		2.6.2.7	Tables and Figures
	2.6.3	Pharmacology Tabulated Summary	
	2.6.4	Pharmacokinetics Written Summary	
		2.6.4.1	Brief Summary
		2.6.4.2	Methods of Analysis
		2.6.4.3	Absorption
		2.6.4.4	Distribution
		2.6.4.5	Metabolism (interspecies comparison)
		2.6.4.6	Excretion
		2.6.4.7	Pharmacokinetic Drug Interactions
		2.6.4.8	Other Pharmacokinetic Studies
		2.6.4.9	Discussion and Conclusions
		2.6.4.10	Tables and Figures
	2.6.5	Pharmacokinetics Tabulated Summary	

(Continued)

TABLE 7.7 (Continued)

Section	Contents			
		2.6.6	Toxicology Written Summary	
			2.6.6.1	*Brief Summary*
			2.6.6.2	*Single-Dose Toxicity*
			2.6.6.3	*Repeat-Dose Toxicity*
			2.6.6.4	*Genotoxicity*
			2.6.6.5	*Carcinogenicity*
			2.6.6.6	*Reproductive and Developmental Toxicity*
			2.6.6.7	*Local Tolerance*
			2.6.6.8	*Other Toxicity Studies (if available)*
			2.6.6.9	*Discussion and Conclusions*
			2.6.6.10	*References*
		2.6.7	Toxicology Tabulated Summary	
	2.7	Clinical Summary		
		2.7.1	Summary of Biopharmaceutic and Associated Analytical Methods	
			2.7.1.1	*Background and Overview*
			2.7.1.2	*Summary of Results of Individual Studies*
			2.7.1.3	*Comparison and Analyses of Results Across Studies*
			2.7.1.4	*Appendix*
		2.7.2	Summary of Clinical Pharmacology Studies	
			2.7.2.1	*Background and Overview*
			2.7.2.2	*Summary of Results of Individual Studies*

Section	Contents				Page numbers
Module 2	**Common Technical Document Summaries**				
			2.7.2.3	*Comparison and Analyses of Results Across Studies*	
			2.7.2.4	*Special Studies*	
			2.7.2.5	*Appendix*	
		2.7.3	Summary of Clinical Efficacy		
			2.7.3.1	*Background and Overview of Clinical Efficacy*	
			2.7.3.2	*Summary of Results of Individual Studies*	
			2.7.3.3	*Comparison and Analyses of Results Across Studies*	
				2.7.3.3.1	*Study Populations*
				2.7.3.3.2	*Comparison of Efficacy Results Across All Studies*
				2.7.3.3.3	*Comparison of Results in Subpopulations*
			2.7.3.4	*Analysis of Clinical Information Relevant to Dosing Recommendations*	
			2.7.3.5	*Persistence of Efficacy and/or Tolerance Effects*	
			2.7.3.6	*Appendix*	

(Continued)

TABLE 7.7 (Continued)

Section	Contents				Page numbers
		2.7.4	Summary of Clinical Safety		
			2.7.4.1	Exposure to the Drug	
				2.7.4.1.1	Overall Safety Evaluation Plan and Narratives of Safety Studies
				2.7.4.1.2	Overall Extent of Exposure
				2.7.4.1.3	Demographic and Other Characteristics of Study Population
			2.7.4.2	Adverse Events	
				2.7.4.2.1	Analysis of Adverse Events by Organ System or Syndrome
				2.7.4.2.2	Narratives
			2.7.4.3	Clinical Laboratory Evaluations	
			2.7.4.4	Vital Signs, Physical Findings, Observations Related to Safety	
			2.7.4.5	Safety in Special Groups and Situations	
				2.7.4.5.1	Intrinsic Factors
				2.7.4.5.2	Extrinsic Factors
				2.7.4.5.3	Drug Interactions
				2.7.4.5.4	Use in Pregnancy and Lactation
			2.7.4.6	2.7.4.5.5	Overdose
				2.7.4.5.6	Drug Abuse
				2.7.4.5.7	Withdrawal and Rebound
				2.7.4.5.8	Effects on Ability to Drive or Operate Machinery or Impairment of
				Postmarketing Data	
			2.7.4.7	Appendix	
		2.7.5	References		
		2.7.6	Synopses of Individual Studies		
Module 3	Quality				
	3.1	Table of Contents of Module 3			
	3.2	Body of data			
		3.2.S	Drug Substance		
			3.2.S.1	General Information	
				3.2.S.1.1	Nomenclature
				3.2.S.1.2	Structure
				3.2.S.1.3	General Properties
			3.2.S.2	Manufacture	
				3.2.S.2.1	Manufacturer(s)
				3.2.S.2.2	Description of Manufacturing Process and Process Controls

(Continued)

TABLE 7.7 (Continued)

Section	Contents				Page numbers
			3.2.S.2.3	Control of Materials	
			3.2.S.2.4	Control of Critical Steps and Intermediates	
			3.2.S.2.5	Process Validation and/or Evaluation	
			3.2.S.2.6	Manufacturing Process Development	
		3.2.S.3	Characterization		
			3.2.S.3.1	Elucidation of Structure and Other Characteristics	
			3.2.S.3.2	Impurities	
		3.2.S.4	Control of the Drug Substance		
			3.2.S.4.1	Specifications	
			3.2.S.4.2	Analytical Procedures (Include but not limited to)	
			3.2.S.4.3	Validation of Analytical Procedures	
			3.2.S.4.4	Batch Analyses	
			3.2.S.4.5	Justification of Specification	
		3.2.S.5	Reference Standards or Materials		
		3.2.S.6	Container/Closure Systems		
		3.2.S.7	Stability		
			3.2.S.7.1	Stability Summary and Conclusions	
			3.2.S.7.2	Postapproval Stability Protocol and Commitment	
			3.2.S.7.3	Stability Data	
	3.2.P	Drug Product			
		3.2.P.1	Description and Composition of the Drug Product		
		3.2.P.2	Pharmaceutical Development		
			3.2.P.2.1	Components of the Drug Product	
				3.2.P.2.1.1	Drug substance
				3.2.P.2.1.2	Excipients
			3.2.P.2.2	Drug Product	
				3.2.P.2.2.1	Formulation Development
				3.2.P.2.2.2	Overages
				3.2.P.2.2.3	Physiochemical and Biological Properties
			3.2.P.2.3	Manufacturing Process Development	
			3.2.P.2.4	Container Closure System	
			3.2.P.2.5	Microbiological Attributes	
			3.2.P.2.6	Compatibility	

(Continued)

TABLE 7.7 (Continued)

Section	Contents			Page numbers
		3.2.P.3	Manufacture	
			3.2.P.3.1 Manufacturer(s)	
			3.2.P.3.2 Batch Formula	
			3.2.P.3.3 Description of Manufacturing Process and Process Controls	
			3.2.P.3.4 Controls of Critical Steps and Intermediates	
			3.2.P.3.5 Process Validation and/or Evaluation	
		3.2.P.4	Control of Excipients	
			3.2.P.4.1 Specifications	
			3.2.P.4.2 Analytical Procedures	
			3.2.P.4.3 Validation of Analytical Procedures	
			3.2.P.4.4 Justification of Specifications	
			3.2.P.4.5 Excipients of Human or Animal Origin	
			3.2.P.4.6 Novel Excipients	
		3.2.P.5	Control of Drug Product	
			3.2.P.5.1 Specifications	
			3.2.P.5.2 Analytical Procedures	
			3.2.P.5.3 Validation of Analytical Procedures	
			3.2.P.5.4 Batch Analyses	
			3.2.P.5.5 Characterization of Impurities	
			3.2.P.5.6 Justification of Specifications	
		3.2.P.6	Reference Standards or Materials	
		3.2.P.7	Container/Closure System	
		3.2.P.8	Stability	
			3.2.P.8.1 Stability Summary and Conclusions	
			3.2.P.8.2 Postapproval Stability Protocol and Stability Commitments	
			3.2.P.8.3 Stability Data	
		3.2.A	Appendices	
			3.2.4.A.1 Facilities and Equipment	
			3.2.4.A.2 Adventitious Agents Safety Evaluation	
			3.2.4.A.3 Excipients	
		3.2.R	Regional Information	
			3.2.R.1 Alcohol Content Declaration	
			3.2.R.2 Porcine Pork—content/origin	
			3.2.R.3 The diluents and coloring agents in the product formula	
	3.3	Literature References		

(Continued)

TABLE 7.7 (Continued)

Section	Contents			Page numbers
Module 4	**Nonclinical Study Reports**			
	4.1	Table of Contents of Module 4		
	4.2	Study Reports		
		4.2.1	Pharmacology	
			4.2.1.1 *Primary Pharmacodynamics*	
			4.2.1.2 *Secondary Pharmacodynamics*	
			4.2.1.3 *Safety Pharmacology*	
			4.2.1.4 *Pharmacodynamic Drug Interactions*	
		4.2.2	Pharmacokinetics	
			4.2.2.1 *Analytical Methods and Validation Reports*	
			4.2.2.2 *Absorption*	
			4.2.2.3 *Distribution*	
			4.2.2.4 *Metabolism*	
			4.2.2.5 *Excretion*	
			4.2.2.6 *Pharmacokinetic Drug Interactions*	
			4.2.2.7 *Other Pharmacokinetic Studies*	
		4.2.3	Toxicology	
			4.2.3.1 *Single-dose Toxicity*	
			4.2.3.2 *Repeat-dose Toxicity*	
			4.2.3.3 *Genotoxicity*	
				4.2.3.3.1 *In vitro Studies*
				4.2.3.3.2 *In vivo Studies*
			4.2.3.4 *Carcinogenicity*	
				4.2.3.4.1 *Long-term Studies*
				4.2.3.4.2 *Short- or medium-term Studies*
				4.2.3.4.3 *Other studies*
			4.2.3.5 *Reproductive and Development Toxicity*	
				4.2.3.5.1 *Fertility and Embryonic Development*
				4.2.3.5.2 *Embryo-Fetal Development*
				4.2.3.5.3 *Pre- and Postnatal Development and Maternal Function*
				4.2.3.5.4 *Offspring, Juvenile, Second and Third-Generation Studies*
			4.2.3.6 Local Tolerance	
			4.2.3.7 Other Toxicity Studies	
				4.2.3.7.1 *Antigenicity*
				4.2.3.7.2 *Immunogenicity*
				4.2.3.7.3 *Mechanistic Studies (not included elsewhere)*

(Continued)

TABLE 7.7 (Continued)

Section	Contents				Page numbers
			4.2.3.7.4	*Dependence*	
			4.2.3.7.5	*Metabolites*	
			4.2.3.7.6	*Impurities*	
			4.2.3.7.7	*Other*	
	4.3	Literature References			
Module 5	**Clinical Study Reports**				
	5.1	Table of Contents of Module 5			
	5.2	Tabular Listing of All Clinical Studies			
	5.3	Clinical Study Reports			
		5.3.1	Reports of Biopharmaceutic Studies		
			5.3.1.1	*Bioavailability (BA) Study Reports*	
			5.3.1.2	*Comparative BA and BE Study Reports*	
			5.3.1.3	*In vitro In vivo Correlation (IVIIVC) Study Reports*	
			5.3.1.4	*Reports of Bioanalytical and Analytical Methods for Human Studies*	
		5.3.2	Reports of Studies Pertinent to Pharmacokinetics using Human Biomaterials		
			5.3.2.1	*Plasma Protein Binding Study Reports*	
			5.3.2.2	*Reports of Hepatic Metabolism and Drug Interactions studies*	
			5.3.2.3	*Reports of Studies Using other Human Biomaterials*	
		5.3.3	Reports of Human Pharmacokinetic Studies		
			5.3.3.1	*Healthy Subject PK and Tolerability*	
			5.3.3.2	*Patient PK and Initial Tolerability*	
			5.3.3.3	*Intrinsic Factor PK Study Reports*	
			5.3.3.4	*Extrinsic Factor PK Study Reports*	
			5.3.3.5	*Population PK Study Reports*	
		5.3.4	Reports of Human Pharmacodynamic (PD) Studies		
			5.3.4.1	*Healthy Subject PD and PK/PD Study Reports*	
			5.3.4.2	*Patient PD and PK1PD Study Reports*	
		5.3.5	Reports of Efficacy and Safety Studies		
			5.3.5.1	*Study reports of Controlled Clinical Studies pertinent to the claimed Indication*	
			5.3.5.2	*Study reports of Uncontrolled Clinical Studies*	
			5.3.5.3	*Reports of Analyses of Data from More than One Study*	
			5.3.5.4	*Other Study Reports*	
		5.3.6	Reports of Postmarketing Experience		
		5.3.7	Case Report Forms and Individual Patient Listings		
	5.4	Literature References			

FIGURE 7.8 Organization structure as per NDA.

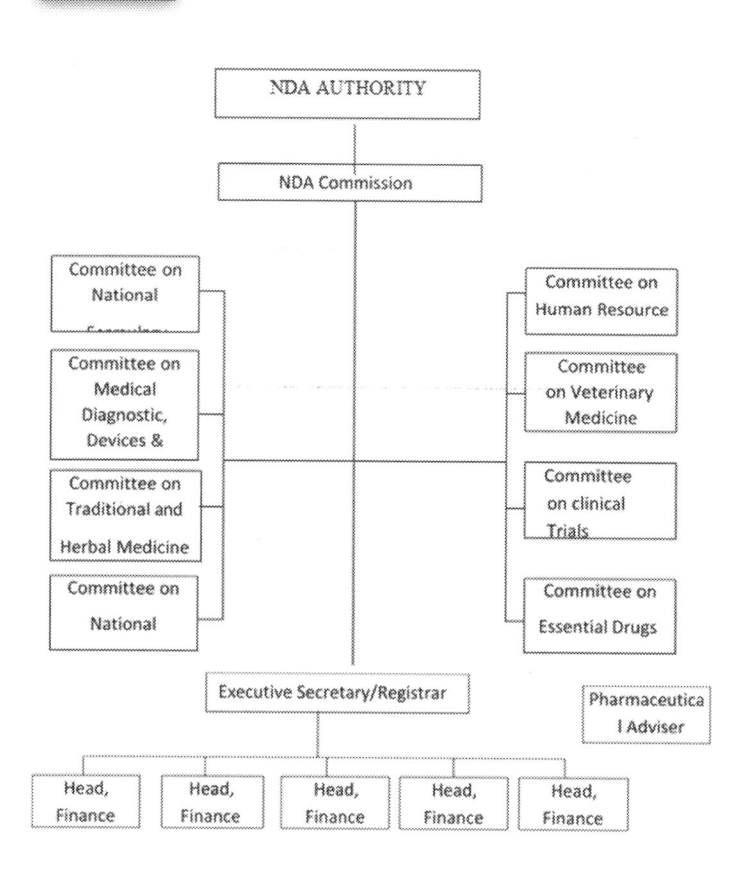

Organisation structure of Uganda as per National Drug Policy & Authority (NDA)

- Committee on Medical Devices and Equipment
- Committee on Veterinary Medicines
- Committee on Traditional and Herbal Medicines
- Audit Committee
- Human Resource Committee
- Legal Committee

NDA secretariat

The Secretariat is headed by the Executive Secretary/Registrar. It is responsible for the day-to-day activities of the Authority. The secretariat is responsible for the implementation of the objectives of the National Drug Policy and Authority Act. It implements the mandate of the Authority through the functions of Drug Assessment and Registration, Inspectorate Services, Drug Quality Control, and Drug Information/Pharmacovigilance (as per NDA).

NDA organization structure as per NDA (Fig. 7.8)

7.10 Zimbabwe

Legal framework and regulations

Medicines Control Authority of Zimbabwe (MCAZ) is a statutory body established by an act of Parliament, *The Medicines and Allied Substances Control Act (MASCA)*. MCAZ is a successor of the Drugs Control Council (DCC) and the Zimbabwe Regional Drug Control Laboratory (ZRDCL). DCC was established by an Act of Parliament in 1969: Drugs and Allied Substances Control Act following which ZRDCL became operational in 1989.

The mandate of MCAZ is to protect public health ensuring that medicines and medical devices on the market are safe, effective, and of good quality.

TABLE 7.8 Registration requirements in Zimbabwe.

Section	Contents			Page numbers
Module 1	Administrative Information			
	1.1	Comprehensive Table of Contents for all Modules		
	1.2	Cover Letter		
	1.3	Comprehensive Table of Contents		
	1.4	Quality Information Summary (QIS)		
	1.5	Product Information		
		1.5.1	*Prescribing information (Summary of Products Characteristics)*	
		1.5.2	*Container labeling*	
		1.5.3	*Patient information leaflet (PIL)*	
		1.5.4	*Mock-ups and specimens*	
	1.6	Information About the Experts		
	1.7	APIMFs and Certificates of Suitability to the Monographs of the European Pharmacopeia		
	1.8	Good Manufacturing Practice (GMP)		
	1.9	Regulatory Status within EAC and in Countries with SRAs		
		1.9.1	*List of countries in EAC and countries with SRAs in which a similar application has been submitted*	
		1.9.2	*Evaluation reports from EAC-NMRA*	
		1.9.3	*Evaluation reports from SRAs*	
		1.9.4	*Manufacturing and Marketing Authorization*	
	1.10	Pediatric Development Program		
	1.11	Product Samples		
Module 2	Common Technical Document Summaries			
	2.1	Table of Contents of Module 2−5		
	2.2	Introduction		
	2.3	Quality Overall Summary—product dossiers (QOS-PD)		
		2.3.S	Overview of Active Pharmaceutical Ingredient (API)	
			2.3.S.1	*General Information*
			2.3.S.2	*Manufacture*
			2.3.S.3	*Characterization*
			2.3.S.4	*Control of Drug Substance*
			2.3.S.5	*Reference Standards or Materials*
			2.3.S.6	*Container/Closure System*
			2.3.S.7	*Stability*
		2.3.P	Overview of Finished Pharmaceutical Product (FPP) *(name, dosage form)*	
			2.3.P.1	*Description and Composition of the Drug Product*
			2.3.P.2	*Pharmaceutical Development*
			2.3.P.3	*Manufacture*

(Continued)

TABLE 7.8 (Continued)

Section	Contents				Page numbers
		2.3.P.4	*Control of Excipients*		
		2.3.P.5	*Control of Drug Product*		
		2.3.P.6	*Reference Standards or Materials*		
		2.3.P.7	*Container/Closure System*		
		2.3.P.8	*Stability*		
2.4	Nonclinical Overview				
2.5	Clinical Overview				
		2.5.1	*Product Development Rationale*		
		2.5.2	*Overview of Biopharmaceutics*		
		2.5.3	*Overview of Clinical Pharmacology*		
		2.5.4	*Overview of Efficacy*		
		2.5.5	*Overview of Safety*		
2.6	Nonclinical Written and Tabulated Summaries				
		2.6.1	*Nonclinical Written summaries*		
		2.6.2	*Introduction*		
		2.6.3	*Pharmacology Written Summary*		
		2.6.4	*Pharmacology Tabulated Summary*		
		2.6.5	*Pharmacokinetics Written Summary*		
		2.6.6	*Pharmacokinetics Tabulated Summary*		
		2.6.7	*Toxicology Written Summary*		
		2.6.8	*Toxicology Tabulated Summary*		
2.7	Clinical Summary				
		2.7.1	*Summary of Biopharmaceutics Studies and Associated Analytical Method*		
Module 3	**Quality**				
3.1	**Table of Contents of Module 3**				
3.2	**Body of Data**				
		3.2.S	**Drug Substance**		
			3.2.S.1	**General Information**	
				3.2.S.1.1	*Nomenclature*
				3.2.S.1.2	*Structure*
				3.2.S.1.3	*General Properties*
			3.2.S.2	**Manufacture**	
				3.2.S.2.1	*Manufacturer(s)*
				3.2.S.2.2	*Description of Manufacturing Process and Process Controls*
				3.2.S.2.3	*Control of Materials*
				3.2.S.2.4	*Control of Critical Steps and Intermediates*
				3.2.S.2.5	*Process Validation and/or Evaluation*

(Continued)

TABLE 7.8 (Continued)

Section	Contents				Page numbers
			3.2.S.3	**Characterization**	
				3.2.S.3.1	*Elucidation of Structure and Other Characteristics*	
				3.2.S.3.2	*Impurities*	
			3.2.S.4	**Control of the Drug Substance**	
				3.2.S.4.1	*Specifications*	
				3.2.S.4.2	*Analytical Procedures (Include but not limited to)*	
				3.2.S.4.3	*Validation of Analytical Procedures*	
				3.2.S.4.4	*Batch Analyses*	
				3.2.S.4.5	*Justification of Specification*	
			3.2.S.5	**Reference Standards or Materials**	
			3.2.S.6	**Container/Closure Systems**	
			3.2.S.7	**Stability**	
				3.2.S.7.1	*Stability Summary and Conclusions*	
				3.2.S.7.2	*Postapproval Stability Protocol and Commitment*	
				3.2.S.7.3	*Stability Data*	
		3.2.P	**Drug Product**		
			3.2.P.1	**Description and Composition of the FPP**	
			3.2.P.2	**Pharmaceutical Development**	
				3.2.P.2.1	*Components of the FPP*	
				3.2.P.2.2	*Finished pharmaceutical product*	
				3.2.P.2.3	*Manufacturing process development*	
				3.2.P.2.4	*Container closure system*	
				3.2.P.2.5	*Microbiological attributes*	
				3.2.P.2.6	*Compatibility*	
			3.2.P.3	**Manufacture**	
				3.2.P.3.1	*Manufacturer(s)*	
				3.2.P.3.2	*Batch Formula*	
				3.2.P.3.3	*Description of Manufacturing Process and Process Controls*	
				3.2.P.3.4	*Control of Critical Steps and Intermediates*	
				3.2.P.3.5	*Process Validation and/or Evaluation*	
			3.2.P.4	**Control of Excipients**	
				3.2.P.4.1	*Specifications*	
				3.2.P.4.2	*Analytical Procedures*	
				3.2.P.4.3	*Validation of Analytical Procedures*	
				3.2.P.4.4	*Justification of the Specifications*	

(Continued)

TABLE 7.8 (Continued)

Section	Contents				Page numbers
			3.2.P.4.5	Excipients of human or animal origin	
			3.2.P.4.6	Novel excipients	
		3.2.P.5	**Control of the Finished Pharmaceutical Product**		
			3.2.P.5.1	Specifications	
			3.2.P.5.2	Analytical Procedures (Include but not limited to)	
			3.2.P.5.3	Validation of Analytical Procedures	
			3.2.P.5.4	Batch Analyses	
			3.2.P.5.5	Characterization of the Impurities	
			3.2.P.5.6	Justification of Specification	
		3.2.P.6	**Reference Standards or Materials**		
		3.2.P.7	**Container/Closure Systems**		
		3.2.P.8	**Stability**		
			3.2.P.8.1	Stability Summary and Conclusions	
			3.2.P.8.2	Postapproval Stability Protocol and Commitment	
			3.2.P.8.3	Stability Data	
		3.2.R	**Regional Information**		
			3.2.R.1	**Production Documents**	
				3.2.R.1.1 Executed Production Documents	
				3.2.R.1.2 Master Production Documents	
			3.2.R.2	Analytical Procedures and Validation Information	
Module 4	**Nonclinical Study Reports**				
	4.1	**Table of Contents of Module 4**			
	4.2	**Study Reports**			
		4.2.1	**Pharmacology**		
			4.2.1.1	Primary Pharmacodynamics	
			4.2.1.2	Secondary Pharmacodynamics	
			4.2.1.3	Safety Pharmacology	
			4.2.1.4	Pharmacodynamic Drug Interactions	
		4.2.2	**Pharmacokinetics**		
			4.2.2.1	Analytical Methods and Validation Reports	
			4.2.2.2	Absorption	
			4.2.2.3	Distribution	
			4.2.2.4	Metabolism	
			4.2.2.5	Excretion	
			4.2.2.6	Pharmacokinetic Drug Interactions	
			4.2.2.7	Other Pharmacokinetic Studies	

(Continued)

TABLE 7.8 (Continued)

Section	Contents			Page numbers
		4.2.3	**Toxicology**	
			4.2.3.1	Single-dose Toxicity	
			4.2.3.2	Repeat-dose Toxicity	
			4.2.3.3	Genotoxicity	
				4.2.3.3.1	In Vitro Studies	
				4.2.3.3.2	In Vivo Studies	
			4.2.3.4	Carcinogenicity	
				4.2.3.4.1	Long-Term Studies	
				4.2.3.4.2	Short- or medium-term studies	
				4.2.3.4.3	Other studies	
			4.2.3.5	Reproductive and Development Toxicity	
				4.2.3.5.1	Fertility and Embryonic Development	
				4.2.3.5.2	Embryo-Fetal Development	
				4.2.3.5.3	Pre- and Postnatal Development and Maternal Function	
				4.2.3.5.4	Offspring, Juvenile, Second- and Third-Generation Studies	
			4.2.3.6	**Local Tolerance**	
			4.2.3.7	**Other Toxicity Studies**	
				4.2.3.7.1	Antigenicity	
				4.2.3.7.2	Immunogenicity	
				4.2.3.7.3	Mechanistic Studies (not included elsewhere)	
				4.2.3.7.4	Dependence	
				4.2.3.7.5	Metabolites	
				4.2.3.7.6	Impurities	
				4.2.3.7.7	Other	
	4.3	**Literature References**		
Module 5	**Clinical Study Reports**			
	5.1	**Table of Contents of Module 5**		
	5.2	**Tabular Listing of All Clinical Studies**		
	5.3	**Clinical Study Reports**		
		5.3.1	Reports of Biopharmaceutics Studies	
			5.3.1.1	Bioavailability (BA) Study Reports	
			5.3.1.2	Comparative BA and BE Study Reports	
			5.3.1.3	In Vitro In Vivo Correlation (IVIIVC) Study Reports	
			5.3.1.4	Reports of Bbioanalytical and Analytical Methods for Human studies	

(Continued)

TABLE 7.8 (Continued)

Section	Contents			Page numbers
		5.3.2	Reports of Studies Pertinent to Pharmacokinetics using Human Biomaterials	
			5.3.2.1 Plasma Protein Binding Study Reports	
			5.3.2.2 Reports of Hepatic Metabolism and Drug Interactions studies	
			5.3.2.3 Reports of Studies Using Other Human Biomaterials	
		5.3.3	Reports of Human Pharmacokinetic Studies	
			5.3.3.1 Healthy Subject PK and Tolerability	
			5.3.3.2 Patient PK and Initial Tolerability	
			5.3.3.3 Intrinsic Factor PK Study Reports	
			5.3.3.4 Extrinsic Factor PK Study Reports	
			5.3.3.5 Population PK Study Reports	
		5.3.4	Reports of Human Pharmacodynamic (PD) Studies	
			5.3.4.1 Healthy Subject PD and PKIPD Study Reports	
			5.3.4.2 Patient PD and PK1PD Study Reports	
		5.3.5	Reports of Efficacy and Safety Studies	
			5.3.5.1 Study reports of Controlled Clinical Studies pertinent to the claimed Indication	
			5.3.5.2 Study reports of Uncontrolled Clinical Studies	
			5.3.5.3 Reports of Analyses of Data from More than One Study	
			5.3.5.4 Other Study Reports	
		5.3.6	Reports of Postmarketing Experience	
		5.3.7	Case Report Forms and Individual Patient Listings	
	5.4	**Literature References**		

Format followed as per MCAZ

CTD format with some country-specific requirements.

An application for registration of a medicine may be made by:

- The prospective holder of the marketing authorization/registration hereinafter referred to as the applicant.
- A nominee of the applicant who must submit evidence of power of attorney.
- The CTD is organized into five modules. Module 1 is region-/country-specific. Modules 2, 3, 4, and 5 are intended to be common for all regions.

Registration procedure for products as per MCAZ

1. When a dossier is evaluated the evaluation summary is presented to an expert conditions, the applicant will be informed by the Director General in writing of such intention. Within a period specified by the Authority, which shall not be less than 14 days, the applicant may make representations in relation to the intentions of the Authority.
2. If the Authority had shown intend to register, a certificate will thereafter be sent to the applicant informing him of registration of that medicine and any conditions subject to which it is registered.
3. If registration is refused, the Director General will inform the applicant in writing stating the reasons and drawing attention to the right to appeal. Finally, the Director General will publish a notice in the Government Gazette notifying the approval or refusal to register as the case may be. The medicine will then be registered and applicants MUST, prior to the sale of the product, fulfill any specified conditions. Failure to comply with the conditions will render applicants liable to prosecution.

TABLE 7.9 Requirements in Zimbabwe.

Section	Contents			Page numbers
Module 1	**Administrative Information and Prescribing Information**			
	1.0	**Cover Letter**		
	1.1	**Table of Contents**		
	1.2	**Application Information**		
		1.2.1	*MC8 Application Form*	
		1.2.2	*Declaration by the Applicant*	
		1.2.3	*Screening Checklist*	
		1.2.4	*Proof of Payment of the Appropriate Fees*	
		1.2.5	*Manufacturing and Marketing Authorizations*	
		1.2.6	*Copy of Certificate of Suitability of the European Pharmacopoeia*	
		1.2.7	*Current Good Manufacturing Practices Certificate*	
		1.2.8	*Biowaiver (Bioequivalence and Bioavailability)*	
	1.3	**Product Information**		
		1.3.1	*Summary of Product Characteristics*	
		1.3.2	*Labeling*	
		1.3.3	*Package Insert and Patient Information Leaflet*	
	1.4	**Regional Summaries**		
		1.4.1	*Bioequivalence Application Form*	
		1.4.2	*Quality Information Summary*	
Module 2	**Common Technical Document (CTD) Summaries**			
	2.1	**CTD Table of Contents (Module 2–5)**		
	2.2	**CTD Introduction**		
	2.3	**Quality Overall Summary—product dossiers**		
	2.3.S	**Overview of Active Pharmaceutical Ingredient [API]**		
		2.3.S.1	**General Information**	
			2.3.S.1.1	*Nomenclature*
			2.3.S.1.2	*Structure*
			2.3.S.1.3	*General Properties*
		2.3.S.2	**Manufacture**	
			2.3.S.2.1	*Name and Address of API Manufacturer*
			2.3.S.2.2	*Description of Manufacturing Process and Process Controls*
			2.3.S.2.3	*Control of Materials*
			2.3.S.2.4	*Controls of Critical Steps and Intermediates*
			2.3.S.2.5	*Process Validation and/or Evaluation*
			2.3.S.2.6	*Manufacturing Process Development*
		2.3.S.3	**Characterization of the API**	
			2.3.S.3.1	*Elucidation of structure and other characteristics*
			2.3.S.3.2	*Impurities*

(Continued)

TABLE 7.9 (Continued)

Section	Contents			Page numbers
		2.3.S.4	**Control of API**	
			2.3.S.4.1 *Specifications*	
			2.3.S.4.2 *Analytical procedure*	
			2.3.S.4.3 *Validation of Analytical procedure*	
			2.3.S.4.4 *Batch analysis*	
			2.3.S.4.5 *Justification of specification*	
		2.3.S.5	**Reference Standards or Materials**	
		2.3.S.6	**Container/Closure System**	
		2.3.S.7	**Stability**	
			2.3.S.7.1 *Stability Summary and Conclusions*	
			2.3.S.7.2 *Postapproval Stability Protocol and stability commitment*	
			2.3.S.7.3 *Stability data*	
	2.3.P	**Overview of Finished Pharmaceutical Product (FPP)** *(name, dosage form)*		
		2.3.P.1	**Description and Composition of the FPP**	
		2.3.P.2	**Pharmaceutical Development of the FPP**	
		2.3.P.3	**Manufacture**	
			2.3.P.3.1 *Manufacturer(s)*	
			2.3.P.3.2 *Batch Formula*	
			2.3.P.3.3 *Description of Manufacturing Process and Process Controls*	
			2.3.P.3.4 *Controls of Critical Steps and Intermediates*	
			2.3.P.3.5 *Process Validation and/or Evaluation*	
		2.3.P.4	**Control of Excipients**	
			2.3.P.4.1 *Specifications*	
			2.3.P.4.2 *Analytical procedure of Excipients*	
			2.3.P.4.3 *Validation of Analytical procedure*	
			2.3.P.4.4 *Justification of specification*	
			2.3.P.4.5 *Excipients of Human or Animal origin*	
			2.3.P.4.6 *Novel Excipients*	
		2.3.P.5	**Control of the FPP**	
			2.3.P.5.1 *Specifications*	
			2.3.P.5.2 *Analytical procedure*	
			2.3.P.5.3 *Validation of Analytical procedure*	
			2.3.P.5.4 *Batch analysis*	
			2.3.P.5.5 *Characterization of Impurities*	
			2.3.P.5.6 *Justification of specification*	

(Continued)

TABLE 7.9 (Continued)

Section	Contents				Page numbers
		2.3.P.6	Reference Standards or Materials		
		2.3.P.7	Container/Closure System		
		2.3.P.8	Stability		
			2.3.P.8.1	Stability Summary and Conclusions	
			2.3.P.8.2	Postapproval Stability Protocol and stability commitment	
			2.3.P.8.3	Stability data	
	2.4	Nonclinical Overview			
	2.5	Clinical Overview			
	2.6	Nonclinical Written and Tabulated Summaries			
	2.7	Clinical Summary			
Module 3	Quality				
	3.1	Table of Contents of Module 3			
	3.2	Body of data			
		3.2.S	Drug Substance		
			3.2.S.1	General Information	
				3.2.S.1.1 Nomenclature	
				3.2.S.1.2 Structure	
				3.2.S.1.3 General Properties	
			3.2.S.2	Manufacture	
				3.2.S.2.1 Manufacturer(s)	
				3.2.S.2.2 Description of Manufacturing Process and Process Controls	
				3.2.S.2.3 Control of Materials	
				3.2.S.2.4 Control of Critical Steps and Intermediates	
				3.2.S.2.5 Process Validation and/or Evaluation	
				3.2.S.2.6 Manufacturing process Development	
			3.2.S.3	Characterization	
				3.2.S.3.1 Elucidation of Structure and Other Characteristics	
				3.2.S.3.2 Impurities	
			3.2.S.4	Control of the API	
				3.2.S.4.1 Specifications	
				3.2.S.4.2 Analytical Procedures (Include but not limited to)	
				3.2.S.4.3 Validation of Analytical Procedures	
				3.2.S.4.4 Batch Analyses	
				3.2.S.4.5 Justification of Specification	

(Continued)

TABLE 7.9 (Continued)

Section	Contents				Page numbers
		3.2.S.5	Reference Standards or Materials		
		3.2.S.6	Container/Closure Systems		
		3.2.S.7	Stability		
			3.2.S.7.1	Stability Summary and Conclusions	
			3.2.S.7.2	Postapproval Stability Protocol and Commitment	
			3.2.S.7.3	Stability Data	
	3.2.P	Drug Product			
		3.2.P.1	Description and Composition of the FPP		
		3.2.P.2	Pharmaceutical Development		
		3.2.P.3	Manufacture		
			3.2.P.3.1	Manufacturer(s)	
			3.2.P.3.2	Batch Formula	
			3.2.P.3.3	Description of Manufacturing Process and Process Controls	
			3.2.P.3.4	Control of Critical Steps and Intermediates	
			3.2.P.3.5	Process Validation and/or Evaluation	
		3.2.P.4	Control of Excipients		
			3.2.P.4.1	Specifications	
			3.2.P.4.2	Analytical Procedures of Excipients	
			3.2.P.4.3	Validation of Analytical Procedures	
			3.2.P.4.4	Justification of the Specifications	
			3.2.P.4.5	Excipients of human or animal origin	
			3.2.P.4.6	Novel excipients	
		3.2.P.5	Control of the FPP		
			3.2.P.5.1	Specifications	
			3.2.P.5.2	Analytical Procedures (Include but not limited to)	
			3.2.P.5.3	Validation of Analytical Procedures	
			3.2.P.5.4	Batch Analyses	
			3.2.P.4.5	Characterization of the Impurities	
			3.2.P.4.6	Justification of Specification	
		3.2.P.5	Reference Standards or Materials		
		3.2.P.6	Container/Closure Systems		
		3.2.P.7	Stability		
			3.2.P.7.1	Stability Summary and Conclusions	
			3.2.P.7.2	Postapproval Stability Protocol and Commitment	
			3.2.P.7.3	Stability Data	

(Continued)

TABLE 7.9 (Continued)

Section	Contents				Page numbers
3.3	3.2.R	Regional Information			
		3.2.R.1	Production Documents		
			3.2.R.1.1	*Executed Production Documents*	
			3.2.R.1.2	*Master Production Documents*	
		3.2.R.2	Analytical Procedures and Validation Information		
	Literature References				
Module 4	Nonclinical Study Reports				
Module 5	Clinical Study Reports				

The penalty for such failure is a fine not exceeding $10,000 or imprisonment for a period not exceeding TEN years or both including risking cancellation of registration of the offending product (Table 7.8).

Requirements for generic registration as per MCAZ (Table 7.9)

7.11 Conclusion

The regulatory requirements for ROW markets are still a matter of concern. There are either no regulations for a few markets or the regulations are not fully understood for the other. Since the requirements differ from one country to the other, there have been conflicts in the easy filing of the dossiers. There have been many government agencies that are trying to harmonize the regulations of these countries. The industry is also facing a big challenge in filing the product dossiers. To ease the filing the regulatory requirements have been discussed in the study.

All selected countries in Pharmaceutical Inspection Cooperation Scheme (PIC/S) (South Africa, Malaysia, and Indonesia) follow their own country guidelines, selected ASEAN (Thailand, Vietnam, Philippines, and Myanmar) countries follow both ACTD- and country-specific guidelines, and selected AFRICAN (Sudan, Uganda, and Zimbabwe) countries follow CTD format which will differ in only Module 1.

Pharma environment in these regions is a big challenge to regulatory professionals. They are feeling it very difficult to adopt to this environment and file a dossier because each region follows different formats to register a drug.

The regions that are selected in this study are not much regulated as the United States, Europe, Australia, Japan, and Canada where some of the countries do not have proper regulations, if they also have that regulations are not well understood so due to this in some countries the drug or plant is getting approval if the drug or plant is already having the approval of regulated market authorities.

As a matter of fact, in these three regions, there is a huge boom in pharma sector, and if companies are in regular touch in these regions, there will a robust platform for them.

This condition may be due to lack of harmonization of pharma regulation in the respective regions. And also if they have the regulations also, some countries fail to implement those regulations.

Pharma experts are saying that there are lots of efforts taken to harmonize these regulations and then they are trying to make everything available in the same roof and then they are telling that this harmonization process is quietly challenging and will defiantly happen but that will take some more time due to various reasons.

As a regulatory professional if this harmonization process happens successfully means it will be beneficial in many ways such as:

- Degenerating and compiling different registration dossiers;
- Common format will exist and reduce time and resources;
- Facilitates simultaneous submission in all regions;

- Facilitates exchange of information;
- Faster availability of medicines in all region.

Keeping in mind, the value of time and money and the requirements of the industry a comparison have been made in between the PIC/S Countries, ASEAN countries, and AFRICAN countries. The comparison studies done will facilitate the easy filing of a product dossier in PIC/S, ASEAN and AFRICAN markets in one go.

Acknowledgment

We acknowledge the generous infrastructure and the Regulatory Suite by the JSS College of Pharmacy, JSS Academy of Higher Education & Research, Ooty.

References

Al Ameri, M.N., Nayuni, N., Kumar, K.A., Perrett, D., Tucker, A., Johnston, A., 2012. The differences between the branded and generic medicines using solid dosage forms: in-vitro dissolution testing. Results Pharma Sci 2, 1–8.

Allen, L., Ansel, H.C., 2013. Ansel's Pharmaceutical Dosage Forms and Drug Delivery Systems. Lippincott Williams & Wilkins.

Anciaux, D., Neves, E., van der Zee, F.A., van der Giessen, A., Rammer, C., Pellens, M., 2016. Mapping the Regional Embeddedness of the NMP Programme: Final Report of the Project "RTD-NMP-2014-Mapping." ZEW-Gutachten und Forschungsberichte.

Buckley, G.J., Riviere, J.E. (Eds.), 2012. Ensuring Safe Foods and Medical Products Through Stronger Regulatory Systems Abroad.

Carpenter, D., 2014. Reputation and Power: organizational Image and Pharmaceutical Regulation at the FDA. Princeton University Press.

Cheema, P.K., Gavura, S., Migus, M., Godman, B., Yeung, L., Trudeau, M.E., 2012. International variability in the reimbursement of cancer drugs by publically funded drug programs. Curr. Oncol 19 (3), e165.

Chomsky, N., 1999. Profit over People: neoliberalism and Global Order. Seven Stories Press.

Davies, E.H., Fulton, E., Brook, D., Hughes, D.A., 2017. Affordable orphan drugs: a role for not-for-profit organizations. Br. J. Clin. Pharmacol. 83 (7), 1595–1601.

Fathelrahman, A., Ibrahim, M., Wertheimer, A., 2016. Pharmacy Practice in Developing Countries: Achievements and Challenges. Academic Press.

Follesdal, A., Wessel, R.A., Wouters, J., 2008. Multilevel Regulation and the EU: The Interplay Between Global, European, and National Normative Processes. BRILL.

Garattini, L., Cornago, D., De, Compadri, P., 2007. Pricing and reimbursement of in-patent drugs in seven European countries: a comparative analysis. Health Policy 82 (3), 330–339.

Hansen, C.H., Doolan, C.J., Hansen, K.L., 2017. Wind Farm Noise: Measurement, Assessment, and Control. John Wiley & Sons.

Harrison, R., Walton, M., Healy, J., Smith-Merry, J., Hobbs, C., 2016. Patient complaints about hospital services: applying a complaint taxonomy to analyse and respond to complaints. Int. J. Qual. Health Care 28 (2), 240–245.

Hassali, M.A., Tan, C.S., Wong, Z.Y., Saleem, F., Alrasheedy, A.A., 2015. Pharmaceutical pricing in Malaysia. In: Pharmaceutical Prices in the 21st Century, pp. 171–188.

Hettle, R., Corbett, M., Hinde, S., Hodgson, R., Jones-Diette, J., Woolacott, N., et al., 2017. The assessment and appraisal of regenerative medicines and cell therapy products: an exploration of methods for review, economic evaluation and appraisal. Health Technol. Assess. 21, 1–204.

Jacob, V., Crawford, C., Cohen-Mekelburg, S., Viladomiu, M., Putzel, G.G., Schneider, Y., et al., 2017. Single delivery of high-diversity fecal microbiota preparation by colonoscopy is safe and effective in increasing microbial diversity in active ulcerative colitis. Inflamm. Bowel Dis. 23 (6), 903–911.

Katsandres, J.T., Hunt, J.M., Ho, C.M., Shoeman, P.D., 2002. Inventors, Intermec IP Corp, assignee. Automatic data collection device that receives data output instruction from data consumer. US patent US 6,356,949.

Phuong, N.C., Nguyen, T.D., 2012. International harmonization and national particularities of accounting: Recent accounting development in Vietnam. J. Account. Organ. Change 8.

Raw, A.S., Furness, M.S., Gill, D.S., Adams, R.C., Holcombe Jr, F.O., Lawrence, X.Y., 2004. Regulatory considerations of pharmaceutical solid polymorphism in abbreviated new drug applications (ANDAs). Adv. Drug Deliv. Rev. 56 (3), 397–414.

Schwartländer, B., Stover, J., Hallett, T., Atun, R., Avila, C., Gouws, E., et al., 2011. Towards an improved investment approach for an effective response to HIV/AIDS. Lancet 377 (9782), 2031–2041.

Schwartzberg, E., Ainbinder, D., Vishkauzan, A., Gamzu, R., 2017. Drug shortages in Israel: regulatory perspectives, challenges and solutions. Isr. J. Health Policy Res. 6 (1), 1–8.

Van Dijk, L., Monteiro, S.P., Vervloet, M., de Bie, J., Raynor, D.T., 2014. Study on the package leaflets and the summaries of product characteristics of medicinal products for human use. PIL's Study. European Union Google Scholar.

Venkateswarlu, B., Nagarjuna, D., Ramaiah, M., Nagabhushanam, M., Akram, M.V., 2014. Regulatory requirements for the registration of generic solid oral in USA, Singapore, Malaysia and Thailand. J. Glob. Trends Pharm. Sci. 5 (4), 2225–2232.

Weiss, E.B., Jacobson, H.K., 2000. Engaging Countries: Strengthening Compliance with International Environmental Accords. MIT Press.

World Health Organization, 2017. Made in Viet Nam Vaccines: Efforts to Develop Sustainable In-Country Manufacturing for Seasonal and Pandemic Influenza Vaccines: Consultation held in Viet Nam, April–June 2016. World Health Organization.

Chapter 8

Drug product performance and scale-up process approval changes

Gulam Mustafa[1], Md Ali Mujtaba[2], Sabna Kotta[3], Abdullah Habeeballah[4], Nabil A. Alhakamy[3,5], Hibah M. Aldawsari[3,5], Shahid Karim[6] and Shadab Md[3,5]

[1]*College of Pharmacy, AD-Dawadmi, Shaqra University, Riyadh, Saudi Arabia, [2]Department of Pharmaceutics, Faculty of Pharmacy, Northern Border University, Rafha, Saudi Arabia, [3]Department of Pharmaceutics, Faculty of Pharmacy, King Abdulaziz University, Jeddah, Saudi Arabia, [4]Department of Clinical Pharmacology, University of Glasgow, Glasgow, United Kingdom, [5]Mohamed Saeed Tamer Chair for Pharmaceutical Industries, King Abdulaziz University, Jeddah, Saudi Arabia, [6]Department of Pharmacology, Faculty of Medicine, King Abdulaziz University, Jeddah, Saudi Arabia*

8.1 Introduction

Performance of the drug product can be characterized as an active pharmaceutical ingredient (API) release, resulting in its systemic availability required to achieve the desired therapeutic response (Scheubel, 2010). Drug product performance trials are used to develop new and generic drugs (Sathe et al., 2005). There are several issues to be addressed by a pharmaceutical company while developing a drug product, starting from the API to the robust production process (Sathe et al., 2005; Scheubel, 2010). This formulation maintains the patient's persistent bioavailability (BA) and treatment over time as separately as possible from the manufacturing process. Dissolution testing is a preferred method of evaluating the potential to develop new APIs and drug formulations (Sathe et al., 2005; Scheubel, 2010). This has proved to be a very useful tool for formulations development, manufacturing control, and quality measurement. Most oral solid dosage forms, including oral suspensions, require dissolution or drug release tests (Singh et al., 2011). For the dissolution test to be useful, it must be quick, accurate, and reproducible and must be able to differentiate between different degrees of product's performance. It is a comprehensive testing and can be viewed as a good indicator of all the processes leading to the dissolution of API in a solution (Singh et al., 2011).

During the initial stages of drug development, APIs' dissolution test serves as an important tool for evaluating drug candidates' physicochemical properties. It helps toxicology selection and clinical trial formulations for animal and human evaluation (Sathe et al., 2005; Singh et al., 2011). At the later stages, dissolution testing is carried out with drug products to compare with the prototype formulation, for elucidating the mechanism involved for drug dissolution that indicates the stability and robustness in the product manufacturing methods and ensures the satisfactory release and reproducibility of the process. In vitro–in vivo correlation (IVIVC) is useful for developing new pharmaceuticals and for decreasing the time and cost of studies (Food and Drug Administration, 1997; Food and Drug Administration/Center for Drug Evaluation and Research, 1997). IVIVC serves as a support to claim biowaivers (Emami, 2006; Hanif et al., 2018). Thus dissolution testing may be a substitute measure for bioequivalence (BE) leading to successful biowaiver (Food and Drug Administration, 2017). It is also recognized for scale-up and postapproval changes (SUPACs) (Food and Drug Administration, 2000).

8.2 In vitro drug product performance

The US Pharmacopoeia (USP) tests for finished dosage forms can be divided into drug product quality and performance tests. The dissolution test is a powerful physiochemical in vitro test that evaluates the consistency and efficiency of drug product (Diaz et al., 2016). Broadly, the solid oral dosage forms can be immediate release (IR) or modified release (MR) (Sathe et al., 2005). The IR dosage forms releases the API quickly after administration (Food and Drug Administration,

Regulatory Affairs in the Pharmaceutical Industry. DOI: https://doi.org/10.1016/B978-0-12-822211-9.00010-1
© 2022 Elsevier Inc. All rights reserved.

2000). Extended-release (ER) forms releases the API available over an extended period. A delayed-release (DR) product is aimed to retard API release, generally until the drug product leaves the stomach (Sathe et al., 2005).

Following oral administration, the drug product is subjected to disintegration, deaggregation, dissolution, solubilization, and finally permeation across the gastrointestinal membrane. They are all considered as the critical elements of API absorption (Amidon et al., 1995, 2014). In vitro dissolution is an indicator of the initial stage of these critical elements, and thus is significantly related to in vivo performance. This is more pronounced in the case of low-solubility APIs and MR products, for which the dissolution of API is mostly the rate-limiting step in the absorption of the API after oral administration (Al Ameri et al., 2011). In vitro dissolution can also be affected by intrinsic property of drug substance, manufacturing process, dissolution testing methods, and drug product formulation. There are several factors related to the dissolution of drug substance which includes salt factor, solubility, surface area, particle size, and polymorphism. Based on Noyes and Whitney equation and Nernst's theory, solubility of drug, diffusion, effective surface area, and hydrodynamics influence the drug dissolution (Abdou, 1989). A drug's dissolution rate is closely correlated with the solubility of the drug product. High-solubility compounds normally exhibit significantly high dissolution. The dissolution of ionizable group compounds depends on the medium pH and the compound pK_a (Singh et al., 2011; Sathe et al., 2005; Diaz et al., 2016).

Organic salts provide an easy way of increasing the rate of dissolution and are often chosen during the production of drugs for this purpose (Morris et al., 1994). Different physical forms of the drug substance can also occur and display solid-state polymorphism. The difference in these polymorphs' lattice energies also results in dissolution (Grant and Higuchi, 1990). Chloramphenicol palmitate polymorphism is a good example (Sathe et al., 2005; Scheubel, 2010). The formulation variables used in the formulation, such as excipients (e.g., disintegrants, surfactants, hydrophilic binders, and fillers), can also significantly impact the dissolution of the drug product. The drug product dissolution can be affected by manufacturing variables. Therefore several manufacturing approaches are needed to enhance dissolution. Spray drying/melt extrusion of API may be employed to produce stable amorphous dispersions with a significantly high dissolution rate (Stavchansky and McGinity, 1989; Yi, 2001).

8.3 In vitro drug product performance evaluation

8.3.1 Disintegration test

Disintegration testing is deemed acceptable when a dissolution relationship is formed or in situations where disintegration is more discriminatory than dissolution (International Conference on Harmonisation, 2000).

8.3.2 Dissolution test

Dissolution testing is mandatory as a condition of product approval. Decision trees are established by the International Conference on Harmonization (ICH) Q6A Guidance document (International Conference on Harmonization, 2000) to assist in the establishment of appropriate conditions and tolerances for dissolution testing (Hanson, 1991).

8.3.2.1 Dissolution method

Dissolution sets the requirements of equipment and working setting for basket apparatus and paddle apparatus. These are the systems mostly used to conduct dissolution testing of solid oral dosage types. The basket is discovered to be discriminatory at 100 rpm and is widely used to test capsules. If the coning effect, which is normal for slow stirring rate, is reduced, then the paddle system at 50 rpm may be discriminatory (U.S. Food and Drug Administration, 2018). The paddle system is widely used for tablets. As the stirring rate is improved, the dissolution rate usually increases. The official USP instruments are given in Table 8.1.

One dissolution test or one dissolution medium cannot always be produced or chosen to ensure batch-to-batch monitoring and to track the biopharmaceutical aspects of the drug product (Sathe et al., 2005; Scheubel, 2010; U.S. Food and Drug Administration, 2018). The drug properties are the basis for choosing a dissolution test medium. effort should be placed to match physiological conditions when choosing the medium. The simulated gastric fluid (SGF) and simulated intestinal fluid (SIF) have been used to provide an environment similar to gastric juice and intestinal fluid. They mainly simulate the average pH of the biological fluid and its ionic strength. Both SGF and SIF are used with or without enzymes too. Therefore media with pHs ranging from 1.2 (gastric pH) to 6.8 (intestinal pH) are favored. Water, 0.1 N hydrochloric acid, acetate buffer (pH 4.5), and phosphate buffer are some of the common media used. A two-stage protocol is followed for enteric-coated solid oral dosage forms, first testing at 0.1 N HCl for 2 h to demonstrate

TABLE 8.1 Various dissolution testing apparatuses and applications.

USP apparatus type	Apparatus description	Dosage form
I	Basket apparatus	Immediate/delayed/extended-release dosage forms
II	Paddle apparatus	Immediate/delayed/extended-release dosage forms
III	Reciprocating cylinder	Immediate/delayed/extended-release dosage forms
IV	Flow-through cell	Extended-release/poorly soluble drugs in IR
V	Paddle over disk	Trandermal patches
VI	Rotating cylinder	Transdermal patches
VII	Reciprocating disk	Extended-release, transdermal patches

acid tolerance, followed by pH 6.8 phosphate buffer testing (Sathe et al., 2005; Scheubel, 2010; U.S. Food and Drug Administration, 2018).

Nevertheless, there are arguments against the use of a constant pH in these media. The presence of a pH range, rather than a specific pH value, in both gastric and intestinal fluids, is observed in actual physiological conditions (Klein, 2010).The presence of an enzyme will make the medium more realistic to actual physiological conditions. Meanwhile, the use of biorelevant dissolution media which can simulate both fed and fasted states would give more approximation of the in vivo performance. Towards this objective, fasted state intestinal fluid and fasted state gastric fluid have emerged as biorelevant dissolution media. They provide a more meaningful estimation of formulation and food effects on absorption of poorly soluble drugs (Kostewicz et al., 2002; Nicolaides et al., 2001). The dissolution rises with increasing pH for drugs that are weak acids, while with increasing pH, the dissolution rate decreases for weak bases (Sathe et al., 2005; Scheubel, 2010).

During the oral administration of drugs, they must undergo inevitable interaction with bile salts and surfactants which are essential in the absorption process and present in the gastrointestinal tract (Lu et al., 2017). Thus the reported biorelevant media contain sodium taurocholate, a bile salt and emulsifier, to provide such a solubilization effect. Nevertheless, overestimation of the dissolution process is also possible with the use of sodium taurocholate (Vertzoni et al., 2007). Meanwhile, sodium taurocholate can also reduce drug absorption (Carmona-Ibáñez et al., 1999). Therefore judicious use of sodium taurocholate and other components of biorelevant media may be needed for a more accurate prediction of in vivo performance. Surfactants may alternatively be applied to the dissolution medium and they can reduce the interfacial tension and induce micellar formation, increasing the dissolution.

Similarly, ionic salts increase dissolution, but hydroalcoholic or other organic solvent-containing media are discouraged (Diaz et al., 2016; Sathe et al., 2005; U.S. Food and Drug Administration, 2018). For gelatin-based dosage forms, specified amounts of enzymes can be applied to the medium (US Pharmacopeia/National Formulary, 2002). By the deaeration process, the air bubbles are removed from the medium (Chapter 711; USP, 2010a). To reflect human body temperature, the dissolution medium is normally maintained at $37°C \pm 0.5°C$. More efforts are needed to predict lipophilic drug plasma levels (Sathe et al., 2005; Scheubel, 2010). The 500-mL dissolution medium is widely used to provide sink conditions for highly soluble, rapidly dissolving drugs. Appropriate justification is required for the option of 900-mL volume (U.S. Food and Drug Administration, 2018).

In addition to tablets, dissolution of other important delivery systems such as transdermal patches, vaginal tablets, suppositories (rectal tablets), and implants are also of relevance. Among these systems, the evaluation of dissolution of transdermal patches has been sufficiently evolved over time. As such, it is difficult to delineate the difference between dissolution testing and drug release evaluation of transdermal patches. In cases where the drug release is favored through a matrix erosion of patches, the dissolution may be in synonym with drug release. But in the case of a matrix diffusion-based patch, diffusion also comes into action, and as such the drug release cannot be directly corroborated with the dissolution of the drug. Nevertheless, USP has suggested several apparatuses suitable for testing transdermal patches. Paddle over disk (USP Type 5), cylinder (USP Type 6), and reciprocating holder (USP Type 7) are among them. The paddle over disk method could be considered as an adaptation of the USP paddle apparatus (Shah et al., 1986). Meanwhile, other advanced or modified methods are also available for the evaluation of transdermal patches. A moisturized synthetic skin simulator is such an example, which provides release resistance. Interestingly, this system was found to be better than USP paddle and paddle over disk methods (Cai et al., 2012).

Vaginal tablets (pessaries) are appropriate delivery systems for microbicides for local action. Like other delivery systems, their evaluation to ascertain sufficient API dissolution is needed. Further, the drug dissolution test is a quality assurance or confirmation of batch uniformity. Similar to tablets, several USP-type apparatuses could be used for dissolution testing of vaginal tablets too. Interestingly, in a comparison between the flow-through cell (USP Type 4) and paddle methods, the former was found to be better for vaginal tablets (Szymańska and Winnicka, 2013). In another adaptation, it was found that providing an amount of vaginal fluid is possible and that too at the rate of daily production and without any rotational movement. This resulted in a simple and more accurate method for the dissolution testing of vaginal tablets (Baloglu et al., 2011).

Rectal delivery systems can be aimed for local or systemic action of drugs. Absorption by rectal route is fast but unreliable, and this marks the importance of the need for dissolution testing. Suppositories are such a rectal delivery system that needs dissolution testing for assessment for product performance (Janicki et al., 2001). Earlier, USP Type 1 or 2 apparatus were used with the suppositories either placed in the basket, medium, or inside a dialysis bag (Hammouda et al., 1993). In an effort to overcome the disadvantages of the use of the USP Type 1 apparatus, a modified basket made of polyurethane was successfully tried for aspirin suppositories (Palmieri, 1981). Later, the flow-through cell is an appropriate testing apparatus for suppositories. Similarly, the dissolution cell described in British Pharmacopoeia 1998 is also useful (Janicki et al., 2001).

The implantable systems represent a plethora of applications and mechanisms. In the case of implants also USP Type 1 and Type 2 apparatuses are used (Balasubramaniam et al., 2008). Nevertheless, the flow-through apparatus is suitable for the dissolution testing of most types of implants (Browne and Kieselmann, 2010; Iyer et al., 2006). In the case of implants, the site of implantation and the purpose of implantation also need serious consideration along with the biological tissue environment in which it is placed. Further, the tailoring of sink conditions in consideration to the drug and the dose needs to be addressed (Iyer et al., 2006).

8.3.2.2 Dissolution acceptance criteria

The importance of dissolution data in the quality control of drug products is evident by the pharmacopoeia specification of acceptance criteria. A three-stage dissolution testing and acceptance are recommended for IR formulations. Here, the stages S1, S2, and S3 are suggested to be performed with 6, 6, and 12 numbers of products, respectively (Table 8.2). The product passes the test if the dissolution acceptance criterion is met under S1, S2, or S3. The term "Q" is the percentage of drug dissolution specified in the monograph. Meanwhile, it is interesting to discuss the chances of passing the acceptance criteria at these three different stages (Chow et al., 2002; Dumont et al., 2007). Several suggestions are placed to enhance the discriminatory power of dissolution testing. Changing the $Q-15\%$ criteria in stages S2 and S3 to $Q-5\%$ were vital among them (Givand, 1980; Tsong et al., 1995).

The acceptance criteria for dissolution of a drug product are based on drug substance's high solubility. Usually, 80% of the drug is defined to be dissolved within 30 minutes for most types of IR oral dosage (U.S. Food and Drug Administration, 2018). When an average of 85% or more drug dissolves within 15 minutes, an IR product is deemed to be called rapidly dissolving drug (Food and Drug Administration, 2000, 2017). If an alternative acceptance criterion is introduced, additional evidence to support the proposed acceptance criterion should be presented by the sponsor/applicant. In addition to dissolution performance data, suitable silico modeling may provide additional supporting details (U.S. Food and Drug Administration, 2018).

TABLE 8.2 Dissolution test acceptance criteria for IR drug products (USP, 2003).

Stages	No. of units to be tested	Total no. of units tested	Acceptance criteria
Stage S1	6	6	All units have $\geq Q+5\%$
Stage S2	6	12	Average $\geq Q$ (with no sample have less than $Q-15\%$)
Stage S3	12	24	Average $\geq Q$ (with not more than two samples have less than $Q-15\%$ and no sample has less than $Q-25\%$)

8.3.3   Dissolution profile comparisons

The comparisons of dissolution profiles are gaining importance for comparative BA studies, that is, BE. The substitution of in vivo BE studies by an in vitro test is the biowaiver. The agency has developed and tested several different profile comparison methods (Sathe et al., 1996, 1997; Tsong et al., 1996; Shah et al., 1998). A reported model such as independent mathematical approach is used for a variety of applications (Mounica et al., 2017).

8.3.3.1   Difference factor and similarity factor

It measures the relative errors occurring between the two dissolution curves (Food and Drug Administration, 2000).

$$f_1 = \left\{ \frac{\left\{ \sum_{t=1}^{n} |Rt - Tt| \right\}}{\sum_{t=1}^{n} Rt} \right\} \times 100$$

$$f_2 = 50 \times \log \left[\left\{ 1 + \frac{1}{n} \sum_{r=1}^{n} wt(Rt - Tt) \right\}^{-0.5} \times 100 \right]$$

where f_2 is the similarity factor, n is the number of observations, Rt and Tt are the cumulative percentage of drugs dissolved from reference formulation and test formulation.

An f_2 value of 50 or greater (50−100) ensures dissolution profile similarity and the sameness or equivalence of the two curves, and thus the performance of the two products. At a minimum, three points, no more than one point exceeding 85%, should be used for similarity profile comparison. A profile comparison is not necessary for products that dissolve very rapidly (85% dissolution in 15 minutes). When the two profiles are exactly identical, $f_1 = 0$ and $f_2 = 50 \times \log(100) = 100$, they are scaled between approximately 0 and 100 (Diaz et al., 2016; Costa, 2001; Mounica et al., 2017).

8.3.3.2   Dissolution efficiency for the comparison of in vitro dissolution profiles

A comparison of dissolution profiles has been essential in both product development and manufacturing stages. The f_1 and f_2 have proved to be useful fit factors for a comparison (Moore and Flanner, 1996). Among these, the similarity factor is widely used for the comparison of dissolution. These fit factors are approved by regulatory agencies for comparison of dissolution profile. Precisely, these fit factors are qualitative in nature and many patterns of dissolution profile can have the same values for a fit factor. Thus many a times, a batch−batch variation cannot be always evaluated using the fit factors. This gap was filled by the parameter called dissolution efficiency (Khan and Rhodes, 1972). The area of the dissolution curve is considered as the dissolution efficiency, similar to the concept of the area under the curve (AUC) in pharmacokinetics (PK) (Anderson et al., 1998). The dissolution efficiency is given by the equation:

$$\text{Dissolution efficiency} = \frac{\int_{t_1}^{t_2} y dt}{y_{100} \times (t_1 - t_2)} \times 100$$

where y and y_{100} represent the percentage of drug being dissolved and maximum percent of drug dissolved, respectively, over the selected time periods of t_1, and t_2 used for the estimation. If the selected initial time point is zero (time of the start of dissolution), then the equation takes the form as given below:

$$\text{Dissolution efficiency} = \frac{\int_{0}^{T} y_t dt}{y_{100} \times T} \times 100$$

where T represents the total time interval considered to evaluate the dissolution efficiency.

To carry out a comparison of the drug products in terms of dissolution efficiency, the mean value and the standard error of mean (or standard deviation) may be used after confirming that the confidence interval is within the acceptable limit (Anderson et al., 1998).

In addition to dissolution efficiency, similarity factor, and the difference factor, comparison of dissolution values at specific time intervals could also serve as a discriminatory method for the assessment of dissolution profile. This could be even used for assessing the batch−batch variation or uniformity. The time taken for the specific percentage of drug dissolution (D) is represented by $t_{D\%}$. For example, the time taken for drug dissolution of 25% is represented by $t_{25\%}$. Similarly, $t_{50\%}$, $t_{70\%}$, and $t_{90\%}$ are also used frequently for comparison of dissolution profiles (Keshaversushetti, 2015).

A study compared the use of such $t_{D\%}$ values and found that these are inferior to the similarity factor (Pillay and Fassihi, 1998). Nevertheless, $t_{D\%}$ values are very easy to calculate and understand and therefore widely used for a direct comparison of dissolution profiles (Shirsand et al., 2012).

8.3.4 Dissolution specification for a new chemical entity

The properties of the dissolution of drugs must be accomplished based on the drug product's pH, solubility profile, and pK_a. Although these factors govern the dissolution methodology, other factors also determine the type of dissolution methodology. The choice of apparatus and dissolution medium is based on the physicochemical characteristics of the drug (including solubility, stability) and the type of formulation (such as IR, enteric coated, ER, and rapidly dissolving) (Suarez et al., 2016).

The dissolution test shall be performed at 50/100 rpm using a basket method or at 50/75 rpm using the paddle method with an interval of 15 minutes to produce a dissolution profile. A reasonable profile sampling at an interval of 5 or 10 minutes would be needed for the fast dissolution products. Approaches for the setting of dissolution requirements of a new chemical entity are shown in Fig. 8.1. If the drug's dissolution profile varies over time, to maintain adherence to SUPAC, the dissolution profile(s) will be compared to the approved biobatch/pivotal clinical trial batch(s) (U.S. Food and Drug Administration, 2018).

8.3.5 Dissolution specification for generic products

The dissolution specifications for the generic medicine are usually similar to the reference-listed drug (RLD). The dissolution performance of the generic medicine as per specification is confirmed from an acceptable BE study (Anand et al., 2011; Food and Drug Administration, 1997; Food and Drug Administration/Center for Drug Evaluation and Research, 1997). Where there is a substantial dissolution of the generic product other than the RLD and there are sufficient in vivo results, a specific requirement for the dissolution of the generic product may be established. If there is a significant variation in the dissolution profile of generic product as compared to RLD and acceptable in vivo data then altered dissolution specification for such generic product could be established (Anand et al., 2011; Food and Drug Administration, 1997a; Food and Drug Administration/Center for Drug Evaluation and Research, 1997). All existing approved new drug product must comply with USP method for dissolution test. The three categories are (Food and

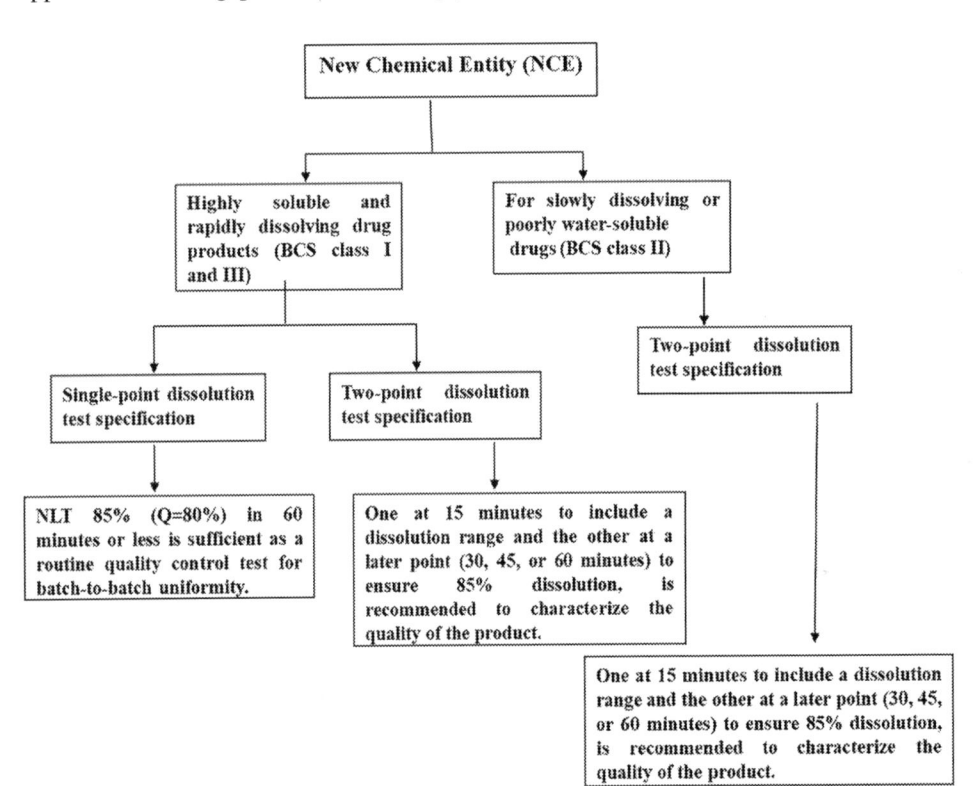

FIGURE 8.1 Flowchart for setting dissolution specifications for a new chemical entity. *NLT*, Not less than.

Drug Administration, 1997a; Food and Drug Administration/Center for Drug Evaluation and Research, 1997) listed below.

8.3.5.1 Dissolution test is available for USP drug product

In this case, quality control dissolution test is the test described in the USP. It is recommended by the Division of Bioequivalence, Office of Generic Drugs, to perform dissolution profile at an interval of 15 minutes or less for both test and reference products (12 units each) using the USP method. The Division of Bioequivalence may recommend an additional dissolution test based on a scientific justification. Examples of this include (1) cases where the USP did not describe dissolution test for combination drug products and (2) cases where the use of disintegration apparatus described in the USP.

8.3.5.2 Dissolution test is not available for USP drug product; dissolution test for reference-listed NDA drug product available publicly

In such cases, it is recommended to perform dissolution profile at 15-minute intervals for both tests and reference products (12 units each) based on the method approved for RLD. The Division of Bioequivalence may also request for approval about six submissions of additional dissolution test results, if scientifically justified.

8.3.5.3 Dissolution test is not available for USP drug product; dissolution test for reference-listed NDA drug product not available publicly

In such cases, comparative dissolution tests for both test and reference products are recommended under various testing conditions. The test conditions which include various dissolution media (pH 1−6.8), surfactant use, and apparatuses 1 and 2 with variable agitation. In all such cases, profiles of dissolution should be produced as recommended. The criteria for the dissolution are set based on the availability of BE and related data.

8.3.6 Biopharmaceutics classification system

It is for the classification of drugs based on its solubility and intestinal permeability (Benet, 2013; U.S. Food and Drug Administration, 2018; Food and Drug Administration, 2017). As per biopharmaceutics classification system (BCS), the drugs are graded under BCS I with high solubility and high permeability, such as diltiazem, propranolol, metoprolol; BCS II with low solubility and high permeability, such as nifedipine, phenytoin, mefenamic acid; BCS III with high solubility and low permeability, such as acyclovir, captopril, ranitidine; and BCS IV with low solubility and low permeability, such as taxol, chlorothiazide, furosemide (Amidon et al., 1995; U.S. Food and Drug Administration, 2018). The drug's solubility is measured by dissolving the full unit dose of the drug in an aqueous solution of ∼250 mL with a pH range between 1.0 and 6.8. High permeability drugs are normally absorbed by 90% or more in the absence of recorded gastrointestinal instability or permeability problems. (Food and Drug Administration, 2000; U.S. Food and Drug Administration, 2018). BCS indicates that 85% of drug dissolution in 0.1 N HCl for Class I and Class III drugs within 15 minutes may warrant that dissolution does not reduce the drug's BA. Gastric emptying is regarded as a rate-limiting step for the absorption of a drug in such cases. Under fasting conditions, the average T50% gastric residence period is 15−20 minutes. According to this conventional assumption, a drug product with a dissolution of 85% in 0.1 N HCl within 15 minutes acts as a solution. It should not have any problems with BA under mild dissolution conditions (U.S. Food and Drug Administration, 2018; Food and Drug Administration, 2017). Multiple time point dissolution profiles in various dissolution media are indicated when the dissolution rate is slower than gastric emptying (Tsume et al., 2014). In the case of class II drugs, drug dissolution may be a rate-limiting step for drug absorption and IVIVC may be required. For medicinal products of that kind, dissolution profiles in different dissolution media are recommended. For Class III drugs, permeability may be the rate-limiting step for drug absorption and a limited IVIVC could be expected, due to relative dissolution rate and bowel movements. Class IV drugs may have a significant problem for oral drug delivery (Food and Drug Administration, 2017; Hofsäss and Dressman, 2019). The BCS, therefore, gives a comparison for which the dissolution test is a replacement for PK studies.

8.4 In vivo performance

In vivo performance evaluation is critical for drug research and development. This can be demonstrated by the high number of drug candidates failing in drug production's clinical process in the last decades. Historically, the percentage of drugs tested that were and reached the market to the extent of almost 14%. In the last few decades, the likelihood percentage for a candidate drug to enter Phase I trial is just 8% (Frantz, 2004). In late Phase III trials, the 20% rate of product failure was common, but this figure now stands at nearly 50% (Crawford, 2004). The most obvious reasons for potential drug candidates' clinical failures are weak or inadequate preclinical forecasting of clinical effectiveness, safety pharmacology, or potential toxicities.

BA is a typical PK parameter determined by estimating the AUC of plasma drug concentration versus time profile (Dietrich et al., 2003). AUC is the most reliable measure of a drug's BA (Rescigno, 2000) and a measure of drug reaching the systemic circulation. At maximum absorption, the maximum plasma concentration (C_{max}) is reached and the elimination rate constant (K_{el}) equals the absorption rate (K_a) (Doogue and Polasek, 2013; Rescigno). BA determinations based on C_{max} may be deceptive since drug elimination starts the moment the drug reaches the bloodstream. The most commonly used parameter for absorption rate is peak time (T_{max}); the slower the absorption is, the later the T_{max} will be (Doogue and Polasek, 2013). Both intrinsic and extrinsic variables influence BA (Reyner et al., 2020).

To measure the concentrations of active pharmaceutical molecules and not their metabolites, the biological fluids (e.g., salivary fluid for estimation of theophylline; cerebrospinal fluid and bile fluids for cephalosporin estimation) obtained throughout BA studies should be analyzed. The only exception to allowing metabolic intermediates to be measured in the presence of an active pharmaceutical agent in extremely small quantities, which can be quantified in plasma, blood, or serum. Both the prodrug and the active moieties should be assessed in the case of prodrugs (Rein et al., 2013). For drug candidates, the concentration profile assesses both the absorption and elimination of the drug compound contained in the biological fluid. Frequent sampling is essential in the beginning in order to compute correctly the rate of absorption, true C_{max} of the compound after dosing for an extravascular dose. From pilot tests, acceptable time courses can be calculated to provide the most accurate estimates for pivotal BA studies (Chow, 2014).

Urinary excretion tests are useful for determining the BA of unchanged excreted drugs and are directly proportional to the drug's plasma concentration. The urine samples are collected regularly to 7 elimination half-lives and estimated (Wesch, 2011). Complete emptying of the bladder is required for each sample collection. Total urinary excretion rate (dXu/dt)max, time for total excretion rate (tu)max, and cumulative substance excreted in urine (Xu) are the main parameters tested (Currie, 2018). If the quantitative analysis of a drug in plasma or urine is unreliable, acute pharmacological effects are used. In the case of topical products, systemic BA has no significance. Here, the acute pharmacological effect approach may be applicable to dosage forms that are not intended for delivery into the systemic circulation of the active drug (Agudelo and Vesga, 2012). Therapeutic reaction monitoring, involving observation of clinical response, is limited by inaccurate BA assessment.

8.4.1 In vivo performance evaluation of generic drugs

In vivo performance evaluation of generic drugs must have the same clinical benefits as reference-listed drugs and follow stringent Food and Drug Administration (FDA) requirements. They must show pharmaceutical, biological, and therapeutic "BE" to an RLD. Their active ingredients, dosage types, routes of administration, strengths, and related properties must be the same (pharmaceutical); their APIs must be similarly available and active at the (biological) site of action; and the medication must provide a similar safety and efficacy profile in a clinical (therapeutic) condition (Chow, 2014; Meredith, 2009).

BE is tested using comparative blood-level profiles for simple orally administered medications, as the therapeutic agent must enter the systemic circulation to reach the site of action (Rescigno, 1992). However, demonstrating BE for complex generic drug products (CGDPs), which represent complicated formulations or routes of administration, is much more difficult and therefore usually needs to be investigated using time-consuming and costly clinical endpoint studies (Chow, 2014). The biomorphological, physical, and structural characteristics of a drug dosage form directly affect a formulation's in vivo parameters, including the rate and extent of the drug delivery at the targeted site. CGDPs have diverse APIs, formulations, routes of administration, drug—device combinations, and dosage types, significantly increasing the complexity in BE research (Chow and Liu, 2008).

Besides, a generic can have an RLD-like formulation but perform differently in vivo, particularly given the amount of intersubject variability within a reference population. Although physicochemical characterization can determine comparability between CGDP formulations, these in vitro tests cannot predict results in vivo (Anderson and Hauck, 1990).

To satisfy regulatory criteria's, drug developers need complete proof of in vivo characteristics and actions of a formulation to validate therapeutic equivalence to an RLD. Integrated approaches like IVIVC—in which bioassays are used alongside existing tests—have proven successful in identifying not only a single property of formulation, but the overall behavior of a multifactorial formulation in a physiological system (Anderson and Hauck, 1990; Chow and Liu, 2008; Suarez-Sharp et al., 2016).

8.5   Bioavailability and bioequivalence regulatory perspective

The regulatory authorities require the manufacturer applicants to provide the BA and BE information as a part of the drug assessment. BE is the term used for the pharmaceutical alternative, and test drug (T) can be claimed pharmaceutically equivalent to the reference drug (R) (Committee for Proprietary Medicinal Products, 2001). Preapproval BE studies of the drug product are required to be conducted for clinical use. Both BA and BE studies are important (Gad, 2008). However, Abbreviated New Drug Application (NDA) approval for generic drug products does not require long clinical assessment as the brand name of the drug product does in the case of NDA approval. It requires chemistry, manufacturing, control, testing, labeling, PK, and BA evaluations but not animal studies and safety/efficacy clinical trials (Chow, 2014). The BE study of a test drug assumed that it is bioequivalent under fundamental BE assumption (Chow, 2014). From ADME (absorption, distribution, metabolism and excretion) process, the concentration of the drug can be determined for the assessment. Mainly, two major PK parameters, C_{max} and AUC, are used for the assessment. However, the overall exposure for single-dose BE study can be determined by $AUC_{0-\infty}$ (area under the plasma concentration–time curve from time zero to infinity), and for multiple-dose study, $AUC_{0-\tau}$ [area under the plasma concentration–time curve during a dosage interval (τ)] can be used (Qiu et al., 2016). Moreover, in vitro tests are considered for determining or anticipating BA and establishing BE assessment. General methods of BE assessment for oral dosage forms are presented in Table 8.3.

8.5.1   Design of bioequivalence studies

It is crucial to design the BE study in such a way to distinguish the effect of the test drug product from the other effects (Committee for Proprietary Medicinal Products, 2001). It is required for either single or multidose BE studies; unless another design, such as parallel design, is scientifically valid (Table 8.4).

TABLE 8.3 General methods of bioequivalence assessment for oral dosage forms.

In vitro	Dissolution	Immediate/extended-release oral dosage forms
	BCS	Highly permeable, highly soluble drugs
In vivo	Pharmacokinetic	C_{max}, AUC, $AUC_{0-\tau}$, and $AUC_{0-\infty}$
	Pharmacodynamic	When drug levels cannot be measured or irrelevant

TABLE 8.4 Represent the parallel group and crossover design (Zhu, 2014).

Types of design	
Parallel group design	**Crossover group design**
• Subjects are divided into treatment groups • Number of treatment groups equals number of treatments to be studied • Each treatment group receives only one treatment randomly	• Subjects receives two or more treatments at different time periods randomly • Number of time periods equals number of treatments to be studied • Number of subjects participating should be a multiple of number of time periods
Comparison	
• More number of participating subjects needed to produce efficient results • Preferred design to study drugs and/or metabolites with long half-life • Missing of some results will not affect the efficiency of design • No fear of subject dropout • No sequence or period effect • Variability in subject is not significant and not included in error variability	• Fewer number of participating subjects needed to produce efficient results • Time-consuming • Missing of some results will affect the efficiency of design • Fear of subject dropout due to long washout periods • Management of treatment order reduces the effect of sequence or period effect • Variability in subject is significant and included in error variability

An appropriate washout period should separate the treatment periods to ensure that at the beginning of the second period all the subjects have blood concentrations of the drug that are below the specified lower limit for that drug that any residual therapeutic effects have worn off Achieving this concentration level usually takes at least 5 elimination half-lives, and this has been demonstrated for drug products which are released immediately. On the other hand, controlled release drug products may require the least 8.5 elimination half-lives (Chow, 2014). In practice, the study design of a randomized two-period (2×2), two-sequence crossover design (RT/TR) is often considered for the comparison of two products. While a scientifically sound, alternative, well-established design, such as a parallel design, can be used for very long half-life products, examining the products of high variability in PK should use replicate designs (CHMP, 2010). A replicate 2×4 (TRTR, RTRT) crossover design is commonly considered under certain circumstances (Chow et al., 2011).

8.5.1.1 Sample size

It is essential to including an appropriate count of subjects in BE studies to provide sufficient power to enable the correct conclusions concerning BE. Several parameters should be considered in calculating the sample size for the trial; BE margins within the range (0.8, 1.25), significance level $P = .05$ one side, Type I error (i.e., the error that shows the equivalence despite the inequivalent formulations), Type II error (i.e., the error that does not show the equivalence despite the equivalence formulations), expected ratio of BE metrics, the coefficient of variation of intraindividuals and total sample size (N) (Ring et al., 2019). The margins and significance level are fixed by regulations/guidelines, while the other parameters can be from previous trials, pilot experiments, or published data (Hauschke et al., 2007). However, there are analytical and clinical imposed standards that may influence the determination of sample size (CHMP, 2010) and other regulatory agencies require the number of evaluable subjects in the trial to be not less than 12 (Qiu et al., 2016).

8.5.1.2 Subjects

The appropriate selection of subjects for BE trials minimizes the variability and permits identification of the differences among the drug products (Hauschke et al., 2007). Therefore official guidelines have been updated to state that subjects should be at least 18 years of age, representative of the general population, and able to give informed consent. The preferred BMI for subjects is between 18.5 and 30 kg/m^2 (Elangovan, 2019). The trial should be carried out in healthy volunteers (when the product can be administrated safely). Healthy subjects are preferred over patients; this can be justified because the use of healthier subjects is considered adequate to allow patient populations to extrapolate the results (Verbeeck and Musuamba, 2012; Elangovan, 2019).

8.5.1.3 Single-dose versus multiple-dose studies

For single-dose studies, AUC can be measured from time 0 to the last sampling time point; this can provide an approximation of the comparison products (Hauschke et al., 2007). FDA guidelines recommend this approach to assess BA and BE since it is incredibly sensitive than multiple-dose studies (Food and Drug Administration, 2014). However, multiple-dose studies should be considered in addition of single-dose studies for some instances, such as where there are dose- and time-dependent PK, or in the case of MR products (Hauschke et al., 2007). In addition, three consecutive trough concentrations (C_{min}) on 3 consecutive days should be calculated to ensure that the steady state is attained in subjects (Food and Drug Administration, 2014; Shargel and Yu, 2016).

8.5.1.4 Role of ± 20 and role of 80/125

In BE studies, test and reference drug products can be compared for their PK metrics after single administration; both parameters (AUC and C_{max}) should be assumed to be log-normally distributed (Ring et al., 2019). The criteria for assessing the average BE, in terms of applying AUC and C_{max} as primary parameters, are the role of ± 20 and role of 80/125 (Chow, 2014); this means that confidence intervals for interpreting BE data are required and should be used for accomplishing BE. Those standards are as follows (Gad, 2008):

- The test product's average BA should be within $\pm 20\%$ of the reference product.
- The confidence interval of 90% of the relative mean AUC of the test product should be within the 80%−125% BE range.
- The relative mean measured C_{max} of the test in comparison with the reference product should be within BE limits of 80%−125%.

- The relative mean measured C_{min} of the test in comparison with the reference product should be within BE limits of 80%−125%. T/R = 80/100 = 80%; R/T = 100/80 = 125%).

8.5.2 Drug interchangeability

As mentioned previously, a branded drug product may be substituted by a generic drug product where the assessment of BE has been approved. However, regulatory authorities have not indicated that two generic product variants of the same branded drug product can be used interchangeably, even if both generic variants show BE to the same branded drug product (Chow et al., 2011).

This concept can be categorized either as "drug prescribability" or "drug switchability." Drug prescribability refers to the physician's options in prescribing either an appropriate branded medication or generic alternative. On the other hand, drug switchability refers to the switching from one branded or generic dosage form to an alternative dosage form within the same subject whose dosage has been titrated to a steady state within an effective and tolerable level (Chen and Chow, 2017). Therefore in those patients who take a prescription for some time, drug switchability is important than prescribability (Chow, 2014). However, drug interchangeability can be determined after studies demonstrating BE between the generic drug product and the brand-name drug. While assessing drug interchangeability, several criteria must be addressed such as average BE, individual BE, variability due to subject−drug interaction, and criteria established on reversing the test and reference drug (Chen and Chow, 2017). The following study illustrates the evaluation of BE and drug interchangeability for a brand name and a generic fixed-dose combination tablet of antihepatitis C drugs sofosbuvir and ledipasvir (400/90 mg) (Bendas et al., 2018). This study shows the effective application of reference scaled average BE for the two formulations, which considered as highly variable drugs amongst Egyptian volunteers from the intrasubject variability, more than 30%. Both products considered clinically irrelevant with a wider difference in C_{max} according to EMA guidelines. This indicates that the replicate crossover design study can be carried out, and larger sample size should be considered (Bendas et al., 2018). The results show no serious adverse effect, similar PK, and more than 85% of the drug dissolves within 15 minutes as the in vitro dissolution data are revealed. Those highly variable products fell within the BE limits of 80%−125%; however, reference scaled average BE approach could be considered for widening the acceptance criteria.

8.5.3 Practical issues

BE studies allow two drug products (test and reference) to be claimed as bioequivalent; thus, if they contain matching quantities of active ingredients in identical dosage forms, it is presumed to be therapeutically equivalent and therefore could be interchanged. This concept is known as the fundamental BE assumption (Chow, 2014). This assumption has been challenged by the brand-name drug innovators using scientific/clinical justifications to criticize the generic drug products. The arguments were whether statistical BE in terms of drug absorption would certainly imply therapeutic equivalence and, conversely, whether therapeutic equivalence equated with BE (Chow et al., 2011). Exposure-response evaluation, or additional data analysis, for example, partial AUC could be required to evaluate the differences in the BA assessment.

In light of this controversy, the FDA introduced a "one-size-fits-all" criterion for BE assessment (Chow, 2014). This does not, however, take into account drugs with a narrow therapeutic index and intrasubject variability. These issues influence both safety and effectiveness of generic drug products, leading to variations in requirements stipulated in the guidelines.

Thus for drugs with a narrow therapeutic index, the ratio of geometric means of the required PK parameters should be reduced to 90.00%−111.11% (Elangovan, 2019). When determining BE of products containing drugs that show high variability, with large fluctuations within individuals, the sample size should be increased, and a large number of volunteers are required. There is international consensus that a drug will be considered highly variable if the intrasubject variation exceeds 30%. As a result, the use of scaled average BE is recommended in such cases (Chow et al., 2011). The replicate study design approach is recommended for BE assessment using wider acceptance range of C_{max}, but not AUC, for 90% CI, with clinical justification (Verbeeck and Musuamba, 2012).

MR drug products are characterized by an initial rapid increase in plasma drug concentration and therefore causes a fast therapeutic onset accompanied by sustained plasma concentrations and activity after drug administration. In such cases, in addition to the regular PK parameters (AUC and C_{max}), the recommendations may include a partial AUC metric or several partial AUC metrics to ensure therapeutic equivalence for early onset and continuous activities. An example of a MR/ER drug is Ritalin LA (methylphenidate HCL), which has been approved by the FDA. This formulation shows a bimodal plasma concentration–time profile, resulting in two separate peaks approximately 4 hours apart following once-daily, oral administration of a MR/ER formulation. It shows a lower second peak concentration (C_{max2}), a higher interpeak minimum concentration (C_{minip}), and less peak and trough fluctuations, as compared to standard Ritalin tablets administered in two doses 4 hours apart (Drugs@FDA, 2020; Wang et al., 2017).

8.6 In vitro–in vivo correlation

IVIVC is a predictable mathematical model describing the relationship between the in vitro characteristic and the corresponding in vivo response (Jayaprakasam et al., 2003). Research on IVIVCs between in vitro dissolution profiles and in vivo dissolution performance and BA was incorporated into drug product development programs to reduce human testing (Emami, 2006; Hanif et al., 2018; Cheng et al., 2020). IVIVCs play a vital role in drug product development and formulation improvement. The IVIVC correlation assay is based on the ability to evolve an in vitro dissolution assay, which can predict the drug product's in vivo effectiveness (Emami, 2006; Hanif et al., 2018). An approved IVIVC may serve as a guide for the development of drug products, processes, and specifications. It can also offer a reliable tool for product quality control and an alternative to in vivo studies to help product and process improvements. In particular, developing the IVIVC model needs special attention in developing new candidates for lipophilic drugs with low solubility in water. IVIVC can be used to reduce the required number of studies in humans in developing new drugs and formulations (Hanif et al., 2018).

In recent years, the pharmaceutical industry, academia, and regulatory have shown increasing interest in the IVIVC. Edwards (1951) and Nelson (1957) were pioneers in introducing the IVIVC by relating the rate of aspirin and theophylline dissolution in vitro with their appearance in vivo after oral administration Several published studies on the development and validation of IVIVC for different drugs and dosage forms exist (Emami, 2006; Zolnik and Burgess, 2008; Chaturvedula and Banga, 2007). So, the main goal of IVIVC is to act as an alternative to human biological equivalence (BE) studies and provide support for claims for biowaivers.

8.6.1 Advantages of IVIVC

- It serves as an alternative to in vivo BA testing.
- It supports biowaivers for BE testing.
- It verifies the dissolution process and sets criteria for dissolution.
- It is an important instrument for drug product research and development.
- The IVIVC model promotes the development and evaluation dosage forms for immediate and sustained release.
- It assists with quality control of some scope and postapproval changes.

8.6.2 Drawbacks associated with IVIVC

The PK of an oral dosage form is a critical factor affecting its effectiveness. Physiological and anatomical conditions are the crucial factors for IVIVC performance. In addition, the absorption of a drug in vivo is also affected by the nutritional content of the gastrointestinal tract, the presence/absence of disease, gastrointestinal enzyme reaction, peristaltic movements, and concurrently administered medications—thus raising objections to the accuracy of the predictive ability of the IVIVC (Sjögren et al., 2014; Mumtaz et al., 2018).

8.6.3 Criteria and classification of IVIVC

IVIVCs are normally demanded when the drug solubility and in vitro dissolution are the rate-determining steps in the drugs in vivo absorption and circulation. Therefore when a drug has high permeability, and the rate-limiting step is in vitro dissolution/release, it is highly expected that a fruitful IVIVC could be established (Food and Drug Administration, 2000, 2018). There are five correlation levels defined in the FDA IVIVC specification (Jayaprakasam et al., 2003). The concept of degree of correlation depends on the capacity of the correlation to represent the complete profile of the plasma drug levels over time as a result of management a particular dose form (Chen et al., 2005). The correlation levels are as follows.

8.6.3.1   Level A

This type of correlation is commonly linear and corresponds to a point-to-point association that connects the in vitro dissolution and in vivo input rate; nonlinear links are acceptable. The correlation at the A level is the most helpful and organizationally very useful. FDA guidelines indicate that two or more formulas should be identified at different launch rates (10% different) by IVIVC. Only one formula combination may be considered if the in vitro degradation is independent of the conditions for the solubility test (Emami, 2006; Hanif et al., 2018). According to the instructions, one should estimate the entire in vivo from laboratory data (Fig. 8.2).

8.6.3.2   Level B

This level is based on statistical moment analysis. The mean dissolution time (MDT) in the laboratory is compared with either the average residence time or the average dissolving time in vivo (Fig. 8.2). Although both laboratory and biological data are used for this kind of correlation, level B correlation is not a point-to-point one. Moreover, the binding of level B does not represent uniquely the curve of the actual plasma level in vivo, which is less useful for regulatory purposes (Emami, 2006; Mumtaz et al., 2018). Level B IVIVC (Uppoor, 2001) includes:

- MDT in vitro to MDT in vivo
- MDT in vivo to mean residence time
- In vitro dissolution rate constant (K_d) to k_a.

8.6.3.3   Level C

A level C correlation involves evaluating the correlation between PK parameters (e.g., C_{max}, AUC, K) and in vitro drug dissolution rate at one point. This kind of correlation can be useful in the early stage of drug development (Emami, 2006; Mumtaz et al., 2018) (Fig. 8.2).

8.6.3.4   Multiple level C

Multilevel C-level correlation with one or more interest-bearing PK parameters (C_{max}, AUC, T_{max}, CL, etc.) is associated with the volume of dissolved drug at various time points. If there can be multiple C-level correlations, the correlation at the A level is most probable. This level can be as functional as level A (Emami, 2006; Mumtaz et al., 2018).

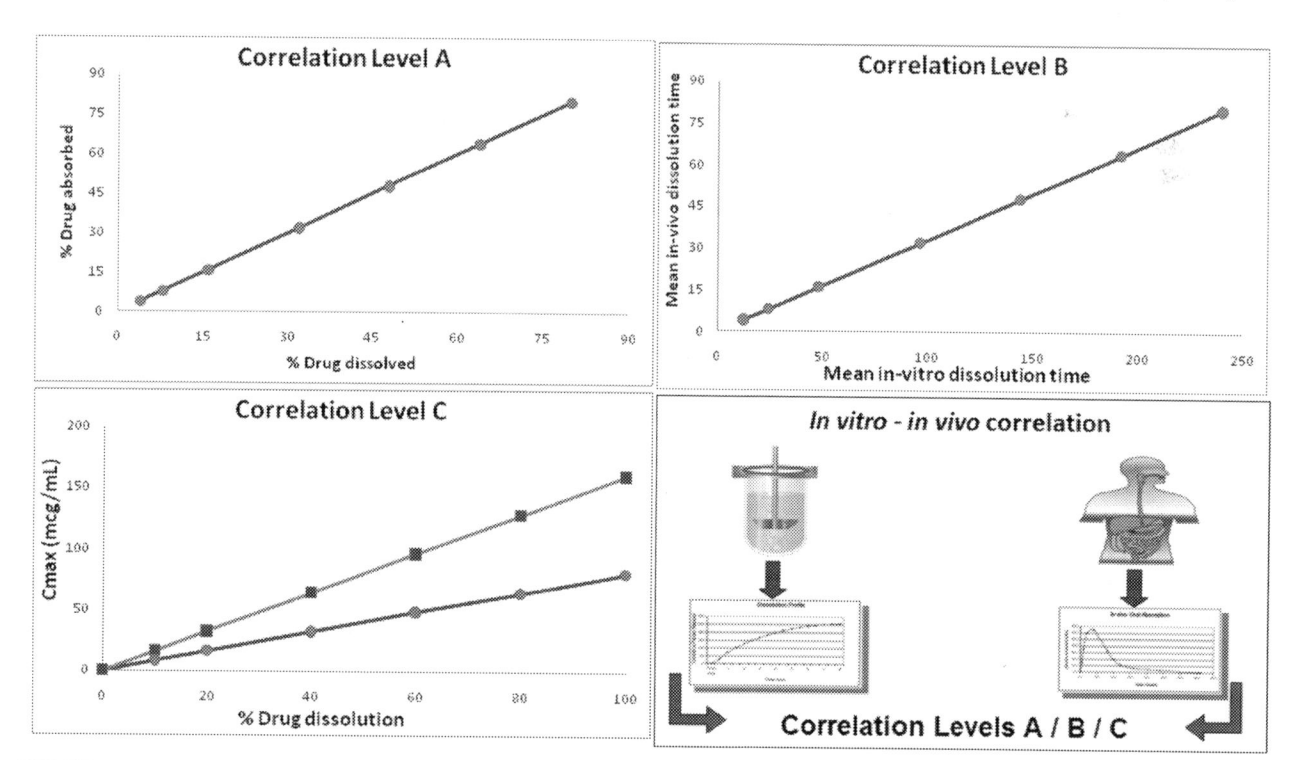

FIGURE 8.2   Different levels of in vitro—in vivo correlation (IVIVC) and pictorial view of IVIVC model.

8.6.3.5 Level D

The D-level correlation is a qualitative analysis and thus not appropriate for regulatory approvals. This is not used as an official tool, but acts as an aid in developing a formulation or procedure (Food and Drug Administration, 1997, 1999; Food and Drug Administration/Center for Drug Evaluation and Research, 1997).

If in vitro dissolution is the rate-limiting step in the drug's absorption process into the systemic circulation, it successfully establishes an IVIVC to employ this dissolution test as a replacement for BE, the IVIVC must be predictive of the product's in vivo performance as shown in Fig. 8.2.

8.6.4 Biowaivers

IVIVC may allow prediction of in vivo BA (Qiu et al., 2016). This can be used to grant biowaiver releases and define specific dissolution criteria that carry the clinical implications to a surrogate. Ideally, one can predict the drug product's performance from its in vitro dissolution. Therefore waivers for in vivo BA studies can be asserted with an extrapolative IVIVC for change of manufacturing location, equipment, manufacturing process, or compositional changes. The biowaiver deals with modifications in medicinal products that range from minor changes that only have a marginal impact on product performance to major changes, where the IVIVC is insufficient to support the changes (Verbeeck and Musuamba, 2012). Tables 8.5 and 8.6 show IVIVC and BCS classifications for IR and ER formulations.

According to the BCS, in vivo BA and BE studies need not to be conducted under the following conditions, so biowaivers for these products are authorized (Food and Drug Administration, 2003; CMPH, 2010).

8.6.4.1 Other criteria for biowaiver and considerations

Ideally, one would like to be able to estimate in vivo performance from dissolution. Consequently, as explained above, biowaivers may be given with a predictive IVIVC for changes in the manufacturing process and location, changes in equipment, and changes in the composition of formulation (Qiu et al., 2016).

8.6.4.2 Biowaiver for excipients

For BCS I drugs, excipients alter the BA due to altered drug absorption. In general, FDA-approved excipients are not expected to affect the BA of drugs with high solubility and high permeability that are formulated as IR formulations. In

TABLE 8.5 IVIVC expectation and BCS classification for IR formulations.

Classifications	Status of IVIVC	Dissolution data and IVIVC prediction status
BCS I	(1) Not expected if dissolution rate is higher than gastric emptying rate.(2) Expected if dissolution rate is slower than gastric emptying rate.	Exists
BCS II	Not required.	Exists
BCS III	No IVIVC with dissolution.	Not exists
BCS IV	Not required.	Not exists

TABLE 8.6 IVIVC and BCS classifications for ER formulations.

BCS class	Solubility modification	Permeability modifications	IVIVC
BCS IA	High and site independent	High and site independent	IVIVC Level A is expected
BCS IB	High and site independent	Dependent on site and narrow absorption window	IVIVC Level C is expected
BCS IIA	Low and site independent	High and site independent	IVIVC Level A is expected
BCS IIB	Low and site independent	Dependent on site and narrow absorption window	Poor IVIVC or no IVIVC
BCS VA (acidic)	Variable	Variable	Poor IVIVC or no IVIVC
BCS VB (basic)	Variable	Variable	IVIVC Level A is expected

order to support a biowaiver claim, the amount of excipients in the IR product must correspond to the intended function. When new, or widely used, excipients are included in the greater quantities than those corresponding to the intended use in the solid IR, the agency may request additional information documenting a lack of effect on the drug's BA. Excess amounts of some excipients like surfactants and sweeteners might produce an obstacle in BA. For BCS III Class drug products, unlike BCS I Class, biological rejection is scientifically justified, provided that the medicinal product tested contains the very same excipients as that of the reference product. This seems to be attributed to the concern that excipients may have a greater effect on the absorption of poorly permeable drugs than highly permeable ones. The test product composition needs to be qualitatively comparable and quantitatively equivalent to that of the composition of the reference product.

8.6.4.2.1 Biowaiver for fixed-dose combinations

1. Where all active ingredients belong to category BCS I Class: BCS-based biological preparations apply to fixed-dose formulation products if all drugs in the group belong to category BCS I, given that the PK interaction between such components is negligible, and excipients achieve the requirements set out in the guidelines. In the event of a PK reaction, the excipients must adhere to the considerations set forth in the explicit guidelines. Otherwise, BE testing is required in vivo and no biowaivers are permitted.
2. Where all components of the formulations belongs to BCS III class or a blend of BCS I class and BCS III class: BCS classification-based biowaiver criteria are applied to IR formulation products, provided the excipients meet the requirements set out in the specific guidelines. If the criteria are not met as per the guidelines, an in vivo BE test is necessary.

8.6.4.3 Exceptions in biowaiver (BCS-based biowaivers are not applicable for the following)

8.6.4.3.1 Narrow therapeutic index drugs

This guide does not apply to medicinal products with a narrow therapeutic range because of the significant relationship between BA and clinical outcome. Sponsors are supposed to consult the opposite review department to ascertain whether the drug falls into the category of narrow therapeutic index.

8.6.4.3.2 Products designed to be absorbed in the oral cavity

A dosage form containing a drug component of BCS class that is meant for absorption in the oral cavity is not appropriate for biowaiver request. Similarly, an orally disintegrating tablet should be considered for a biowaiver based on BCS, only to be considered if absorption is ruled out through the oral cavity.

The following example illustrates an attempt to apply for a biowaiver based on in vitro dissolution assay; this was undertaken for sildenafil citrate, which has been classified in different ways by several authors in the published literature. The data collected for the solubility and intestinal permeability show that it has been classified as BCS class I or BCS class III. However, according to the WHO, FDA, and EMEA guidelines, this drug can be classified as BCS class II depending on different experimental solubility conditions. Miranda et al. (2018) attempted to characterize this drug product according to the BCS. Their study showed sildenafil citrate to have a low solubility at high pH (pH = 6.8) under the prescribed condition of the guidelines (pH range of 1.2–6.8 at 37°C in aqueous media); they showed the drug to have high permeability and oral absorption to be complete using the closed loop in situ perfusion method. Therefore this product cannot undergo a BCS-based biowaiver procedure, and BE studies in human are required to demonstrate therapeutic interchangeability.

8.7 Scale-up and postapproval changes

8.7.1 EMA guidelines

Postapproval changes are a vital part in the life cycle of a pharmaceutical formulation. These changes should be clearly scrutinized and should follow the proper regulatory guidelines. All kinds of postapproval changes should be informed to the agency by variation filing. The Variations Regulation governs the procedure for the variation of marketing authorizations and is concerned with the evaluation of changes (Official Journal of the European Union, 2013).

A variation or postapproval change to a prequalified profile means an alteration in the content of its records. The competent authority must approve those modifications. In Europe, the EMA (European Medicines Agency) has published a regulatory framework called "variation filing." The variations are categorized as four types, namely Type IA, Type-IA$_{IN}$, IB and Type II. The procedure for the submission of minor variations are mentioned in Type IA, for moderate changes in Type IB and for major variations in Type II. The major changes need a letter of approval, while minor variations can be included after reporting to the agency.

8.7.1.1 Different types of variations or postapproval changes

Type IA and Type-IA$_{IN}$ relate to minor variations, which include variations having a minor effect on efficiency, security, and quality of the product. On the other hand, moderate, as well as major, variations might have an unfavorable effect on the safety, efficacy, and quality of the approved pharmaceutical product and are classified as Type IB and Type II. Different types of variations are summarized in Fig. 8.3.

8.7.1.1.1 Type-IA (minor variation)

This type of minor variation does not need any previous approval. These types of changes have negligible effect on the superiority, safety, and efficacy of the pharmaceutical ("Do and Tell" procedure).

8.7.1.1.2 Type-IA$_{IN}$ (minor variation)

This requires immediate notification after implementation.

8.7.1.1.3 Type IB (moderate variation)

Until implementation, these types of minor variation must be notified.

8.7.1.1.4 Type II (major variation)

This type of changes needs approval from the concerned authority before execution (European Medicines Agency, 2013; Mallu and Anand, 2014; Kumar et al., 2015).

8.7.1.1.5 Extensions

This type of application will be evaluated by same procedure as that used for granting the initial marketing authorization. Some types of deviation to the formulation should be considered as basically a change in the conditions of the sanction and hence cannot be executed as a variation procedure. These kinds of change must be considered as a new marketing approval as "extension filing." The details are given in EC No. 1234/2008 as Annex I. The major variations

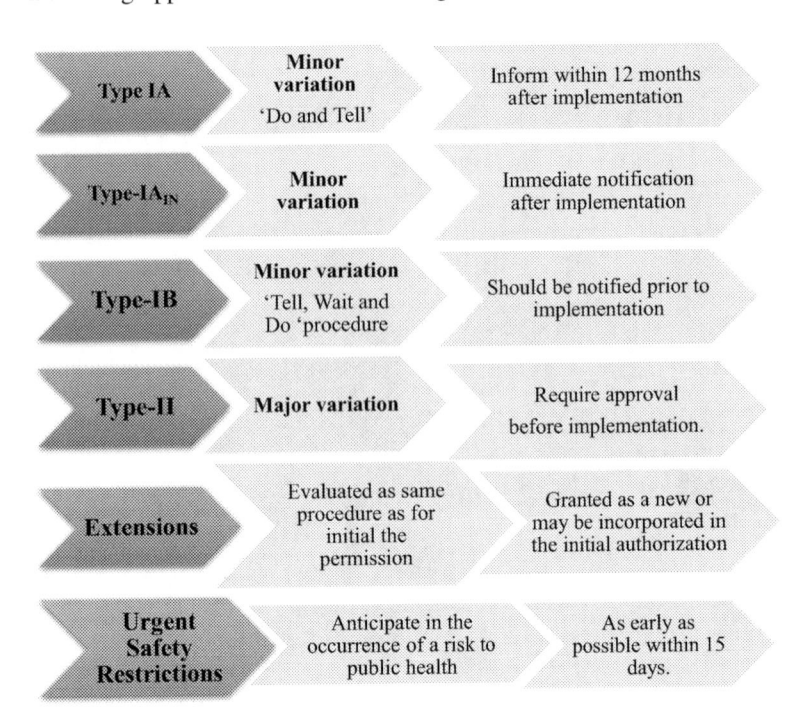

FIGURE 8.3 Different types of variations.

demanding an "extension application" includes change to the active ingredient, change in its quantity, dosage form as well as route of administration (Official Journal of the European Union, 2013).

8.7.1.1.6   Urgent safety restrictions

This regulation anticipates the occurrence of a risk to public health. The application with the urgent safety restrictions should be submitted by the owner as early as possible within 15 days.

8.7.1.2   Submission of the variation notification

In Directive 2001/83/EC the variation guidelines are given in detail for medicines of human use and animal use to assist the holder to plan, set the file and submit for postapproval changes (Mallu and Anand, 2014; Kumar et al., 2015). Table 8.5 summarizes the definition of various variation classifications and the detailed description along with examples can be seen in annexure I to IV.

The variation filing should be submitted by the marketing authorization holder using the Centralized Procedure, Mutual Recognition Procedure or as national procedures (Procedures and Fees for Prequalification | WHO— Prequalification of Medicines Programme, 2020). Submission procedure of various modifications and outcomes are detailed in the form of flowcharts. Fig. 8.4 shows three types of *Type IA Variation* application procedure. Fig. 8.5 shows three types of *Type IB Variation* application procedure.

Fig. 8.6 shows three types of *Type II Variation* application procedure. These flowcharts represent the step-by-step procedures for the application of variation filing under Central procedure, mutual recognition procedure as well as national procedure for different types of variations (EUR-Lex, 2003; European Medicines Agency, 2013; Type-IA variations: questions and answers | European Medicines Agency; Type-IB variations: questions and answers | European

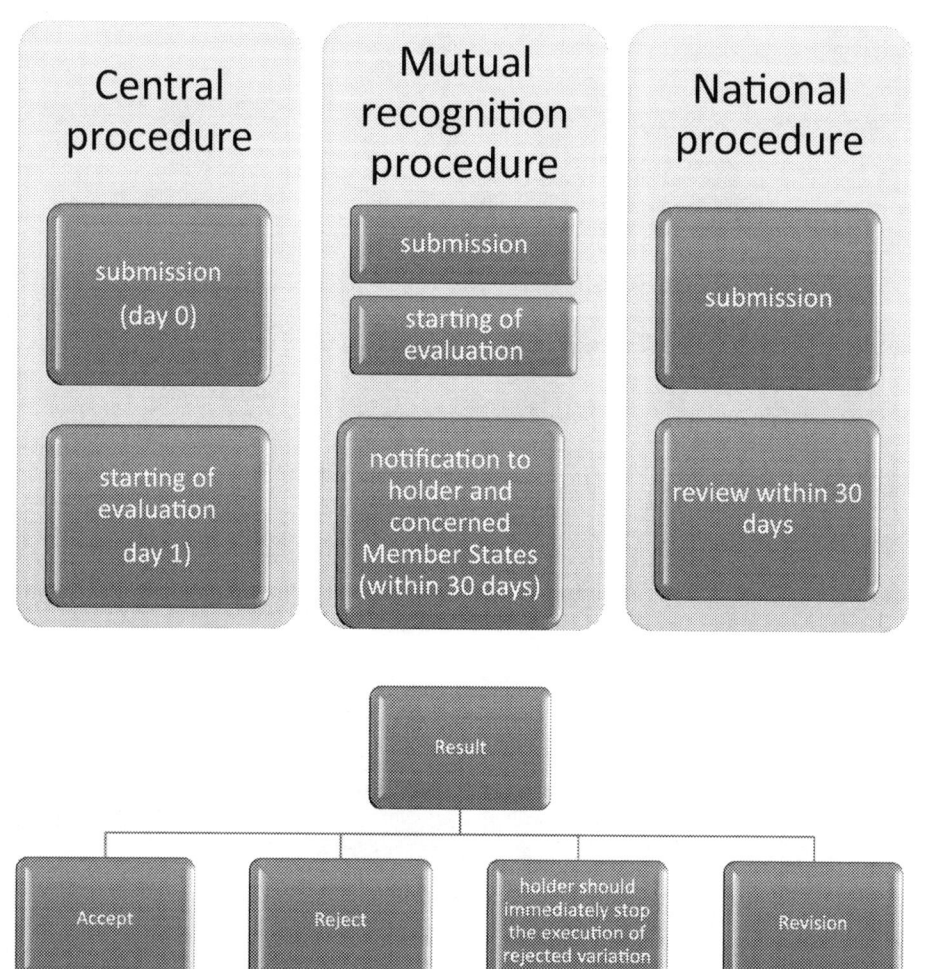

FIGURE 8.4   *Type IA Variation* application procedure.

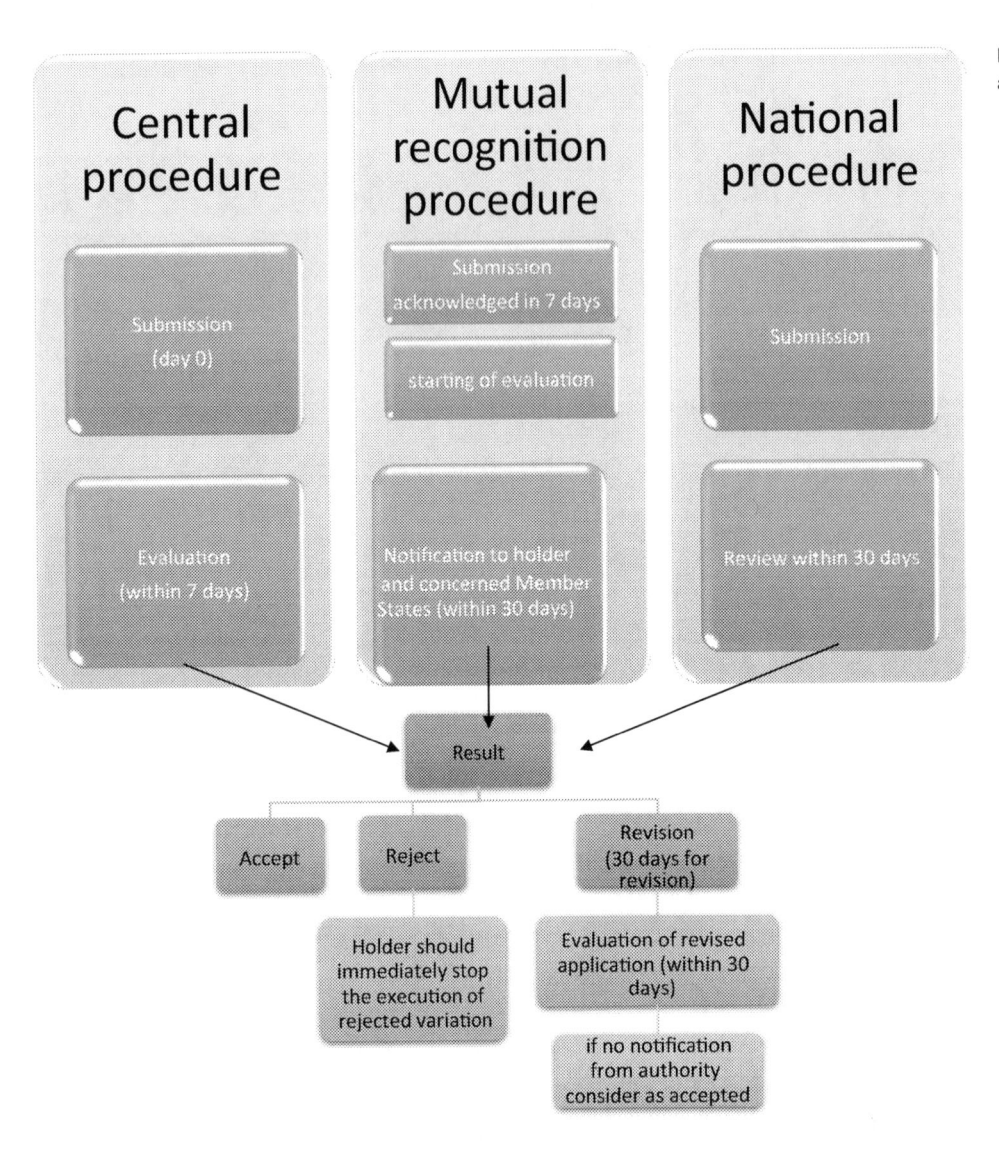

FIGURE 8.5 *Type IB Variation* application procedure.

Medicines Agency; Official Journal of the European Union, 2013; Q&A: Type II variations | European Medicines Agency; Kumar et al., 2015; EudraLex—Volume 6).

8.7.2 US FDA guidelines

The US FDA also requires certain guidelines to be followed if the manufacturer wants to change the composition or components, manufacturing site, production scale-up/down, or the process during the postapproval period. These guidelines are named the SUPAC (SUPAC-IR: Food and Drug Administration, 1995a,b).

The guidance specifies the change levels; this covers chemistry, manufacturing, and controls tests for each change level, as well as in vitro dissolution tests and/or in vivo BE tests for each change level, along with the necessary documentation information that might support the changes.

8.7.2.1 Components and composition changes

It details only the changes in excipients in the formulation.

- *Level 1*: No measurable effect on quality and performance.
- *Level 2*: Major impact on product quality and performance.
- *Level 3*: Which significantly the performance and quality of the product.

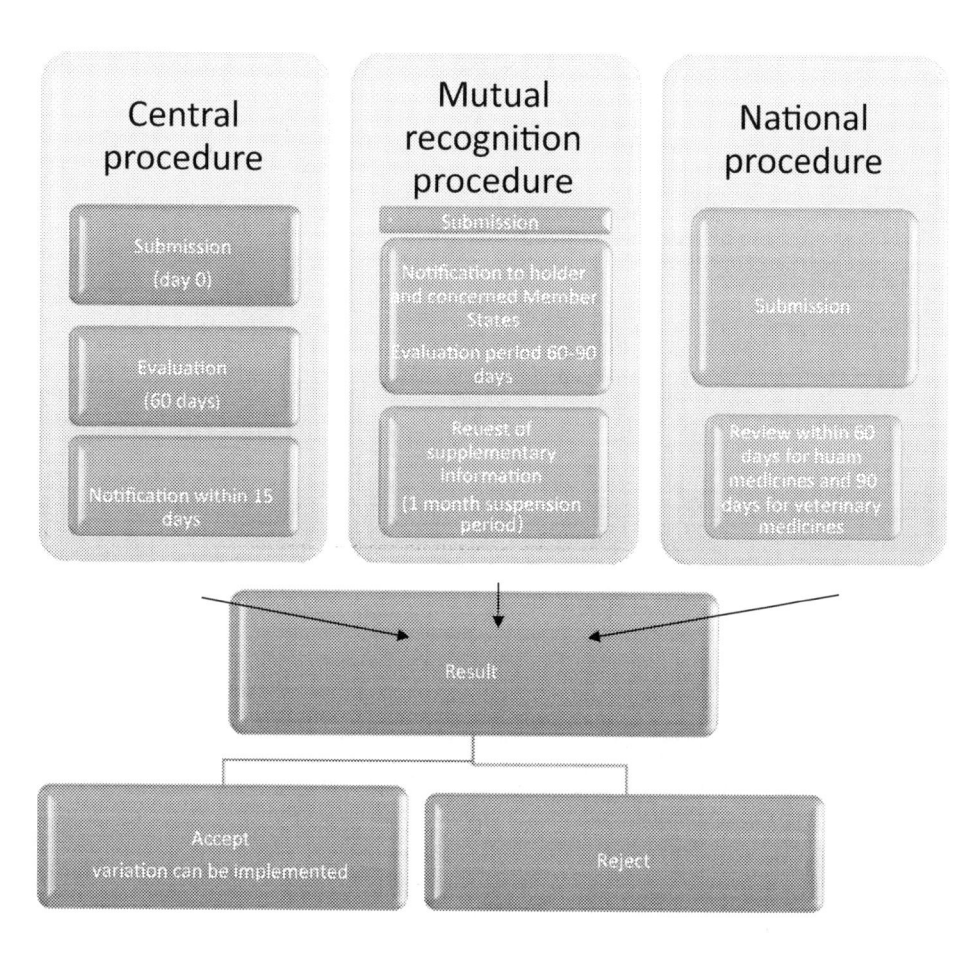

FIGURE 8.6 *Type II Variation* application procedure.

The details of test documentation required for different types components and composition changes as per US FDA is given in Table 8.7.

8.7.2.2 Site changes

This covers changes in the company owned manufacturing site as well as facilities for contract manufacturing. Scale-up changes, process and/or equipment modifications, and changes in ingredients or their quantities will not come under site change. The new locations for the manufacturing must be approved by an acceptable CGMP (current good manufacturing practice) inspection. The details of test documentation required for different types of site changes is given in Table 8.8.

8.7.2.3 Scale-up/scale-down

Change in the amount of a batch postapproval require additional data. There should be proper validation and inspection of changes by a qualified personnel. Table 8.9 describes the details of test documentation required for changes in batch size.

Level 1

Batch size changes up to 10 times of the pilot batch with same equipment with all other parameters same, including SOP (standard operating procedures), and in full compliance with CGMP.

Level 2

A batch size change more than 10 times of the size of a pilot/biobatch with same equipment with all other parameters being the same, including SOP, and in full compliance with CGMP.

8.7.2.4 Manufacturing changes

Changes in the manufacturing equipment as well as the manufacturing process come under this.

TABLE 8.7 Details of test documentation required for components and composition changes as per US FDA.

	Chemistry documentation	Dissolution documentation	In vivo bioequivalence documentation	Filing documentation
Level 1	Application/compendial release requirements and stability testing.	None beyond application/compendia requirements are needed.	Not required	Annual report with long-term stability data.
Level 2	Application/compendial release requirements and batch records. Stability testing: 3 months accelerated stability study data for one batch and long-term stability data of one batch as supplement.	*Case A*: For drugs with high solubility and permeability, 85% should be dissolved within 15 min in dissolution medium Failure to meet this should go for case B. *Case B*: for drugs having low permeability and a high solubility, a dissolution profile should be performed in the compendia medium at 15, 30, 45, 60, and 120 min or until an asymptote is reached. *Case C*: For drugs with high permeability and low solubility, dissolution (in water, 0.1 N HCl, USP buffer at pH 4.5, 6.5, and 7.5) should be performed at different times with an interval, including 15, 30, 45, 60, and 120 min until 90% of drug is dissolved.	None: If the condition does not meet the above descriptions, refer the case to Level 3 changes	Annual report and prior approval supplement.
Level 3	Three months accelerated stability study data up to three batches and long-term stability data of one batch.	Dissolution profile is required as per case B.	Full BE study is needed; this may be waived if a satisfactory IVIVC can be verified.	All information together with accelerated stability test data (prior approval supplement) and long-term stability study data (annual report).

TABLE 8.8 Details of test documentation required for site changes as per US FDA.

	Chemistry documentation	Dissolution documentation	In vivo bioequivalence documentation	Filing documentation
Level 1	Not needed other than application/compendial release requirements	Not needed other than application/compendial release requirements	Not needed	To be filed in annual report
Level 2	Place of new site as well as updated batch records are required. Nothing other than application or compendial release requirements. Data of long-term stability for one batch in annual report	Not needed other than application or compendial release requirements	Not needed	Changes which are affected as supplement and annual report
Level 3	Updated batch records with new site location are required	Case B: A multipoint dissolution profile should be performed in the compendia medium at 15, 30, 45, 60, and 120 min, or until an asymptote is reached The dissolution profile of the product in the new site should be similar to that of old site	Documentation not needed	Changes which are affected as supplement and long-term stability data are required

1. Equipment
   a. *Level 1*: It includes machinery or equipment changes with a different capacity with same design and operating principles.
   b. *Level 2*: It involves changes in the equipments to another with a dissimilar design and different operating theories.
2. Process
   a. *Level 1*: Changes like change in mixing times and operating speeds.
   b. *Level 2*: Includes process changes.

TABLE 8.9 Details of test documentation required for change in batch size as per US FDA.

	Chemistry documentation	Dissolution documentation	In vivo bioequivalence documentation	Filing documentation
Level 1	Application/compendial release requirements Announcement of changes and surrender of updated batch records	Not needed other than application or compendial release requirements	Not needed	Long-term stability test data are required in annual report
Level 2	Application/official release requirements. All changes should be notified with an updated batch record	Dissolution Documentation as per Case B	Not required	Data of changes which are affected as supplement and long-term stability data in annual report

TABLE 8.10 Details of test documentation required for manufacturing changes as per US FDA.

	Chemistry documentation	Dissolution documentation	In vivo bioequivalence documentation	Filing documentation
	A. Changes in equipment			
Level 1	Application/ official release requirements changes should be notified with an updated batch record.	Nothing other than application/ compendial release requirement	Not needed	Long-term stability test data as annual report
Level 2	Application or official requirements. Changes should be notified with an updated batch records.	Documentation as per Case C dissolution profile	Not needed	Previous approval supplement along with explanation for changes as well as long-term stability data to be filed
	B. Changes in process			
Level 1	Nothing other than application/ compendial release requirements.	Not needed other than application/ compendial release requirements	Not needed	Annual report
Level 2	Application/compendial release requirements. Changes should be notified along with an updated record of the batch. Long-term stability study data of one batch.	As per Case B	Not needed	Data of changes which are affected as supplement and long-term stability data in annual report should be filed
Level 3	Application or official release requirements. Changes should be notified along with updated batch record.	As per Case B	In vivo bioequivalence test can be waived if an appropriate IVIVC is established	Prior approval supplement along with explanation and annual report for long-term stability test data

c. *Level 3*: Change in the type of procedure used in the manufacture of formulation like shifting to direct compression from wet granulation.

Table 8.10 describes the details of test documentation required for manufacturing changes (SUPAC-IR: Food and Drug Administration, 1995a,b; Uppoor, 2014).

8.8 Conclusion

Dissolution test is a powerful in vitro tool for assuring dosage form quality. Its testing is most suited for BCS I and III APIs, based on that they have comparable dissolution characteristics. Thus the in vitro dissolution testing would provide a better and more meaningful relationship with the in vivo performance. Meanwhile, many hurdles will be solved in obtaining a precise and accurate result. Factors such as dissolution test apparatus design, working, dosage form placement and position, sampling position, dissolution medium can influence the dissolution testing's precision and accuracy. An IVIVC is absolutely necessary, without which predicting in vivo response is difficult.

Interestingly, for IR drug products, dissolution testing of BCS I and III drugs would be over-discriminating. In contrast, testing of BCS II and IV by single-point dissolution test might be nondiscriminating. Both these situations lead to a poor prediction of in vivo performance. While BA studies are useful for new dosage forms, BE testing compares the developed product with an innovator product. Thus BE testing involves test and reference. The BA and BE testing depends on the guidelines of the concerned regulatory authorities; these guidelines are regularly updated in light of scientific evidence. IVIVC relates the in vitro results to the in vivo counterparts and can be used for predicting the in vivo response. Thus it can form the basis for a biowaiver.

Further, establishing and validating the dissolution test methodology and specifications is possible using IVIVC. This has application in both scale-up and postapproval changes too. Thus this is in compliance with SUPAC guidelines.

References

Abdou, H.M., 1989. Evolution of dissolution testing, theory of dissolution, theoretical concepts for the release of a drug from dosage forms and factors affecting rate of dissolution. Abdou, H.M. (Ed.), Dissolution Bioavailability & BioequivalenceMack Publishing Company, Easton, PA, pp. 1–105.

Agudelo, M., Vesga, O., 2012. Therapeutic equivalence requires pharmaceutical, pharmacokinetic, and pharmacodynamic identities: true bioequivalence of a generic product of intravenous metronidazole. Antimicrob. Agents Chemother. 56 (5), 2659–2665.

Al Ameri, M.N., Nayuni, N., Anil Kumar, K.G., Perrett, D., Tucker, A., Johnston, A., 2011. The differences between the branded and generic medicines using solid dosage forms: in-vitro dissolution testing. Results Pharm. Sci. 2, 1–8.

Amidon, G.L., Lennernas, H., Shah, V.P., Crison, J.R., 1995. A theoretical basis for a biopharmaceutic drug classification: the correlation of in vitro drug product dissolution and in vivo bioavailability. Pharm. Res. 12 (3), 413–420.

Amidon, G.L., Lennernas, H., Shah, V.P., Crison, J.R., 2014. A theoretical basis for a biopharmaceutic drug classification: the correlation of in vitro drug product dissolution and in vivo bioavailability. Pharm. Res. 12, 413–420. 1995-Backstory of BCS, AAPSJ., 16(5):894–898.

Anand, O., Yu, L.X., Conner, D.P., Davit, B.M., 2011. Dissolution testing for generic drugs: an FDA perspective. AAPS J. 13 (3), 328–335.

Anderson, S., Hauck, W.W., 1990. Consideration of individual bioequivalence. J. Pharmacokin. Biopharm. 18 (3), 259–273.

Anderson, N.H., Bauer, M., Boussac, N., Khan-Malek, R., Munden, P., Sardaro, M., 1998. An evaluation of fit factors and dissolution efficiency for the comparison of in vitro dissolution profiles. J. Pharm. Biomed. Anal. 17, 811–822.

Balasubramaniam, J., Srinatha, A., Pandit, J.K., 2008. Studies on indomethacin intraocular implants using different in vitro release methods. Indian J. Pharm. Sci 70, 216–221.

Baloglu, E., Ay Senyigit, Z., Karavana, S.Y., Vetter, A., Metin, D.Y., Hilmioglu Polat, S., et al., 2011. In vitro evaluation of mucoadhesive vaginal tablets of antifungal drugs prepared with thiolated polymer and development of a new dissolution technique for vaginal formulations. Chem. Pharm. Bull. 59, 952–958.

Bendas, E.R., Rezk, M.R., Badr, K.A., 2018. Drug interchangeability of generic and brand products of fixed dose combination tablets of sofosbuvir and ledipasvir (400/90 mg): employment of reference scaled average bioequivalence study on healthy Egyptian volunteers. Clin. Drug Invest. 38 (5), 439–448.

Benet L.Z., 2013. The role of BCS (biopharmaceutics classification system) and BDDCS (biopharmaceutics drug disposition classification system) in drug development. J. Pharm. Sci. 102 (1), 34–42.

Browne, D., Kieselmann, S., 2010. Low-level drug release-rate testing of ocular implants using USP apparatus 4 dissolution and HPLC end analysis. Dissolution Technol. 17, 12–14.

Cai, B., Söderkvist, K., Engqvist, H., Bredenberg, S., 2012. A new drug release method in early development of transdermal drug delivery systems. Pain Res. Treat. 2012, 953140.

Carmona-Ibáñez, G., Bermejo-Sanz, Md.V., Rius-Alarcó, F., Martin-Villodre, A., 1999. Experimental studies on the influence of surfactants on intestinal absorption of drugs cefadroxil as model drug and sodium taurocholate as natural model surfactant: studies in rat colon and in rat duodenum. Arzneimittelforschung 49, 44–50.

Chaturvedula, A., Banga, A.K., 2007. In vitro—in vivo correlation: transdermal drug delivery systems. In: Chilukuri, D.M., Sunkara, G., Young, D. (Eds.), Pharmaceutical Product Development: In vitro—In vivo Correlation. Informa Healthcare, New York, pp. 153—176.

Chen, M., Chow, S., 2017. Assessing bioequivalence and drug interchangeability. J. Biopharm. Stat. 27 (2), 272—281.

Chen, J.C., Chiu, M.H., Nie, R.L., Cordell, G.A., Qiu, S.X., 2005. Cucurbitacins and cucurbitane glycosides: structures and biological activities. Nat. Product. Rep. 22 (3), 386—399.

Cheng, X., Gao, J., Li, J., et al., 2020. In vitro-in vivo correlation for solid dispersion of a poorly water-soluble drug efonidipine hydrochloride. AAPS PharmSciTech 21, 160.

CHMP, 2010. Committee for Medicinal Products for Human Use (2010), Guideline on the Investigation of Bioequivalence, EMEA, London.

Chow, S., 2014. Bioavailability and bioequivalence in drug development. Wiley Interdiscip. Rev. Comput. Stat. 6 (4), 304—312.

Chow, S., Liu, J., 2008. Design and Analysis of Bioavailability and Bioequivalence Studies. Taylor & Francis Ltd, Hoboken, pp. 451—452.

Chow, S.-C., Shao, J., Wang, H., 2002. Probability lower bounds for USP/NF tests. J. Biopharm. Stat 12, 79—92. Available from: https://doi.org/10.1081/bip-120005781.

Chow, S.C., Endrenyi, L., Chi, E., Yang, L.Y., Tothfalusi, L., 2011. Statistical issues in bioavailability/bioequivalence studies. J. Bioequivalence Bioavailab. S1, 1—8.

Committee for Proprietary Medicinal Products, 2001. Note for Guidance on the Investigation of Bioavailability and Bioequivalence. EMEA, London.

Crawford, L.M., 2004. http://www.fda.gov/oc/speeches/2004/bascrty0707.html.

Currie, G.M., 2018. Pharmacology, part 2: introduction to pharmacokinetics. J. Nucl. Med. Technol. 46 (3), 221—230. Available from: https://doi.org/10.2967/jnmt.117.199638. Epub 2018 May 3. PMID: 29724803.

Costa, P., Sousa Lobo, J.M., 2001. Modeling and comparison of dissolution profiles. Eur. J. Pharm. Sci. 13 (2), 123–133.

Diaz, D.A., Colgan, S.T., Langer, C.S., Bandi, N.T., Likar, M.D., Van Alstine, L., 2016. Dissolution similarity requirements: how similar or dissimilar are the global regulatory expectations? AAPS J. 18 (1), 15—22.

Dietrich, C.G., Geier, A., Oude Elferink, R.P., 2003. ABC of oral bioavailability: transporters as gatekeepers in the gut. Gut 52 (12), 1788—1795.

Doogue, M.P., Polasek, T.M., 2013. The ABCD of clinical pharmacokinetics. Ther. Adv. Drug Saf. 4 (1), 5—7.

Drugs@FDA, 2020. [Online]. Available from: https://www.accessdata.fda.gov/drugsatfda_docs/label/2015/010187s080,018029s049,021284s027lbl.pdf (accessed 02.12.20).

Dumont, M.L., Berry, M.R., Nickerson, B., 2007. Probability of passing dissolution acceptance criteria for an immediate release tablet. J. Pharm. Biomed. Anal. 44, 79—84.

Edwards, L.J., 1951. The dissolution and diffusion of aspirin in aqueous media. Trans. Faraday Soc 47, 1191—1210.

Elangovan, E., 2019. Bioequivalence guidelines requirements for orally administered generics (IR products) in Gulf Cooperation Council Countries, European Union and United States of America. J. Bioequivalence Bioavailab. 11 (387).

Emami, J., 2006. In vitro—in vivo correlation: from theory to applications. J. Pharm. Pharm. Sci. 9, 169—189.

EudraLex - Volume 6 Notice to applicants and regulatory guidelines for medicinal products for veterinary use | Public Health (not dated). Available from: https://ec.europa.eu/health/documents/eudralex/vol-6_en (accessed 26.03.20).

European Medicines Agency, 2013. Transitional provisions for implementation of Commission Regulation (EU) No 712/2012 amending variations regulation (EC) No 1234/2008, 44 (712), p. 626908. Available from https://ec.europa.eu/health/sites/health/files/files/eudralex/vol-1/reg_2012_712/reg_2012_712_en.pdf.

EUR-Lex, 2003. Commission Regulation (EC) No 1084/2003 of 3 June 2003: Concerning the examination of variations to the terms of a marketing authorisation for medicinal products for human use and veterinary medicinal products granted by a competent authority of a Member State (Text with EEA relevance)'. Available from https://eur-lex.europa.eu/legal-content/EN/ALL/?uri = CELEX%3A32003R1084

Food and Drug Administration, 1995a. November Guidance for Industry: Immediate Release Solid Oral Dosage Forms: Scale-Up and Post-Approval Changes. United States Department of Health and Human Services, FDA, Center for Drug Evaluation and Research, Rockville, MD.

Food and Drug Administration, 1995b. Guidance for Industry: SUPAC-IR: Immediate Release Solid Oral Dosage Forms Scale Up and Post Approval Changes: Chemistry Manufacturing and Controls In Vitro Dissolution Testing and In Vivo Bioequivalence Documentation. FDA, Center for Drug Evaluation and Research, Rockville, MD.

Food and Drug Administration, 1997. Guidance for Industry: Modified Release Solid Oral Dosage Forms: Scale-up and Post-Approval Changes. United States Department of Health and Human Services, FDA, Center for Drug Evaluation and Research, Rockville, MD.

Food and Drug Administration, 1999. Draft Guidance for Industry: Waiver of In vivo Bioavailability and Bioequivalence Studies for Immediate Release Solid Oral Dosage Forms Containing Certain Active Moieties/Active Ingredients Based on Biopharmaceutics Classification System.

Food and Drug Administration, 2000. FDA Guidance for Industry: Bioavailability and Bioequivalence Studies for Orally Administered Drug Products—General Considerations. United States Department of Health and Human Services, FDA, Center for Drug Evaluation and Research, Rockville, MD.

Food and Drug Administration, 2003. Guidance for Industry: Guidance on Bioavailability and Bioequivalence Studies for Orally Administered Drug Products—General Considerations. United States Department of Health and Human Services, FDA, Center for Drug Evaluation and Research, Rockville, MD.

Food and Drug Administration, 2014. Center for Drug Evaluation and Research Guidance for Industry: Bioavailability and Bioequivalence Studies Submitted in NDAS or INDS—General Considerations. United States Department of Health and Human Services, FDA, Center for Drug Evaluation and Research, Rockville, MD.

Food and Drug Administration, 2017. Waiver of In vivo Bioavailability and Bioequivalence Studies for Immediate-Release Solid Oral Dosage Forms Based on a Biopharmaceutics Classification System Guidance for Industry United States Department of Health and Human Services Food and Drug Administration Center for Drug Evaluation and Research (CDER).

Food and Drug Administration/Center for Drug Evaluation and Research, 1997. Guidance for Industry: Extended Release Oral Dosage Forms: Development, Evaluation, and Application of In vitro/In vivo Correlations. Food and Drug Administration, Rockville.

Food and Drug Administration, 2018. Dissolution Testing and Acceptance Criteria for Immediate-Release Solid Oral Dosage Form Drug Products Containing High Solubility Drug Substances. United States Department of Health and Human Services, FDA, Center for Drug Evaluation and Research, Rockville, MD.

Frantz, S., 2004. 2003 approvals: a year of innovation and upward trends. Nat. Rev. Drug Discov. 3, 103−105. Available from: https://doi.org/10.1038/nrd1327.

Gad, S.C., 2008. Preclinical Development Handbook—ADME Biopharmaceutical Properties. Wiley, Hoboken, New Jersey.

Givand, T.E., 1980. An evaluation of the dissolution test acceptance sampling plan of USP XX. Pharmacopeial Forum (Mar-Apr), 186−190.

Grant, D.J.W., Higuchi, T., 1990. Solubility Behavior of Organic Compounds. John Wiley & Sons.

Hammouda, Y.E., Kasim, N.A., Nada, A.H., 1993. Formulation and in vitro evaluation of verapamil HCl suppositories. Int. J. Pharm 89, 111−118.

Hanif, M., Shoaib, M.H., Yousuf, R.I., Zafar, F., 2018. Development of in vitro−in vivo correlations for newly optimized nimesulide formulations. PLoS One 13 (8), e0203123.

Hanson, W.A., 1991. Handbook of Dissolution Testing, second (ed.) Aster Publishing Corporation, Eugene, OR.

Hauschke, D., Steinijans, V., Pigeot, I., 2007. Bioequivalence Studies in Drug Development: Methods and Applications. Wiley, Chichester, West Sussex, England.

Hofsäss, M.A., Dressman, J.B., 2019. The discriminatory power of the BCS-based biowaiver: a retrospective with focus on essential medicines. J. Pharm. Sci. 108 (9), 2824−2837.

International Conference on Harmonisation, 2000. Guidance on Q6A specifications: test procedures and acceptance criteria for new drug substances and new drug products: chemical substance. Federal Register 65 (251), 83059−83061.

Iyer, S.S., Barr, W.H., Karnes, H.T., 2006. Profiling in vitro drug release from subcutaneous implants: a review of current status and potential implications on drug product development. Biopharm. Drug Dispos 27, 157−170.

Janicki, S., Sznitowska, M., Zebrowska, W., Gabiga, H., Kupiec, M., 2001. Evaluation of paracetamol suppositories by a pharmacopoeial dissolution test—comments on methodology. Eur. J. Pharm. Biopharm. 52, 249−254.

Jayaprakasam, B., Seeram, N.P., Nair, M.G., 2003. Anticancer and antiinflammatory activities of cucurbitacins from *Cucurbita andreana*. Cancer Lett. 189 (1), 11−16.

Keshavshetti, G., 2015. Design and evaluation of fast dissolving tablets of ergotamine tartarate. Int. J. Curr. Pharm. Res. 7, 101−104.

Khan, K.A., Rhodes, C.T., 1972. Effect of compaction pressure on the dissolution efficiency of some direct compression systems. Pharm. Acta Helv. 47, 594−607.

Klein, S., 2010. The use of biorelevant dissolution media to forecast the in vivo performance of a drug. AAPS J. 12, 397−406.

Kostewicz, E.S., Brauns, U., Becker, R., Dressman, J.B., 2002. Forecasting the oral absorption behavior of poorly soluble weak bases using solubility and dissolution studies in biorelevant media. Pharm. Res. 19, 345−349.

Kumar, P., Yadav, V., Kaushik, D., 2015. Post-approval changes in pharmaceuticals: regulatory perspectives in Europe. Appl. Clin. Res. Clin. Trials Regul. Aff. 2 (2), 60−68. Available from: https://doi.org/10.2174/2213476x02666151013203029.

Lu, J., Ormes, J.D., Lowinger, M., Mann, A.K.P., Xu, W., Patel, S., et al., 2017. Compositional effect of complex biorelevant media on the crystallization kinetics of an active pharmaceutical ingredient. Cryst. Eng. Comm. 19, 4797−4806.

Mallu, U.R., Anand, K., 2014. Variation filing procedure in Europe: a complete review. Available from: https://www.semanticscholar.org/paper/VARIATION-FILING-PROCEDURE-IN-EUROPE%3A-A-COMPLETE-Mallu-Anand/009fc1c862623010ee45e971828310330f874636.

Meredith, P.A., 2009. Potential concerns about generic substitution: bioequivalence versus therapeutic equivalence of different amlodipine salt forms. Curr. Med. Red. Opin. 25 (9), 2179–2189.

Miranda, C., Pérez-Rodríguez, Z., Hernández-Armengol, R., Quiñones-García, Y., Betancourt-Purón, T., Cabrera-Pérez, M.Á., 2018. Biowaiver or bioequivalence: ambiguity in sildenafil citrate BCS classification. AAPS Pharm.Sci.Tech. 19 (4), 1693−1698.

Moore, J.W., Flanner, H.H., 1996. Mathematical comparison of dissolution profiles. Pharm. Technol. 20, 64−75.

Morris, K.R., Fakes, M.G., Thakur, A.B., Newman, A.W., Singh, A.K., Venit, J.J., et al., 1994. An integrated approach to the selection of optimal salt form for a new drug candidate. Int. J. Pharm. 105 (3), 209−217.

Mounica, N.V.N., S. Reddy, V., Anusha, S., Evangeline, L., Nagabhushanam, M.V., Nagarjunareddy, D., et al., 2017. Scale up and post approval changes (SUPAC) guidance for industry: a regulatory note. Int. J. Drug Regul. Aff. 5 (1), 13−19.

Mumtaz, H., Batool, M.A., Syed, A.A., 2018. Significance of in vitro and in vivo correlation in drug delivery system. Res. Pharm. Health Sci. 4 (4), 523−531.

Nelson, E., 1957. Solution rate of theophylline salts and effects from oral administration. J. Am. Pharm. Assoc. 46 (10), 607−614.

Nicolaides, E., Symillides, M., Dressman, J.B., Reppas, C., 2001. Biorelevant dissolution testing to predict the plasma profile of lipophilic drugs after oral administration. Pharm. Res 18, 380−388. Available from: https://doi.org/10.1023/A:1011071401306.

Official Journal of the European Union, 2013. '2013/C 223/01', (C). Available from: https://eur-lex.europa.eu/LexUriServ/LexUriServ.do?uri = OJ:C:2013:223:FULL:EN:PDF.

Palmieri, A., 1981. Suppository dissolution testing: apparatus design and release of aspirin. Drug. Dev. Ind. Pharm. 7, 247−259.

Pillay, V., Fassihi, R., 1998. Evaluation and comparison of dissolution data derived from different modified release dosage forms: an alternative method. J. Control. Release 55, 45—55.

Procedures and Fees for Prequalification | WHO - Prequalification of Medicines Programme, 2020. Available from: https://extranet.who.int/prequal/content/prequalification-procedures-and-fees-0 (accessed 20.06.20).

Q&A: Type II variations | European Medicines Agency, not dated. Available from: https://www.ema.europa.eu/en/veterinary-regulatory/post-authorisation/variations/qa-type-ii-variations (accessed 26.03.20).

Qiu, Y., Chen, Y., Zhang, G.G., Yu, L., Mantri, R.V. (Eds.), 2016. Developing Solid Oral Dosage Forms: Pharmaceutical Theory and Practice. Academic Press.

Rein, M.J., Renouf, M., Cruz-Hernandez, C., Actis-Goretta, L., Thakkar, S.K., da Silva Pinto, M., 2013. Bioavailability of bioactive food compounds: a challenging journey to bioefficacy. Br. J. Clin. Pharmacol. 75 (3), 588—602.

Rescigno, A., 1992. Bioequivalence. Pharm. Res. 9 (7), 925—928.

Rescigno, A., 2000. Area under the curve and bioavailability. Pharmacol. Res. 42 (6), 539—540.

Reyner, E., Lum, B., Jing, J., Kagedal, M., Ware, J.A., Dickmann, L.J., 2020. Intrinsic and extrinsic pharmacokinetic variability of small molecule targeted cancer therapy. Clin. Transl. Sci. 13 (2), 410—418.

Ring, A., Lang, B., Kazaroho, C., Labes, D., Schall, R., Schütz, H., 2019. Sample size determination in bioequivalence studies using statistical assurance. Br. J. Clin. Pharmacol. 85 (10), 2369—2377.

Sathe, P., Tsong, Y.I., Shah, V., 1996. In vitro dissolution profile comparison: statistics and analysis model dependent approach. Pharm. Res. 13 (12), 1799—1803.

Sathe, P., Tsong, Y.I., Shah, V., 1997. In vitro dissolution profile comparison and IVIVR_carbamazepine case. In: Young, D., DeVane, J.G., Butler, J. (Eds.), In vitro-In vivo Correlations. Plenum Press, New York, pp. 31—42.

Sathe, P.M., Raw, A.S., Ouderkirk, L.A., Yu, L.X., Hussain, A.S., 2005. Drug Product Performance, In vitro. Marcel Dekker, Inc.

Scheubel, E., 2010. Predictive In vitro Dissolution Tools: Application During Formulation Development. Pharmacology. Université d'Auvergne, Clermont-Ferrand I, pp. 12—25.

Shah, V.P., Tymes, N.W., Yamamoto, L.A., Skelly, J.P., 1986. In vitro dissolution profile of transdermal nitroglycerin patches using paddle method. Int. J. Pharm. 32, 243—250.

Shah, V., Tsong, Yi, Sathe, P., Liu, J.-P., 1998. In vitro dissolution profile comparison: statistics and analysis of the similarity factor f2. Pharm. Res. 15 (6), 889—896.

Shargel, L., Yu, A.B.C., 2016. Applied Biopharmaceutics and Pharmacokinetics, Seventh ed. McGraw-Hill Medical, New York.

Shirsand, S., Suresh, S., Keshavshetti, G., Swamy, P., Reddy, P.V.P., 2012. Formulation and optimization of mucoadhesive bilayer buccal tablets of atenolol using simplex design method. Int. J. Pharm. Investig. 2, 34—41.

Singh, S.K., Prakash, D., Srinivasan, K.K., 2011. Dissolution testing of formulations: a regulatory, industry and academic perspective. Asian J. Biochem. Pharm. Res. 1 (1), 1—8.

Sjögren, E., Abrahamsson, B., Augustijns, P., Becker, D., Bolger, M.B., Brewster, M., et al., 2014. In vivo methods for drug absorption—comparative physiologies, model selection, correlations with in vitro methods (IVIVC), and applications for formulation/API/excipient characterization including food effects. Eur. J. Pharm. Sci. 57, 99—151.

Stavchansky, S.A., McGinity, J., 1989. Bioavailability and tablet technology. In: Lieberman, H.A., Lachman, L., Schwartz, J.B. (Eds.), Pharmaceutical Dosage Forms: Tablets, Vol. 2. Marcel Dekker, NewYork, pp. 349—553.

Suarez, S.S., Marroum, P.J., Hughes, M., 2016. Biopharmaceutic considerations in drug product design and in vitro drug product performance, Seventhth (ed.) Shargel, L., Yu, A.B.C. (Eds.),Applied Biopharmaceutics and Pharmacokinetics, McGraw-Hill Education, New York, pp. 415—467.

Suarez-Sharp, S., Li, M., Duan, J., Shah, H., Seo, P., 2016. Regulatory experience with in vivo in vitro correlations (IVIVC) in new drug applications. AAPS J. 18 (6), 1379—1390.

Szymańska, E., Winnicka, K., 2013. Comparison of flow-through cell and paddle methods for testing vaginal tablets containing a poorly water-soluble drug. Trop. J. Pharm. Res. 12.

Tsong, Y., Hammerstrom, T., Lin, K., Ong, T.E., 1995. Dissolution test acceptance sampling plans. J. Biopharm. Stat. 5, 171—183. Available from: https://doi.org/10.1080/10543409508835106.

Tsong, Y., Sathe, P., Hammerstrom, T., Shah, V., 1996. Statistical assessment of mean differences between two dissolution data sets. Drug Information Journal 30 (4), 1105—1112.

Tsume, Y., Mudie, D.M., Langguth, P., Amidon, G.E., Amidon, G.L., 2014. The biopharmaceutics classification system: subclasses for in vivo predictive dissolution (IPD) methodology and IVIVC. Eur. J. Pharm. Sci. 57, 152—163.

Type-IA variations: questions and answers | European Medicines Agency, not dated. Available from: https://www.ema.europa.eu/en/human-regulatory/post-authorisation/variations/type-ia-variations-questions-answers (accessed 26.03.20).

Type-IB variations: questions and answers | European Medicines Agency, not dated. Available from: https://www.ema.europa.eu/en/human-regulatory/post-authorisation/variations/type-ib-variations-questions-answers (accessed 26.03.20).

Uppoor, R., 2014. Guidance for industry: CMC postapproval manufacturing changes to be documented in annual reports. Available from: https://www.fda.gov/media/79182/download (accessed 27.03.20).

Uppoor, V.R.S., 2001. Regulatory perspectives on in vitro (dissolution)/in vivo (bioavailability) correlations. J. Control. Release 72 (1—3), 127—132.

US Pharmacopeia/National Formulary, 2002. USP 26-NF 21. Rockville, MD: United States Pharmacopeial Convention Inc.

USP, 2003. The United States Pharmacopoeia XXVI. The United States Pharmacopeial Convention, Inc., Board of Trustees, Webcom Limited, Toronto, Ontario.

USP Chapter 711: Dissolution. In: United States Pharmacopeia 31 (USP 31): National Formulary 26 (NF 26). 2008. p. 267–274. 2010a.

U.S. Food and Drug Administration, 2018. Dissolution Testing and Acceptance Criteria for Immediate-Release Solid Oral Dosage Form Drug Products Containing High Solubility Drug Substances. United States Department of Health and Human Services, FDA, Center for Drug Evaluation and Research, Rockville, MD.

Verbeeck, R.K., Musuamba, F.T., 2012. The revised EMA guideline for the investigation of bioequivalence for immediate release oral formulations with systemic action. J. Pharm. Pharm. Sci. 15 (3), 376.

Vertzoni, M., Pastelli, E., Psachoulias, D., Kalantzi, L., Reppas, C., 2007. Estimation of intragastric solubility of drugs: in what medium? Pharm. Res. 24, 909–917.

Wang, R., Conner, D.P., Li, B.V., 2017. Bioavailability and bioequivalence aspects of oral modified-release drug products. AAPS J. 19 (2), 360–366. 10.1208/s12248-016-0025-9.

Wesch, R., 2011. Absolute and relative bioavailability. Vogel, H.G., Maas, J., Gebauer, A. (Eds.),Drug Discovery and Evaluation: Methods in Clinical PharmacologySpringer, Berlin, Heidelberg.

Yi, L., 2001. Amorphous pharmaceutical solids: preparation, characterization and stabilization. Adv. Drug Delivery Rev. 48 (1), 27–42.

Zhu, S., 2014. In vivo and in vitro bioequivalence testing. J. Bioequivalence Bioavailab. 06 (02), 69–70.

Zolnik, B.S., Burgess, D.J., 2008. In vitro–in vivo correlation on parenteral dosage forms. Biopharmaceutics Applications in Drug Development. Springer, Boston, MA, pp. 336–358.

Chapter 9

Regulatory affairs in clinical trials

Mohammad Ahmed Khan, Sadat Shafi, Syed Sufian Ahmad and Faraha Ahmed

Department of Pharmacology, School of Pharmaceutical Education and Research, Jamia Hamdard, New Delhi, India

9.1 Introduction

Ancient civilizations trusted herbs prescribed by the medical practitioner. The modernization of medical science in the early 20th century and drug-associated medical mishaps led to the advent of concept of drug trial. With the refinement of the process over the years, the practitioner and patients now have substantial trustworthy clinical data. Today, a clinical trial is mandatory to acquire drug approval. Since, every drug is ought to pass through the essential trial process, the demand for the drug trial is high, but the availability is minimal and slow due to the limited setup. This slow clinical trial process also affects the supply of pharmaceutical products globally and increases the burden especially on the regulated markets. Other factors such as the climbing disease prevalence, shortage of essential medicines, the surging metabolic diseases especially in developing countries and limited orphan drug availability also poses important challenges (ICH-GCP, 2016). Infectious and tropical diseases have become more common over the world. In the last two decades, three pandemics (SARS, MERS, and COVID-19) claimed millions of lives. Global warming has increased the induced respiratory and skin disease with soaring incidence worldwide (ICH-GCP, 2016). These issues propel the process of clinical trials and the clinical research market.

Pharmaceutical industry invests billions of dollars into drug discovery and filing for generic drug production. Regulatory agencies like Food and Drug Administration (FDA), Pharmaceutical and Medical Devices Agency (PMDA), and European Medicine Agency (EMA) have now focused on risk-based approaches in clinical trial monitoring to accelerate the trial process. The regulatory market believes that risk-based centralized monitoring will minimize the oversight errors. The risk-based approach of monitoring focuses on risks of critical data of clinical trials. Centralized monitoring ensures the subject safety and study quality. Several studies have also shown that the risk-based centralized monitoring also helps detect data fabrication, subject rights violations, and frauds with ease. The United States (US), Europe, and Japan have also introduced the new process of clinical trial monitoring.

9.2 Regulatory submissions of new drugs

Drug development is a complex and time-consuming process. This process involves comprehensive cooperation between external and internal stakeholders. Cross-functional departments within a pharmaceutical establishment, starting from research and development (R&D) to marketing, supply chain and sales, must collaborate together to transform drug compounds from original development to storage cabinets. Organizations are obliged to validate the efficacy and safety of their products for human use before making them available to the patients. Because of this, it is essential that regulatory affairs (RA) departments collaborates closely with healthcare administration on the dossiers which are part of regulatory submissions (RS) (Joubert Shayna, 2018).

RS is a set of documents submitted to the health authority by a drug manufacturer as proof of compliance. RS start with preclinical research, which is many years earlier than investigational drug is approved for human use and continue for the complete product life cycle. "Investigational New Drug Applications (INDs)" and "New Drug Applications (NDAs)" represent the two major types of RS required to receive and retain drug approval. The initial IND is a RS that is a mandatory requirement for a pharmaceutical company to scientifically advance to clinical testing. In addition to manufacturing and administrative information, these submissions contain exhaustive and broad range of nonclinical data of multidisciplinary nature which can even surpass 10,000 pages. The initial NDA permits a pharmaceutical

Regulatory Affairs in the Pharmaceutical Industry. DOI: https://doi.org/10.1016/B978-0-12-822211-9.00006-X
© 2022 Elsevier Inc. All rights reserved.

company to manufacture, distribute, market and sell its product. The completion and approval of the NDA permits commercialization of clinically validated drugs. The IND and NDA collectively establish that drug development in itself is a complex process requiring interconnectedness of multidisciplinary groups and competence of experienced RA professionals. Timely submission of IND enables a faster clinical investigation of potentially life-saving drugs, resulting in the earlier availability of efficacy and safety information, critical for an NDA. Finally, effective NDA submission allows a clinically approved drug to reach market sooner (Joubert Shayna, 2018).

9.2.1 Role of regulatory professionals in regulatory submissions

Individuals involved in preparing, designing, and submitting a theoretically complex set of RS are recognized as RA professionals. Throughout the drug development process, these professionals are ultimately responsible for IND and NDA maintenance, and are important for regulating the clinical approval of drugs. RA professionals develop cross-functional collaborations and regular communications with R&D, nonclinical, clinical, medical, and marketing departments on a regular basis to develop an integrated regulatory dossier. RA professionals have the responsibility to remain up-to-date with new regulatory developments and regularly familiarize themselves with current regulations and guidelines related to the company's area of operations. Given the multifaceted role of these professionals in pharmaceutical company, a RA specialist must possess the following skills:

9.2.1.1 Strong communicators

As the core contacts between government and industry, RA professionals play a crucial role in defining the reputation of their company. Excellent oral and written communication are thus regarded as foundational skills for regulatory work. To involve the internal departments more efficiently during the planning of RS, RA professionals need to specifically express the intent of the submission by describing the applicable laws, regulations, and guidelines. The provision of straightforward and clear regulatory guidance and development of enforceable regulatory compliance plan enhances the integrity of the regulatory affairs department within the company.

9.2.1.2 Expert organizers

RA professional should have the capacity to coordinate with stakeholder, gather information, prepare reports, and submit the same in accordance with regulatory requirements, while at the same time keeping track with ever-evolving national and international regulations.

9.2.1.3 Cross-culturally sensitive

The regulatory affairs has a significant international dimension especially from the clinical trial perspective; for example, Phase III studies require participation from around the world. Pharmaceutical companies must follow the guidelines of local regulatory authority of any particular country where they plan to carry out testing or sell their products. Local health agencies have different standards, policies, regulations, schedules, and evaluation system all across the world. Pharmaceutical companies frequently hire local regulatory consultants for deconstructing the country's regulatory setup. Therefore, it is very important for RA specialists to stay culturally aware and interact efficiently at the global level.

9.3 Clinical trial regulation in regulated markets: the United States, Japan and Europe

In 1938, the Food, Drug, and Cosmetic Act (FDCA) was the pioneer to make clinical trials mandatory for the introduction of any new drug. Today, China and India are promising pharmaceutical markets, but the United States stands as a leading player in the pharmaceutical drug development industry. The United States claims around 51% of the global market share, and it is projected to grow from $5.65 billion (2020) to $8.08 billion (2025) (Market Report Analysis, 2020). This huge market size also poses challenges; for example, approval process takes a long period in the United States than any contemporary market. Nevertheless, the drug approval laws of the United States are considered stringent. The FDA in the United States holds the responsibility to protect public health and manage clinical trials. Organizations willing to conduct clinical trial under FDA regulation are required to fulfill its good clinical practice (GCP) guidelines to procure drug approval.

Any new drug approval in the United States market is accomplished after submitting the written approval for clinical trials for an IND and NDA. There is a lengthy list of processes to follow to obtain IND and NDA. Similarly, the

Office of Generic Drugs (OGDs) certifies the safety, efficacy, and quality of generic drugs and approves Abbreviated New Drug Application (ANDA) through a regulatory process (CMIC, 2018). FDA has recently introduced the several innovative methods for the clinical trial monitoring: The sponsor conducts on-site monitoring at the clinical investigation site to ensure the data integrity. In centralized monitoring, sponsor carries out monitoring remotely, and FDA also recommends this process. Around 30% of clinical trial studies sponsored by the companies situated in the United States are being conducted outside the States, especially in developing countries due to the saturation of in-house facilities.

Japan is an expanded pharmaceutical market following the United States and the Europe (Fig. 9.1). Since, the past decade, the demand for pharmaceutical products has soared swiftly in Japan, due to the perpetual rise in the number of old population. Other compelling circumstances (environment and infectious diseases) have also invoked Japan to improve its pharma sector. Previously, the "Ethical Guidelines for Medical and Health Research Involving Human Subjects" was less stringent. Before the commencement of new regulatory laws, the clinical trials in Japan held regulated under the investigator-initiated registration-directed trial (IIRDT) under the PMD. However, several incidences of clinical misconduct, like the Valsartan incident, invoked the demand for stricter clinical trial regulation. Since then, Japan has renewed its clinical trial segment, adopted new clinical trial regulation act enacted in 2018. Also, the intervention of government also improved resource availability such as funding clinical trials, flexible regulatory guidelines, removal of obstacles like brokers, and bureaucrats, prioritized highly required unmet drug trials, acknowledging the significance of orphan drug development, financing health insurance, eliminating the complexities in NDA and ANDA approvals. In early 2000, the average time spend on new drug approval in Japan happened about 2−3 years, more than any other country. Today, the time has been slashed to a few months, only less than the United States and Europe (average 2−3 years) (CMIC, 2018). Japan's drug regulatory agency PMDA, Japanese Good Clinical Practice (J-GCP), and the government of Japan unitedly brought various reforms in clinical studies. The clinical study qualities of Japan are synchronized with universal standards, and trials are now being conducted as per the standards of International Council on Harmonization (ICH)-GCP (CMIC, 2018).

The European Union (EU) has also amended their clinical trial regulations (CTRs); recently EMA has announced the Clinical Trials Information System (CTIS) to establish a more affirmative atmosphere for the clinical trial operations in Europe by 2020. The EMA trial regulation (introduced in 2014) guarantees the quality standards of patient safety and clinical trial data transparency (Official Journal of EU, 2014). Before the introduction of EU-CTR, EU was following the EU Clinical Trials Directive (EUCTD), implemented in 2001. Despite the affirmative objective, EUCTD missed to achieve its objective of harmonizing the clinical trial in EU countries. Interpretation of EUCTD working procedure varied across all member states, eventually that led to a delay in clinical trial and increased the cost of the whole process in multicenter trials. EUCTD caused a decline in clinical trials across European member countries by 25%. EU has introduced a universal database for each clinical trial conducted in European countries, which will be live by 2021 (TranspariMED and Health Action International, 2019). Strict timelines were set for the approval of new drug applications. To prioritize transparency in clinical trial data, the EMA made the mandatory publication of all clinical studies,

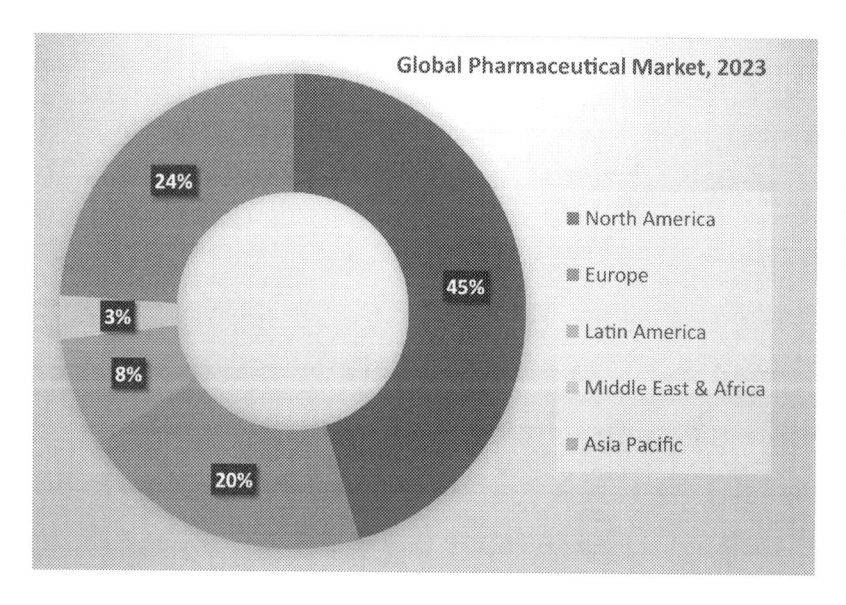

FIGURE 9.1 Geographical distribution of pharmaceutical market share, 2023 projections (Verma, 2019). *From Verma, A., 2019. Global pharmaceuticals market forecast: drivers, value chain analysis & trends. Market Research Reports® Inc., Market Research Report. Available from: https://www.marketresearchreports.com/blog/2019/01/31/global-pharmaceuticals-market-forecast-drivers-value-chain-analysis-trends (accessed 09.03.21.).*

regardless of results (TranspariMED and Health Action International, 2019). Moreover, introduction of new CTR has simplified the application submission procedure for the new drug trial. Sponsors have been enabled to submit the single application to the concerned authority at EU portal. The CTR encourages the safety reporting. Moreover, reporting of clinical trial is also simplified. Now, only one report will be required to be submitted even if more than one investigational product are being used in the single clinical trial.

The global clinical trial market size has increased by 44.3 billion in 2020 (Market Report Analysis, 2020). Many countries have collaborated in the growth of globalization of clinical trials (Market Report Analysis, 2020). The contribution of India further propels the growth, and it is anticipated to expand at even faster rate in the future. Therefore, India is adopting new technology, improving R&D, promoting GCP, and revising regulatory requirements. Regardless of the nature of the research (Regulatory Clinical Trials or IISs), knowing the requirements of clinical trials is necessary and vital for GCP (Gogtay et al., 2017).

The public health mission in India assured by the national regulatory authority is Central Drugs Standards Control Organization (CDSCO, 2019), counterpart of USFDA (Gogtay et al., 2017). Drug and Cosmetics Act in India first came into existence in 1940 to regulate the export, import, manufacture, and distribution of drugs in the country (Imran et al., 2013). The schedule Y along with 122A, 122B, 122D, 122DA, 122DAC, and 122E are the important statutes regulating the clinical trials in the country. In 2006, Indian Council of Medical Research (ICMR) has released the "Ethical guideline for biomedical research on human participant" which was further revised in 2017 (Gogtay et al., 2017). This document covers general and special guidance for children or herbal research and ensures that every clinical trial should be in compliance with GCP; Ethics Committee and Drug Controller General of India (DCGI) approved the protocol. The scope of clinical research in India is enormous: 17% of world population lives here, having 20% of global disease burden of both communicable and noncommunicable diseases. Today, India is strengthening its clinical trials regulations and amending its regulatory laws to alleviate disease burden (Market Report Analysis, 2020).

The regulatory requirement for clinical trial mechanism is varied globally due to the economics, population, and company requirements. For example, the United States follows the guidelines of the FDA, Japan prioritizes PMDA, India adheres to CDSCO, and European countries abide by EMA instructions. But, the EU, the United States, and Japan have decided to initiate the harmonization of their regulations through International Conference on Harmonization (ICH)-GCP guidelines (ICH-GCP, 2016).

9.4 Regulatory collaboration: developing new reliance model

As the requirement of medicine is growing every day and consequently the number of clinical trials are increasing, there are numerous drugs undergoing trials. Moreover, the same investigational drug is under the supervision of different jurisdictions and regulatory agencies (Condran, 2017). As a consequence, it becomes difficult for an innovator to maintain the variability in case the regulations have significant variation. In a complicated working environment, coordination between the regulatory agencies is necessary. EMA has already shown the best example of effective coordination between different European countries (Condran, 2017). There is a need for the system that can work in effective coordination. Several initiatives have been taken by the major regulatory agencies to maintain quality and consistency. The new collaborative 2020 plan proposed by EMA is directed towards the cooperation between the regulatory agencies to work in reliance (ICDRA, 2016). It will also be helpful is removing the duplication in work. In the reliance plan, the details related to the study will be shared by the regulatory agency through an assessment or inspection report. However, this new reliance initiative is still limited to a few regulatory agencies. Additionally, various formal and informal collaborative forums have also come into existence (Table 9.1).

EMA took the initiative of sharing the assessment and inspection reports with other regulatory agencies. Therefore, it has started a pilot project under the name International Generic Drug Regulators Program (IGDRP) in July 2014 (Condran, 2017). Currently, Canada Health Authority, Swiss Medic, Regulatory Agency of Taiwan [Taiwan Food and Drug Administration (TFDA)], and the Therapeutic Goods Administration (TGA) of Australia are working along with EMA (ICDRA, 2016).

9.5 Harmonization of clinical trial regulation: principles of ICH-GCP

Since 1996, ICH-GCP guidelines have defined the safety, efficacy, and quality of scientific standards in clinical studies. Approximately 14% of the global population from around 16 developed, and developing nations have adopted ICH-GCP (ICH-GCP, 2016). The remaining countries use ICH-GCP guidelines as a reference. ICH-GCP is an international quality standard for *designing, conducting, recording, and reporting* clinical trial data. It

TABLE 9.1 Formal and informal forums developed by the collaboration of countries.

S. no.	Forum	Description
1	Pan American Network for Drug Regulatory Harmonization (PANDRH)	The regulatory agencies of 55 American countries form a forum for harmonized clinical trial practice.
2	Caribbean Community (CARICOM)	Caribbean countries develop a regional regulatory agency.
3	East-African Community (EAC)	The regulatory agencies of African region (Zambia, Zimbabwe, Botswana, and Namibia) collaborated under the ZaZiBoNa project, to work toward harmonization.
4	Association of Southeast Asian Nations (ASEAN)	The initiative taken by Asian nation towards harmonization.
5	Gulf Central Committee for Drug Registration (GCC-DR)	Similarly, Gulf countries also started considering the importance of drug trial harmonization and form a committed committee for that.
6	African Vaccine Regulatory Forum (AVAREF)	It is an initiative started by different regulatory agencies in collaboration with WHO to address public health emergencies. It is a joint review committee.

reduces the complexity from drug approval process. ICH-GCP monitors the data integrity, adverse event reporting, and protection of rights of human trial volunteers globally (ICH-GCP, 2016). The significance of ICH-GCP in the clinical trials is given below:

- ICH guidelines improve the awareness towards the ethical aspects of the trial.
- Improvement in the quality of data, concepts of trials, and methods is now possible.
- Cost-effectiveness of trial checks the aftermarket pricing of the product.
- Clinical trial with ICH-GCP regulations is less prone to frauds and fabrication.
- Prioritization of risk-benefit analysis for every subject.
- ICH-GCP also ensures that the trial product should be manufactured under good manufacturing practices (GMPs).
- Faster access of the drug at lower cost due to avoidance of duplicity of data.

As per the latest revised guidelines in 2007, the core principle of ICH-GCP confirms that confidentiality, integrity, and rights of human subjects are protected. It mentions that:

- Clinical trials should be consistent with GCP and ethical principles enshrined in it which are applicable for specific regulatory requirement(s).
- Prior to the clinical study, a risk-benefit analysis for individual subjects should be done. Only if the risks are lower than the anticipated benefits, then only the trials will proceed further.
- Safety and interest of human volunteers participating in the trial should be kept on top, over the interest of anything.
- All the information (clinical or nonclinical) about the investigational product should be mentioned in the protocol.
- A clinical trial should be scientifically justified in the protocol.
- A trial protocol should be approved by the responsible authorities [institutional review board (IRB)/independent ethics committee (IEC)], and a clinical trial should be conducted as per the protocol.
- Each participant involved in performing the clinical trial should be properly educated and well trained to carry out their responsibilities.
- Qualified personnel have the responsibility of medical treatment given to the subject.
- Before the trial, each participant must fill the consent form.
- All information on the clinical trials should be responsibly recorded, patiently handled, and accurately documented.

Besides that, the confidentiality of every subject should be respected, and GMP should be followed as per the protocol. Qualifications of the investigators should be evaluated by the IRB/IEC. However, there are many challenges to the existing ICH guidelines. Major limiting factor in executing the ICH guideline is a large capacity difference and expertise in between developed and developing nations. There is a lack of key infrastructure in regional harmonization initiatives. So, interregional cooperation is required. Due to the differences in local regulatory norms, there is a variation in results despite the utilization of same data. Following milestones serve as important goals for better implementation and harmonious working of ICH-GCP:

- To develop a suitable framework for better and common understanding of ICH for all.
- Universal acceptance of ICH-GCP guidelines for the better execution of clinical trial of same standards.
- Spread of economic benefits and rationale of harmonization application in countries that are away from the participation in ICH-GCP.
- Evaluation of impact of ethical and cultural impacts on harmonization.

9.6 Clinical trial protocol

A document prepared according to the ICH-GCP guidelines and updated with the development of every clinical trial is known as clinical trial protocol (CTP). CTP signifies the essential document to secure the integrity of trial. It is prepared before the commencement of a clinical trial. It contains significant objectives such as rationale, study design, treatment regimen, safety and efficacy, adverse events, ethics, and quality assurance, related to the trials (GCP-CTP, 2016; ICH-GCP, 2016).

9.6.1 Significance of clinical trial protocol

CTP promises the safety of trial participant. Before the trial, sponsor thoroughly reviews the trial protocol. The respective authority from investigator to the number of departments like nursing, pharmacy, and IRB reviews and approves the protocol. The ethical committee approves the safety, clarity, accuracy, and completeness of the trial for each volunteer (GCP-CTP, 2016).

To enhance the integrity, and content of protocol, a team of experts drafted a "Standard Protocol Items: Recommendations for Interventional Trials (SPIRIT) statement" in the year 2013. The statement provides guidance related to the clinical trial in form of checklist of recommendations. SPIRIT guideline provides accurate protocol and encourages the publishing of protocol for public to get benefit for patient, and users. Table 9.2 summarizes the content of CTP.

TABLE 9.2 Content of the clinical trial protocol.

S. no.	Title	Information
1	General Information	This section should include the name of the protocol, information related to the sponsor, and trial center, etc.
2	Background Information	Description of the investigational product should be mentioned, such as name, indication, potential risk, and any relevant study regarding the product.
3	Trial Objectives and Purpose	• Reasons and objectives for conducting the clinical trial.
4	Trial Design	Description of trial such as blinding, randomization, and comparator drug information are included in this section.
5	Treatment	Treatment-related information, such as treatment regimen, route of administration, inclusion, and exclusion criteria are included in this section.
6	Assessment of Safety & Efficacy	• Proper documentation of safety and efficacy parameters is required in this section
7	Statistics	The number of subjects enrolled, significance level, and termination criteria are documented in statistics section.
8	Ethics	Clear description of ethical considerations applied to the trial.
9	Financing and Insurance	Source of funding and insurance of clinical trial.
10	Publication Policy	Describes the policies of publication.

9.7   Ethical aspect of clinical trial

9.7.1   Informed consent form

Informed consent (IC) represents one of the most crucial elements of research ethics, which justifies the "principle of autonomy" in clinical research (Gupta, 2013). IC should be obtained from every participating subject or legally acceptable representative (LAR) (if applicable), prior to the trial. IC process must give ample opportunity to the participating subject to consider his/her participation in the clinical trial (Gupta, 2013). The research subjects should be informed about the research protocol, research purpose, their role in the study, the fact that their participation in the study is voluntary, predictable discomforts or risks they may face, compensation (if any), for participation or injury/treatment and reasons which may lead to termination from the trial (Roberts, 2002). Additionally, the language of the IC form should be nontechnical, nonexculpatory, and understandable to the participant or LAR. The process of obtaining informed consent must occur in environment that underplay the possibility of coercion or undue influence.

9.7.1.1   Components of informed consent

An IC is composed of three main components including voluntarism, disclosure of information, and decision-making capacity (Meisel et al., 1977). For IC to be ethically valid, these components should be essentially implemented while IC is sought expressly from a participating subject (Gupta, 2013).

- *Voluntarism*: It is described as the capacity of a person to independently judge what is best, subject to his or her own values and circumstances (Roberts, 2002). The concept and significance of voluntarism in the area of clinical studies have not been fully practiced, despite being documented in numerous biomedical codes and regulations (Zaubler et al., 1996; Sugarman et al., 1999). For a legitimate and ethically valid IC, the decision of the subject must be a voluntary one. Various factors have been reported to affect individual's voluntarism such as emotional and intellectual ability to take critical decisions, disease-related considerations such as the impact of incurable or dreaded illnesses or severe mental disorders, cultural, and religious beliefs and values, relation with caregiver including care and economic burden, and coercion to participate in research (Ganzini et al., 1994; Dresser, 1996; Roberts, 2002; Geppert and Abbott, 2007). Owing to these obstacles to voluntarism, additional measures are intended to secure and strengthen the autonomous decision-making of these subjects, to whatever extent possible (Levine, 1981; Dresser, 1996; Brody and Jaworski, 1998; Roberts, 2002). Moreover, vulnerable subjects are more prone to compromised voluntarism. Therefore, special precautions are to be taken in case of such subjects. Lastly, the mode of consent should be approved by IRB/IEC (Aday, 2002; Gupta, 2013).
- *Information disclosure*: Information disclosure, one of the basic components of legitimate IC, refers to providing necessary information to the research subject to make an informed decision (Manti and Licari, 2018). For an ethically valid IC, information disclosed to a subject must include, but not confined to, purpose and nature of the study, health condition for which the study is proposed, experimental research procedures, study interventions or treatment, potential benefits and risks related to nature of illness and its complications if not treated, availability of alternative treatment and its benefits, research participation, voluntary nature and right to withdraw from trial at any stage, and other relevant information enabling participants to make an informed decision (Shrestha, 2012; Ryan Kenneth, 2014; ICH-GCP, 2016). Specific information to the participating subject must be provided if the research projects involve illiterate populations, children, adults who cannot give informed consent due to disability, etc. The purpose of information disclosure is to aid subjects in making logical, informed, and rational choice whether to participate/not participate in the study.

    The process of information disclosure seems fairly simple; but, in actual situation, it possesses difficulties, such as to what extent or how much information on different research aspects should be provided, and the presentation of research information in a biased manner with the intention of obtaining the consent in accordance with the wish of researcher. Therefore, researchers should ensure that the research information strikes a balance between ethics and anticipated benefits and risks of the research intervention under investigation (Abdussalam, 2003).
- *Decision-making capacity*: The capacity of a research subject to logically understand and analyze the information which is essential to make an informed decision, concerning study participation (Barstow et al., 2018). An individual's decisional capacity relies on a combination of voluntarism, cognitive ability, and emotional state. Decisional capacity consists of four basic components: (1) understanding the information being disclosed, (2) assessment of the information, (3) rational processing, and (4) evidencing or communicating the decision (Appelbaum and Grisso, 1988; Fisher et al., 2006; VHA, 2009). It is important to underline here that the subjects must realize that the purpose is research and not the treatment which may have positive or negative consequences (Gupta, 2013).

9.7.1.2 Obtaining informed consent

The process of obtaining IC has always been one of the most sensitive and complex ethical challenges in clinical research (Manti and Licari, 2018). Commonly, it is believed that researchers provide the potential participants all the necessary study-related information and sought their consent for participation in research; however, this is not so always. While performing clinical research study, various situations or circumstances can be encountered, based on patient's capabilities and abilities that require special intervention while obtaining consent. Various guidelines and regulations have been developed on how and in what way the IC should be obtained from study participants in those particular circumstances (Gupta, 2013). For example, conditions such as medical emergency complicates the situation making it difficult to obtain informed consent from a practically incompetent subject (such as patients with serious psychological disabilities, minors, etc.). Incompetent subjects can only be allowed to participate in research after obtaining consent from their LAR, preferably guardians. In such cases, IC protocol should be customized to adapt to the understanding and abilities of participating subject. It is recommended that the subject should personally give written consent along with the consent of his LAR to get enrolled in the study. Various measures can be employed, such as using easily understandable language, disclosure of information in small sequential units, and providing sufficient time and facility to raise questions related to research and sought justifications. The information about LAR's consent and/or objections, if any, should be taken into consideration and communicated to the participant (National Bioethics Advisory Commission, 2002). An unbiased witness shall be provided for subjects/LAR in case he/she is not able to read the information given in the IC. The participating subject shall also be given the choice to consult or want investigator to discuss the study with his/her personal physician.

9.7.1.2.1 Procedure

While encouraging participants to engage in clinical study and securing consent, prospective subjects are provided an IC document (ICD), consisting of patient information sheet (PIS), containing all vital information related to the clinical trial in a simplified and easy to understand language. It also contains format for IC format (ICF). Clinical researchers have recognized that it is imperative to have an interactive session with the participants (ICH-GCP, 2016). The investigator will analyze the information and will allow the participants to understand and evaluate the same to reach a decision on participation in the study. The investigator has to satisfactorily answer individual queries in simple language which can be understood by a nontechnical person. After understanding the study information assessing the effects of participation, if the subject agrees to participate then he is asked to sign the ICF stating his voluntary and informed decision.

9.7.2 Exceptions to informed consent

While IC is a mandatory process, there are certain exceptions to this general rule, wherein the disclosure of information can be reduced in part or whole. This includes research in emergency situations or therapeutic privilege, etc. However, it is important to note that the subject still has the right to decline research participation.

Medical Emergencies: Medical emergencies are situations that needs immediate medical attention during a patient's life-threatening condition, and where the period needed for information to be disclosed will trigger possible harm to the patient. Obtaining consent prior to such medical intervention may be excused stating that any interruption of care may jeopardize the patient's existence (Hartman and Liang, 1999). Regulations have included a limited exception to the provision of informed consent for these emergency testing studies. A comprehensive guide on emergency studies based on informed consent has been issued by the USFDA (FDA, 2019). According to this guidance, the following requirements should be fulfilled to enable such an intervention.

- Human participants are in a life-threatening condition that requires immediate intervention.
- Available therapeutic options are unsatisfactory or unproven.
- Compilation of important scientific data to assess the efficacy and safety of the treatment.
- Obtaining IC from participant is not possible due to his/her critical medical condition.
- The intervention needs be administered before obtaining consent from the subject's LAR.
- Study participation holds potential advantage to the subject.
- The clinical research could not be performed, practicably without the waiver.

Therapeutic privilege: Therapeutic privilege applies when the investigator cannot reveal, typically a portion of, clinical information to a patient, relating to the treatment or diagnosis because they feel that information disclosure will inflict possible damage to the patient's physical, emotional, or social well-being, to the extent of being a contraindication to the therapeutic intervention. It is, however, different from cases where disclosure of knowledge is withheld on the grounds such as emergencies. However, therapeutic privilege should not be applied except in case where there is a confirmed threat to the wellbeing of patient, for example, if the physician, based on his experience and expertise, can demonstrate the development of suicidal behavior. The situation should also be carefully examined to ensure that the therapeutic privilege is not applied in the anticipation that the IC would lead to denial to participation in a clinical study which investigators consider to be of benefit to the subject (Hodkinson, 2013).

9.8   Protection of human subjects

The healthy volunteers/person on whom research is conducted by potential investigator is referred to as *Human Subject* (1). The data/research information and biospecimens to be utilized, studied, and analyzed are acquired by them through (Hodge, 2005) two options:

1. Intervention or interaction;
2. Identifiable personal information.

Intervention with respect to research involves physical procedures (e.g., electrocardiogram, phlebotomy) and orchestration of subject and its environment (Code of federal regulations, 2009).

Interaction during research is the contact between subject and investigator which is both communicative and interpersonal (Code of federal regulations, 2009).

Identifiable personal information is the exclusive information associated with and provided by the subject that may be established by the investigator with respect to the information obtained regarding research (Code of federal regulations, 2009) (see Fig. 9.2).

9.8.1   The common rule

The research involving human volunteers/subjects needs to be under the purview of "The Common Rule" which sets down certain specifications in context to research and IC to be obtained by subjects (FDA, 1991). The Central Intelligence Agency (CIA) adopted "the common rule" after it was published on June 18, 1991 as final common federal policy (FDA, 1991). Section 45 CFR 46(A) affirms policy considering protection of research subjects by Department of

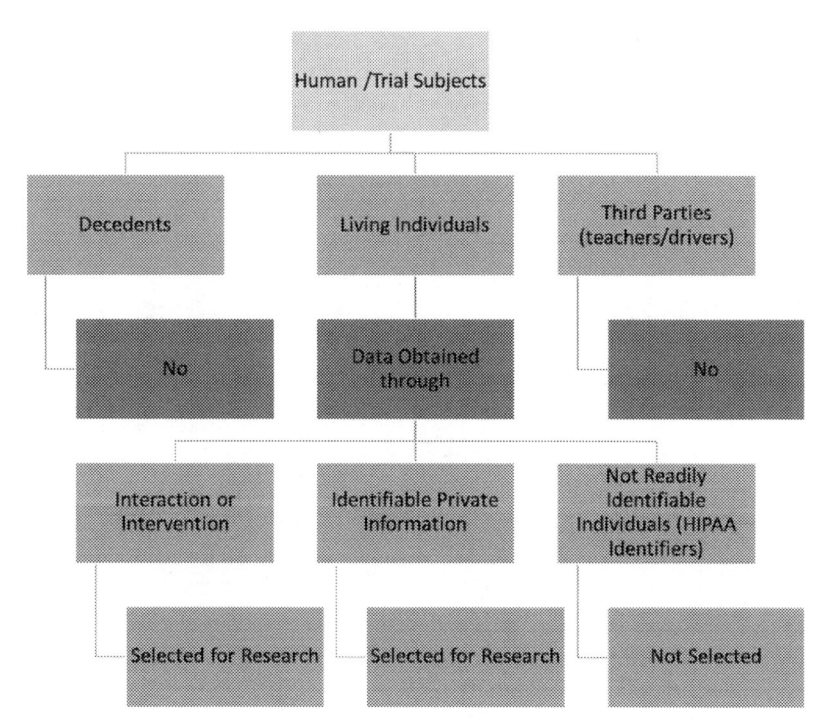

FIGURE 9.2   Selection of human subject for clinical trial.

Health and Human Services (DHHS) (Code of federal regulations, 2009). The common rule has been revised by DHHS, and final rule was published on January19, 2017 (45 CFR Part 690, 2017). The final rule aims to ensure that low-risk researches are not burdened by administrative obligations and also the protection of subjects participating in research is strengthened (Hodge, 2005). Federal policy 45 CFR 46(101) describes in detail the rules formed for welfare of public and mentioned under protection of human subjects (45 CFR Part 690, 2017).

This Common Rule applies to all publicly funded research, wherein institutions conducting the research are directed to enforce the protection of human subjects. Before selecting the human subjects and securing IC, the research proposals are evaluated by institutes for their benefits and risks, and also it is mandatory for the institutes to converge upon the requirements stated through the Common Rule (ICH-GCP, 2016)

To gain the federal support for research, the Common Rule prerequisites the set up for IRB by research institute. IRB is commissioned to review, ratify or reject, specify changes if any, and assures for the security of human subjects during the research. The team of IRB is a well-read experienced team of scientists, medical practitioners, administrators, and members from local community or agencies managing extra mural researches (Code of federal regulations, 2009; ICH-GCP, 2016)

9.8.2 Institutional review board

According to ICH, IRB is "an independent body composed of medical, scientific, and nonscientific members, to protect the rights, safety and wellbeing of human subjects in a trial. It approves the material and method for obtaining inform consent. It also reviews and approves protocols and subsequent amendments and informed consent of the trial subjects." IRB can also be called IEC (ICH-GCP, 2016). The ethics committee is constituted and registered under rules 7 and 8, respectively, with central licensing authority (CDSCO, 2019). The purpose of the IRB is to review the protocol for clinical trial to establish its safety for human subjects. It aims to ensure maximum benefits and minimal risks to the participants involved in the research (ICH-GCP, 2016).

- It reviews all data before and during the clinical trial.
- It functions in agreement with ICH GCPs guidelines along with domestic legislations.

IRB functions at two levels (Amdur, 2010) as given below:

1. *Local IRB*: This is exclusively responsible for review of research and clinical trials conducted at academic institutions.
2. *Central IRB*: It functions for multiple organizations/institutes.

If the investigator does not have access for local IRB, then they may seek review from central IRB. In case local IRB exists, still the clinical trial investigator seeks central IRB opinion; it may be required to justify the need for the same (ICH-GCP, 2016; Amdur, 2010).

9.8.2.1 Members of institutional review board

All members of IRB should be qualified enough to review the various aspects of clinical trials which may be ethical, scientific, behavioral, or medical (ICH-GCP, 2016; 45 CFR Part 690, 2017; Amdur, 2010). Team of IRB is composed of (CDSCO, 2019) a minimum of seven members. Members should be from various backgrounds such as medical, scientific, nonmedical, and nonscientific areas with at least:

- One lay member;
- One woman member;
- One legal expert;
- One independent member related to any other field (such as ethicist).

9.8.2.2 Responsibilities of institutional review board

IRB performs initial review followed by periodic reviews. Initial review is carried out before the enrollment of human subjects in clinical trial followed by periodic reviews which are executed at least once a year but throughout the conduction of clinical trial (45 CFR Part 690, 2017). The IRB may further inquire about IC as well as remunerations for the participants in the trial (ICH-GCP, 2016; 45 CFR Part 690, 2017). For biomedical research entailing human subjects, FDA employs IRB to analyze and observe the trial. IRB, in accordance with FDA regulations, may modify, approve/disapprove the proposed research. IRB serves as an important authority for welfare of human subjects involved in research (Code of federal regulations, 2009). Review and analysis by IRB promise that suitable measures for the protection of human subjects are being taken. IC and investigator's brochure (IB) serve as important tools for IRB. To review the research, IRB uses a few processes (21 CFR, 2019):

- *Regulations*: It is an umbrella which encompasses the regulations for clinical trials and GCP regarding supervision of clinical trials and protection of human subjects.
- *Guidance*: This guidance focusses on IRB and interrelationships among sponsor-investigator-IRB, protocols and essential documentation required for trial, all sanctions made and inspections performed by FDA investigator. It provides directions to secure people who are enrolled as subjects for the trial.
- *Information*: It provides supplementary information to health professionals from FDA and alternative government bodies for the protection of subject.
- *Clinical Safety Data Management*: To ease the reporting of adverse drug events, these data dispense essential terminology and definitions related to clinical safety.

The accountability for conforming with IRB requirements is taken care by principal investigator (PI). It is the responsibility of a PI to inform IRB if any modifications are made in the protocol. In an attempt, to avoid immediate safety hazard, the PI may deviate from the submitted protocol (GCP IB, 2016; ICH-GCP, 2016).

9.9   Investigator's brochure

IB contains all product-related information, including nonclinical and clinical data. IB is a multidisciplinary document, which summarizes information regarding drug's development (GCP IB, 2016; ICH-GCP, 2016).

The section 7 of ICH E6 (R1) guidelines (10) on GCP provides the official guidance for producing an IB. It contains a suggested layout for the document's required elements, which establishes a table of contents that nearly all IBs follow (GCP IB, 2016; ICH-GCP, 2016).

FDA guidance states that even though "common rule" 21 CFR 56 does not mention the IB by name, much of the information contained in such brochures is "clearly required to be reviewed by the IRB." Investigator's drug brochure (IDB) is a mandatory requirement as per FDA [(21 CFR 312.23(a)(5) and 312.55)] (Fiebig, 2014; ICH-GCP, 2016).

IB serves as a comprehensive record comprising of relevant and necessary information regarding the investigational drug. In relevance to the study on human subjects, IB is a compendium of both clinical and nonclinical information about investigational drug (Fiebig, 2014). The rationale, compliance, procedures related to safety and certain key features of the protocol including the dose of drug, frequency of dosing, and routes of drug administration are the various parameters which could be well understood by PI and others involved in the trial with the help of IB. It also serves as essential document for imparting awareness in relevance to clinical management of human subjects (Fiebig, 2014). For significant assessment by PI for the proposed study for trial, the structure of information provided by IB should be in impartial, condensed, uncomplicated, balanced, easy, and in nonpromotional form (Fiebig, 2014).

The qualified researchers shall generate and approve the IB content. IB should be updated as soon as noteworthy data are received or it should be reviewed at least once a year. In compliance with GCP, before the inclusion of new data in revised IB, it is foremost that it must be also communicated to IRB or local regulatory authorities (Fiebig, 2014). The sponsor prepares the IB and checks its distribution. National competent authority (NCA) holds approval of IB once it is submitted along with Clinical Trial Application (CTA) (GCP IB, 2016). The IB should include the following information (GCP IB, 2016):

- Name of the sponsor and identity of investigational new drug (e.g., research number);
- Statement mentioning confidentiality and exclusivity of the document;
- Results obtained from study of drug both clinical and nonclinical studies;
- History, property, and background information of investigational new drug.

9.9.1   Contents of investigator's brochure

There must be a version number and date of release of every IB. It should contain the following data along with citations of literature (CDSCO, 2019) (Table 9.3):

- *Summary*: It provides insights for the investigator highlighting relevant information regarding development of drug.
- *Introduction*: This has the information about drug, rationale for the study, and objective of the planned study.

TABLE 9.3 Content of investigator's brochures.

S. no.	Title	Description
1	• Table of contents	• It illustrates the agenda of investigator's brochure.
2	• Summary	• This part summarizes important properties of investigational drug, including its pharmacology, toxicology, pharmacokinetics, clinical information, etc.
3	• Introduction	• It briefs about chemical name, active ingredients, rationale of the proposed research, indications along with approach for evaluating the investigational product.
4	• Physical, chemical, and pharmaceutical properties and formulation	• This segment describes the investigational drug with chemical name and structural formula. Information regarding pharmaceutical, physical, and chemical properties is also mentioned. Inclusion of excipients, safety measures incorporated, and instructions about handling and storage of dosage form are also revealed.
5	• Nonclinical studies Introduction	• It describes the detailed information of the study and relevant findings. The information includes number, sex and species of animals, unit dose, dosing interval, route and duration of drug administered, systemic distribution, and postexposure follow-up. The information about result includes type, frequency, and severity of pharmacological/toxicological effects as well as onset and duration of action and dose response.
5.1	• Nonclinical pharmacokinetics	• Pharmacology of investigational drug and its metabolites studied on animals are mentioned briefly. The summary also includes researches that evaluated mechanism through receptor binding, models, and specificity along with safety studies.
5.2	• Pharmacokinetics and product metabolism in animals	• Physiological modification and pharmacokinetics of drug in all species is reviewed.
5.3	• Toxicology	• Toxicological effects in the research conducted is mentioned specifying the studies such as single dose, repeated dose, reproductive toxicity, carcinogenicity, etc.
6	• Effects in humans	• Effects of investigational drug regarding known pharmacokinetic parameters, effects in population subgroups (age, gender, sex, etc.) are specified.
6.1	• Known effects	• Known pharmacokinetic effects of drugs obtained from completed clinical trials are mentioned
6.2	• Pharmacokinetics and metabolism in humans	In this segment, pharmacokinetic information such as absorption, distribution, biotransformation and excretion, bioavailability of drug, population subgroup, and drug interaction are mentioned.
6.3	• Safety and efficacy	• The information about drug and its metabolite obtained from the clinical trials regarding its pharmacodynamics, safety, dose response, and efficacy is mentioned in condensed form. This helps in anticipation of possible risks and adverse events.
6.4	• Marketing experience	IB identifies the countries where investigational new drug is unapproved or approved and marketed. Any information received through marketing such as adverse events and dosages is also summarized.
7	• Summary	• This section discusses and summarizes the data and published reports and interprets the information provided. The focus of this section is to apprise investigator about the potential risks or adverse reactions and precautions and tests required during clinical trial.

- *Properties and formulation*: Various physical and chemical properties of investigational drug and pharmaceutical properties of drug and excipients, including specifications for handling and storage.
- *Nonclinical studies*: It includes animal studies, doses, methodology employed, and key findings. Results of pharmacological, toxicological, and metabolic studies are also included. This section gives the information on favorable and unfavorable effects in humans.
- *Effects in humans*: It mentions and summarizes the outcome of various studies such as toxicology, metabolism, safety, and efficacy. It also gives the information about market experience from other countries.
- *Summary*: Summary holds the discussion about all data to foresee the adverse drug reactions (ADRs) and other issues related to clinical trials.

9.10 Clinical trial: quality assurance

The quality of a clinical study depends upon the data integrity and subject's rights. Increased global demand of pharmaceutical product has put the pressure on industry to increase and accelerate the process of clinical trial. To supplicate the increased requirements, clinical trials industries tend to outsource their clinical trial process to other countries. Outsourcing remarkably reduces the cost and time of clinical trials. However, redistribution of trials to other countries compromises the compliance of clinical trials. Developing countries are the major partners of conducting clinical trials on the behalf of the industrious countries. According to a report, outsourcing of clinical trial to other countries have been doubled from 1995 to 2005 (Glickman, 2009). This symbiotic relationship of developed and developing countries sometime is unable to assure the quality of the trial.

The questions highlighted on the quality of clinical trials conducted in developing countries is due to the discrepancies in regulatory, ethical, medical, and trial guidelines. Besides that, inadequate infrastructure in developing countries has made the situation even more difficult. The outsourcing of clinical trials to developing nations decreases the cost and duration. However, maintaining the international quality of the product becomes difficult (Bhatt, 2011).

9.10.1 Good clinical practice: requirement of quality clinical trial

GCP is globally accepted and is the applied standard for conducting the quality checks on clinical trials. To maintain the universal standard of clinical trial, GCP should be applied from the beginning till the end of the trial (Glickman, 2009). It ensures the designing and recording of the clinical trials in a scientific manner. GCP is also of significance in the preparation and following up of CTP (Glickman, 2009). Adhering to the GCP is necessary for trial integrity and for the assurance of accuracy of data. The rights and confidentiality of subject are also protected under the GCP guidelines. The data collected according to the GCP guidelines are widely acceptable (Glickman, 2009). There are various quality issues in clinical trial that are mainly visible during the regulatory and sponsor inspections. Some of such quality issues recoded in clinical trials are as follows:

- Deviation from protocol,
- Subject's right violation,
- Poor keeping of trial records,
- Improper adverse event reporting, and
- Lack of knowledge of GCP.

The quality is essential in designing, conducting, recording, and evaluating the clinical trials. CRO and sponsors involved in a clinical study are responsible for the maintenance of clinical trial's quality. Maintaining quality in clinical trials requires proper training, education of trial coordinators, proper mentioning of policies and procedure in trial protocol, and appropriate documentation (Bhatt, 2011). FDA has advised four approaches for the improvement of clinical trial quality (Bhat, 2011).

1. *Say what you do*: It is the role of the sponsor to prepare and communicate the SOP and protocol. Qualified and educated professional should be enrolled in the process who can direct the procedure and guidelines of clinical trials. Also the sponsors should be able to describe the potential risk in SOPs (Bhatt, 2011).
2. *Do what you say*: The staff of sponsor, CROs, and trial site coordinators involved in clinical trials should be trained and educated. They should be well versed with policies, procedures, and responsibilities. According to a survey, most professionals involved in clinical trial process are from nonmedical background. This lack of required knowledge is responsible for malpractice (Bhatt, 2011).

3. *Prove it*: Risk management analysis that is focused on trial process should be conducted as per the protocol. Trend analysis monitors the data compliance across all the trials sites. Risk analysis and analysis of data trend revolutionize the central monitoring process, and it proved out to be useful for quality.
4. *Improve it*: The corrective actions are necessary in improving the quality, and it should be effective in correcting the root cause of the problem.

The quality issues in clinical trials are dynamic in nature, and thus the quality guidelines with reference to the clinical trials must be updated periodically. Sponsors and regulatory agencies also continuously work on inspection approaches to build the quality of trials (Bhat, 2011).

9.11 Safety monitoring in clinical trials

Assessment of safety is a key component in all phases of the drug discovery and development process. Prior to drug's marketing authorization, comprehensive safety evaluations and monitoring are needed at each and every stage starting from bench side to the clinic. To gain regulatory approval as well as marketing authorization, pharmaceutical sponsors are required to adequately describe the product's safety profile. The authorized product label provides an important information regarding advantages and risks of the product. The continued monitoring is also important to gather wider experience and data from a larger population once the drugs are approved for clinical use. In certain cases, new safety information can be contrary to the established conclusions about risks and benefits. These are evidenced in several high-profile products which have been withdrawn from the market, such as Rofecoxib (Vioxx), Troglitazone (Rezulin), and Rosiglitazone (Avandia). In 2005 USFDA released guidance documents regarding *risk management practices, including premarket risk evaluation, postmarketing/pharmacovigilance and pharmacoepidemiologic assessments* (GCP-PV, 2005; GCP-RMP, 2005; Shauren, 2005). Regulatory agencies and the pharmaceutical industries globally are taking a more holistic and thorough approach to safety assessment in drug development (Yao et al., 2013).

9.11.1 Role of Data and Safety Monitoring Board in monitoring safety in clinical trials

The Data and Safety Monitoring Board (DSMB), also known as Data Monitoring Committee (DMC), is a specialist committee, established for safety evaluation of clinical trials, independent of the sponsor. The DSMB periodically evaluates clinical trial data to assess the overall safety of the current study participants as well those yet to be registered. The DSMB periodically reviews efficacy data to ensure that sufficient proof of efficacy or the lack thereof. The additional function of DSMB is to inform the study sponsor about the continuing validity and clinical credibility of the trial. However, it is not mandatory to have a formal DSMB for all clinical trials. The role of DSMB is very significant during the Phase 3 double-blind randomized trials. Members of DSMB include clinical trial specialists, physicians with expertise in the relevant area, biostatisticians, and persons from other research fields such as basic science/pharmacology, biomedical ethics, or law. Additionally, sponsors can opt to select data analysis team with multifunctional expertise to perform review of safety data. This autonomous data analysis team is empowered to conduct similar tasks as the DSMB on later stage trials (Yao et al., 2013).

9.11.2 Role of regulatory authorities in monitoring safety of clinical trials

Pharmaceutical sponsors in the United States are required to submit an IND application to the regulator, prior to initiating a clinical trial. The FDA reviews the submitted IND for safety (usually within 30 days) to ensure that study participants are not subjected to unreasonable risk. The FDA released various guidance documents in 2010 to the clinical trial investigators and sponsors regarding requirements of safety reporting for drugs and biologicals for human use under an IND and also for drugs subject to bioequivalence (BE) and bioavailability (BA) studies (US Food and Drug Administration, 2010). The guidance documents implemented internationally harmonized the reporting standards and definitions provided the agency's expectations for timely review, assessment, and submission of useful and relevant safety information. In Europe, safety evaluation of new drug applications from pharmaceutical sponsors is carried out by various scientific committees of EMA. Pharmaceutical sponsors need to submit risk management plans (RMPs) to the EMA during drug approval process. An RMP provides a description of significant established risks of the therapeutic product, possible risks, and missing/incomplete information, which provides a basic framework for risk minimization measures and pharmacovigilance. Regulatory authorities in other countries mostly follow the same protocol under different local legislation.

9.11.3 Postmarketing surveillance (pharmacovigilance)

Postmarketing surveillance (PMS), or pharmacovigilance, means the drug safety monitoring process. This surveillance starts once the drug is approved for market use, after successful clinical trial completion. The prime objective of PMS is to detect previously undiscovered adverse as well as positive effects of the newly approved drug (Sharrar and Dieck, 2013). Other important components can include the use of off-label drugs, problems with orphan drugs and issues associated with performing clinical trials in the pediatric population. Although the premarketing trials are performed to establish the toxicity profile of drug, these trials are reported to lack the capacity of detecting some serious ADRs. This can be due to limitations in the number of trial participants, as certain ADRs can be detected at rates of 1 in 10,000 or fewer drug exposures. The WHO describes ADRs as "an unintended and noxious reaction" to a drug that occurs usually at doses used in humans for prophylaxis, therapy, or diagnosis of disease, or for physiological function modification. They have multiple types including nondose-related, dose-related, time-related, and unexpected treatment failure. Follow-ups are vital for the detection of noxious reactions coupled with the prolonged use of drugs or drug intake at broadly separated intervals. In general, the limitations posed by premarketing trials necessitate the need of continuous safety investigation even after drug approval.

PMS is a vital tool for correlating the intensity of the exposed drug with the initiation of adverse events, thereby providing a clearer picture regarding the types of negative or positive effects which a drug may pose over a long-term usage. Over the years, PMS procedures have advanced considerably, with regulatory authorities recognizing the significance of applying suitable measures to suppress the increasing adverse reaction incidences (US -FDA PSP, 2020).

9.11.4 Postmarketing reporting of adverse experiences

Routine postmarketing monitoring of adverse events provides updated safety data for newly approved drugs. For this purpose, four main databases are used. The Uppsala Monitoring Center which is WHO collaborating center for International Drug Monitoring, uses VigiBase. The VigiBase has collected more than 7 million case reports on individual safety from 144 countries (Lindquist, 2013). The Adverse Event Reporting System was launched by USFDA in 1969 and has around 4 million safety reports. USFDA initiated Vaccine Adverse Event Reporting System (VAERS) in the year 1990. The VAERS has also collected more than 400,000 reports (VAERS, 2013). EudraVigilance is the EMA database which was launched in 2001. All four information databases are digitized to monitor the safety profile of approved products in the postmarketing setup. They are voluntary reporting systems that gather information from physicians, manufacturers, patients (consumers), and the scientific literature regarding medicinal product's usage associated adverse effects.

These systems contain reports of serious, related, or unexpected adverse effects from clinical trials, voluntary reports from consumers, medical experts, legal experts, and others. The reported adverse experience are initially associated with the usage of drugs which may or may not establish a causality with the drug. Moreover, there may be inaccurate reporting of adverse event by nonmedical persons as no standard medical descriptions are available for adverse event terms and coding of event is purely based on reporter's terminology. Some factors to be considered in the evaluation of individual reports include the temporal correlation, the frequency of reports, the adverse event with the use of drug, the timing/duration of the adverse event (an anaphylactic reaction occurs spontaneously after drug administration while cancer development require relatively longer duration), adverse event on rechallenge, consistency of the incidence with therapeutic effect of the drug or other drugs of the same class, and consistency with reported clinical data. Spontaneous report assessment should also focus on rare/unusual adverse effects that are usually linked with drug use, for example, toxic epidermal necrolysis, Stevens—Johnson syndrome, etc. These adverse effects can alter the drug's benefit—risk profile (Sharrar and Dieck, 2013).

For adverse events that require further review, a set of case reports may be generated and evaluated to assess the clinical continuum of the adverse effects, its outcome as well as its pattern of occurrence (Sharrar and Dieck, 2013).

9.12 Outsourcing of clinical trials

Clinical trial is a long and expensive process, and outsourcing has proven to being a most cost-effective. So, the assessment of effectiveness is necessary to plan and execute the trial properly. Study sponsors outsourced the trial process to clinical research organizations (CROs) to achieve the aspired expectations (MoDezfuli, 2018). As of 2017, more than one lakh clinical trials for IND were conducted outside the sponsor facility, and less than ninety thousand clinical studies were recorded at the sponsor's land, that is in the United States (Fisher et al., 2006; ICDRA, 2016).

After the 1970s, the yearly number of filling new drug applications has increased remarkably. The requirement of the clinical trial structure moved up. To reduce the burden of workload, the sponsors distributed it to the CROs, because outsourcing companies operate enormous staff to implement end-to-end service to the sponsors (FDA, 1991; ICH-GCP, 2016). Also, it has been recorded that developing a new drug is a billion-dollar process, and with outsourcing the liability drops down the expenditure of the complete clinical study. Outsourcing the clinical trials accelerates the process of trial and ensures the data integrity and transparency. The outsourcing charges depend on the services provided to the sponsors. Sometimes, CROs ask around 20% of the total cost of the trial. Therefore, this extra spending increases the fixed and variable cost of the whole study, ultimately the market price of the drug increases and burden on the patient also increases (MoDezfuli, 2018).

CROs and sponsor are independent entities, but the relationship between them is symbiotic: one cannot thrive without the other. Both have their roles and responsibility to conduct transparent clinical trials and to built the trust of individuals participating in the trials though, respect the confidentiality and integrity (MoDezfuli, 2018).

9.12.1 Contract research organizations

Increased requirement of pharmaceutical products globally pushes the race of drug delivery process. CROs support the pharmaceutical companies to conduct their clinical trials. Outsourcing the clinical trial is an ongoing trend towards drug development (Bhatt, 2011). The trial numbers significantly increase from the past decades, so as the number of CROs, more than 700 CROs are offering their services worldwide (5). Sponsors are pouring dollars in the clinical trial processes, flourishing the growth of CRO industries (MoDezfuli, 2018). From biopharmaceutical studies to pharmacovigilance, CROs caters full or niche range of services to sponsors. CROs guarantee the clinical data credibility and ensure compliance with GCP, good laboratory practices, and other regulatory guidelines. Rather than hiring permanent staff and investing capital in infrastructure, pharmaceutical companies prefer to take the services of CROs (Bhatt, 2011). Table 9.4 addresses some of the advantages and disadvantages of outsourcing to CROs.

It is anticipated that working models of CROs will be strong and strategically more sound with the sponsor. In future with the advancement in clinical trial procedure, the process will be shorter and less complicated than it is today. Deadlines will be respected so that the drug can reach to the market sooner. These prospective approaches will have an positive impact on the public healthcare (ICH-GCP, 2016).

9.12.2 Outsourcing of bioavailability and bioequivalence studies

The safety and efficacy of generic drugs requires the same standards to its innovative counterpart. BA and BE studies confirm the therapeutic equivalency of generic drugs (Midha and McKay, 2009). Failing or passing the BA/BE standards of the drug is considered insignificant for clinical use. Bioavailability is an in vivo study. It is designed to

TABLE 9.4 Advantages and disadvantages of choosing the services of clinical research organization (CRO).

Advantages	Disadvantages
• Reduces the burden on the sponsor to establish the designated department for clinical trials.	• The sponsor holds the responsibility for the quality and integrity of the outcome of the trial (ICH-GCP, 2016).
• Outsourcing R&D to CROs empowered the sponsors to conduct research in those therapeutic areas where their company doesn't have expertise.	• Necessary rapid audits are time-consuming for the sponsors, but it is mandatory to protect their interests.
• CROs accelerate the process of clinical trials, help in the submission of NDA and ANDA to regulatory agencies, hence reducing burden on sponsors.	• In case the deadline is being missed by the CROs, they would raise the overall expenditure of the trial. In this scenario, sponsor would raise the market price of the product (Fiebig, 2014).
• Clinical research organization has the responsibility to ensures the quality control and integrity of trial data.	• Sponsors are directly not involved in the trial process; therefore they loss control on the clinical trial, resulting in possible loss of the quality of trial.
• CROs provide the required services to the sponsor.	• Sometimes outsourcing the trials offshore may raise ethical issues.

evaluate the pharmacokinetic parameters such as absorption rate, absorption extent, excretion rate, metabolism, and half-life of a new drug (ICH-GCP, 2016). BE studies are conducted on healthy volunteers. It is designed to determine the pharmacokinetic parameters of generic drugs in contrast to the reference or brand drug.

BE study was required when the innovative drug went off the patent. The BE data necessitated filing ANDA for generic drug approval (Official Journal of EU, 2014). Sponsors, or pharmaceutical companies, have the sufficient availability to conduct BE and BA studies under their facility. Big pharma industries have many products in the pipeline; therefore, their facility is mostly drenched. Moreover, small or generic pharma companies are deprived of the privilege to own a trial facility. Hence, pharma companies prefer to outsource BA and BE studies to CROs (MoDezfuli, 2018).

9.13   Health Insurance Portability and Accountability Act

The Health Insurance Portability and Accountability Act (HIPAA) was implemented in the year 1996 by the United States Congress, primarily to permit people with chronic or serious illness to change their jobs without risk of losing their health insurance coverage due to the exclusion of "preexisting conditions" in their health care plans. The law incorporated further provisions concerning health care reform, including steps designed to enhance the functioning of the health system and minimize administrative costs by "administrative simplification" (Patrick, 2004). Although the law was drafted and merits were addressed in Congress, privacy advocates raised concerns about a potential risk to privacy from the standardization mandates set out in the rules for administrative simplification. However, in the final HIPAA law, congressional efforts to address these misgivings and in following years ultimately failed. Finally, under the 1996 HIPAA, it was left to the Secretary of the Department of Health and Human Services (HHS) to implement privacy regulations. HHS released a guideline entitled *Standards for Privacy of Individually Identifiable Health Information* in response to a congressional mandate under the HIPAA. Compliance with this guideline known as the Privacy Rule was needed as of April 14, 2003, for most covered entities (HIPAA, 1996).

The Privacy Rule is a response to public distress about alleged misuse of the health information privacy. The Privacy Rule describes a form of health information known as protected health information (PHI) that can be used or revealed to anyone under certain circumstances or only in certain conditions. PHI is a subgroup of what is called as *individually identifiable health information*. With some exceptions, the Privacy Rule applies to individually identifiable health information generated or sustained via covered entity. The covered entities include health care providers, health care clearing houses, health plans as well as those transmitting electronically health information, for example, claims or eligibility queries, in relation to specific HIPAA transactions. PHI contains information from the medical chart or test findings of a patient and the billing information of a person for the medical treatment that is given when the information is retained or communicated by a covered entity. PHI also contains identifiable health information of clinical research subjects compiled by an investigator who is a covered health care professional (45 CFR Part 690, 2017).

The Privacy Rule specifies the way by which the individuals are informed about their medical information usage and disclosures for research purposes as well as the right to access information maintained by covered entities about them. The Privacy Rule safeguards the confidentiality of individually identifiable health records when research is involved, however at the same time ensures that the researchers are able to continue to have access to the health information required to carry out critical research (HIPAA Privacy Rule, 2004). The Privacy Rule allows a covered entity to use or disclose PHI for research, under the conditions and circumstances mentioned in the Fig. 9.3:

It should be noted that the Privacy Rule also allows the covered entities to use or disclose PHI for payment, treatment, and medical care operations without authorization.

9.13.1   HIPAA compliance in clinical trials

9.13.1.1   Preresearch review of medical records

A potential sponsor shall establish if a physician's practice is suitable site for clinical trial for which it may ask for detailed description about his/her patients. The Privacy Rule provides scope for inspection patient's medical records by the physician for "preresearch" ensuring PHI is masked from the sponsor. However, to record HIPAA compliance for third-party review of medical and billing history, for example, by CROs, the practitioner should get representations in writing that:

1. During the review, no PHI should be removed from the protected entity.
2. The PHI that is being reviewed by the researcher or CROs essential for review.

Alternatively, the "de-identified" details of patient can be exchanged without restrictions. The de-identification standard of the Privacy rule is very stringent, usually involving the elimination of eighteen specific identifiers that vary from zip codes, treatment dates to names, and social security numbers (Kulynych, 2008) (see Fig. 9.3 for conditions for disclosing PHI under Privacy Rules).

9.13.1.2 Recruitment

The Privacy Rule allows a physician to recruit his/her own potentially eligible and willing patients through in person or indirect communication, though the recruitment plan must be approved by the IRB.

If a CRO wants to utilize physician's patient record to recruit patients, the PI of the study should request to IRB to partly waive HIPAA authorization. (*The Privacy Rule waiver criteria, 45C.F.R.* Section 164.512 *[i][1][i]*). Such a waiver should be used by the CROs to use PHI in recruitment. However, IC and written HIPAA authorization will still be obligatory to enroll a subject.

9.13.1.3 Enrollment and conduct of study

Physicians must obtain HIPAA research authorization to register a patient in a clinical study. Though a study sponsor may give a template consent form, however the HIPAA authorization must be provided by the research site (which is the covered entity). The consent forms and authorization can also be combined, provided that the all the elements needed by the Privacy Rule and federal research regulations are included in the combined form. The HIPAA research authorization should include all components of a "valid general HIPAA authorization" as per 45 C.F.R. Section164.508

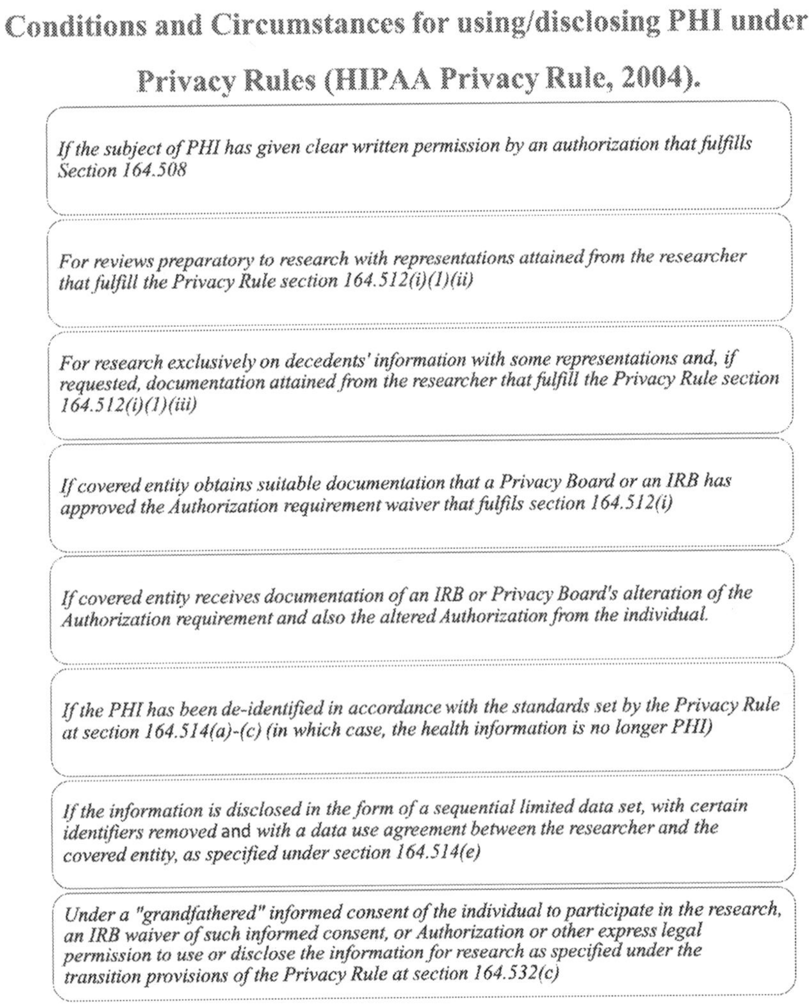

Conditions and Circumstances for using/disclosing PHI under Privacy Rules (HIPAA Privacy Rule, 2004).

FIGURE 9.3 Conditions and circumstances for using/disclosing protected health information under Privacy Rules (HIPAA Privacy Rule, 2004).

If the subject of PHI has given clear written permission by an authorization that fulfills Section 164.508

For reviews preparatory to research with representations attained from the researcher that fulfill the Privacy Rule section 164.512(i)(1)(ii)

For research exclusively on decedents' information with some representations and, if requested, documentation attained from the researcher that fulfill the Privacy Rule section 164.512(i)(1)(iii)

If covered entity obtains suitable documentation that a Privacy Board or an IRB has approved the Authorization requirement waiver that fulfils section 164.512(i)

If covered entity receives documentation of an IRB or Privacy Board's alteration of the Authorization requirement and also the altered Authorization from the individual.

If the PHI has been de-identified in accordance with the standards set by the Privacy Rule at section 164.514(a)-(c) (in which case, the health information is no longer PHI)

If the information is disclosed in the form of a sequential limited data set, with certain identifiers removed and with a data use agreement between the researcher and the covered entity, as specified under section 164.514(e)

Under a "grandfathered" informed consent of the individual to participate in the research, an IRB waiver of such informed consent, or Authorization or other express legal permission to use or disclose the information for research as specified under the transition provisions of the Privacy Rule at section 164.532(c)

[c][1]–[2]. A HIPAA research authorization has an expiry date of "none" (if authorized by state law), unlike general HIPAA authorization. All the patients who are willing to participate should sign the research authorization and submit it to the physician. The research authorization must specify to patient about the suspension of his right to access research information documented medical or billing records till the completion of the trial. Every HIPAA authorization should also inform the patient about authorization withdrawal. If a patient wish to withdraw authorization, the physician performing the trial can continue to use and disclose PHI acquired before the withdrawal. After withdrawal the physician can use and disclose the new PHI of patient only as necessary to preserve the research integrity (e.g., adverse event reporting or the death of a participant).

9.13.1.4 Publication or presentation of results

HIPAA is also applicable when the findings of clinical trials or case studies are published or presented making it mandatory for a physician to obtain written HIPAA authorization, if presentation/publication contains PHI (except for internal medical education). An IRB may not waive authorization for the presentation or publication of clinical research. Physicians must ensure to delete HIPAA identifiers before presentation or publication and check if residual information has the potential to reveal the identification of the participant upon being merged with other publicly available information. Materials such as photographs of highly publicized cases or rare diseases should be utilized with caution (Kulynych, 2008).

9.14 Conclusion

The pharmaceutical and medical devices sector is undergoing dynamic changes at fast pace. The collection and analysis of patient and population data has been revolutionized. The personalized medicines has gained interest in the recent times. Regulation of clinical trials need to become even more dynamic today to match with these evolving sectors. The review of safety and efficacy should also move towards data-intensive technologies to capture patient experience and collection of clinical data. The wider disparity and duplicacy of clinical studies in various regions is still a reality despite best efforts to harmonize the regulations and recognition of data generated in other regions. The regulations shall be revised to atleast narrow down, if not bridge this gap.

References

21 CFR, 2019. CFR—Code of Federal Regulations Title 21.

45 CFR Part 690, 2017. National Science Foundation 45 CFR Part 690 Department of Transportation 49 CFR Part 11 Federal Policy for the Protection of Human Subjects. Available from: <https://www.gpo.gov/fdsys/pkg/FR-2011-07> (accessed 06.12.20.).

Abdussalam, M., 2003. Informed consent in clinical practice and biomedical research. eolss.net. Available from: <http://www.eolss.net/Sample-Chapters/C03/E1-14-04-03.pdf> (accessed 06.12.20.).

Aday, L.A., 2002. At Risk in America: The Health and Health Care Needs of Vulnerable Populations in the United States, second ed. Wiley.

Amdur, R., 2010. Institutional Review Board Member Handbook. Jones & Bartlett Learning.

Appelbaum, P.S., Grisso, T., 1988. Assessing patients' capacities to consent to treatment. N. Engl. J. Med. 319 (25), 1635–1638. Available from: https://doi.org/10.1056/nejm198812223192504.

Barstow, C., et al., 2018. Evaluating medical decision-making capacity in practice. aafp.org. Available from: <https://www.aafp.org/afp/2018/0701/p40.html> (accessed 06.12.20.).

Bhatt, A., 2011. Quality of clinical trials: a moving target. Perspect. Clin. Res. 2 (4), 124. Available from: https://doi.org/10.4103/2229-3485.86880.

Brody, B., Jaworski, L., 1998. The Ethics of Biomedical Research: An International Perspective.

CDSCO, 2019. New drugs and clinical trials rules. Available from: <https://cdsco.gov.in/opencms/export/sites/CDSCO_WEB/Pdf-documents/NewDrugs_CTRules_2019.pdf> (accessed 09.03.2021).

CMIC, 2018. How to run successful clinical trials in Japan.

Code of federal regulations, 2009. Title 45- Public welfare, Department of Health and Human Services; Part 46- Protection of. Human Subjects.

Condran, G., 2017. IGDRP overview. Available from: <https://www.edqm.eu/sites/default/files/20092017-g_condran-igdrp_initiative.pdf> (accessed 6.12.2020).

Dresser, R., 1996. Mentally disabled research subjects. JAMA 276 (1), 67. Available from: https://doi.org/10.1001/jama.1996.03540010069034.

FDA, 1991. FDA policy for the protection of human subjects. FDA. Available from: <https://www.fda.gov/science-research/clinical-trials-and-human-subject-protection/fda-policy-protection-human-subjects> (accessed 06.12.20.).

FDA, 2019. Abbreviated new drug application (ANDA). FDA. Available from: <https://www.fda.gov/drugs/types-applications/abbreviated-new-drug-application-anda> (accessed 06.12.20.).

Fiebig, D., 2014. The Investigator's Brochure: a multidisciplinary document. Med. Writ. 23 (2), 96–100. Available from: https://doi.org/10.1179/2047480614z.000000000212.

Fisher, C.B., et al., 2006. Capacity of persons with mental retardation to consent to participate in randomized clinical trials. Am. J. Psychiatry 163 (10), 1813−1820. Available from: https://doi.org/10.1176/ajp.2006.163.10.1813.

Ganzini, L., Lee, M.A., Heintz, R.T., 1994. The capacity to make decisions in advance and borderline personality disorder. J. Clinical Ethics. Available from: <https://pubmed.ncbi.nlm.nih.gov/7749189/> (accessed 06.12.20.).

GCP-CTP, 2016. ICH GCP—Clinical trial protocol and protocol amendment(s)—ICH GCP. Available from: <https://ichgcp.net/6-clinical-trial-protocol-and-protocol-amendments> (accessed 06.12.20.).

GCP IB, 2016. ICH GCP-7. Investigator's brochure—ICH GCP. Available from: <https://ichgcp.net/7-investigators-brochure> (accessed 06.12.20.).

GCP-PV, 2005. Good pharmacovigilance practices and pharmacoepidemiologic assessment. FDA. Available from: <https://www.fda.gov/regulatory-information/search-fda-guidance-documents/good-pharmacovigilance-practices-and-pharmacoepidemiologic-assessment> (accessed 10.12.20.).

GCP-RMP, 2005. Development and use of risk minimization action plans. FDA. Available from: <https://www.fda.gov/regulatory-information/search-fda-guidance-documents/development-and-use-risk-minimization-action-plans> (accessed 10.12.20.).

Geppert, C.M.A., Abbott, C., 2007. Voluntarism in consultation psychiatry: the forgotten capacity. Am. J. Psychiatry 164 (3), 409−413. Available from: https://doi.org/10.1176/ajp.2007.164.3.409.

Glickman, S., 2009. Ethical and scientific implications of the globalization of clinical research.

Gogtay, N.J., Ravi, R., Thatte, U.M., 2017. Regulatory requirements for clinical trials in india: what academicians need to know. Ind. J. Anaesth. 61 (3), 192−199. Available from: https://doi.org/10.4103/ija.IJA_143_17.

Gupta, U., 2013. Informed consent in clinical research: revisiting few concepts and areas. Perspect. Clin. Res. 4 (1), 26. Available from: https://doi.org/10.4103/2229-3485.106373.

Hartman, K.M., Liang, B.A., 1999. Exceptions to informed consent in emergency medicine. Hosp. Physician 2 (March), 53−59. Available from:. Available from: http://citeseerx.ist.psu.edu/viewdoc/summary?doi = 10.1.1.432.6678 (accessed 06.12.20.).

HIPAA, 1996. Health Insurance Portability and Accountability Act of 1996 (HIPAA). CDC. Available from: <https://www.cdc.gov/phlp/publications/topic/hipaa.html> (accessed 06.12.20.).

HIPAA Privacy Rule, 2004. HIPAA privacy rule and its impacts on research. Available from: <https://privacyruleandresearch.nih.gov/clin_research.asp> (accessed 6.12.2020).

Hodge, J.G., 2005. An enhanced approach to distinguishing public health practice and human subjects research. J. Law Med. Ethics 33 (1), 125−141. Available from: https://doi.org/10.1111/j.1748-720X.2005.tb00215.x.

Hodkinson, K., 2013. The need to know—therapeutic privilege: a way forward. Health Care Analysis. Springer, pp. 105−129. Available from: http://doi.org/10.1007/s10728-012-0204-5.

ICDRA, 2016. WHO Drug Information, 28 (1), pp. 1−70.

ICH-GCP, 2016. International Council for Harmonisation of technical requirements for pharmaceuticals for human use (ICH), ICH harmonised guideline integrated addendum to ICH E6(R1): guideline for good clinical practice E6(R2).

Imran, M., et al., 2013. Clinical research regulation in India-history, development, initiatives, challenges and controversies: still long way to go. J. Pharm. Bioallied Sci. 5 (1), 2−9. Available from: https://doi.org/10.4103/0975-7406.106553.

Joubert Shayna, 2018. FDA regulatory submissions: a closer look. Available from: <https://www.northeastern.edu/graduate/blog/fda-regulatory-submissions-overview/> (accessed 08.12.21.).

Kulynych, J., 2008. HIPAA compliance in clinical trials. J. Oncol. Pract. 4 (1), 9−10. Available from: https://doi.org/10.1200/JOP.0812505.

Levine, R.J., 1981. Ethics and Regulation of Clinical Research. Yale University Press.

Lindquist, M., 2013. Director's message. Available from: <http://www.peoplespharmacy>. (accessed 10.12.20.).

Manti, S., Licari, A., 2018. How to obtain informed consent for research. Breathe 14 (2), 145−152. Available from: https://doi.org/10.1183/20734735.001918.

Market Report Analysis, 2020. Clinical trials market size, share & growth report, 2021−2028. Available from: <https://www.grandviewresearch.com/industry-analysis/global-clinical-trials-market> (accessed 06.02.21.).

Meeker-O'Connell, 2017. A Enhancing clinical trial quality: CDER.

Meisel, A., Roth, L.H., Lidz, C.W., 1977. Toward a model of the legal doctrine of informed consent'. Am. J. Psychiatry 134 (3), 285−289. Available from: https://doi.org/10.1176/ajp.134.3.285.

Midha, K.K., McKay, G., 2009. Editorial: Bioequivalence; its history, practice, and future. AAPS J. 11, 664−670. Available from: https://doi.org/10.1208/s12248-009-9142-z.

MoDezfuli, 2018. Outsourcing clinical trials outside of the United States. Available from: <https://www.pharmatechglobal.net/industry/articles/outsourcing-clinical-trials-outside-of-the-us> (accessed 06.12.20.).

National Bioethics Advisory Commission, 2002. Research involving persons with mental disorders that may affect decisionmaking capacity, national bioethics advisory commission. J. Int. Bioethique 13 (3−4), 173−179. Available from. Available from: https://scholarworks.iupui.edu/handle/1805/21 (accessed 06.12.20.).

Official Journal of EU, 2014. Regulations (EU) No 536/2014 of the European Parliament of the Council of 16 April 2014 on clinical trials on medicinal products for human use, and repealing directive 2001/20/EC

Patrick, G., 2004. The Health Insurance Portability and Accountability Act Privacy Rule: A Practical Guide for Researchers on JSTOR. Available from: <https://www.jstor.org/stable/4640745?seq = 1> (accessed 06.12.20.).

Roberts, L.W., 2002. Reviews and overviews informed consent and the capacity for voluntarism. Am. J. Psychiatry 159 (5), 705−712.

Ryan Kenneth, 2014. The Belmont Report: ethical principles and guidelines for the protection of human subjects of research. Available from: <https://pubmed.ncbi.nlm.nih.gov/25951677/> (accessed 10.12.20.).

Sharrar, R.G., Dieck, G.S., 2013. Monitoring product safety in the postmarketing environment. Ther Adv. Drug Saf. 4 (5), 211–219. Available from: https://doi.org/10.1177/2042098613490780.

Shauren, J., 2005. Guidance for industry on premarketing risk assessment; develoment and use of risk minimizarion action plans; and good pharmacovigilance practices and pharmacoepidemiologic assessment; availability. Federal Register 70 (59), 15866–15867.

Shrestha, B.M., 2012. View of the declaration of Helsinki in relation to medical research: historical and current perspectives. Available from: <http://jnhrc.com.np/index.php/jnhrc/article/view/343/342> (accessed 10.12.20.).

Sugarman, J., et al., 1999. Special supplement: empirical research on informed consent: an annotated bibliography. The Hastings Center Report. doi: 10.2307/3528546.

TranspariMED and Health Action International, 2019. Clinical trials in the European Union a roadmap to greater transparency.

US Food and Drug Administration, 2010. Guidance for industry and investigators: safety reporting requirements for INDs and BA/BE studies. US Food and Drug Administration. Available from: <http://www.fda.gov/downloads/Drugs/GuidanceComplianceRegulatoryInformation/Guidances/UCM227351.pdf%5Cnhttp://www.fda.gov/downloads/Drugs/GuidanceComplianceRegulatoryInformation/Guidances/UCM257976.pdf> (accessed 10.12.20.).

US-FDA PSP, 2020. Postmarketing surveillance programs. FDA. Available from: <https://www.fda.gov/drugs/surveillance/postmarketing-surveillance-programs> (accessed 10.12.20.).

VAERS, 2013. VAERS—about us. Available from: <https://vaers.hhs.gov/about.html> (accessed 10.12.20.).

Verma, A., 2019. Global pharmaceuticals market forecast: drivers, value chain analysis & trends. Market Research Reports® Inc., Market Research Report. Available from: <https://www.marketresearchreports.com/blog/2019/01/31/global-pharmaceuticals-market-forecast-drivers-value-chain-analysis-trends> (accessed 09.03.21.).

VHA, 2009. VHA Handbook 1004.01, Informed Consent for Clinical Treatments and Procedures.

Yao, B., et al., 2013. Safety monitoring in clinical trials. Pharmaceutics 5 (4), 94–106. Available from: https://doi.org/10.3390/pharmaceutics5010094.

Zaubler, T.S., Viederman, M., Fins, J.J., 1996. Ethical, legal, and psychiatric issues in C CO envy, and informed consent: an annotated bibliography. Gen. Hosp. Psychiatry 18.

Index

Note: Page numbers followed by "*f*" and "*t*" refer to figures and tables, respectively.

Printed in the United States
by Baker & Taylor Publisher Services